Robert Louis Stevenson,

WRITER OF BOUNDARIES

Robert Louis Stevenson,

WRITER OF BOUNDARIES

edited by

RICHARD AMBROSINI

and

RICHARD DURY

THE UNIVERSITY OF WISCONSIN PRESS

This book was published with the support of the Università degli Studi di Milano
and the University of Wisconsin–Madison Library.

The University of Wisconsin Press
1930 Monroe Street
Madison, Wisconsin 53711

www.wisc.edu/wisconsinpress/

3 Henrietta Street
London WC2E 8LU, England

Library of Congress Cataloging-in-Publication Data
Robert Louis Stevenson : writer of boundaries / edited by
Richard Ambrosini and Richard Dury.
p. cm.
Includes bibliographical references and index.
ISBN 0-299-21220-3 (alk. paper) — ISBN 0-299-21224-6 (pbk. : alk. paper)
1. Stevenson, Robert Louis, 1850–1894—Criticism and interpretation.
I. Ambrosini, Richard. II. Dury, Richard.
PR5496.R64 2005
828'.809—dc22
2005011165

CONTENTS

PART IV

Textual and Cultural Crossings

PREFACE

The small town of Gargnano (with its dependent villages of Villa and Bogliaco) lies on the northwestern side of Lake Garda in Italy, on a sliver of shore between a low shoulder of hillside to the south, around which the road curves on an oleander-lined *corniche,* and a mighty headland of precipitous lake-cliffs to the north. With mountain slopes beginning right behind the little town, there is no room for expansion and, the local people miraculously having managed to hold on to many of the houses, the place retains the charm and coherence of a traditional community. Everyday life goes on, with much meeting and talking outside, especially in the inner street parallel to the lakefront. Just to the south, Villa is even prettier and (unlike other picture-postcard villages) is without busloads of trippers looking for something to photograph or buy. From five until dinner and then in the evening, the mothers in their floral pinafores meet to chat and knit, while their children run around or sit on the harbor wall and play cards in their outdoor communal living room.

It was here at the end of August 2001 that the editors of the present volume organized a Robert Louis Stevenson conference that aimed both to continue the interest already shown at a series of Stevenson conferences in centenary-year 1994 (at Guelph and Yale) and 2000 (at Stirling, Little Rock, and Cerisy), and to lay the foundations for a series of biennial conferences.

The venue was Palazzo Feltrinelli, the University of Milan's small conference center on the lakefront at the northern end of the short Gargnano *lungolago*, a square Beaux-Arts palazzo of beige and orangey brown. In the center of the ground floor and extending out to the back is the main conference hall, ending in three French windows, the central one left open, so that those on the dais at the other end had a constant view of the changing sparkling blue of the lake and, twice in the morning, and twice in the afternoon, could see the arriving or departing ferry, with its colorful passengers at the rails, glide seemingly just past the end of the room. Those in the audience could hear the gentle ruffling beat of the propellers and were perhaps unconsciously aware of a slight change of luminosity and the sound of the wash against the terrace. This was no distraction: the passage of the ferry was like a passing breeze on the face while reading at an open window in summer: allowing you to continue still absorbed with what you are doing, yet concurrently aware of—yourself—this place—this time.

And a memorable time it was. Part of the magic of Gargnano was ending a session and stepping out to the flowery gravel terrace for coffee or lunch or to meet there in the long Gargnano twilight for an *aperitivo* or dinner. We talked around the tables, in friendly groups or at the terrace edge in a frieze of moving figures against the shining lake (understanding, by glances that informed as unconsciously as breathing, the simple pleasure of living inside such a landscape, always the same, always different); and as we talked the atmosphere of the place fused with an easy conviviality that helped the free exchange of ideas and opinions. But it was also a memorable conference because of the high level of all the papers and the way that themes were taken up and added to by different speakers. This we will leave readers to discover for themselves.

The two organizers and co-editors would like to thank all those who took part for helping to create such a successful event, with a special thanks to the University of Milan, to Paolo Mantegazza, then president of the university, to Fabrizio Conca, dean of the Faculty of Letters and Philosophy, for providing the financial support that in part went also into helping produce the present volume, and to the Dipartimento di Scienze del Linguaggio e Letterature Straniere Comparate for institutional support. In Gargnano, Francesca Cuojati, Cinzia Giglioni, Paolo Cassinari, Sara Rizzo, and Marco Manunta, students and graduates from the University of Milan, with brio and savvy dealt with all sorts of emergencies plus giving at least as much as they got in the exchange of ideas that characterized life there in between sessions. When more complex problems arose, Alda Gandini was always present to sort them out. Very special thanks to Marina Gardumi, the friendly and ever-helpful manager of Palazzo Feltrinelli, provider of excellent food and wine.

Thanks also to Barry Menikoff for his paper on how Stevenson imaginatively recreates history in *Kidnapped* (which he decided not to publish here because it is the basis of a chapter in his *Narrating Scotland* [2005]). Dick Ringler (who gave a memorable evening talk on James Dutton and Stevenson) made a fundamental contribution to this volume with his contagious enthusiasm in the idea of its publication with the University of Wisconsin Press. This was taken up by Ken Lee Frazier, director of the General Library System at the University of Wisconsin, and by Steve Salemson at the University of Wisconsin Press, who has followed the whole project through. Our special thanks to these three.

Villa di Gargnano,
APRIL 2003

INTRODUCTION

RICHARD AMBROSINI AND RICHARD DURY

Many were the geographical and social boundaries that Robert Louis Stevenson crossed in person. And many more as a writer: mixing genres, combining elements of high literature and popular narratives, introducing the personal and subjective into the "scientific" genres of biography and anthropology, repeatedly returning to situations and characters of ambiguous categorization, passing from one kind of writing to another in a continuous process of innovation. Indeed, it seems that he crossed too many artistic boundaries, and early twentieth-century literary taxonomists punished him for his repeated trespassing by relegating him to a lowly and marginal position in the academic canon—way down, on the boundary between serious literature and boys' stories and other products of popular culture.

Stevenson continues to remain out of bounds even for those who claim to be engaged in revising and opening up the canon—like the compilers of the *Norton Anthology of English Literature*, who still in the seventh edition cannot find a place for him in their selection. The fact is, a writer whose first essays were written in the style of William Hazlitt, and last published novel was the first colonial fiction in the language, simply cannot be forced into the ready-made categories of old canons or new fashions.

And yet, precisely the ex-centric nature of Stevenson's diversified and provocative opus, with its conscious intertwining of the "popular" and the "artistic," can turn into an asset. Even though, along with Walter Pater, he was the supreme prose stylist of his age and could have continued in a

xiii

belle-lettrist ivory tower, Stevenson reacted to the new mass-consumption market not by rejecting it but by repeatedly and self-consciously exploring the world of penny literature; and he did so because he saw in the popular subgenres a modern version of atavistic narrative forms. This aspect of his work was repeatedly explored at the Gargnano conference, and his creative engagement with popular literature set in contexts that have made possible fascinating crossovers between literary and cultural studies. As a result, Stevenson, the *marginal* novelist, gradually emerged, rather, as a *liminal* writer, a cultural actor who in opening door after door located himself on a number of thresholds connecting—and dividing—the realm of literature with the world of experience, politics, and history.

The vistas that open up once we view Stevenson as a "writer of boundaries" make past calls for a "revaluation" appear somewhat anachronistic, since they assumed a continuing validity for hierarchies set up by the literary system founded on modernism. This does not mean, however, that the issue of a revaluation—which, incidentally, is never mentioned once in the essays collected in this book—is no longer relevant; if only because the reasons behind his exclusion from the Anglo-American twentieth-century academic canon have become today as many motivations for re-reading his texts today, and thus discovering their particular significance for all students and scholars of age-of-transition British literature and culture.

An ideal frame for moving from "re-valuation" to "re-reading" can be found in the controversy about Stevenson, which Gerard Manley Hopkins engaged in with Robert Bridges a few months after the publication of *Jekyll and Hyde* and *Kidnapped*. Bridges, who wasted his technical skill in trying to recreate the syllabic meter of Greek and Latin, was concerned that his friend was spending his time reading modern fiction instead of studying Dante and the classics. Hopkins replied that Stevenson, alone among his contemporaries, wrote "continuously well," and was such "a master of a consummate style" that each of his phrases was as "finished as in poetry." When Bridges became too pressing with his remonstrance, Hopkins lost his patience: "Your sour severity blinds you to his great genius," and put an end to the polemical exchange with a good piece of advice: "You need not in writing join issue about Stevenson any more: instead of that you can read a book or two more of his and ripen a while" (Abbott 1935: 238–39, 243).

The origin of the "sour severity," which resulted in his critical exclusion, is to be found in the cultural context that led to the "Fall of Stevenson," registered with satisfaction and complacency by Leonard Woolf in a 1924 essay where he described how the style of the writer who had been "just the man to captivate the taste of the romantic 'nineties," sounded by then "drearily thin and artificial." (Stevenson's old friend, Edmund Gosse, could not believe that such things were being said by "the son-in-law of our old friend Leslie Stephen, having married Virginia"; Maixner 1981: 515.) In the same year, from the other side of the Atlantic, H. L. Mencken dealt a blow of greater severity: "The typical Stevensonian is . . . a sort of gaper over the fence of beautiful letters . . . I can detect no passion for Stevenson among the men and women who are actually making the literature of today. . . . His customers, beginning with literary college professors, often female, fade into collectors of complete library sets. . . . Stevenson, alas, wrote a great deal of third-rate stuff . . . an air of triviality hangs about all his work and even at times, an air of trashiness. He is never very searching, never genuinely profound" (Mencken 1924: 378–79).

The rejection of Stevenson's style, however, was not simply a reaction against the tastes of the earlier generation. In the aftermath of the Great War, the world of masculine, individual adventure, which in the last years of the *pax Britannica* could still appear innocuously liberating and playful, was now identified with the rhetorical orgy of war propaganda. Those who had been stirred to action and had had firsthand experience of the fighting now felt betrayed. A front-page article in *The Times Literary Supplement* in 1919 reports that "the generation which has grown up with such tragic suddenness under war conditions" regards Stevenson with "[an] attitude of kindly and agreeable patronage" (Fausset 1919: 701). Stevenson of course had nothing to do with the message implicit in Henry Newbolt's ethical-imperialist invocation to "Play up, play up, and play the game." But, as G. K. Chesterton warned, "when we look back up the false perspective of time, Stevenson does seem in a sense to have prepared that imperial and downward path," even though "he would not have liked it if he had lived to understand it" (Chesterton 1913: 110). Indeed, Rupert Brooke seems to have embodied Stevensonianism and patriotism when, after seeking to relive Stevenson's romantic myth by living in Samoa between the end of 1913 and early 1914, he came back to join the navy and died the following year.

Other voices spoke for the "Lost Generation," but this was not the only reason why from the 1920s Stevenson was relegated to the status of second-rate writer. His critical misfortune had already been settled long before the war. Unsurprisingly, given the embarrassing posthumous glorification

orchestrated by his family and friends, which had transformed him—
as William Ernest Henley bitterly remarked in 1901—into a "Seraph in
Chocolate." This backlash culminated in 1914 when a young critic, Frank
Swinnerton—in a monograph pointedly titled *R. L. Stevenson: A Critical
Study* to distinguish it from earlier readings of Stevenson's life and personality—demolished both the man and his work with arguments that
would recur throughout the century. G. K. Chesterton took on himself
the task of rejecting Swinnerton's trenchant onslaught, in a defense not
only of the writer but also of the values of his own generation. His epigrammatic brilliance, however, undermined his defense—leaving readers
like T. S. Eliot with the feeling that what was still needed was "a critical
essay showing that Stevenson is a writer of permanent importance, and
why" (Maixner 1981: 42–43).

By the time of Eliot's death in 1965, only one English-language monograph had appeared that could have fulfilled his wish. Two more were
published the following year, another in 1974, and a fifth in 1996.[1] A mere
handful, during a century that has seen the rise of an academic publishing market. Such neglect cannot be explained by reference to some absolute value-standard of Stevenson's worth.[2] There must be other reasons.
Stevenson had been a model writer for the first-generation holders of
chairs of English literature at the two historic English universities: Sir Walter Raleigh (Merton Chair, Oxford, 1904), author of one of the first major
studies on his style (1895), and Sir Arthur Quiller-Couch (King Edward
VII Professor, Cambridge, 1912) who wrote the final chapters of *St. Ives*, a
novel Stevenson's left unfinished at his death. These two quintessential
late-Victorian men of letters had established their reputation in the field
of literary journalism, and their successors in the academy later rebelled
against what they rightly perceived as their amateurish approach to literary criticism. The first professional scholars, committed to protecting values supposedly endangered by the voracious appetites of the newly literate
masses, taught their students how to understand the difficult techniques
and obscure language of the new modernist novel. And by so doing, they
succeeded in making literature no longer dependent on the market but on
professional readers. Ironically, the men now paid to teach literature could
not accept an author who considered himself a professional writing for the
market: he had to belong exclusively to the empyrean world of art, which
the professors were modeling according to their critical premises. And in
that world there was no space for Stevenson, the professional writer beloved by amateur professors.

Once a new canon of high literature began to be established, the authors vying to be accepted in it started using Stevenson to signal to their readers how different they were from this romantic stylist, by then irrevocably démodé. In E. M. Forster's *Howards End*, Leonard Bast betrays his lack of culture by enthusing over Stevenson's essays and travel books, thus creating great embarrassment and a ripple of laughter among the young intellectuals gathered around the Schlegel sisters (Forster 1910: 111–13). A generation later, George Orwell, in his first novel, *Burmese Days*, has the protagonist, Mr. Flory, pay a visit to an Indian expatriate, Dr. Veraswami, in whose house he finds on display a "rather unappetising little library, books of essays, of the Emerson-Carlyle-Stevenson type." The Indian is a fervent supporter of the British empire, and his masochistic adoration of the colonial power is brought out by the narrator in an harangue in the course of which, "the doctor searched for a phrase, and found one that probably came from Stevenson . . . 'torchbearers upon the path of progress.'" This jingoistic phrase, of course, is nowhere to be found in Stevenson, but its association serves Orwell's purpose: if Flory himself has become a detached and cynical opponent of imperialist ideology, it is also because he has read better books—as is revealed when he asks the doctor, "You've read Ibsen, of course?" and the other can only reply: "Ah, no, Mr Flory, alas!" (Orwell 1934: 34, 40–41).[3] Both Forster and Orwell use an appreciation of Stevenson as synonymous with cultural pretensions on the part of those—the low-class clerk, the colonized—who want to ape the taste of the bourgeoisie without having the means to understand which authors are now accepted in the predominant literary canon.

Scholars from non-English-speaking countries are in a better position to explain why Stevenson was singled out with such "sour severity," and why this ostracism proved so enduring. If Marcel Proust had been present at the Schlegel sisters' party, the London intellectuals would have felt less *à la page*. In a passage of *Le Temps retrouvé* claimed to be taken from a Goncourt *Journal*, Swann hears someone describe Stevenson as a children's writer—and this slighting comment, "met dans la bouche de Swann cette affirmation péremptoire: 'Mais c'est tout à fait un grand écrivain, Stevenson, je vous assure, monsieur de Goncourt, un très grand, l'égal des plus grands'" [led Swann to the following peremptory affirmation: "Not at all, he is a really great writer, Stevenson, I assure you monsieur de Goncourt, a very great writer, on a level with the greatest"] (Proust 1927: 716).[4]

Later in the century, Italo Calvino—an avowed "Stevenson worshipper" who repeatedly praised the Scottish author for his "marvelous lightness"—

wrote: "I love Stevenson because he gives the impression he is flying";[5] while Jorge Luis Borges, in his poem, "Los justos" [The Righteous], thanked the "ignored persons who are saving the world"—among whom he includes "El que agradece que en la tierra haya Stevenson" [Whoever is glad that on earth there is a Stevenson] (Borges 1981). These tributes to Stevenson bear witness to an admiration of his unique ability to combine stylistic artistry and the pleasure of reading—an ability, indeed, that has been focused on by a number of the conference participants.

The idea of having the University of Milan host an international conference on Robert Louis Stevenson in Gargnano was launched at the end of the conference, "Stevenson, Scotland, and Samoa," organized by Eric Massie at the University of Stirling in July 2000—a thrilling experience for those who had been working on Stevenson without being aware that they in fact belonged to a community of Stevensonians. The stimuli created by Stirling were confirmed when a few months later, in November 2000, some of us met again at an international symposium, "RLS 2000: R. L. Stevenson in Literature and Popular Culture," held at the Public Library of Little Rock, Arkansas. The symposium was a brainchild of Bill Jones, who later edited a collection of essays (*R. L. Stevenson Re-Considered*, Jefferson, NC: McFarland, 2003), based on the symposium papers. In the same year Gilles Menegaldo and Jean-Pierre Naugrette organized a conference on Doyle and Stevenson at the famous Cerisy conference center in Normandy and published the proceedings (*R. L. Stevenson & A. Conan Doyle. Aventures de la fiction*, Rennes: Terre de Brume, 2003). In the context of this new interest, it was no surprise to us that the proposals submitted for the Gargnano Conference went beyond the thematic categories traditionally applied to him. Stevenson, at the conference and in the papers in this volume, is seen instead as a catalyst for a variety of critical approaches, a writer who forces the rethinking of conventional categories, in his texts and in his own relation to the literary system: a "writer of boundaries."

When it came to preparing the program and dividing the papers into sessions, the change of focus from traditional divisions made it necessary to create new categories to accommodate themes such as masculinity, intertextuality, anthropology, Stevenson in film and TV, the pleasure of reading, popular culture, and evolutionary psychology. Then, when we started to assemble the present collection of essays, we soon realized that even the sessions into which we had organized the papers had become themselves boundaries that the participants had crossed and recrossed in a number of ways—and that, perhaps unsurprisingly, retracing these boundary-crossings to give coherence to the collection was turning out to be a problematic process. The four sections into which we have divided the essays collected in this volume serve therefore the primary purpose of attracting the reader's attention to the transitions within and among them—transitions that reflect the changes the field of Stevenson studies is undergoing today.

The Pleasures of Reading, Writing, and Popular Culture

Stephen Arata opens this section with an essay on "mental abstraction, idleness, reverie, and pleasure" in the writings of Stevenson and William Morris and their relation to late nineteenth-century theories of reading. Both writers are opposed to the professionalization of reading (associated with the new "serious" novel), and to activity not uniquely centered on one simple end (as in the tedious tasks of industrial production). Stevenson worked carefully to produce texts that reward close attention yet at the same time seems to discourage it, creating a playful relationship with the reader and encouraging a reading process that is a pleasure, not a task.

For Robert Louis Abrahamson, Stevenson's own reading involved crossing a boundary from the self to the other, eliminating the ego in order to be refined in an almost mystical way. The good reader (like one of Stevenson's own heroes) encounters the other and locates meaning and value in personal experience not in conventional morality. The cheerful banter and emotional effusion of Stevenson's own remarks about reading are encouragements to face the challenge and the purifying ordeal of escaping the boundaries of the self.

Stevenson's entire approach to fiction, according to Richard Ambrosini, was grounded on an "anthropologically informed reader-response model," which he kept modifying throughout his life as he searched for the atavistic pleasure found in narrative forms for children, "uneducated readers," and South Seas Islanders. The extent to which Stevenson's anthropological approach to fiction shaped his novel writing becomes clear once we retrace the four main thresholds he crossed during his writing career. Each of these occurred in conjunction with a physical journey (in France, twice to the United States, and during his Pacific cruises) but, most importantly, they marked as many redirections in the ongoing experimentation with literary forms and genres out of which his extraordinarily polygraphic output took shape. In a number of his essays and travel writings Stevenson recurrently presents himself as an ethnographer, describing or interviewing various kinds of others, and especially testing his aesthetic and narratological theories. His fiction shows how he applied the lessons he learned from such encounters to construct a series of reading-models. His final aim seems to have been the creation of a modern version of the epic, conceived as a narrative form both popular and artistic.

In her essay, Liz Farr provides insight into Stevenson's seductive quest of aesthetic pleasure in the biographical essays collected in *Familiar Studies of Men and Books* (1882). By crossing the boundaries between biography and fiction, he rejected the dominant scientific and moral approach to biographical writing of the time. Stevenson's essays, subjective and amoral, openly celebrate the provisional and subjective nature of impressions, and are conducted not in the spirit of judgment but aim to cultivate the familiarity of friendship.

Nathalie Jaëck's investigation of Stevenson's tendency to multiply and scatter the text uncovers a further way in which pleasure operates in his works, subverting the way textual guardians—in *Treasure Island, Jekyll and Hyde,* and *The Master of Ballantrae*—try to enclose and control language. Yet, she argues, the texts proliferate out of their narrators' control, and subjectivity is shown to be inevitable, textual integrity a myth. Stevenson's stories thus become "textual adventures"—proliferating, opaque, a rhizome, their own reflective subject, the real treasure to be found.

Glenda Norquay writes about Stevenson's ambivalent attitudes toward professional and popular writing with reference to *Treasure Island.* In "My First Book" Stevenson recognizes influences on *Treasure Island,* yet at the same time his ability to recognize them keeps him on a high literary plane. In "Popular Authors" he accepts the pleasure of commercial art, but stays at an amused distance; in addition, he does not include the popular *Tom Holt's Log* in the influences on *Treasure Island* despite a number of affinities, nor does he mention its elements of textual sophistication. He does, however, accept the popular into his aesthetic, unlike Sidney Colvin and other defenders of his reputation, who tried to present him as the high artist, distant from the rejected "popular."

Stephen Donovan gives us an overview of Stevenson's attitudes toward popular entertainment. Though the expansion of such forms of entertainment in the late nineteenth century was often seen as a threat, Stevenson saw it as valuable because of its links to the instinctive imaginative life. His own works have affinities with popular text-types, and they also contain numerous references to popular genres. While contemporaries condemned popular entertainment as infantile, Stevenson saw its childishness as a thing of great value, since writers express the daydreams of common men and create, as in child's play, the precious experience of "pure delight."

In explaining the financial and cultural background to *The Wrong Box*, Gordon Hirsch reveals how this farcical text contains a criticism of a new commercial culture and betrays Stevenson's doubts about his own position after returning to the United States in 1887. The "tontine" was a matter of current concern, since by the 1880s the most popular form of life insurance contained an inequitable tontinelike gambling element. Stevenson, in rewriting a short story his stepson Lloyd Osbourne had sketched out, took the tontine system as a symbol of greedy competition and the replacement of traditional social ties with market forces.

Scotland and the South Seas

This section traces a trajectory between Scotland and the South Seas linking not places but forms of writing. It is framed by two essays, respectively by Jean-Pierre Naugrette and Oliver Buckton, which outline a movement, from "writing as en-graving " to "writing as cruising," that also further enrich the theme of the pleasure of writing.

Jean-Pierre Naugrette's densely woven essay on " *The Master of Ballantrae*, or the Writing of Frost and Stone" starts by drawing out the intertextual references to Shakespeare's *A Winter's Tale*—the novel's subtitle—and Schubert's *Winterreise*, which Stevenson was studying in this period. From "cold" Naugrette then turns his analysis to the associated lexical field of stone and petrification, related to male fear of the female Medusa, and shows us how Alison, the only woman in the novel, retains her plasticity and humanity while the men "turn to stone." Mackellar finally cuts his prose in stone, just as Stevenson himself "graves" a personal epitaph in his poem, "Requiem." The notch cut by Billy Bones, Alison's thrust with the sword, and Mackellar's chiseling of the epitaph all seem close to Stevenson's art of writing as en-graving, writing as epitaph.

Luisa Villa uses an early Scottish tale, "The Merry Men," to suggest new directions for investigating the father-son conflict so pervasive in Stevenson's works. In the story, the shapeless feminine sea overcomes the patriarch, just as, in Stevenson's case, paternal authority must have been weakened by Thomas Stevenson's greatest failure, the collapse of the Wick harbor wall, followed scarcely a month later by the pivotal father-son quarrel, which soured their relationship for years. In "The Merry Men," and a series of criminal father figures, anger at patriarchy is expressed without challenging its structures, since the more virtuous sons are ready to replace the fathers. In later narratives, however, generational ethical roles are reversed or more nuanced. The abandonment of binary ethical distinctions, the reversals and confusion of roles, and a flirting with the female element of water are forbidden pleasures, made possible following the collapse of generational differences.

In "Figures in a Landscape: Scott, Stevenson, and Routes to the Past," Jenni Calder gives us an extended reflection on how, while both Scottish writers responded to the clear diversity of landscape in Scotland (onto which oppositions of characters, plot, and cultures could easily be mapped), the half-century that divides them marks a clear change in approach. If for Scott the "other country" of the past was part of a mythic history that he was attempting to recover, for Stevenson the landscape is a scene for trials and personal development. So, while Scott describes Highlands and clan members organically united, Stevenson presents Cluny in *Kidnapped* as isolated and in a temporary construction, and in *Ballantrae* he shows the American wilderness as harshly indifferent to human life.

The question of Scotland's divided relationship with England is central to Caroline McCracken-Flesher's essay on "The Body Snatcher." In this text, Stevenson presents the confrontation of Dr. MacFarlane (the wealthy and anglicized "London doctor") and Fettes (the drunken Scotsman, nicknamed "the Doctor") in a protagonist-vs.-double configuration that suggests the anxieties of a Scottish elite in the face of a "buried" national identity that refuses to go away—with Fettes returning to take the place of the original corpse last seen carried off crazily toward Edinburgh.

Ilaria Sborgi sees this same open ending and its association with the return of the repressed as expression of a more general cultural anxiety concerning degeneration and easy reversion to primitive behavior. This she links up with the racial anxieties that we find in the open ending of the South Sea tale "The Beach of Falesá" and with the Imperial Gothic fantasy of *Jekyll and Hyde*. The open endings in all these texts show that the body of the other can be temporarily removed but not eliminated; in the end, the attempt to create boundaries by dividing and suppressing does not work.

Manfred Malzahn establishes a further link between the South Seas and Scotland in his interrogation of the links between Scots (including Stevenson) and the Empire. Certainly Scots were important agents of the British Empire, yet they have a double experience of being colonized as well as colonizing. There is also a Scottish cultural tradition of lack of pretentiousness and tolerance for others that, Malzahn argues, is embodied in John Wiltshire, the first-person narrator of "The Beach of Falesá," who while unable to overcome his racist feelings learns to put individual loyalty above what he has been taught by his culture.

The ambiguous but on balance positive figure of Wiltshire is contrasted with his antagonist, Case, by Robbie Goh. Case has linguistic abilities and cultural knowledge, but in the absence of values he uses them merely to exploit others. His acceptance of the dehumanizing logic of profit (treating women as a commodity, for example) is his downfall, while Wiltshire is redeemed through his emotional relationship with Uma. Despite his prejudices, Wiltshire has a degree of open-minded acceptance of local culture and is willing to negotiate. Stevenson does not see individuals as necessarily imprisoned in one language and culture: like Wiltshire he is ready to explore the value of cultural, imaginative, and social exchanges.

Ann Colley examines how Stevenson exploited the discontinuous island nights' lamplight and mingling of light, darkness, and shadow as powerful symbols of imperfect knowledge and understanding. The disconnected details revealed by partial lighting present a challenge of interpretation to the viewer in the fictional world and to the reader of the text. In Stevenson, darkness is the foundation of knowing, and it is the obscure moment that brings significance.

The theme of attitudes to colonialism is continued with Ralph Parfect's paper on Stevenson's use of violence in his South Seas works, in particular in relation to the eye: dominating gazes, threatening gazes, excluding stares, and (following Bataille) the eye as locus of both seductiveness and horror. Hostile gazes are often reinforced by the universal gaze of a harsh sun. And, as always in Stevenson, violence (and here, violence and the eye) is connected with desire.

Oliver Buckton's "Cruising with R. L. Stevenson: The South Seas from Journal to Fiction," opens with a development of the idea of pleasure in reading and writing discussed in the previous section. For Stevenson, cruising, travel for sensual pleasure, was associated with a new and fragmentary kind of writing in which travel writing and fiction are complementary. Buckton then goes on to examine how the South Sea letters were quarried for fictional texts.

Evolutionary Psychology, Masculinity, and *Dr. Jekyll and Mr. Hyde*

Stevenson, associated as he is to buoyant adventure romances, is perceived as the antithesis of the psychological realistic writer—with the exception, perhaps, of his portrait of the double and of male perversion in *Strange Case of Dr. Jekyll and Mr. Hyde*. This section shows how this picture is outdated by pointing out his engagement with some of the most innovative psychological thinking of his times.

In the 1880s, Julia Reid reminds us, Stevenson wrote a series of essays in which he argued for the connection of modern individuals with early evolutionary states. In contrast to the evolutionary scientists, however, he did not see human development as a story of progress from savagery to civilization. Instead, he saw the creative unconscious as gaining new life from a renewed contact with "the sincerity of savage life," which could beneficially counter "the comfortable fictions of the civilised." The revived romance form, for Stevenson, heralded at least a partial return to an unaffected oral culture. Stevenson's originality, Reid suggests, lies in his rejection of any idea of gradual progress in psychological history, and his celebration of primitive states of consciousness. For him there were no clear boundaries between savagery and civilization, low and high culture, the unconscious and the conscious mind.

Olena Turnbull writes that Stevenson, despite his interest in evolutionist ideas, opposed simple evolution theory as a new inflexible doctrine, irreconcilably opposed to the constant variety that constituted for him the essence of both life and art. Scientific ideas could never be sufficient guides in life, since they could not provide an answer to the problems of existence; they are idealizations, and in the end must needs be expressed in imperfect language. A similar basic feeling of a final dignity and inner essence of mankind also led him to oppose naturalism, with its view of life as merely an objective phenomenon. In a way, his own variety of styles is a statement against any superiority of one style, and *The Master of Ballantrae*, apparently dark and pessimistic, is also a celebration of heterogeneity and an argument against simple interpretation and in favor of the centrality of chance.

The extent to which French psychological texts influenced the ideas and the textual forms of *Jekyll and Hyde* is the subject of Richard Dury's contribution. Stevenson's wife claims that he was influenced by an article in a French scientific journal, but Stevenson in an interview seems to exclude this possibility. A study of French scientific journals of the period and of the interest in double personality cases after 1876, leads Dury to the conclusion that the article, though it can never be identified, was probably one dedicated to the double-personality case of Félida; he also identifies some interesting feature of scientific discourse that are echoed in Stevenson's text. Returning to the interview, he interprets Stevenson's denial as a strategy to avoid discussing connections between double personality cases and *Jekyll and Hyde,* and suggests that this was to avoid providing any simple key to a text deliberately constructed to have no clear interpretation.

Linda Dryden sets *Jekyll and Hyde* in the context of contemporary perceptions of London. The size and population of the metropolis caused alarm, as did the opportunities that this divided, labyrinthine, and imperfectly lit city gave for crimes, committed both by an underclass and by apparently respectable gentlemen. Fiction and reality merge a few years later when *Jekyll and Hyde* was evoked in public discussions of Jack the Ripper, another frightening criminal with the power to disappear into the "City of Dreadful Night."

According to Richard Walker, in *Jekyll and Hyde* Stevenson undermines Victorian ethic-aesthetic coherence and paves the way for modernism. The Romantics' search for a single authentic self and their belief that art should be sincere, natural, and ethical was increasingly questioned in the second half of the century. Rimbaud's "Je est un autre" challenges the ideal of sincerity and the aesthetic movement sees art as a pleasurable activity. In this context, Hyde is a cool dandy who invents himself, lives for the fleeting moment, and challenges bourgeois stability. He is also a satanic literary critic, scrawling blasphemous comments on a "pious work," impatient with fake sincerity like some angry, avant-garde writer.

In "A 'Men's Narrative' of Hysteria and Containment," Jane Rago presents *Jekyll and Hyde* as a hysterical text of attempted professional containment. The lawyer, Utterson, his cousin, Enfield, "a man of the world," and Dr. Lanyon and Dr. Jekyll, represent the homosocial professional world, which asserts the right to examine, analyze, and define reality through the authority of their written texts. The professionals agree on aspects of themselves remaining invisible, but their attempts to identify the marks of otherness and degeneracy are undermined because Hyde is similar to themselves and, though rejected, refuses to remain hidden and unsaid.

Dennis Denisoff retraces the theme of ageist masculinity in *The New Arabian Nights.* Stevenson, Denisoff argues, rebelled against the Victorian masculine ideal of the mature gentleman (virile in his self-mastery and restraint, powerful in his ability to define what was real and important) by emphasizing boyishness, unfixed identity, ambiguity, and an absence of constraint by economic and social imperatives. In *The New Arabian Nights*, for example, we have a series of dandies and aesthetes who are "sick of the performance" they are expected to keep up all their lives and refuse the model of middle-class masculinity.

Michela Vanon draws attention to the main literary influences on "Markheim," especially Shakespeare, Hogg, and Dostoevsky. The moral dualism familiar to Stevenson from his upbringing is used here as a tool of psychological penetration and self-analysis, given that the central character has the same age as the author. In a modern way that reminds us of writers like Albert Camus and Franz Kafka, man is shown to be a stranger to himself, with inevitably ambiguous motivations and a drive to self-annihilation.

Textual and Cultural Crossings

Alan Sandison reminds us of Richard Le Gallienne's prediction that Stevenson's "final fame will be that of the essayist." A comparison with Robert Musil is useful to show the attraction for both writers of the essay form, by its very nature incomplete and fragmentary. Another writer with a similar temperament is Roland Barthes, who in his aphoristic style reproduces "the design of thought." This might be applied to Stevenson too, a writer ever aware of form, who in his essays foregrounds taste and subjectivity, and revels in the freedom given by the essayist's amateur status. The essays that Musil incorporates into his major work emphasize the mobility and incompleteness of personality and perceived phenomena, and are opposed to the despotic reductionism of philosophers. Stevenson too is "a master of the hovering life," attracted like Musil to ideas embedded in lived experience, who views with suspicion those (like Attwater in *The Ebb-Tide*) who have no doubts.

The American literary tradition, Wendy Katz reminds us, was an important influence on Stevenson's writing. The recurrent association of sunrise and dawn with New World optimism by Thoreau and Whitman is taken up by Stevenson in his description of sunrise at the arrival in California in *The Amateur Emigrant* and his optimistic "dawning of the stars" at the end of *The Silverado Squatters*. Another influence can be seen in the generous Whitmanesque understanding of ordinary lives of the fellow passengers on ship and train, and the Thoreau-like exultation in independence and the emphasis on the pleasure of simple physical activities in

Silverado. Even the language has Whitmanesque cadences in the litany of place-names and the proverblike overviews of human life.

Ann Lawson Lucas's essay is devoted to the tradition of piracy in European literature, *Treasure Island,* and the Italian literary tradition. Salgari's pirates Sandokan (1883–84) and "il Corsaro Nero" (1898) do not apparently derive from *Treasure Island.* In the twentieth century, however, Calvino (who was to write his second novel as a variation on *Jekyll and Hyde*) creates numerous parallels with *Treasure Island* in his first novel *Il sentiero dei nidi di ragno* (1947).

Daniel Balderston starts by telling us how both Borges and Bioy Casares were enthusiastic readers of Stevenson and in 1943 included the "Was that murder?" episode from *Ballantrae* in their anthology of "the best detective stories." The narrative in question is notably enigmatic, leaving the reader to fill in the gaps, and it clearly appealed to both Borges and Bioy and thus anticipates some of their own later experiments in fiction. The idea of "murder by suggestion" is used in three stories by Borges, but the closest parallel with the *Ballantrae* story is found in Bioy's *El sueño de los heroes* (1954).

NOTES

1. David Daiches, *Robert Louis Stevenson* (1947); Robert Kiely, *Robert Louis Stevenson and the Fiction of Adventure* (1965); Edwin M. Eigner, *Robert Louis Stevenson and Romantic Tradition* (1966); Irving Saposnik, *Robert Louis Stevenson* (1974); Alan Sandison, *Robert Louis Stevenson and the Appearance of Modernism* (1996). To these five, we should add four monographs in other languages: Horst Dölvers, *Der Erzähler Robert Louis Stevenson* (1969); Jean-Pierre Naugrette, *Robert Louis Stevenson: L'aventure et son double* (1987); Burkhard Niederhoff, *Erzähler und Perspektive bei Robert Louis Stevenson* (1994); Richard Ambrosini, *R. L. Stevenson: La poetica del romanzo* (2001).

2. The MLA Bibliography lists, for the years 1963–2000 384 essays on R. L. Stevenson, 6,552 on James Joyce, 3,193 on Conrad, 2,747 on Virginia Woolf, and 1,103 on Oscar Wilde.

3. Orwell's description of the doctor's tastes, however, reflects the reality of the Imperial educational system. Harish Trivedi refers that Stevenson was "the only prose writer prescribed for study in the B.A. English Literature syllabus at the University of Allahabad from the 1890s through to the 1970s" (Trivedi 1993, 204).

4. Proust was not the only French modernist writer to recognize Stevenson's value. Two years after Stevenson's death, Mallarmé wrote in support of a group of writers and intellectuals who proposed building a monument to honor his memory (Mallarmé 1896, 879–80).

5. Calvino 1955, 968, and Calvino 1959, 1528; cf. also Anderson 1991, McLaughlin 1999.

REFERENCES

Abbott, Claude Colleer, ed. 1935. *The Letters of Gerard Manley Hopkins to Robert Bridges*. Oxford: Oxford University Press.

Anderson, Carol. 1991. No Single Key: The Fiction of Robert Louis Stevenson and Italo Calvino. *English Studies 3*. Ed. J. J. Simon and Alain Sinner. Luxemburg: Centre Universitaire de Luxemboug.

Borges, Jorge Luis. 1981. *La cifra*. Buenos Aires: Emecé.

Barenghi, Mario, ed. 1995. *Italo Calvino, Saggi 1945–1985*, vol. 1. Milano: Mondadori.

Calvino, Italo. 1955. L'isola del tesoro ha i suoi segreti. In Barenghi 1995, 968–69.

———. 1959. Risposte a 9 domande sul romanzo. In Barenghi 1995, 1528–29.

Chesterton, G. K. 1913. *The Victorian Age in Literature*. London: Home University Library.

[Fausset, Hugh l'Anson]. 1919. Stevenson To-Day. *Times Literary Supplement* 933 (4 December): 701–2.

Forster, Edwin Morgan. 1910. *Howards End*. 1953. Harmondsworth: Penguin.

Maixner, Paul. 1981. *Robert Louis Stevenson: The critical heritage*. London: Routledge & Kegan Paul.

Mallarmé, Stéphane. 1896. Sur Robert-Louis Stevenson. In *Œuvres complètes*, vol. 2: 879–80. 1979. Paris: Gallimard (La Pléiade).

McLaughlin, Martin. 1999. Dr Calvino and Mr Stevenson. *Italia&Italy* 2 (April–June): 15.

Mencken, Henry L. 1924. Tusitala [review]. *American Mercury* 3(2) (November): 378–80.

Orwell, George. 1934. *Burmese Days*. 1989. Harmondsworth: Penguin.

Proust, Marcel. 1927. *Le Temps retrouvé*. 1954. *À la recherche du temps perdu*. Paris: Gallimard (La Pléiade).

Trivedi, Harish. 1993. *Colonial Transactions: English Literature and India*. Calcutta: Papyrus.

Woolf, Leonard. 1924. The Fall of Stevenson. *Nation and Athenaeum* 34 (5 January). Also in 1927. *Essays on Literature, History, Politics, Etc.* London: Hogarth Press. 33–43.

ABBREVIATIONS

Edinburgh Edition

Stevenson, Robert Louis. 1894–98. *The Works of Robert Louis Stevenson.* 28 vols. Edinburgh Edition. London: Constable/Longmans/Seeley/Scribner's/Chatto & Windus.

Skerryvore Edition

Stevenson, Robert Louis. 1924–26. *The Works of Robert Louis Stevenson.* 30 vols. Skerryvore Edition. London: Heinemann/Chatto & Windus/Cassell/Longmans.

South Seas Edition

Stevenson, Robert Louis. 1925. *The Works of Robert Louis Stevenson.* 32 vols. South Seas Edition. New York: Charles Scribner's Sons.

Thistle Edition

(i) First issue: Stevenson, Robert Louis. 1895–99. [*The Works of Robert Louis Stevenson*]. 24 vols. Thistle Edition. New York: Charles Scribner's Sons. 1911: vols 25–26 (Balfour's biography). 1912: vol. 27 ('New Letters'). (ii) Second issue, 1901: Reprint of the Thistle Edition in 27 vols. (iii) Third issue, 1924: reset version in 25 vols., without the biography and with "New Letters" as vol. 25. (The edition in its various versions lacks a general title and is called the Thistle Edition only in its prospectuses (a name evoked, however, by thistle decorations on the cover), hence may be catalogued in libraries in various ways. Each volume has a mid-level title that assigns it to a section of the whole edition: *The Novels and Tales of Robert Louis Stevenson, The Travels and Essays of Robert Louis Stevenson*, etc.).

Tusitala Edition

Stevenson, Robert Louis. 1923–24. *The Works of Robert Louis Stevenson.* 35 vols. Tusitala Edition. London: Heinemann.

Vailima Edition

(i) Vailima Edition (1912): Stevenson, Robert Louis. 1912. *The Works of Robert Louis Stevenson.* 15 vols. Vailima Edition. New York: P. F. Collier & Son. (ii) Vailima Edition (1922–23): Stevenson, Robert Louis. 1922–23. *The Works of Robert Louis Stevenson.* 26 vols. Vailima Edition. London: Heinemann.

Ltrs

Booth, B. A. and E. Mehew, eds. 1994–95. *The Letters of Robert Louis Stevenson.* 8 vols. New Haven/London: Yale University Press.

PART I

The Pleasures of Reading, Writing, and Popular Culture

Stevenson, Morris, and the Value of Idleness

STEPHEN ARATA

I would like to begin by drifting idly down one river and then rowing vigorously—but not at all strenuously—up another. The ultimate destination of both journeys is a certain abstraction of mind. That abstraction, I will argue, is an important component of Stevenson's aesthetic theory. Using Stevenson as a touchstone, I will then make some general claims about the place of mental abstraction, idleness, reverie, and pleasure in late-nineteenth-century theories of reading. At the moment, however, those claims are still well downstream. So let us embark.

First, upon the Oise river, site of *An Inland Voyage*. The climax of that book comes when Stevenson and his traveling companion, paddling effortlessly with the river's current through long empty eventless days, finally achieve what Stevenson calls "the apotheosis of stupidity." Now, he writes, "when the river no longer ran in a proper sense, only glided seaward with an even, outright, but imperceptible speed, and when the sky smiled upon day after day without variety, we began to slip into that golden doze of the mind which follows much exercise in the open air. I have stupefied myself in this way more than once: indeed, I dearly love the feeling; but I never had it to the same degree as when paddling down the *Oise*. It was the apotheosis of stupidity" (Stevenson 1878: 110).

In this golden doze, somewhere "between sleeping and waking" (112), the muscles, even the voluntary ones, perform their duties without supervision, and the brain goes off-line altogether. "The central bureau of nerves," Stevenson writes, "what in some moods we call *Ourselves*, enjoyed

3

its holiday without disturbance, like a Government Office. The great wheels of intelligence turned idly in the head, like fly-wheels, grinding no grist" (113). Impressions from the landscape impinge on the senses, but no answering consciousness rises to meet them, and so they drift unattended in some interior space Stevenson can give no name to. Likewise, "thoughts presented themselves unbidden," but they are not his own thoughts, because he is not there to think them. "I considered them like a part of the landscape" (114). Moreover, as Stevenson contemplates "the depth, if I must not call it the intensity, of my abstraction," he notices that it leaves him with "less *me* and more *not-me* than I was accustomed to expect" (113). Indeed, "a province of my proper being had thrown off allegiance and set up for itself" (114). His usual self has now "dwindled into quite a little thing" (114), and he responds to this secession of the *me* with a benign placidity that almost, but never quite, amounts to actual interest. Landscapes glide by, thoughts arise, impressions impinge, and someone paddles a boat. An "ecstatic stupor," Stevenson calls it. Cultivating it, he says, was "the farthest piece of travel [we] accomplished." All in all, "this frame of mind was the great exploit of our voyage" (114).

What a strange thing to say. But then *An Inland Voyage* is an odd book. It does almost none of the things travel books do. It is not a voyage of discovery in any conventional sense. Stevenson takes, literally, only passing interest in the topography he traverses, the communities he encounters, the people he meets. Nor does he take more than a passing interest in himself: this is not an inward journey into his own psyche. Instead the book seems to have been written in precisely the state of ecstatic stupor it describes. And, if I may take my own experience as representative, it seems designed to induce a like frame of mind in readers as well. This is not a criticism. I take seriously Stevenson's claim that achieving such utter mental abstraction was a goal of his voyage, as it would be a goal of many of his subsequent travels. Clearly it is a state of mind Stevenson was intrigued by, and it is one he pursued assiduously. In his essay "Walking Tours" he says that the true walker is never "in quest of the picturesque," for landscape "is quite accessory" to his aims (Stevenson 1876: 150). The true walker learns to *stop* paying attention and "surrender himself to that fine intoxication that comes of much motion in the open air" (152). "[O]nce you have fallen into an equitable stride, it requires no conscious thought from you to keep it up, and yet it prevents you from thinking earnestly of anything else. Like knitting, like the work of a copying clerk, it gradually neutralises and sets to sleep the serious activity of the mind" (154).

What are we to make of this? How are we to understand it? In *An Inland Voyage* Stevenson suggests that this "calm, golden, and incurious" mental state is akin to what Buddhists call Nirvana (114). Maybe, but I think there are other more relevant contexts closer at hand. Here is where we embark on the second inland voyage I mentioned, on the Thames this time, headed upriver, and accompanied not by Robert Louis Stevenson but by William Morris, or rather by William Guest, Morris's alter ego in *News from Nowhere*. The second half of that book depicts a long beautiful journey up the Thames from London to Morris's beloved Kelmscott Manor. It is a secular pilgrim's progress, with Kelmscott as the New Jerusalem. During the journey Guest finally gives himself over, not just intellectually but physically, emotionally, spiritually, to the utopian world he has landed in. Rowing up the river, he momentarily succeeds in producing in himself the state of consciousness appropriate to that utopia. Like Stevenson on the Oise, Guest learns to cultivate an emptiness that is not vacuity but instead a kind of balance or integration of body and psyche. His traveling companion, the wise and lovely Ellen, echoes Stevenson when she counsels Guest not to confuse this condition with "mere dreamy musing" (Morris 1890: 204). She proposes a better definition: "repose amidst of energy" (204). Rowing is the perfect example of what she is talking about. Her larger point—and Morris's as well—is that all activities in Nowhere are so defined. Indeed, at the heart of Morris's socialism is the belief, as he puts it in his 1889 essay "How Shall We Live Then?" that we must be "free to enjoy all . . . exercises of the body without any sense of shame" and "without any suspicion that our mental powers are so remarkable and god-like that we are rather above such common things" (Morris 1889: 261). "We shall not be happy," he writes, "unless we live like good animals" (261). One name for these exercises of the body is, simply, work—not useless toil or degrading labor but genuine work, which, as Morris writes in "How We Live and How We Might Live," we experience at a deep level as the pleasure of "moving one's limbs and exercising one's bodily powers" (Morris 1884: 17). What in *News from Nowhere* he calls "work-pleasure" (Morris 1890: 134) is for Morris the source of all human value, and it is among other things the precondition for art. Yet work-pleasure is precisely what the modern world no longer offers us. That alone, says Morris, is a sure sign of our degradation. By contrast, he says, imagine a social order so arranged that every human act is one of repose amidst of energy. That would be utopia. It would be the earthly paradise.

I introduce Morris here because he helps to illuminate an important aspect of Stevenson's aesthetic theory. That aesthetic theory in turn is, like Morris's, grounded in a political insight. I am not suggesting that Stevenson was a socialist in Morris's sense. But the two men do share an interest in a cluster of keywords that they invest with a weight and a significance— political *and* aesthetic—that is likely to strike us as counterintuitive. Two of those words are idleness and pleasure. They are in fact among Morris's favorite words, recurring with unmissable frequency throughout his political writings, his long narrative poems, and his prose romances, as well as throughout *News from Nowhere.* Contrary to common usage, Morris does not associate idleness with passivity or pleasure with escapism. He instead charges them, consciously and systematically, with revolutionary energy. Less consciously and far less systematically, Stevenson does the same.

To see what is at issue here, consider both writers' seemingly perverse insistence on the value of not paying attention. Stevenson on the Oise, William Guest on the Thames, both slide into states of mind in which they no longer attend consciously to their surroundings or to themselves. At best their attention is diffused, not centered on any one object or set of objects or ideas. We have all been in that state and can attest to its pleasures. But its value? The value—as our parents, teachers, mentors, and employers have always told us—lies precisely in learning to pay attention, in cultivating the discipline needed to accomplish that always-difficult task. The idea that paying attention is at once a virtue in itself and the fount of other virtues is so deeply engrained in our thought that it is difficult to see the connection as anything but natural. Yet it was not always so. For a long time—from, roughly, the late eighteenth century to the early twentieth—attention was a *problem*, or rather it was the site of a series of problems that cut across intellectual disciplines. During this period, attention attracted the attention of numerous thinkers, great and small. What *is* attention, anyway? How is it produced? In what contexts is it needed, and why? How might it be prolonged? How is it related to will? to discipline? to education? to temperament? to physiology? to environment? These and related questions were posed by philosophers, physiologists, political economists, aestheticians, psychologists, sociologists, and others, all of whom were for different reasons attempting to define and to theorize this phenomenon, this problem, of attention.[1]

There were some practical incentives for doing so. It is no coincidence that attention emerges as an object of inquiry during a period when new forms of industrial production were transforming the conditions and experience of work. In the first volume of *Capital,* Marx points out that factory managers had long since recognized that the conditions of factory- and millwork made attentiveness a problem (Marx 1867: 407–17). For industrial workers, paying attention was essential but often nearly impossible to do. For their own safety, mill-hands needed to concentrate as they interacted with ever larger, ever more complex machines. Yet the very nature of their tasks fostered *in*attention, since those tasks were often literally mind-numbing in their tedium and repetitiveness. In Morris's terms, industrial labor under these conditions is the epitome of useless toil. Concentration is required, but no other faculties of mind are engaged. Indeed, the intensity of the concentration required of industrial laborers leaves no room for any other mental activity. The need to pay attention drives out everything else. Paying attention is all they can do, yet conversely, because of the tedium of their tasks, it is also all they can do to pay attention.

In Morris's utopia, useless toil has given way to genuine work, which always involves the integration of body and mind in tasks that engage the full range of human faculties. "Men whose hands were skilled in fashioning," writes Morris in "The Lesser Arts of Life," "could not help thinking the while, and soon found out their deft fingers could express some part of the tangle of their thoughts, and that this new pleasure hindered not their daily work, for in the very labour they lived by lay the material in which their thought could be embodied; and thus, though they laboured, they laboured somewhat for their pleasure and uncompelled, and had conquered the curse of toil" (Morris 1882: 236). Note Morris's insistence on "pleasure," which is invariably his term for the sensuality, amounting at times to a kind of erotics, of work. Implicit too in this passage is the altered status of attention in the context of work. Genuine work engages the attention, but it is always a multiple, relaxed, and diffused attention rather than a focused and intense one. The craftwork Morris most enjoyed, weaving especially, called for an attentiveness that still allowed plenty of room for attending to other things too. Morris was himself famously adept at "multitasking": making sketches for wallpaper patterns at the same time that he was mentally composing poetry, all while engaged in vigorous conversation. Far from finding this taxing or wearying, Morris was invigorated by it, in part because his faculties were agreeably diffused across a range of objects and tasks, in part because like Stevenson he found a release in being decentered, in giving himself over to the "not-me," which for him was a defining effect of pleasurable work. Repose amidst of energy.

For Morris, then, learning not to pay attention could be a political act. In a properly-ordered world, social and economic relations would be so arranged that the kind of attention required by, say, a factory manager or by my teachers in grade school would no longer serve any function. In the world as it is presently ordered, refusing to submit to the regime of attention can be a gesture of defiance, an indication that one recognizes the need to pay attention as a symptom of larger social ills. Morris's deliberately provoking term for such a refusal is idleness.

So too is it Stevenson's. At the beginning of "An Apology for Idlers" Stevenson foregrounds the political dimension of his argument concerning the "utility" of idleness. "Idleness so called," he writes, "which does not consist in doing nothing, but in doing a great deal not recognized in the dogmatic formularies of the ruling class, has as good a right to state its position as industry itself" (Stevenson 1877: 67). The essay as a whole works by wittily reversing the valuations of those familiar Victorian keywords, industry and idleness. Idleness is shown to be a form of vigorous activity and a vehicle for self-development, while industry produces only mental torpor and physical lassitude, what Stevenson calls a "dead-alive" kind of existence (73). "Extreme *busyness*," he writes, "is a symptom of deficient vitality" (73). The world tells you to work hard, buckle down, attend only to your business, let nothing divert your attention or your energy. Yet those who follow this advice "have no curiosity; they cannot give themselves over to random provocations; they do not take pleasure in the exercise of their faculties for its own sake. . . . It is no good speaking to such folk: they *cannot* be idle, their nature is not generous enough" (73). Like Morris, Stevenson sees "industry" as an ideologically charged term, and like him he wants to strip it of its accustomed virtues. To be industrious is finally to be, in Stevenson's phrase, "paralysed or alienated" (74), the two conditions open to workers in the modern world. It is to exist "in a sort of coma" that makes "the whole breathing world . . . a blank" (73–74). To be idle, to be deliberately and self-consciously idle, is on the other hand to resist the ideology of work and all it entails in order to cultivate the pleasures of "random provocations" and "the exercise of one's faculties for its own sake." Where Morris offers his resistance in the name of socialism, in "An Apology for Idlers" Stevenson, we might say, resists on behalf of the Republic of Bohemia: a not wholly serious undertaking, in other words. But as so often in his writings, the seemingly inconsequential air and not-quite serious tone of this essay mask an incisive critique of a type I would be willing to call socialist if only Stevenson were willing to do the same.

The issues I have been raising thus far bear directly on key developments in late-Victorian literary theory. Consider again the word "idleness," this time in the context of the history of criticism of narrative fiction, the novel in particular. Advocates of the novel from the early eighteenth century onward have always had to fend off the charge that reading stories is mere idleness, the product as well as the source of mental vacancy. The connection between idleness and immorality is too familiar to need rehearsing. It would be an exaggeration—but not much of one—to say that narrative theory over the last three hundred years has largely been an effort to refute Samuel Johnson's claim in *Rambler* 4 that novels appeal exclusively to "the young, the ignorant, and the idle" (Johnson 1750: 21). What Henry James in "The Art of Fiction" called "the old evangelical hostility" (James 1884: 45) to the novel still lingered in the 1880s and '90s, though by this time the genre as a whole enjoyed—thanks in no small part to James—a new-won legitimacy. James says the novel earned that legitimacy by at last learning how to take itself seriously. True enough, but legitimation also depended on the emergence of a new class of professionalized readers, whose business it was to read seriously. I am referring not just to the professional reading that rapidly became the norm in the academic departments of modern literature, which sprouted up in the last decades of the century, but more generally to the kinds of reading practiced by anyone who took to heart Matthew Arnold's strictures concerning the function of criticism in the contemporary world.[2]

In the 1880s and '90s the activity of reading—what it is, how it is best done and by whom, and to what ends—began to be theorized in new, indeed in unprecedented, ways. Among other changes, this was the moment when some forms of reading began to be described as labor. Reading—not in the sense of mere literacy, but as a set of higher-level skills having to do with judgment, taste, perception, sensibility, discrimination—was now something you could be trained to do. You could be evaluated at it, and you could earn professional credentials with it. You could make your living by it. Viewed in this way, reading is the very opposite of idleness. To call reading work, to give it that dignity, is to invest it with all the virtues Victorians associated with the term. It would be difficult to overestimate the importance of that shift. Yet to call reading work is also to assimilate it into larger institutional structures, to open it to the possibility of becoming routinized, bureaucratized, mere "toil" in Morris's sense. Not surprisingly, the new theories of reading that emerged in the last decades of the century continually returned to the issue of attention. A quite extensive body of literature on the physiology of reading became available, not just in medical or other specialist journals but also in the popular periodical press. Much of it focused on attention, and on the vital importance of its development in the teaching of reading skills.[3]

Both Morris and Stevenson had significant reservations about the regularization of reading. In the late 1870s Morris turned down the chance to succeed Arnold as professor of poetry at Oxford; in the mid 1880s he was among the very few to oppose the establishment of Oxford's first chair of literary studies, the Merton Professorship of Literature.[4] To turn literary study into a profession would inevitably make the writing and reading of literature mere toil: tasks imposed by the dominant culture for its own purposes and ends. In his own writing from the 1860s onward, especially his poetry, Morris consciously endeavored to produce works that could be read without effort or concentration, works that could, in effect, be read idly. Needless to say, this runs utterly counter to some of the most basic of our own notions of literary artistry.[5] Morris, we recall, often composed his verses while he was doing other things too. His attention was dispersed, not concentrated, and it was precisely this dispersal that facilitated his creativity and enhanced his pleasure. "If a chap can't compose an epic poem while he's weaving a tapestry," Morris is reported to have said one day, "he had better shut up, he'll never do any good at all" (Mackail 1899, vol. 1: 186). The pleasures Morris's poems offer to readers are never intense. Instead they are placid, continuous, and very much attuned to the rhythms of the body. I am certain that Morris had in mind the practice of many traditional craftsmen—weavers and cobblers especially, if the period's working-class autobiographies are accurate indications—of propping up books beside them to read while they worked. Poems composed by a body occupied by the rhythms of tapestry-weaving might best be read by a body occupied by rhythms of a similar kind. They certainly do *not* repay the kind of close reading we usually practice, which is one reason Morris's poetry is so seldom today read by academic readers. What we find scandalous in Morris's method is precisely that he is not giving his full attention to the act of composition. He is weaving, and he is composing. But perhaps we should instead call his a different mode of attention, one that works to integrate body and mind, hand and brain. To appreciate the products of that labor might require a more diffused attention, a somatic attention, perhaps.

Stevenson presents a more complex case, and in many ways a more interesting one. As Alan Sandison (1996) among others has ably documented, Stevenson was thoroughly committed to the virtues we associate with modernist literary artistry: elegance, austerity, indirection, compression, irony, and so on—the kinds of things you cannot achieve without paying close attention to what you are doing. And as a result Stevenson's works amply reward our close attention as readers. Yet often Stevenson seems actively to discourage that kind of readerly response. Unlike Walter Pater or Henry James, Stevenson asks us simply to revel. The commitment to stylistic perfection is in his case wholly in the service of pleasure, of literature as play, of reading as idleness. As his essays and letters repeatedly show, Stevenson did not see literature as a vehicle of moral improvement, as an instrument of useful knowledge, or as a form of engagement with one's historical moment. Indeed he can seem positively Nabokovian in this respect. Unlike Nabokov, though, Stevenson committed himself to popular culture and to mass market genres. He did so because he saw in popular literature a (perhaps) last refuge from the routinization of reading. Indeed, it took another century for such literature to become the object of professional readerly scrutiny. Like Morris, Stevenson tries to relieve us of the burden of paying attention, or more precisely, he encourages us to re-imagine attention as a more dispersed and decentered phenomenon, one capable of inducing that ecstatic stupor he so valued. Reading ought not to be work, though writing must be. It is that combination which makes Stevenson so intriguing. It is also one source of the challenge he offers to contemporary critical theory. At the close of *An Inland Voyage*, having paddled idly down the Oise to the end of his journey, having so carefully cultivated a state of pleasurable mental abstraction, Stevenson suddenly discovers "I was weary of dipping the paddle. . . . I wished to get to work" (Stevenson 1878: 134–35). That work presumably refers to the writing of *An Inland Voyage*, and it is the sole acknowledgment within the book of the labor that went to produce it. Yet it is labor that seeks to efface itself, and in so doing coaches us to remake ourselves as readers, to reposition ourselves under the sign of pleasure, not work.

NOTES

1. For an incisive account of the status of attention in nineteenth-century thought, see Crary (1999: 11–79).

2. There is a sizable, and still growing, body of work on the rise of institutional literary studies in late-Victorian Britain and America. See, e.g., Baldick, Court, Parrinder.

3. The culmination of late-Victorian research on reading was E. B. Huey's massively influential *Psychology and Pedagogy of Reading* (1908), which is still worth consulting for its synthesis of the previous two generations' worth of speculation on the psychological and physiological processes involved in the development of what Huey was among the first to call "reading skills."

4. See Morris's November 1, 1886 letter to the *Pall Mall Gazette* (Kelvin 1884–96, vol. 2: 589–90), in which he outlines his objections to establishing the Merton Professorship in particular and departments of modern literature in general.

5. I am drawing here on Skoblow's stimulating discussion of Morris's poetics and its relation to his political beliefs.

REFERENCES

Baldick, Chris. 1983. *The Social Mission of English Criticism 1848–1932*. Oxford: Clarendon Press.

Court, Franklin. 1992. *Institutionalizing English Literature: The Culture and Politics of Literary Study 1750–1900*. Stanford, CA: Stanford University Press.

Crary, Jonathan. 1999. *Suspensions of Perception: Attention, Spectacle, and Modern Culture*. Cambridge, MA: MIT Press.

Huey, E. B. 1908. *The Psychology and Pedagogy of Reading*. London: Macmillan.

James, Henry. 1884. The Art of Fiction. In *Henry James: Literary Criticism: Essays on Literature, American Writers, English Writers*. 1984. Washington, DC: Library of America. 44–65.

Johnson, Samuel. 1750. *Rambler*. In *Works of Samuel Johnson*. Vol. 3. Ed. E. L. McAdams, Jr. 1968. New Haven, CT: Yale University Press.

Kelvin, Norman, ed. 1984–96. *The Collected Letters of William Morris*. 4 vols. Princeton, NJ: Princeton University Press.

Mackail, J. W. 1899. *The Life of William Morris*. 2 vols. London: Longmans, Green & Co.

Marx, Karl. 1867. *Das Kapital. Kritik der politischen Oekonomie*. English translation: *Capital: A Critical Analysis of Capitalist Production*. Trans. Samuel Moore and Edward Aveling. 1887. London: Swan Sonnenschein.

Morris, William. 1882. The Lesser Arts of Life. In Morris 1910–15. Vol. 22, 235–69.

———. 1884. How We Live and How We Might Live. In Morris 1910–15. Vol. 23, 3–26.

———. 1889. How Shall We Live Then? In "An Unpublished Lecture of William Morris," by Paul Maier. 1971. *International Review of Social History* 16: 217–40.

———. 1890. *News from Nowhere*. In Morris 1910–15. Vol. 16, 1–211.

———. 1910–15. *The Collected Works of William Morris*. London: Longmans, Green & Co.

Parrinder, Patrick. 1991. *Authors and Authority: English and American Criticism 1750–1990*. London: Macmillan.

Sandison, Alan. 1996. *Robert Louis Stevenson and the Appearance of Modernism: A Future Feeling*. New York: St. Martin's Press.

Skoblow, Jeffrey. 1993. *Paradise Dislocated: Morris, Politics, Art*. Charlottesville: University Press of Virginia.

Stevenson, Robert Louis. 1877. "An Apology for Idlers." Thistle Edition, first issue. Vol. 13, 67–79.

———. 1878. *An Inland Voyage*. Thistle Edition, first issue. Vol. 12, 1–135.

———. 1876. "Walking Tours." Thistle Edition, first issue. Vol. 13, 150–59.

Living in a Book

RLS as an Engaged Reader

R. L. ABRAHAMSON

The way to read a book, Stevenson often seems to say, is to treat it as if it were life itself. Writing to John Addington Symonds about *Crime and Punishment*, "the greatest book I have read easily in ten years," Stevenson contrasts his way of reading the book with Henry James's way of reading. "James did not care for it because the character of Raskolnikov was not objective; and at that I divined a great gulf between us and, on further reflection, the existence of a certain impotence in many minds of today, which prevents them from living *in* a book or a character, and keeps them standing afar off, spectators of a puppet show. To such I suppose the book may seem empty in the centre; to the others it is a room, a house of life, into which they themselves enter, and are tortured and purified" (*Ltrs* 5: 220–21).

What might it mean to "live *in* a book or a character"? What is wrong with "standing afar off, spectators of a puppet show"? What is the connection between reading and being "tortured and purified"? And why did it mean so much to Stevenson? Let us take a survey of Stevenson's reading habits and see how far we can answer some of these questions.

The first thing that strikes us is *how much Stevenson read*. He read favorite books like the *Vicomte de Bragelonne* (in six volumes!) "either five or six" times (Stevenson 1887b: 119), and—so at least he told Mark Twain —he read *Huck Finn* "four times, and am quite ready to begin again tomorrow," including a kind of double reading on the first occasion when he "read it straight through, [and] began again at the beginning and read

13

it straight through again without a break" (*Ltrs* 6: 161). We have pictures of him reading at the dinner table at Heriot Row when his parents were away, reading amid a severe bout of diarrhea just before the *Devonia* set out for New York, reading again at solitary dinners in San Francisco when he was living alone before Fanny's divorce, and, though he does not give us many pictures of this, we must imagine him also reading on his sickbed, on his many journeys by train and boat, and on his walking tours. His letters are filled with references to books he is reading and with requests for more books to be sent to him when he was abroad.

Anyone can read a lot, but not everyone can summon up from memory so many apt quotations—often just tossed out in passing—as Stevenson does in his letters.[1] Here is a list of some of the authors he quotes from in the letters (I exclude quotations from the Bible and Shakespeare): Virgil, Browning, Coleridge, Byron, Burns, Horace, Luther, Lady Grizel Bailie, Montaigne, Hugo, Milton, Ovid, Longfellow, Browne, Goethe, Poe, Whitman, Villon, Watts, Scott, Marvell, Heine, Molière, Henley, Dickens, Cicero, Pliny, Addison, Smollet, Disraeli, Pope, Wordsworth, Herrick, Cowper, Bret Harte, W. S. Gilbert, Thoreau, Marlowe, Tacitus, Butler, Twain, George Eliot, Marryat, Tennyson, Dryden, de Musset, Lamb, Goldsmith, Galt, Bayley, Racine, Persius, "Sir Patrick Spens," Carlyle, Hood, Shelley, Barnfield, Bunyan, Spenser, Gay. You have to read intensely to be able to carry so much literature in your head.

Stevenson often read books to match his moods. Horace, he reported, feels too urban to suit the atmosphere of the hillside olive groves above Mentone; he reads *Maud* when feeling his love for Mrs. Sitwell particularly keenly. Only certain books would do when the "black dog" melancholy gripped him. In a "state of intellectual prostration," the nineteen-year-old RLS announces to his cousin Bob that he was "fit for nothing but smoking, and reading Charles Baudelaire" (*Ltrs* 1: 372; 2: 3; 1: 193–94).

One in a long series of poignant disagreements with his father involved a debate, near the end of Thomas Stevenson's life, over the relative merits of reading Lockhart's *Life of Scott* as opposed to the Waverley Novels when one was depressed. Just come from reading Lockhart, Stevenson advises his father, sunk deep in gloom, "*not* to read [the *Life*]; as it has made me very ill and would make you worse." He's thinking of the ending of the biography, with its graphic depictions of Scott's failing mental faculties, to which "no Waverley novel approaches in power, blackness, bitterness and moral elevation . . . and yet the Waverley novels are better reading for every day than the life. You may take a tonic daily, but not phlebotomy" (*Ltrs* 4:

221). Stevenson apologized to his father at the end of this letter for having sent him a sermon, but in many ways this was not a sermon but a prescription: Reading as therapy. It even worked for serious physical illnesses: Sherlock Holmes, as he told Conan Doyle, provided a "for the moment effectual" cure for pleurisy (*Ltrs* 8: 50).

Besides the reading Stevenson did to raise his spirits or to pass the time, there was the copious reading he needed to do as research for his own writing, reading that ranged from a missionary's account of traveling in the Western Hebrides in the late eighteenth century to his grandfather's diaries and letters to books on hot-air balloons. And of course there were all those times as a sedulous ape, when books were not companions, or therapy, or research, but textbooks on style.

I said the first thing that strikes us about Stevenson's reading habits is the sheer volume, range, and depth of his reading. The next thing might be the enthusiasm with which he spoke about the books he had read. He opened his "Gossip on Romance" with a sustained cry of enthusiasm about the joy of reading: "In anything fit to be called by the name of reading, the process itself should be absorbing and voluptuous; we should gloat over a book, be rapt clean out of ourselves [pay attention to this phrase], and rise from the perusal, our mind filled with the busiest, kaleidoscopic dance of images, incapable of sleep or of continuous thought. The words, if the book be eloquent, should run thenceforward in our ears like the noise of breakers, and the story, if it be a story, repeat itself in a thousand coloured pictures to the eye" (1882: 52). We can find this excitement throughout his letters, too. Here are some moments, taken almost at random, from some of the letters. His tone varies with the different correspondents, but the immediacy of the experience is always there at a high pitch:

> To Fanny Sitwell in 1873: "I have found here a new friend, to whom I grow daily more devoted—George Sand. I go on from one novel to another and think the last I have read the most sympathetic and friendly in tone, until I have read another. It is a life in dreamland. Have you read *Mademoiselle Merquem*? I have just finished it and I am full of happiness."[2]
>
> To James Payn in 1881, in praise of the hero of his novel *A Grape from a Thorn*: "Hip, hip, hurrah for Charles Edward! . . . Vive le prince! . . . Bully for you! . . . James Payn for ever . . ." [the last three phrases composing a spiral of enthusiastic cries drawn on the page, followed by a postscript only slightly more sober] Do not let my childishness blind you to the serious

nature of my admiration; Charles Edward is really a fine thing: the devil a man alive that could have looked near it!"

To Sidney Colvin in 1883 about J. R. Seeley's *The Expansion of England*: "O!—Seeley is a man of hell's talent; I went insane over his book; he is too clever to live, and the book a gem."

To W. E. Henley in 1885 of *Crime and Punishment*: "it is not reading a book, it is having a brain fever, to read it." (*Ltrs* 1: 384; 3: 258–59; 4: 199; 5: 151)

Two metaphors seem to predominate in Stevenson's discussions of reading. In the one, a book becomes a house, or a location that one inhabits—appropriate language from a writer whose fiction contains such vivid attention to place. We have seen how, when contrasting his reading of *Crime and Punishment* with Henry James's, Stevenson spoke about "living *in* a book or character," a book "is a room, a house of life, into which [readers] enter, and are tortured and purified." In "A Gossip on a Novel of Dumas's" he discusses those books he used to read but reads no longer as "houses which were once like home to me, but where I now rarely visit" (1887b: 118). Notice the way reading is taking on a sense of placement (home) and movement outward from oneself (visiting).

Another example of reading as the act of visiting a locale comes in reply to Sidney Colvin, who, writing in 1891 from Lochinvar in the far north of Scotland to Stevenson in Samoa, a little tactlessly asked Stevenson if he were ever "homesick for the Highlands and the Isles." (Was he goading his friend to come back to Britain?) Stevenson did not rise to the bait but replied that he had in fact just been visiting these areas himself: "Conceive that for the last month I have been living there between 1786 and 1850, in my grandfather's diaries and letters" (*Ltrs* 7: 152).

Most commonly, however, Stevenson talks about reading in the language we use for personal relationships. He speaks of authors as though they are intimates of his. Montaigne, for instance, "is the most charming of table-companions." Rather than a friend, someone like Chateaubriand appears as the kind of person we want to avoid in the streets, a *cad*, in nineteenth-century terms: "What a miraculous ideal of literary demerit Chateaubriand is. Of course, he is very clever to the last degree; but he is such a—liar, that I cannot away with him. He is more antipathetic to me than anyone else in the world" (*Ltrs* 1: 335–36, 360).

Not just authors but books themselves take on the language of human relationships. Here, taken from the opening of "A Gossip on a Novel of Dumas's" is a short list of some his remarks about reading:

We "revisit" books "as we choose and revisit human friends."

Scott, Shakespeare, Molière, Montaigne, *The Egoist*, and *Vicomte* "form the inner circle of my intimates."

Some books "look at me with reproach as I pass them by on my shelves."

"I am on . . . sad terms" with some old favorites.

Reading alone in the Pentlands during "a long, silent, solitary lamplight evening by the fire" was not really solitary since "I gained so many friends."

The characters in Dumas interact with him, as he with them: "Aramis, although he knows I do not love him, yet plays to me with his best graces, as to an old patron of the show . . . my acquaintance with Raoul has never gone beyond a bow." (1887b: 118–20)

Just as he speaks of the male characters as friends ("Perhaps my dearest and best friend outside of Shakespeare is d'Artagnan—the elderly d'Artagnan of the *Vicomte de Bragelonne*," 1887a: 111), so we find him speaking of female characters as objects of his love. How else to tell Henry James of his delight in the character of Adela Chart from the story "The Marriages" than to proclaim: "I could live and die with Adela" and to include in his letter a love poem to her:

Adela, Adela, Adela Chart
What have you done to my elderly heart?
Of all the ladies of paper and ink
I count you the paragon, call you the pink. (*Ltrs* 7: 292–93)

The man would be crazy if he actually loved Adela or actually thought d'Artagnan was his friend. Blurring boundaries is a common sign of madness. But Stevenson was not mad; he was not deluded about the boundaries between life and art. His argument in "A Humble Remonstrance" against James's claim that books "compete with life" should remind us of this (1884: 84).

And so ought the many moments in his letters when (often just after he has given one of his enthusiastic outbursts) he offers an objective, critical assessment of what he has just read. Most of his youthful letters to his cousin Bob, for instance, contain attempts at sophisticated literary criticism, such as the way, at age sixteen, and in contrast to how he was later to write about the book, he judges Dumas's *Vicomte de Bragelonne* a disappointing novel. "The conversations are certainly wonderful, but the strength of the plot is frittered away, and the whole story is lengthened out to a most unconscionable and dreary extent. The strength of Porthos, and the furiously acute intellects of Aramis and D'Artagnan are singularly overdone." Even when he turns to praise the book for a few sentences, he retains a dispassionate, objective tone—and, incidentally, offers a very astute comment about Dumas's literary skill. "In spite of all these defects," he goes on, ". . . the book displays a wonderful amount of genius, and imagination. Did you ever observe the different ranges of intellect displayed by Aramis and D'Artagnan?" (*Ltrs* 1: 112).

In later letters, Stevenson's tone seldom remains so consistently objective. The common pattern seems to be some sort of enthusiastic outburst about how the book has moved him (usually in the language as we have seen that speaks of the book as another human being), and then shifting to some objective criticism, then perhaps closing the discussion with one more outburst. This is what happens, for instance, in a letter to William Archer, praising George Bernard Shaw's early novel *Cashel Byron's Profession*. First comes the extravagant praise, especially for the character Bashville. "Over Bashville the footman I howled with derision and delight; I dote on Bashville—I could read of him forever; *de Bashville je suis le fervent*; there is only one Bashville, and I am his devoted slave; *Bashville est magnifique*." Then, however, comes a different note, the voice of the serious critic: "the author has a taste in chivalry like Walter Scott's or Dumas's, and then he daubs in little bits of socialism; he soars away on the wings of the romantic griphon . . . and I believe in my heart he thinks he is labouring in a quarry of solid granite realism." But before he finishes, he gives one final shout (in all caps): "It is HORRID FUN," adding just before the signature, like one *flâneur* to another watching the girls go by, "I say, Archer, my God, what women!" (*Ltrs* 5: 225). Stevenson can offer a sound critical assessment of the quality of the literature, but his final response comes in the language of personal experience. What made this way of talking about books so important to Stevenson?

What Stevenson saw happening when he read was—here comes another boundary crossing—some sort of crossing over from the self to the other. Reading was so important to Stevenson precisely because crossing that boundary to the world of the other took him out of himself, not just intellectually but on a deep, emotional level. In a sense this is escapism; in a sense it is that naïve activity of identifying with a character. But there is a lot more going on. An important passage from "A Humble Remonstrance" takes this farther. Here Stevenson describes the action of reading a romance: "Something happens as we desire to have it happen to ourselves; some situation, that we have long dallied with in fancy, is realised in the story with enticing and appropriate details. Then we forget the characters; then we push the hero aside; then we plunge into the tale in our own person and bathe in fresh experience; and then, and then only, do we say we have been reading a romance" (1884: 61). We are both in and not in the story. This is not our life but the life of d'Artagnan or whoever, and yet we "plunge into the tale in our own person"; we merge with that character.

Books of fiction "disengage us from ourselves," he says in "Books Which Have Influenced Me"; they are like life "but with a singular change—that monstrous, consuming *ego* of ours being, for the nonce, struck out" (1887a: 111). Here, of course, we find the same pattern as Stevenson gave us in his archetypal image of escaping from the self: Jekyll's taking the potion in order to leave his own self behind and live in the life of that other, Mr. Hyde. If this were just escapism, then the game would be over. We would enjoy our spell with the book and return through the small door in the courtyard, drink our chemicals, and return to our old selves like Jekyll unchanged. But here is where Stevenson's reading diverged from the Jekyll–Hyde pattern. While living in a book, we undergo some sort of moral change that Jekyll never experienced. The influence of the books "is profound and silent, like the influence of nature; they mould by contact; we drink them up like water, and are bettered, yet know not how" (1887a: 111). This is no longer Jekyll's chemical transformation but something more like an alchemical transformation that, once the ego is out of the way, refines us in a mysterious, not to say mystical, way. What happens when you read *Crime and Punishment*? You enter a "house of life" and are "tortured and purified" (*Ltrs* : 220–21); Do you want to develop the delicate and fine traits of a gentleman? Then read Thackeray's *The Newcomes*. "[W]hat experience is more formative, what step of life is more efficient, than to know and weep for Colonel Newcome?" (1888: 160).

It is not only in fiction that this alchemical merging occurs. Reading biographies, Stevenson merged himself into the person whose life he was reading. Sometimes a change worked upon him unawares, as reading the lives of Goethe and Balzac contributed to that subtle change in his own life from "one whose business was to shirk into one whose business was to strive and persevere," but "I was never conscious of a struggle, nor registered a vow, nor seemingly had anything personally to do with the matter" (1880: 90).

Sometimes the character you encounter in fiction or biography will startle you as some people in real life do, by acting as a mirror and externalizing your own characteristics—usually the less attractive ones. *The Egoist* does this especially. "It is yourself that is hunted down; these are our own faults that are dragged into the day and numbered . . . . I think Willoughby an unmanly but a very serviceable exposure of myself" (1888: 115). Reading Dowden's biography of Shelley, Stevenson confesses to Lady Taylor: "I was uneasy at my resemblances to Shelley; I seem but a Shelley with less oil, and no genius; though I have had the fortune to live longer and (partly) to grow up" (*Ltrs* 5: 339).

Sometimes, especially when reading nonfiction, you develop a friendship with the author (no distinction here, of course, between the author and the author's voice), who then influences, no, inspires your life for the better. Such a friend was Montaigne, "in a dozen ways a finer fellow, [who] held in a dozen ways a nobler view of life" than anyone we could meet today. Or Marcus Aurelius, reading whom is like making a new friend: "when you have read, you carry away with you a memory of the man himself; it is as though you had touched a loyal hand, looked into brave eyes, and made a noble friend; there is another bond on you thenceforward, binding you to life and to the love of virtue" (1887a: 112, 114).

This process of encountering something other than oneself and adjusting and growing from the encounter gets its fullest attention in the essay "Books Which Have Influenced Me." Here it becomes plain that Stevenson has not been talking about mere identification with the character or confusion of a literary voice with a real person. What matters is how we move on after engaging so closely with a character or an author. We need what he calls "the gift of reading," which "consists, first of all, in a vast intellectual endowment—a free grace, I find I must call it—by which a man rises to understand that he is not punctually right, nor those from whom he differs absolutely wrong. . . . Something that seems quite new, or that seems insolently false or very dangerous, is the test of a reader. If he tries to see what it means, what truth excuses it, he has the gift, and let him read. If he is merely hurt, or offended, or exclaims upon his author's folly, he had better take to the daily papers; he will never be a reader." (1887b: 115). The point, then, is not that the book or character we are living in is the same as ourselves, but that it is different, and this difference stretches us. Identifying with Colonel Newcome stretches us to practice the attributes of a gentleman. Reading Whitman, engaging with those ideas so radically at odds with conventional nineteenth-century morals, "tumbled the world upside down for me, blew into space a thousand cobwebs of genteel and ethical illusion, and, having thus shaken my tabernacle of lies, set me back again upon a strong foundation of all the original and manly virtues" (1887a: 112).

This "gift of reading" challenges our complacency and pulls us across the limits of conventional values by a process that is individual and unique, an act of "grace," as he says, not something to be picked up in Sunday school or any other kind of external learning. It distinguishes us from the "average man," who "lives, and must live, so wholly in convention, that gunpowder charges of the truth are more apt to discompose than to invigorate his creed" and who is either offended by the *otherness* of the book or character, or is seduced by it (1887a: 112). No alchemy takes place for this kind of reader, no growth beyond the boundaries of the self or of the age.

The gift of reading, we might say, connects us with those same transforming Brownies of our unconscious that shape our creative imagination. Or to put it another way, being a good reader is like being a hero in Stevenson's fiction, encountering the other and locating meaning and value in personal experience, not in received cultural mores.

But this gift of reading is not a comfortable or easy gift. It may be fun to throw your self into d'Artagnan for a time (though what Stevenson loved, remember, was not the swashbuckling musketeer but the later d'Artagnan, who wrestled with moral complexities and knew compromise and defeat). It can, however, only be painful to enter the house of *Crime and Punishment* and experience the torture of living with Raskolnikov, or in reading the biography of Shelley to confront one's own shortcomings. (Should we picture the Stevensonian reader undergoing the agonies of transformation similar to Jekyll's?)

Perhaps here we find a clue about why the letters are so effusively emotional about his reading when they might have been more objectively critical. He needed to build up the emotional excitement of reading to spur himself on through this intensive ordeal of reading. So too it may explain the real significance for Stevenson of that "particular crown and triumph of the artist—not to be true merely, but to be lovable; not simply to convince, but to enchant" (1887b: 125). The enchantment in books is needed not as an end for its own sake, as Andrew Lang ("who denies the influence of books"; Stevenson 1888: 160) argued, but as a goad to keep one motivated to continue in the arduous inner work of "liv[ing] *in* the book or character." Stevenson never made things easy for himself. Beneath the cheerful banter with which he speaks about his reading, we find that agonizing struggle to escape the boundaries of the self that we recognize as perhaps the most distinctive characteristic of all aspects of Stevenson's life and work.

NOTES

1. And it was not the thing to identify the quotations. Very early on, in a letter to his mother, he mocks those who nudge the reader with the source of their quotations as followers of Dr. Pangloss, the pompous tutor in George Colman's play *The Heir-at-Law* (1797), who was "fond of using quotations and then identifying the author" (*Ltrs* 1: 163 and n). Is it worth noticing the shared reading experience here between the seventeen-year-old RLS and his mother in this reference to a minor play from seventy years earlier?

2. He overdid this reading. A week and a half later he is telling Baxter that he was reading a history of the French Revolution, "having somewhat surfeited myself on George Sand. Even the most wholesome food palleth after many days banqueting" (*Ltrs* 1: 398).

REFERENCES

Norquay, Glenda, ed. 1999. *R. L. Stevenson on Fiction: An Anthology of Literary and Critical Essays*. Edinburgh: Edinburgh University Press.

Stevenson, Robert Louis. 1880. "Reflections and Remarks on Human Life." Tusitala Edition. Vol. 26. 76–90.

———. 1882. "A Gossip on Romance." In Norquay 1999. 51–64.

———. 1884. "A Humble Remonstrance." In Norquay 1999. 80–91.

———. 1887a. "Books Which Have Influenced Me." In Norquay 1999. 110–16.

———. 1887b. "A Gossip on a Novel of Dumas's." In Norquay 1999. 117–25.

———. 1888. "Some Gentlemen in Fiction" In Norquay 1999. 151–60.

The Four Boundary-Crossings of R. L. Stevenson, Novelist and Anthropologist

RICHARD AMBROSINI

Recent research on the affinities between certain passages in Robert Louis Stevenson's writings and specific anthropological theories of his time has revealed to what extent his South Seas and Scottish works are to be located within the history of Victorian anthropology. Particularly significant, in this sense, are the studies that have assessed the writer's indebtedness to Edward Tylor's theories on primitive culture as well as his position within the "Scottish tradition of anthropological assemblage" linking Walter Scott and James Frazer (Crawford 1992: 170).[1] Indeed, there are striking signs of a continuity between Stevenson's ethnographic imagination and the scientific or pseudoscientific hypotheses underlying a discipline such as anthropology, devoted to the study of that other, which the Victorians firmly associated with the "primitive." Just as significant, however, are the discontinuities. It is no coincidence if, once confronted in the South Seas with what appeared to him as a clash between "barbarism" and "civilization," the author of *Dr. Jekyll and Mr. Hyde* did not side with the latter. (In a letter to Sidney Colvin from Samoa, Stevenson wrote that we all are a product of "two civilizations—or, if you like, of one civilization and one barbarism. And as usual the barbarism is the more engaging," *Ltrs* 8: 185.) And this is why, when in the Marquesas Islands he first witnessed the effect of European colonization on Polynesian culture, he felt he could establish a comparative link between the Scottish Highlands in the eighteenth century and the Pacific Islands, thus ethnologizing his country's past while historicizing the colonial present. In moving beyond the physical and mental boundaries of late-nineteenth-century bourgeois British culture, Stevenson, unlike his contemporary anthropologists, did not focus his gaze on a series of juxtapositions; his search, rather, was aimed at uncovering analogies, based on his repeated refutation of conventional oppositions between the primitive and the civilized, children's and adults' reading practices, high and low literature. His intellectual engagement with ideas and theories shaping the anthropological discourse of his times acquires its full signifi-cance, therefore, only once set in the context of his writerly interests—made apparent, especially, by his recurrent use of the term "epic" to describe those qualities, in certain narrative forms, which could appeal to readers of every class, age, education, and race.

In his search for a common root underlying not only cultures distant in time and space but also social classes and human psyches, he repeatedly crossed the boundaries between anthropology and fiction writing while experimenting with the narrative forms available in the editorial market. The universal effectiveness he was seeking was based on his personal expe-rience of the pleasure of reading, which he viewed as the primitive core of all responses to narratives. A pleasure, this, which he initially associated with his own earliest responses in his childhood to imaginative stories and to the written word.[2] The link with these ontogenetically primitive reading experiences remained throughout his life the basis of his overall approach to fiction, which he gradually evolved by combining the point of view of a professional author and of a cultural anthropologist.

As a contribution toward a reassessment of how Stevenson's anthropo-logical approach to fiction shaped his novel-writing, the present essay will map out the four main thresholds he crossed in his writing career. Each one of these occurred in conjunction with a physical journey—his first stay in France, his two trips to the United States, and his cruise of the Pacific—but most importantly, they marked as many redirections in the ongoing experimentation with literary forms and genres out of which his extraordinarily polygraphic output took shape. By putting into sequence these four crossings, the essays and travel accounts he wrote at the time all appear to share a common feature, in that Stevenson recurrently presents himself in them as an ethnographer, describing or interviewing various kinds of others, always with an eye on the lessons he can derive from them for his aesthetic or narratological theories. Upon turning to the fiction written after these crossings, one finds how he applied these lessons by constructing a number of different reading-models based on, first, chil-dren, then "uneducated readers" (Stevenson 1888: 342), and finally South Seas Islanders—thus testing what can be defined as an anthropologically informed reader-response theory. His aim in doing so was the creation of a modern version of the epic, which he conceived as a literary form both popular and artistic. And this, I believe, is the key to understanding Stevenson's liminal position in late-Victorian British culture and literature.

Boundaries were something Stevenson took very seriously. The hardest to cross was the one dividing nonfiction-writing from fiction-writing. So hard, indeed, that for the first half of his twenty-year long career he stubbornly refused to write a novel, even though everyone around him was urging him to do so. Once he had published his first novel, *Treasure Island,* only five years later, in the Pacific he resisted the combined pressure put on him by family and friends to write South Seas idylls *à la* Melville, and chose instead to describe the life of the Islands through the medium of an impersonal, scientific language.

It is strange, this resistance to fiction, in an author who was only four years old when he started dictating stories to his nurse and his mother. In looking back, his mother proudly recalled that at the time, "it was the desire of his heart to be an author" (*Ltrs* 1: 87). But if "being an author" implies being a *writer*, I very much doubt it was the "desire of his heart." Rather, it would seem that it was to be a listener and reader of tales, and—especially because, precocious as his storytelling talent was, he learned to read and write relatively late—an indulger in the pleasure of inventing stories for an audience of adoring scribes. The first time he put down in writing the outpourings of his fancy was when he was thirteen—and that only because he had no amanuensis available, having been sent to an English boarding school. The result was "The School Boys Magazine," a collection of fragments with prophetic titles like "A Ghost Story," "The Wreckers," and "Creek Island or Adventures in the South Seas." When three years later he did make his debut as a published author it was with a pamphlet, *The Pentland Rising,* which is a tribute to the first Covenant martyrs and murderers, perfectly in line with the "desire," rather, of his rigorous Presbyterian father, who acted both as financial sponsor and implied reader of the pamphlet. One wonders what had happened to his earlier flights of the imagination, apparently sacrificed on the altar of a religious upbringing that led him later to remark: "One thing, indeed, is not to be learned in Scotland, and that is the way to be happy" (Stevenson 1895: 39).

No surprise, then, that when at seventeen he launched on an obsessive literary apprenticeship, he erased from his creative horizon all traces of imaginative storytelling, and in honing his expressive tools he devoted himself exclusively to perfecting his artistic prose. Crossing, years later, the boundary between elegant essayist and purveyor of adventure yarns, involved therefore a radical rethinking of the artistic and professional identity it had taken him so long to construct. Once crossed, however, he was able to combine the pleasure associated with his childhood dictation, listening to and reading stories, with those skills on which he had staked his chances to free himself from his family's expectations. But he was destined never to overcome the conflicts lying behind his problematic relationship with the novel form.

We should be grateful for this unresolved conflict, because out of it evolved the point of view of a master of stylistic prose whose artistic identity was not based on the dominant art form of his age, the novel. Thus it was that he could behold the breaking up of the Victorian three-volume novel, and the proliferation of popular subgenres aimed at a mass editorial market, as an interesting opportunity—and not as a writing on the wall, a warning that the barbarians were at the gate.

Detached as he may have been, he found in these developments suggestions for a theory of the novel. Ideas tested during his literary apprenticeship developed into a poetics of prose that guided his essay writing throughout the 1870s. When with *Treasure Island* he completed his long-delayed transition to novel writing, he reformulated some of those ideas as a "poetics of fiction" (Ambrosini 2001). The dynamics underlying this transition emerges once we recognize the continuity between his first two crucial crossings of cultural and geographical thresholds, in France and in the United States.

Shortly after his debut as an essayist, Stevenson spent the winter of 1873–74 in Menton, on the French Riviera, where he was joined, twice, by Sidney Colvin, then Slade Professor of Fine Arts at Cambridge, and, especially, the person who had discovered his talent, introduced him to the London literary circles, and found him his first publisher. The young writer's letters to his mentor from Menton capture his excitement in finally being able to set forth ideas he had obviously been working on during his long, solitary apprenticeship. One can imagine, then, how he felt when, through Colvin's offices, the editor of the *Cornhill Magazine*, Leslie Stephen, asked him to review Victor Hugo's latest novel, *Quatrevingt-treize*. And indeed, the offer does seem to have gone to his head, since, with vaulting ambition, he used this, his first literary essay, to set Hugo, Sir Walter Scott, and Nathaniel Hawthorne within an evolutionary line culminating in himself—or at least in his theories. Such confidence was based on his being able, he writes, to "throw in relief . . . this idea which underlies and issues from a romance, this something which it is the function of that form of art to create, this epical value"—which "is not to be found . . . in every so-called novel" (Stevenson 1874c: 26).

This extraordinarily self-assured claim signals to what extent Stevenson's view of fiction—which would lead him, years later, to write romances of adventure rather than realistic novels—was based on an insight into the potentials of romance for revitalizing timeless forms of archetypal story-telling. What makes that winter in Menton a crucial boundary-crossing in his career, however, is that other essays he wrote within a few weeks in the spring of 1874 suggest that at the time this ideal model of romance was closely associated with the psychology of the child—an association that would lead him in *Treasure Island,* eight years later, to address himself, as he later wrote, "to the building up and circumstantiation of [youthful day-dreams]" (Stevenson 1884: 352). Some light as to why, ideally, in the late nineteenth-century, "primitive" narrative forms ought be actualized in children's literature comes from a second essay dating from the same period— "Notes on the Movements of Young Children"—on the face of it, poles apart from the Hugo review. In this short essay, Stevenson recalls the combined effect of observing three young girls dancing in the drawing-room of his Menton hotel and a group of equally young girls—but this time "quite common children," the daughters of Italian immigrants in London—"busy over a skipping-rope." The aim of these observations is to point out ways to escape from an automatic association between beauty and contemporary aesthetic conventions—and to this end, the "impulsive truth . . . that shows throughout all imperfection" of the children's "free gestures" is invaluable, in that, he writes, "it is to us a reminiscence of primitive festivals and the Golden Ages" (Stevenson 1874b: 94, 98). In 1878, Stevenson would write a longer, more complex essay, "Child's Play," constructed on a repeated parallel between "us," the adults, and "them," children; but in early 1874, obviously, his priority was rather to link together the psychology of the child and the atavistic components of all narrative. (A few weeks before, in a book review he had argued that the short-story form is in fact nothing else than a post-Darwinian version of classical fable (Stevenson 1974a: 193–96).

Throughout the later half of the 1870s, it was difficult for his contemporaries to understand why, given his success as an essayist, Stevenson did not graduate to novel writing. The most revealing document of the kind of expectations he was raising is a letter written to him on June 7, 1878, by Leslie Stephen—who as editor of the *Cornhill* had been the first person to learn about the young writer's theories of romance. "It has occurred to me lately," Stephen writes, "that you might possibly help me in an ever recurring difficulty. I am constantly looking out rather vaguely for a new novelist. I should like to find a Walter Scott or Dickens or even a Miss Brontë or G. Eliot. Somehow the coming man or woman has not yet been revealed. Meanwhile I cannot help thinking that, if you would seriously put your hand to such a piece of work you would be able . . . to write something really good and able to make a mark in the *Cornhill*" (*Ltrs* 2: 257 n. 1). (One wonders how Stephen reacted the following day, June 8, 1878, when the first of Stevenson's *Latter-Day Arabian Nights* appeared, certainly a far cry from anything worthy of the Great Victorians.)

If he did eventually take this step, it was as a consequence of his second boundary-crossing—his 1879 transatlantic and transcontinental voyage from Liverpool to California—which had the effect of enlarging for the first time his notion of an ideal readership of his romances. While he was writing *The Amateur Emigrant*, the book in which he re-created his experiences aboard the *Devonia*, the emigrant ship that took him to America, he wrote to Colvin, back in London: "There shall be no more books of travel for me" (*Ltrs* 3: 59–60)—and he was true to his word. Indeed, *The Amateur Emigrant*[3] marks a dramatic break from his earlier walking-tour essays and travel books set in Belgium and France, with their painterly renditions of landscapes seen through the eyes of a carefree vacationer. This was to be, he announced, a book written by a man who had given a lot of attention "to contemporary life, and not through the newspapers" (*Ltrs* 3: 30). If he felt he could make such a claim, it was because living as he had for the past months at close quarters with the broken men of Europe and their families, aboard an emigrant ship and emigrant trains, he had come face to face for the first time with a reality that he had "known" only at a distance. "Labouring mankind," he writes at the beginning of *Emigrant*, "had in the last years, and throughout Great Britain, sustained a prolonged and crushing series of defeats. I had heard vaguely of these reverses. . . . But I had never taken them home to me or represented these distresses livingly to my imagination. A turn of the market may be a calamity as disastrous as the French retreat from Moscow; but it hardly lends itself to a lively treatment, and makes a trifling figure in the morning papers." Only now, he adds, "when I found myself involved in the rout, I began to appreciate how sharp had been the battle" (Stevenson 1895: 11–12).

In his interviews with the emigrants, and his descriptions of their patterns of behavior, Stevenson does not seek a purported impersonality. The discoveries he is making are all the more significant, in that he makes his growing admiration for the working-class passengers—and, more dangerously, his identification with them—interact with the class prejudices he continues to share with his readers whom he addresses at one point with the formula, "We gentlemen of England" (55). As usual with Stevenson, it is in the implications he finds for his own writing that his work as social ethnographer acquires its proper interest. A fever-stricken fiddler, or the stories the emigrants tell each other during the long, tedious days and nights aboard, are what make him react imaginatively to their sufferings and, as his letters to his friends written from America show, taught him to respect what could give them a rare moment of happiness. Suddenly, pleasure-inducing stories appeared far more serious to him than the aestheticizing stylistic exercises he had engaged in throughout the 1870s. As he announced in a letter to Colvin: from now on, "I'll stick to stories . . . My sympathies and interests are changed . . . I care for nothing but the moral and the dramatic, not a jot for the picturesque or the beautiful, other than about people" (*Ltrs* 3: 59–60). The novel he planned in San Francisco, "Adventures of John Carson," based on the life of his landlady's husband may have been a false start. But when one year after his return to Scotland he began *Treasure Island*, he was finally on the way of proving the universal effectiveness of the pleasure that as a child he had derived from purely imaginative stories.

In the very same days in which he decided to revise the boys' story for an adult readership, Stevenson started working on an essay, "A Gossip on Romance," in which he made explicit the continuity between his first novel and the epic model theorized in Menton. The "highest and hardest thing to do in words," he writes here, is to strike the reader's mind with "epoch-making scenes," thus filling up, "our capacity for sympathetic pleasure." This, which he defines as "the plastic part of literature . . . once accomplished, equally delights the schoolboy and the sage, and makes, in its own right, the quality of epics" (Stevenson 1882: 332–33). The reference to the "schoolboy" could be taken as a justification of the boys' adventure yarns he was about to rewrite if it were not for the fact that he had opened this passage by claiming that "the great creative writer" is the one who "shows us the realisation and the apotheosis of the day-dreams of common men" (332). Something had changed, in his conception of the epic since his days in Menton, and, over the following years, his engagement with

the novel-reading public was to further broaden the horizon of his writing.
And this is why in another essay, "Pastoral," he would rephrase, five years
later, the same ideas found in "A Gossip on Romance," when he asserts
that novels "begin to touch not the fine *dilettanti* but the gross mass of mankind [only when they] leave off to speak of parlours and shades of manner
and still-born niceties of motive, and begin to deal with fighting, sailoring,
adventure, death or child-birth." When this happens, they have the power
"to lift romance into a near neighbourhood with epic" (Stevenson 1887: 238).

Viewed from the perspective of his later works, *Treasure Island* marks the
arrival point of his theories of an abstract romance model; after this, we
see a basic change in favor of a more professional manipulation of myths
already encoded in literary forms or in the pleasure-inducing mechanisms of popular fiction. We can recognize the outcome of this evolution
in *Kidnapped* and *Strange Case of Dr. Jekyll and Mr. Hyde*. Anthropological subject matter—such as the clash between a Celtic Highlander and an
Anglicized Lowlander, or the eruption of a primitive double in a Faustian
doctor, scientist and man of law—are here thematized; however, the genres
he employed for these inquiries into psychological and cultural doubles
reveal that at the same time he was also making use of his self-awareness
as a cultural anthropologist to intervene in the editorial market. His interest in the primordial mechanisms of storytelling was helping him find a
location between high and low culture.

When he returned for the second time to the United States—in his
third boundary-crossing—he discovered that his playing with commercial
subgenres had made him into a valuable commodity. The lessons he drew
from this discovery can be found in the seven essays—out of a total of
twelve—he wrote in America for *Scribner's Magazine*, in which he registers the perplexities of an upper-class British writer caught in the mechanism of the American popular press. How his idiosyncratic artistic project
has led him to a specious kind of popularity is the theme in particular of
one of these essays, "Popular Authors," in which at one point he adopts
the stance of a field anthropologist conducting research into the world
of penny-literature, interviewing the "natives" of this world to discover
what readers' expectations and needs had made possible the rise of a mass-
consumption publishing market.

The essay opens aboard the *Devonia*, during the same journey Stevenson had described in *The Amateur Emigrant*. It is night, and two men are
alone on deck, one of them a sailor, the other, "an emigrant of an inquiring

turn of mind," who, turning to the deckhand, asks him if there is a book "that gives a true picture of a sailor's life." The answer is deliberate and emphatic: "there is *one*; that is *just* a sailor's life. You know all about it, if you know that. . . . They call it *Tom Holt's Log*." The "amateur anthropologist" conscientiously "enter[s] the fact in his note-book" while anticipating that the book must either be a "solid, dull, admirable piece of truth, or mere ink and banditti" (Stevenson 1888: 329). But, as it turns out, the evidence provided by his 'native' informant proves both these hypotheses wrong: *Tom Holt's Log*, he later discovers, is a novel by a Stephens Hayward, the dullest of hacks—a book "always acutely untrue to life as it is, often pleasantly coincident with childish hopes of what life ought to be." And yet, "this was the work that an actual tarry seaman recommended for a picture of his own existence!" (333).

Stevenson is uniquely positioned to solve this contradiction, since for years now, as he confesses, he has been "a student of our penny press" (336). In pursuit of his studies, "It was once my fortune to have an interview with Mr. HAYWARD's publisher: a very affable gentleman in a shady court off Fleet Street"; and, he recalls, "it was strange to hear him talk for all the world as one of our publishers might have talked of one of us" (334). His use of possessive adjectives and pronouns signal an irreconcilable separateness between the worlds of high and low literature; but, as in *The Amateur Emigrant*, Stevenson is actually more interested in presenting himself as someone willing to traverse this boundary. Having written *Treasure Island* and the *Strange Case of Dr. Jekyll and Mr. Hyde*, isn't he "an upper-class author, bound and criticised" who longs nonetheless "for the penny number and the weekly woodcut"? "Well, I know that glory now," he concludes; "I have tried and on the whole failed" (335), not having met with the kind of real popularity enjoyed instead by penny-writers.

As he then proceeds to pay his tribute to the "great men of the dust," whose names he puts in capitals throughout the essay, for "their day is past, the poor dogs" (334, 330). Stevenson's scandalous erudition casts a fascinating light on the transformations occurring in the nineteenth-century editorial market. But his humorous reveries gradually move toward a question—"What kind of talent is required to please this mighty public?" (340)—which echoes all his past theories on reading and his attacks on realistic fiction. He returns then to the contradictions posed by the seaman's response to Tom Holt's adventures, and by invoking what is for him a similar instance—those barmaids who pore over *The Young Ladies' Journal*—he suggests that the tales preferred by working-class readers are not those that are "true to what men see," but those "true to what the readers dreamed" (342).

As to the reasons for this rejection of realistic fiction on the part of working-class readers, Stevenson falls back on the theories based on the psychology of the child that he had expounded in "A Gossip on Romance" and "A Humble Remonstrance"; but he does so, here, only to launch on an analogy between proletarians and children—fairly common in Victorian anthropology—the purpose of which is to make his bourgeois readers understand what he takes to be "the mind of the uneducated reader," who requires from an author "scenery and properties for autobiographical romancing" (343).

As if unsure whether the child:proletarian analogy may be effective enough, Stevenson invokes an even stronger argument to bring home his point to "readers of an upper class"—that of race. Even for them, he writes, "a writer may be too exotic," as Melville would have been for the *Devonia*'s seaman; and in an "exogamous romance," the "villain, even the heroine, may be a Feejee islander, but only on condition the hero is one of our-selves." (The reverse case that disorients the reader comes of course from his beloved *Arabian Nights*, "where the Moslem hero carries off the Chris-tian amazon.") The "question of exogamy is foreign to the purpose," how-ever, and rather than pushing the analogy to the point of frightening his readers by evoking the fear of miscegenation, he returns to his initial argu-ment: "Enough that we are not readily pleased without a character of our own race and language; so that, when the scene of romance is laid in any distant soil, we look with eagerness and confidence for the coming of the English traveller" (343). The sexual overtones return, however, when he goes to explain why, with the penny-press reader the thing goes farther: "Burning as they are with the desire to penetrate into the homes of the peerage," it is not with "one of us," an "English traveller," they can iden-tify, but with "one of them"—since "they must still be conducted there by some character of their own class" (343–44).

Nowhere else in his investigations into the analogies among so-called primitive readers does Stevenson so dramatize his anthropological approach to the working class, setting it up, for the benefit of his own public, as the ultimate other, whose intellectual abilities can be gauged through the psy-chology of the child, even though its primitiveness appears far more threatening. But his investigation was not over yet. Only a few pages be-fore he had publicly acknowledged that in writing *Treasure Island* he was consciously trying to replicate the pleasure-engendering potentials of the wish-fulfillment mechanisms underlying popular fiction. Reading models based on working-class readers or on children, then, are simply different stages in his search for narrative forms endowed with that "epical value," which alone can make them universally effective.

All dreams of a universal epic form combining the popular and the artistic were eclipsed by the reality he discovered in the South Seas. He had now escaped, he wrote, "out of the shadow of the Roman empire" (Stevenson 1896: 7), and this his fourth boundary-crossing was to be his most dramatic. He went on to complete the work he had begun in America and recorded in *The Wrecker* how radically he was questioning his previous identity as an artist. Indeed, for some time he stopped writing fiction altogether. The ethnological stance he adopted in the essays, which in his previous crossings had preceded his new experiments in fiction, had now become his chosen form of expression. And no wonder: The new experiences were providing him with materials for nonfictional writing vastly superior to anything he had ever dreamed of—to the point that the only equivalents he could think of for his ethnographic treatise, *In the South Seas*, were "the epics, and the big tragedies, and histories, and the choice lyric poetics, and a novel or so" (*Ltrs* 6: 335).

When he did return to imaginative literature, it was clear that he had reached a new balance in his anthropologically informed reader-response theory. Rather than writing up the mythopoetic elements in adventure stories, he started collecting and translating Polynesian myths and folktales, and fashioned out of them ballads and long poems for the "civilized" readers at home. Then, reversing the process, he went back to the "barbaric" origins of Western culture and adapted Northern European sagas and folktales to the Islanders' "savage psychology" (*Ltrs* 7: 187): for "The Bottle Imp," he transposed to Hawaii a German folktale; with the help of a British missionary, he started writing in Samoan "Eatuina," a tale set at the times of the Saxons; for "The Waif Woman" he was inspired by a collection of Nordic sagas. In all these cases, he was positing a reading model based on the "recapitulation theory," according to which "primitive cultures" correspond to earlier stages of Western civilization (Tylor 1871).

Thus transforming an anthropological hypothesis into specialized narrative techniques aimed at racially different readers, he was trying to create for himself a space in between Polynesian and European cultures. When, however, he became aware of "the unjust (yet I can see the inevitable) extinction of the Polynesian Islanders by our shabby civilization"

(Swearingen 1980: 176), the received notions he derived from armchair anthropologists proved untenable. He then went back to writing only for Western readers, but at that point what he had to offer them was either a realistic representation of their shabby civilization's standard-bearers or a denunciation of German colonialists—in angry letters to the London *Times* that proved to be such a nuisance for all colonial powers that the Foreign Office tried to have him deported.

Many of his readers at home were puzzled or disappointed—like Oscar Wilde, who commented: "In Gower Street Stevenson could have written a new *Trois Mousquetaires*. In Samoa he wrote letters to *The Times* about Germans" (Hart-Davis 1962: 520). Stevenson's own view of his accomplishments was different. After finishing *A Footnote to History*, his chronicle of the colonial wars in Samoa, he wrote to Henry James: "You don't know what news is, nor what politics, nor what the life of man, till you see it on so small a scale and with your own liberty on the board for stake. I would not have missed it for much. And anxious friends beg me to stay at home and study human nature in Brompton drawing-rooms! And anyway you know that such is not my talent. . . . I am an Epick Writer with a k to it, but without the necessary genius" (*Ltrs* 7: 449).

In the past, he had invoked "epics" as an encoded term for the kind of fiction he was striving after. But never before had he dared define himself an epic writer. Now he felt he could, albeit self-mockingly, perhaps inevitably, in making such a claim to Henry James, his hyper-civilized sparring partner in the realism vs. romance controversy of the mid-1880s. The hybrid forms of life created by European colonialism contained the potentials for an epic subject. More importantly, however, in the South Seas all theories of fictional representation of reality appeared equally remote— including the abstract romance model he had first envisaged in Menton. Having rejected it, he wrote the first colonial fictions in the language, "The Beach of Falesá" and *The Ebb-Tide*, thus crossing one last threshold—one he had erected himself. A fitting conclusion for the creative and existential journey of this novelist-anthropologist.

NOTES

1. Robert Crawford argues that "we should link Stevenson, one of the descendants of Scott in the Scottish Romantic Novel, and J. G. Frazer, one of the descendants of Scott in the Scottish tradition of anthropological assemblage—or even epic" (Crawford 1992: 170). On his ethnographic writings on the South Seas, see Smith 1997 and Edmond 1997; further light on the issue is cast by Ashley 2000.

2. See the 1893 essay, "Random Memories: Rosa Quo Locorum," for his most explicit link of his fiction writing to his childhood reading.

3. *The Amateur Emigrant* was first published as part of the Edinburgh Edition in 1895, in conformity with the instructions Stevenson gave before his death. It consists of two parts: the transatlantic crossing, "From the Clyde to Sandy Hook," and the journey on the emigrant train, "Across the Plains." This second part had already been published (with some differences) in *Longman's Magazine* (1883) and then again as part of *Across the Plains With Other Memories and Essays* (1892).

REFERENCES

Ambrosini, Richard. 2001. *R. L. Stevenson: la poetica del romanzo*. Rome: Bulzoni.

Ashley, Scott. 2000. Primitivism, Celticism and Morbidity in the Atlantic *fin de siècle*. In *Symbolism, Decadence and the* Fin de Siècle*: French and European Perspectives*. Ed. Patrick McGuinness. Exeter: University of Exeter Press. 175–93.

Crawford, Robert. 1992. *Devolving English Literature*. Oxford: Clarendon Press.

Edmond, Rod. 1997. *Representing the Pacific: Colonial Discourse from Cook to Gauguin*. Cambridge: Cambridge University Press.

Hart-Davis, Rupert, ed. 1962. *The Letters of Oscar Wilde*. New York: Harcourt.

Smith, Vanessa. 1997. *Literary Culture and the Pacific: Nineteenth-Century Textual Encounters*. Cambridge University Press: Cambridge.

Stevenson, Robert Louis. 1874a. "Lord Lytton's 'Fables in Song.'" Thistle Edition, third issue. Vol. 22. 193–204.

———. 1874b. "Notes on the Movements of Young Children." Thistle Edition, third issue. Vol. 22. 92–98.

———. 1874c. "Victor Hugo's Romances." Thistle Edition, third issue. Vol. 14. 17–45.

———. 1882. "A Gossip on Romance." Thistle Edition, third issue. Vol. 13. 315–326.

———. 1884. "A Humble Remonstrance." Thistle Edition, third issue. Vol. 13. 344–358.

———. 1887. "Pastoral." Thistle Edition, third issue. Vol. 13. 231–240.

———. 1888. "Popular Authors." Thistle Edition, third issue. Vol. 14. 329–345.

———. 1895. *The Amateur Emigrant*. Thistle Edition, third issue. Vol. 15. 1–92.

———. 1896. *In the South Seas*. Thistle Edition, third issue. Vol. 19.

Swearingen, Roger G. 1980. *The Prose Writings of Robert Louis Stevenson: A Guide*. Hamden, CT: Archon Books; London: Macmillan.

Tylor, Edward B. 1871. *Primitive Culture: Researches into the Development of Mythology, Philosophy, Religion, Art, and Custom*. 2 vols. London: John Murray.

Stevenson and the (Un)familiar

The Aesthetics of Late-Nineteenth-Century Biography

LIZ FARR

The recent publication of the definitive edition of Lytton Strachey's *Eminent Victorians* (Levy 2002) is a testament to the enduring significance of a work regarded as a landmark in modern biographical practice. First published in 1918, Strachey's collection of essays is seen as signaling a break with both High Victorian values and scientific conceptions of truth (Marcus 1994: 90–91). By satirizing four key figures, Cardinal Manning, Florence Nightingale, Thomas Arnold and General Gordon, Strachey set out to expose the hypocrisies of the preceding generation and to redefine biography as a record of "haphazard visions," governed only by the "simple motives of convenience and art."[1] In Strachey's hands life-writing becomes an aesthetic act, enabling him to shape his portraits of individual lives according to his own subjective predilections, with scant regard for scholarship or accepted facts.

In this chapter I explore the ways in which Stevenson's neglected volume of biographical essays *Familiar Studies of Men and Books,* published in 1882, actually anticipated Strachey's work by nearly four decades by staging a critique of those same Victorian values and the practice of life-writing as a science. However, unlike Strachey, Stevenson was not writing with hindsight but at the very moment when such practices were becoming established as a form of biographical orthodoxy. Stevenson's opposition to the *status quo* therefore took the form of a more covert immanent critique, exemplified in his use of the adjective "familiar" in the title of the collection, which takes on a rhetorical doubleness. While superficially conventional (alluding to the essay "On Familiar Style," in which Hazlitt recommended—rather than a florid or vulgar style—the conversationally straightforward use of English as an "unvarnished medium to display ideas," Hazlitt 1821: 211), the term simultaneously alerts the careful reader to ways in which Stevenson's approach to late-Victorian life writing was also decidedly unfamiliar in potentially subversive ways.

A Design for Life: The Science of Biography

Although, as Richard Altick has observed (1965: 77), the nineteenth century was the age of biography, it was only during the second half of the century that the Victorian orthodoxy, which Strachey later sought to undermine, was established. By the 1860s, institutional shifts in the universities resulted in the emergence of recognizably modern subject areas, including psychology, historiography, and literary criticism (Small 1991). As David Amigoni has shown (1993: 37–38), these shifts also produced a schism in the cultural circulation of knowledge, between scholars practicing particular university specialisms and the more widely disseminated and often undisciplined mediocrity of what passed for learning in the periodical press. Two figures of particular significance for Stevenson, John Morley and Leslie Stephen, both editors of periodicals, and therefore outside the university system, sought to bridge this gap and mediate between the professional specialisms of academia and a general reading public who had neither the time nor inclination to pursue intellectual inquiries in such a rigorous fashion. For both men, popular biography was to serve as an important mechanism by which to promote certain values and attitudes to a middle-class reading public: values and attitudes that, as Amigoni demonstrates (1993: 79–90), were heavily inflected by positivist desires for social progress. Influenced by Mill, Comte, and Darwin, both were agnostics who sought to employ methods borrowed from science to counter any vestiges of metaphysical beliefs in historical and literary critical writing. In this way they hoped to further human evolutionary progress toward a final stage of scientific enlightenment, and they used their editorships of middle-class periodicals to this end. Morley was the editor of the evening newspaper, the *Pall Mall Gazette* (1880–3), *Macmillan's Magazine* (1883–85), and the *Fortnightly Review* (1867–82), while Stephen edited the *Cornhill Magazine* (1871–82). Even more significantly they both became editors of popular biographical series: Morley was the founding editor of the hugely popular *English Men of Letters* series (1878–92), which was to run to thirty-nine volumes, and to which Stephen was the major contributor. Early in his career Stevenson had hoped that Morley would invite him to write the volume on Keats (cf. *Ltrs* 2: 331), but he was passed over in favor of the more reputable Sidney Colvin. In 1882, the year in which *Familiar Studies of Men and Books* came out, Leslie Stephen left the *Cornhill* to become the commissioning editor of the new *Dictionary of National Biography* (1885–1900), a philanthropic project on the part of George Smith, its publisher, which was to become the epitome of Victorian biographical endeavor.[2]

Taken together, the periodical editorships and biographical projects of both Stephen and Morley reveal the moral and intellectual thrust of their mission. Employing positivist methods, which treated critical practice as the application of a disinterested model of scientific surveillance, they encouraged the accumulation of data and careful deliberation before arriving at any judgment of the life and work of the individual under scrutiny. These were the constituent practices of an approach to life-writing that Stephen, in his essay on Charlotte Brontë, likened to gazing at a fossil: "Though criticism cannot boast of being a science, it ought to aim at something like a scientific basis, or at least proceed in a scientific spirit. The critic therefore, before abandoning himself to the oratorical impulse, should endeavor to classify the phenomena with which he is dealing as calmly as if he were ticketing a fossil in a museum" (Stephen 1877: 723). In this manner, the life and works of a writer could be carefully appraised before he (or exceptionally, she), was finally inserted into his rightful place in the evolutionary hierarchy or archive, such as the *Dictionary of National Biography* or the *English Men of Letters* series.

From a present-day perspective, these pretensions toward scientific detachment can be seen as partial instruments of an ideology and a mechanism by which biography served as a tool for middle-class hegemony. The dispassionate observer is encouraged to classify the geographically or historically distant in terms of the present or the near, so that the past or the culturally different is always viewed from the point of view of the imperial center, toward which everything is seen to be progressing. Like painterly realism, which relied upon the conventions of Cartesian perspectivism to imply true depth, this mode of representation, and the positivist beliefs that underpinned it, often co-opted the dispassionate eye of the camera as a metaphor (Jay 1993: 146–47; Jenks 1995: 5–7; McQuire 1998: 33–43). Both Stephen and Morley took great pains to insure objectivity in their contributors, railing at length against subjective bias and all forms of relativism, both in terms of the opinions expressed and idiosyncratic styles

of writing.[3] They equally distrusted the potential of aestheticism to suc-
cumb to an "effeminate and flaccid mannerism" (Morley 1873: 229) and
"immorality" (Stephen 1875: 91–92), and also the stylistic excesses of earlier writers such as Carlyle, whom Morley roundly condemned for his
rhetorical flourishes, which he considered could lead the naïve reader—or
the willful misreader—to arrive at the wrong conclusions concerning the
moral and intellectual values of a life (Amigoni 1993: 34–37). In this way
both the *English Men of Letters Series* and the *Dictionary of National Biography* provided improving examples of lives that served to promote a particular conception of middle-class English masculinity, emphasizing the
rewards of hard work and the sanctity of family life (Kijinski 1991: 205–
25). It is against this background that I wish to examine Stevenson's *Familiar Studies of Men and Books*.

Biography as an Aesthetic Act

Stevenson failed to undertake any significant revisions of this collection of
nine previously published biographical essays, the majority of which had
appeared in the *Cornhill Magazine*.[4] This is perhaps surprising, as a number had received negative criticism on their original publication. His essay
on Thoreau, for example, had been roundly criticized for faulty scholarship by Thomas de Quincey's biographer, Alexander Japp.[5] Stevenson did,
however, attempt to yoke these previously discrete studies together by
means of the aptly titled "Preface, By Way of Criticism," in an effort to
defend himself against similar accusations for a second time.

   In writing a preface Stevenson was, in one sense at least, following a
widely accepted scholarly convention. Together with the title, the preface,
as D. A. Miller, has argued (1988: xiii–iv), attempts to give formal unity to
a collection of previously discrete events. By this means the late-nineteenth-
century author was able to emerge from the impersonality of the periodical press to lay claim to his potentially ephemeral productions and defend
them against critical scrutiny, primarily by situating his work within an
institutional matrix that might lend them authority (Miller 1988: vii). By
selecting the adjective "familiar" for the title, Stevenson not only alludes
to his informal critical style but also suggests that the reader may have
encountered these essays before, and that they might be considered recognizable examples of a popular genre, late-nineteenth-century biography.
From the outset he is at pains to locate himself within a respectable scientific background by noting his affiliation to two paternal figures, his father

and his editor. The dedication to Thomas Stevenson at the beginning of the volume suggests parallels between his father's "devices," the optical inventions that have the ability to shed light upon "every quarter of the world," and the son's literary ability as "the author" to critically illuminate a number of lives. In the opening paragraph of the preface he acknowledges Leslie Stephen, another father to thank, a figure of authority and quality control "under the eye" of whom, Stevenson points out, the bulk of these essays were produced (Stevenson 1882: xi). Up to this point the volume would appear to be yet another untroubling example of the familiar, a collection of late-nineteenth-century biographical essays, but as the preface continues it becomes apparent that a certain doubleness is at work, not least in the rhetorical sleight of hand that Stephen and Morley so deplored. While superficially apologetic for the shortcomings of the essays, "Stephen's-son" goes on covertly to attack the very precepts and models of authority that his literary father held so dear in order to propose a subjective and impressionistic conception of biography as a pre-eminently aesthetic act.

Adopting a tone of self-ironizing flippancy, he reveals an approach to life writing that is less a matter of disinterested surveillance (or fossil-gazing, or a testament to the moral superiority of English manhood) than the works of "a literary vagrant" (xii)—records of random, subjectively selected encounters with men and their books across a range of cultures and historical periods. Stevenson readily admits that the resulting studies "teem with error," for they are not the product of sustained professional scholarship but of cursory and random reading, fuelled only by the amateur enthusiasms of youth. Rather than concluding that this apparent weakness in terms of lack of knowledge or academic credentials should dissuade him from embarking upon such studies in the first place, Stevenson prefers to blame the periodical press, which invites young men such as himself to undertake what he describes as a series of literary quests: "a kind of roving judicial commission through the ages" by which he sets out to "right the wrongs of universal history and criticism." Similarly, he argues that to pass true judgment on the a range of his chosen subjects—an eclectic mix including Charles of Orleans, Pepys, Whitman, Thoreau, Knox, Burns, Villon, Hugo, and a little-known Japanese hero, Yoshida Torajiro—one would have to have a comprehensive knowledge of the cultures of Scotland, France, and America, not to mention Japan, and such a wealth of knowledge is beyond the capacity of the "most erudite of men" (xi). However, in his declarations of ignorance it becomes apparent that Stevenson has another aim in view, to which end he is less than honest, downplaying his actual knowledge of, and keen interest in, all of the cultures concerned. He was not only a Scot, steeped in the history of his country, but he had also traveled widely in France and was well versed in "the growth and liberties of art" in that country. Having recently married an American with two children, he had "a large habit of life among modern Americans" (xi–xii), and, finally, although he claimed to have no firsthand knowledge of his Japanese hero, he was one of the early Western collectors of Japanese prints.[6] In fact, Stevenson had selected these figures as a surrogate literary family, a means to promote his own literary interests and aetheticist agenda, particularly concerning the relationship between art and life and the ways in which the artist/writer might both resist and accommodate some of the norms and values of the society in which he lives.

If these overdetermined excuses were not enough, Stevenson goes on to blame his shortcomings on the exigencies of the marketplace. Not only does the periodicals market actively encourage a young man to wander unsystematically through cultural repositories of texts: the required form of publication—the periodical essay—imposes limitations of time and space. The speed of production and the brevity required mean that the resulting essays can only be an impressionistic record of such encounters with selected men and their books, as they fleetingly imprinted themselves upon the biographer's mind (xii–xiii). In this sense Stevenson's essays, like Strachey's "haphazard visions," are deliberately unsystematic, governed only by "the principles of convenience and art." Rather than employing the slow deliberation and ethical scruples of the fossil gazer, the writer of short biographical essays prefers to follow the model of the portrait painter, which is more suited to his scholarly limitations and the constraints of the periodical press. A lack of space forces him to omit details, not of the morally suspect, like Stephen and Morley, but of the mundane, so that the resulting portrait that emerges is both "logical and striking," while the omission of "neutral circumstances" produces a "negative exaggeration" that "lends the matter in hand a certain false and specious glitter," a simulacrum of the truth (xii–xiii).

By appealing to market forces and human limitations, Stevenson is able implicitly to demonstrate the unsuitability of the scientific and scholarly models of biography his editors sought to promote. However, his is not a naïve attempt to revert to earlier Romantic conceptions of the artist as transcendental genius. By the late nineteenth century, confidence in Romantic conceptions of the artist as the autonomous repository of superior truths was less secure. The arguments that Stevenson rehearses here are symptomatic of a more general feeling of disempowerment, the experiences of a late-nineteenth-century subject decentered by market forces and advances in knowledge, particularly in the area of science, which are perceived as an excess, beyond mastery or full comprehension. Romantic faith in the integrity of the individual is seen only as a necessary fiction and a substitute for an ungraspable reality. Rather than opposing the hegemony of scientific models or market forces, Stevenson, like Pater, conducts an immanent critique of positivist models (fast becoming critical orthodoxy), using the language of empirical method and the concepts of the latest evolutionary-psychological models of aesthetics. Like Pater, as Jonathan Freedman has shown (1990: 65–67), Stevenson draws upon recent psychological models to eschew objective judgments and focus on the ways in which the subjective discriminating mind might treat the world as a resource through which it should quest after pleasurable impressions. According to this psychological model, art is less a quality of objects than the product of the discriminating mind of the observer, who is able to derive aesthetic stimulation from a range of objects including the "engaging personality in life or in a book" of another man (Pater 1888: xiii).[7]

While fossil-gazing lays claim to impartiality and objective distance in its record of "scientific truths," impressionist portrait painting openly acknowledges the constraints of the medium, of the flat surface and the frame, and omits details (as Carlyle and Macaulay did) in order to present a rhetorically charged and subjective point of view. Rather than a sustained and careful analysis over a length of time, this form of representation demands speed of perception and execution, becoming a portrait of the artist/biographer as much as his sitter. Instead of practicing detachment, he is expected to rearrange his chosen subject to conform to a particular conception of his own, if necessary resorting to violence, even breaking the sitter's neck, so that he may be represented from a particular, partial point of view (Stevenson 1882: xiii). In the short study, the writer returns to his point of view, so that "by sheer force of repetition, that view is imposed upon the reader" (xiii), as a recognizable or familiar impression upon his or her mind.

Familiarity is crucial to this psychological model of life-writing, because, as Stevenson argues in his essay on Charles of Orleans, he is less interested in the public records of a man's achievements than to conduct more intimate encounters, described as "the art of making friends," and which invites "a sort of personal seduction" between the artist and his sitter in an effort to produce a "portrait of his soul" (46). This structuring principle of empathy between men as conducive to aesthetic pleasure draws upon the work of James Sully, the late-nineteenth-century psychologist and fellow *Cornhill* contributor, specifically his study of aesthetics, *Sensation and Intuition* (1874).[8] In a chapter on the aesthetics of human character, Sully explains the ways in which a yield of pleasurable impressions might accrue from the feelings of sympathetic identification between one man and another. Sully articulated a form of psychological aestheticism that was endorsed by Stevenson, Pater, and Wilde, and that severed any direct connection between aesthetic judgments and orthodox ethical judgments (Small 1991: 64–88). The aesthetic pleasure an individual life may give, Sully argues, has little if any relation to the ways in which a life may be judged according to the precepts of conventional morality (Sully 1874: 273–82). Rather, pleasure derives from the ways in which an individual's character might seem familiar, echoing one's own, and shows evidence of harmonious adaptation to its larger surrounding cultural or historical environment (268). A good example of Stevenson's attempt to deploy this psychological method can be found in his essay on Robert Burns.

As the title of this essay indicates, a large proportion of "Some Aspects of Robert Burns" concerns itself not with Burns' writings, or an attempt to arrive at some rounded judgment of the man, but with the more scandalous details of his life, often tactfully omitted by other Victorian biographers. In Stevenson's portrait the young Burns initially cuts a familiar figure, as we recognize details of his life that echo those of his biographer. We are told that Burns, like Stevenson, adapted his name, and similarly loved "dressing up" for its own sake, a bohemian sartorial style that Stevenson also affected in his velvet jacket. These flamboyant characteristics cause Stevenson, the Francophile, to suggest that Burns would have fitted well in Gautier's Latin Quarter (Stevenson 1882: 28). In considering Burns's racier output, Stevenson defends his subject by asserting the doctrine of aestheticism according to which Burns's work should be judged by its style, rather than its content.[9] In this manner, Stevenson attempts to rescue Burns, who was always a controversial character for Victorian biographers, from the moral Mrs. Grundyism that would condemn him outright for his political beliefs and scandalous behavior. However, in his attempt to derive aesthetic pleasure from such a character, even Stevenson cannot ignore what he calls a growing number of "blots, exceptions, inconsistencies, and excursions into the diabolic" (24), which prevent his sympathetic identification with the man and threaten to obscure his portrait. Burns's

"Don Juanism," according to Stevenson, eventually causes his "unconscious suicide" (34, 49), not due to the immoral nature of the acts themselves, which were roundly condemned by many of his other biographers, most notably Principle Shairp in his volume for Morley's *Men of Letters* series (1879), but because Burns lived in a society that forced him to conform to certain bourgeois standards at odds with the nature of an artist. Forced by convention to marry the mother of his children, a "facile and empty-headed girl" (23), and to take up work as an exciseman to support his family, Stevenson's Burns provides a critique of bourgeois social structures as his romantic nature is forced to find outlets in illicit affairs, smuggling, and alcoholism, subsequently leading to his demise. This approach was, of course, in direct conflict with the ways in which Stephen and Morley sought to deploy biographical studies as a didactic tool to promote the rewards of hard work, the sanctity of marriage, and the pleasures of family life. At the close of the essay Stevenson is forced to conclude that his portrait was a failure, for which he does not blame himself but the contradictions in his sitter. The blots and inconsistencies, which derive from Burns's internal psychological contradictions, eventually overwhelm this attempted representation of the man and plunge him into shadow.

Looking at the volume as a whole, it seems that many, if not all, of Stevenson's portraits suffer the same fate, records of a series of failed seductions as each of his subjects is found wanting in some aspect of their character that fails to coincide with his own psychological projections or to by an inability to adapt to the social environments in which they lived. Although Stevenson is forced ultimately to condemn the immorality of writers such as Burns and Villon, his portraits all focus on the ways social structures create a schism between art (aesthetic production) and life (social conformity). This is a subjective and impressionistic approach to history and biography, which might seem to prefigure more recent concerns with the relative and textual nature of truths. Stevenson's painterly model of biography, which actively encourages the omission of facts and admits to the subjective and textual nature of all forms of writing, defines an attitude that he extended across his fictional and nonfictional production. We find it echoed in his essay "A Humble Remonstrance," where this approach is used to promote romance over realism and distinguish art from life. Here Stevenson argues that without aesthetic shaping life, and history, would be a confusing chaos of details, or an unfocussed excess (Stevenson 1884: 135). He argues that in order to describe the past, historians are forced to borrow techniques from the novel, as a formal artifice that gives the narrative shape (134). Instead of attempting to catalogue every detail, like the realist novelist or the fossil gazer, Stevenson dispenses with bogus claims to scientific detachment and impersonality, openly celebrating the provisional and subjective nature of his impressions recorded not in the spirit of judgment but the familiarity of friendship. In interrogating the boundaries between biography and fiction, art and science, and painting and writing, the past in this sense becomes a familiar country, providing a variety of landscapes and figures that a young man can seek out on a series of chivalric quests in pursuit of seduction and aesthetic pleasure.

NOTES

1. In his introduction to *Eminent Victorians,* Strachey explicitly appeals to art and the subjective vision of the artist/biographer as the model that he wishes to pursue in his biographical studies: "I have attempted, through the medium of biography, to present some Victorian visions to the modern eye. They are, in one sense, haphazard visions—that is to say, my choice of subjects has been determined by no desire to construct a system or prove a theory, but by simple motives of convenience and art" (Strachey 1918: 3).

2. According to Gillian Fenwick (1990: 182), George Smith expected to lose money on this project but underwrote it with the profits from his investments, most notably the Apollinaris table water company, which he advertised with the same fervor as the *Dictionary* in the *Athenaeum.* In this respect his intentions were philanthropic, but he also hoped that, unlike the table water, the *Dictionary* would provide his own epitaph by leaving a lasting mark on nineteenth-century literature.

3. Stephen and Morley were members of a large group of late-Victorian intellectuals influenced by positivist ideas and scientific methods, who stressed the importance of manly fellowship in opposition to the rhetorical and "literary" uses of language that they deemed feminine and deviant (Amigoni 1993: 37–40, 138–39). As editor of the *Cornhill,* Stephen, unlike Morley at the *Fortnightly,* clung on to the policy of anonymous contributions in an effort to remove subjective bias and personal prejudice (Brake 1994: 23). His instructions to potential contributors to the *Dictionary of National Biography* in a letter to the *Athenaeum,* 23 December 1882, make his "scientific" preoccupations plain. He condemns any philosophical or critical disquisition on the part of the writer, together with "picturesque description" or any controversial or subjective opinions. Finally he stresses the importance of impersonality as synonymous with the practice of life-writing itself: "He must, as a rule, say nothing which would be equally appropriate under several other names; in short he must be strictly biographical" (Fenwick 1990: 182–83).

4. "John Knox and his Relations with Women" was published in *Macmillan's Magazine* in September 1875 and "The Gospel According to Walt Whitman" in the *New Quarterly Magazine* in October 1878; the other essays were all published in the *Cornhill Magazine* under the editorship of Leslie Stephen: "Victor Hugo's Romances"

(August 1874), "Charles of Orleans" (December 1876), "François Villon, Student, Poet, Housebreaker" (August 1877), "Some Aspects of Robert Burns" (October 1879), "Henry David Thoreau" (June 1880), "Yoshida Torajiro" (March 1880), and "Samuel Pepys" (July 1881).

5. In a letter to the *Spectator* on 12 June 1880, Alexander Japp criticized Stevenson's essay, suggesting that he favored style over serious, or even accurate, scholarship (Swearingen 1980: 47).

6. With his earnings from *Treasure Island* he bought thirteen volumes of prints by Hokusai (about who he hoped to write an article that never materialized) (*Ltrs* 4: 122, 130, 132); his review of Japanese book illustrations, "Byways of Book Illustration: Two Japanese Romances" appeared in the November 1885 edition of the *Magazine of Art* (8–15).

7. Jonathan Freedman identifies ekphrasis, the use of verbal description to describe natural scenes as if they were artworks, as one of the identifying marks of British aestheticism that subverted the boundaries between painting and writing established by Lessing (Freedman 1990: 19). He goes on to examine the links between aestheticism and a growing culture of consumption, including the literary marketplace. Stevenson can be seen to exemplify both of these aspects of British aestheticism. For links between late-nineteenth-century models of market economics, consumption, and aestheticism, see also Small (1991) and Gagnier (2000).

8. This was probably the work by Sully that Colvin sent to Stevenson in June 1874 (*Ltrs* 2: 21).

9. Stevenson, who declares that "there is indeed, only one merit worth considering in a man of letters—that he should write well; and only one damning fault—that he should write ill" (Stevenson 1882: 53), is probably paraphrasing Victor Hugo's preface to *Les Orientales* (1829) where he asserted that there were neither good nor bad subjects, only good and bad poets (Bell-Villada 1996: 40). This contention was subsequently and more famously espoused by Oscar Wilde in his preface to *The Picture of Dorian Gray* (1891).

REFERENCES

Altick, Richard. 1965. *Lives and Letters*. Westport, CT: Greenwood Press.
Amigoni, David. 1993. *Victorian Biography*. London: Harvester Wheatsheaf.
Bell-Villada, Gene. H. 1996. *Art for Art's Sake and Literary Life*. Lincoln: University of Nebraska Press.
Brake, Laurel. 1994. *Subjugated Knowledges*. London: Macmillan.
Fenwick, Gillian. 1990. The *Athenaeum* and the *Dictionary of National Biography. Victorian Periodicals Review* 23 (4): 180–88.
Freedman, Jonathan. 1990. *Professions of Taste*. Stanford, CA: Stanford University Press.
Gagnier, Regenia. 2000. *The Insatiability of Human Wants*. Chicago: University of Chicago Press.
Hazlitt, William. 1821. On Familiar Style. In *Selected Writings*. Ed. Ronald Blythe. 1970. Harmondsworth: Penguin.
Jay, Martin. 1993. *Downcast Eyes. The Denigration of Vision in Twentieth-Century French Thought*. Berkeley: University of California Press.

Jenks, Chris, ed. 1995. *Visual Culture.* London: Routledge.

Kijinski, John. 1991. John Morley's "Men of Letters" Series and the Politics of Reading. *Victorian Studies* 34 (winter): 205–25.

Korsten, F. J. M. 1992. The "English Men of Letters" Series: A Monument to Late-Victorian Literary Criticism. *English Studies* 73 (6): 503–16.

Marcus, Laura. 1994. *Auto/Biographical Discourses.* Manchester: Manchester University Press.

McQuire, Scott. 1998. *Visions of Modernity.* London: Sage Publications.

Miller. D. A. 1988. *The Novel and the Police.* Berkeley: University of California Press.

Morley, John. 1873. Mr Pater's Essays. In *Nineteenth Century Essays.* Ed. Peter Stansky. 1970. Chicago: University of Chicago Press.

Pater, Walter. 1888. *The Renaissance: Studies in Art and Poetry.* 1959. London: New English Library.

Small, Ian. 1991. *Conditions for Criticism.* Oxford: Oxford University Press.

Stephen, Leslie. 1875. Art and Morality. *Cornhill Magazine* 32: 91–101.

———. 1877. Charlotte Brontë. *Cornhill Magazine* 36: 723–39.

Stevenson, Robert Louis. 1882. *Familiar Studies of Men and Books.* London: Chatto & Windus. Tusitala Edition. Vol. 27.

———. 1884. "A Humble Remonstrance." *Longman's Magazine.* Tusitala Edition. Vol. 29.

Strachey, Lytton. 1918. *Eminent Victorians.* Ed. Paul Levy. 2002. *Eminent Victorians: The Definitive Edition.* London: Continuum.

Sully, James. 1874. *Sensation and Intuition.* London: Henry S. King and Co.

Swearingen, Roger G. 1980. *The Prose Writings of Robert Louis Stevenson, A Guide.* Hamden, CT: Archon Books; London: Macmillan.

The Greenhouse vs. the Glasshouse

Stevenson's Stories as Textual Matrices

NATHALIE JAËCK

Jekyll's groundbreaking masterstroke of metamorphosis can be read as an intratextual metaphorical clue: indeed, his fascination with bodily prolif-eration, and his transgression of the taboo of individual integrity mirror Stevenson's own fascination with textual proliferation and his transgres-sion of the contemporary naturalist taboo of textual integrity. Transposing Jekyll's most famous statement thus comes very close to defining Steven-son's literary manifesto: "*Text* is not truly one but two. . . . Others will fol-low, others will outstrip me on the same lines; and I hazard the guess that *text* will be ultimately known for a mere polity of multifarious, incongru-ous and independent denizens" (Stevenson 1886: 82).[1] Concentrating on *The Master of Ballantrae, Strange Case of Dr. Jekyll and Mr. Hyde*, and *Trea-sure Island*, Stevenson nurses a constant literary obsession: just as Jekyll wants to launch an assault on the "fortress of identity" (Stevenson 1886: 83), Stevenson seems to be eager to dismember, to scatter the text. Stig-matizing as an illusion the naturalist effort to barricade the text, to turn it into an authoritative and indisputable stronghold, Stevenson becomes a literary outlaw and opens a new, modern, literary way. In his stories the text is dislocated, it is made to proliferate; to escape narrative control, it becomes heterogeneous, opaque, essentially unstable. Stevenson's novels invalidate and outmode Zola's contemporary ideal of the text as a trans-parent and transitive "glasshouse": "Je voulais . . . une composition sim-ple, une langue nette, quelque chose comme une maison de verre laissant voir les idées à l'intérieur . . . , les documents humains donnés dans leur nudité sévère" [I wanted . . . a simple composition, a clear language, something like a house of glass that allow you to see the ideas inside . . . , human documents presented directly and unadorned] (Zola 1881, vol. ii: 92). Instead, he invents a text that is more like a self-contained greenhouse, its own reflexive and dynamic literary fertilizer that experiments with random developments, with textual heterogenesis.

Stevenson playfully insists on the same routine in his narratives: he ironically stages, story after story, the desperate and pathetic fortification of the text, a fortification that he entrusts to dutiful servants of the Realist system, those interchangeable lawyers and mere copyists for whom the text is an authoritative way to testify reality. But the text soon becomes a demolition site, it escapes the lawyers' control and assaults the stronghold from the inside; it starts proliferating, and dissolves narrative integrity as well as textual linearity. Morbid "testification," defeated and proved a delusive fake, thus gives way to dynamic "textification": reality disappears behind its several versions, it becomes mere compost to the text. In Stevenson's transgressive greenhouse, the text thus prophetically bears all the characteristics of the modern Deleuzian ideal of the rhizome; and in the same way as Jekyll transposes Stevenson's method, "the Captain" comes up with an ideal text-to-be: his logbook and his map, folded together in the chest, constitute a treasured literary model, the never-ending, heterogeneous, discontinuous, nonreferential surface that Stevenson wants to write.

The Text as a Demolition Site

The same pre-text postpones the beginning of the story in *Treasure Island*, *Strange Case of Dr. Jekyll and Mr. Hyde*, and *The Master of Ballantrae*, to the point that it becomes a sort of metatextual ritual, a text-lock that triggers the entry into fiction: in all three stories, Stevenson stages the same procedure of textual fortification, the same barricading of the text. In *Treasure Island*, the Captain's papers consist in a resisting "bundle tied up in oilcloth" (Stevenson 1883: 22), "sewn together" (32), and Doctor Livesey adds a personal level of protection: "The doctor looked it all over, as if his fingers were itching to open it; but instead of doing that, he put it quietly in the pocket of his coat" (31). The same ceremonial opens *Strange Case*: Utterson radically locks up a text from Jekyll in "the most private part" of his safe (35), and takes another, already "sealed in several places" and strives even to suppress knowledge of its existence: "The lawyer put it in his pocket. 'I would say nothing of this paper'" (72, 73). But Peter M'Brair, in the preface to *The Master of Ballantrae*, is clearly the most efficient in this series of censoring lawyers and textual undertakers. Here, the text is pad-locked, "a packet, fastened with many seals and enclosed in a single sheet of strong paper" (Stevenson 1898: 7), and it has remained buried in a tex-tual cemetery for the past hundred years, shrouded in other dead texts.[2]

The lawyers very clearly strive to contain texts that are by essence mul-tiple, disorderly, and heterogeneous, and reduce them to an artificial and censoring unity. But the attempt proves delusive, the texts run wild, they escape the frame and irresistibly multiply. The Captain's bundle is dis-membered and divided into two discontinuous fragments, a logbook that is in turn quite heterogeneous, and a map; Utterson's single envelope is no match for Jekyll's dissident text that buds out: "several enclosures fell to the floor" (Stevenson 1886: 73); and the scattering of the text is further rad-icalized in *The Master of Ballantrae*, where the unity carefully preserved by the lawyer ("a single sheet of strong paper") is irrepressibly scattered: the self-contained packet is turned into miscellaneous material, into a literary hybrid, a collage of odds and ends that the "editor/author" insists "shall be published as it stands," resisting the wish of another lawyer (Mr. Thom-son) that a synthesis should be made. The preface is thus very clear: *The Master of Ballantrae* is going to be the story of a literary revival as much as the story of the bodily revival of the Master. In the insubordinate text-lock of the preface, a new type of text is being born, excavated, resuscitated from the literary cemetery collected by generations of dutiful lawyers, whose function was to make sure that these texts were written by the rules. A single clue is given as to the respective nature of these two competing texts: novel and challenging *baldness* ("there is nothing so noble as bald-ness. I would have all literature bald"; Stevenson 1898: 8) vs. inherited habits of *accumulation* ("I succeeded to a prodigious accumulation of old law-papers and old tin-boxes, some of them of Peter's hoarding, some of his father's"; 6). The line of opposition clearly reminds the reader of Steven-son's major grievance about the naturalists' method and particularly about Zola's plea for a minute, documentary, accumulative, panoptic writing that he hoped would "compete with the registry office": "He would leave noth-ing undeveloped, and thus drowned out of sight of land amid the multi-tude of crying and incongruous details. Jesus, there is but one art: to omit!" (*Ltrs* 4: 169). The preface can thus read as an ironical edification of a tombstone to naturalism and its immediate profanation;[3] the editor is like a text-snatcher, and the excavation of Mackellar's subversive manuscript amounts to a desecration: from then on text is under self-attack, it is turned into a demolition site, it deconstructs and scatters the myth of textual integrity, and experiments on its own precariousness and instability.

The first move of the assault is to dissolve narrative integrity. As opposed to the lawyers whose indisputable voice aims at giving a close and continuous account of reality, the narrators in Stevenson's texts stage the defeat of fake authoritative omniscience, and experiment in a very modern way on the instability of focalization. An exponential multiplication of narrators fragments the text and flattens the viewpoint: two juxtaposed narrators in *Treasure Island*, three embedded narrators in *Strange Case*, an unspecified number of juxtaposed and embedded narrators in *The Master of Ballantrae*, plus an acceleration of the process toward the end of the novel, in which a crowd of narrators contribute shorter and shorter inconsistent fragments. Not only do they multiply but their status becomes quite confused, nearly improper as we can best see with the anonymous editor of *The Master*, apparently a mere copyist whose function is to pass the text on, to be a link in its making, and who no longer claims authority over the text. In fact, the editor's main function is metatextual: he is meant to denounce narrative omniscience as a sham, to unmask the third-person narration, proving that it is bound to be a subjectivity in hiding, and to enact the emergence of first-person narration. In the preface, the use of the third-person narration jars from the beginning, since it is contradicted by the present tense that does not enact the grammatical break: "Although an old, consistent exile, the editor of the following pages revisits now and again the city of which he exults to be a native" (Stevenson 1898: 5). And indeed, the third-person singular is an intruder, that it will take less than three pages to expel: after a couple of regular occurrences ("The editor," "he"), the "I" breaks into the text, unannounced, and cracks the uniformity of the narrative voice: "'A Mystery?' I repeated" (6). Absolutely heterogeneous here, the "I" reads like a slip of the tongue and is immediately wiped out, corrected by the possessive adjective: "Yes, said his friend, 'a mystery'" (6). But the check is of no avail, and the third person is truly under attack, stigmatized as the odd one out ("*the other* remarked"; 6), before it finally gives in, irreversibly supplanted by the first person singular: "cried I . . . said I . . . replied I" (6–8). *Strange Case of Dr. Jekyll and Mr. Hyde* obtrusively radicalizes the deconstruction since the use of the "I" proves essentially unstable and delusive, besieged and thus dissolved by both Jekyll and Hyde ("Jekyll was now my city of refuge; but let Hyde peep out an instant . . . ," says a narrator of uncertain identity; Stevenson 1886: 92), to become what Naugrette called "une pure fonction narrative vidée de toute identité" [a purely narrative function void of all identity] (Naugrette 1987: 71), thus completing Stevenson's prophetical and meta-textual panorama of the dislocation of focalization.

The collapse of the fortress of third-person omniscience triggers the vaporization of the text, which is nowhere so obvious as in *The Master of Ballantrae*. Within the novel, as a sort of anecdotal metonymy of the over-all structural dislocation, the numerous books, letters, notes, and papers are invariably misused and endangered: Alison's express to the Master is dropped and trampled over by a horse, the Master's letter to Alison is burned unopened and condemned to remain a dead letter, thus creating a hole in the text, a textual deficit. But these inner immolations are embed-ded in a text the structure of which is absolutely routed. The distribution of the narrative voice brings about the dismembering of the text, that becomes a literary mille-feuilles, an appropriate dessert indeed for the edi-tor's dinner.[4] The text is essentially precarious: it is an unbound manu-script, it consists in a patching up of heterogeneous fragments,[5] growingly disordered, often at odds with one another ("Here follows a narrative which I have compiled out of three sources, not very consistent in all points"; Stevenson 1889: 194), and eventually obtrusively missing, either because they are forgotten (Mackellar admits to forgetting a crucial date and informs the reader that the present manuscript is in fact a secondhand copy, a rewriting of a previous diary—"It is a strange thing that I should be at a stick for a date . . . But the truth is, I was stricken out of all my habitudes, and find my journals very ill redd-up"; 133), or because they are censored. Indeed, Mackellar plays the biased role of narrator-in-chief and literary critic, and highlights his own unreliability by editing others' texts; the Chevalier Burke, as his main literary rival, is also his favorite scapegoat. He repeatedly footnotes his text, stresses the weaknesses of the Chevalier's account, and randomly and rashly expurgates his text, which thus begins in the middle of nowhere, hooked on to the main text by frustrating sus-pension marks, and cut short just before the climax of his fight with the Master ("I have refrained from comments on any of his extraordinary and (in my eyes) immoral opinions . . . But his version of the quarrel is really more than I can reproduce"; 60). But the process is embedded, and the editor repays Mackellar in kind, by wiping five pages clean out of the text: "*[EDITOR'S NOTE.—Five pages of Mr Mackellar's MS. are here omitted. I have gathered from their perusal an impression that Mr Mackellar, in his old age, was rather an exacting servant. Against the seventh Lord Durrisdeer (with whom at any rate, we have no concern) nothing material is alleged.—R. L. S.]*" (125).

This sibylline and understated note efficiently completes the vacancy of the text: highly heterogeneous, written in italics, it digs holes in the transcript and thus breaks it apart, suggesting it might all be a fake, all the more so since the intervention unmasks the manipulative "show-man" behind the puppet-editor. It insists that writing is always a matter of subjective vision, it is always "a version" of reality, an opaque re-vision, and that textual integrity is a myth.

Thus efficiently dispersed, proved "multifarious," "incongruous," and "independent," freed from Zola's delusive glasshouse, the text, initiated to its own precariousness, is ready for a new adventure. And indeed, Stevenson's stories can be read as textual adventures, as quests for a new text: the yoke of the sterile glasshouse, in which the text was only meant as a objective and servile documentation of reality, is thus turned into an opaque self-generating greenhouse that strives to expel extra-organic reality, interested only in textual proliferation and exploration, and in which reality becomes an anecdotal content, a useful fertilizer. Stevenson is repeatedly very clear, in his letters and critical texts, about the fact that in a novel reality is a mere stand-in, that realism is "a mere question of method" (*Ltrs* 4: 169), i.e. a methodological necessity of internal coherence: "People suppose it is the 'stuff' that interests them, . . . not understanding that an unpolished diamond is but a stone" (*Ltrs* 5: 42), or "[The writer must be] disengaged from the ardent struggle of immediate representation, or realistic and *ex facto* art. [Art lies in] the crystallisation of day dreams; in changing, not in copying fact; in the pursuit of the ideal, not in the study of nature" (*Ltrs* 4: 170). The text thus develops into an unpredictable, incidental rhizome, it become its own reflexive subject, the actual treasure to be found, the only surface worth exploring.

The Greenhouse vs. the Glasshouse

As opposed to the sterilized but barren glasshouse, the text as greenhouse opens a place of incubation: it reads as if the text, before developing, needed a period of fermentation in a closed textual environment. Stevenson's stories often pause on their own threshold, to build a sense of textual imminence, to delay and at the same time concentrate, intensify, the budding of the main text. Through several strategies of postponement, Stevenson creates a metatextual inflation of the liminary state, a text-lock in which the only topic is the impending development of the text to come, and the only function is paradoxically to draw out the absence of the text.

This textual holdup may be more or less elaborated: in *Treasure Island,* the stalling space of the text lasts only as long as it takes for Jim to eat a pigeon-pie, and then for the Doctor to unpick the text. But in *The Master of Ballantrae,* the whole preface is meant as a holding area, as an in-between antechamber whose main function is to insist on the fact that the text is imminent, that, being suspended for a century, it is on the brink of starting—and at the same time delaying it even more. Such a dilation of textual imminence is a theoretical transposition: it imports in the form of the text a suspense device that is used in its contents. It reminds the reader of the first story of "The Suicide Club," the "Story of the Young Man with the Cream Tarts," in which Prince Florizel and Colonel Geraldine are suspended on the edge of their adventure, neither inside nor outside the club, paradoxically willing prisoners in the middle of open doors: "The outer door stood open; the door of the cabinet was ajar; and there, in a small but very high apartment, the young man left them once more" (Stevenson 1878: 38). The preface to *The Master* reads like a formal transcription of this passage: it is the text itself, and no longer the characters, that is delayed, suspended. Illustrating Rivière's statement that "L'aventure, c'est la forme de l'œuvre plutôt que sa matière" [Adventure is the form of the work rather than its content] (Rivière 2000: 69), the text becomes adventurous, it conforms to Jankélévitch's definition: "L'aventure infinitésimale est liée à l'avènement de l'événement. . . . L'avènement est l'instant en instance: . . . l'actualité sur le point de se faire" [The infinitesimal adventure is tied to the advent of the event . . . The advent is the instant at its birth . . . the actual on the point of taking place] (Jankélévitch 1998: 830). The preface expands the pending birth of the text, it is the transitory intransitive pre-text that fosters a sense of textual emergency; the text is both in and out of the lawyer's cemetery, it is still the one and only adventure.[6] Stevenson's reticence to yield to the linear logic of the story, his lingering in what Barthes called "un espace dilatoire, dont l'emblème pourrait être la reticence" [a dilatory area, whose emblem might be named "reticence"] (Barthes 1970: 82) builds a reality-proof lock, what I called a textual greenhouse, where the text takes over its contents and is allowed to develop.

Once out of their respective stalling spaces, the texts indeed can no longer be confined to the sterile testification of reality, and a reversal of the traditional order of dependence takes place: testification develops into textification, reality is reconstructed, reinvented by proliferating texts that wildly experiment in "changing, not in copying facts." In *The Master of Ballantrae,* the actual events of the story seem to stammer over these invading literary intruders. Yet Mackellar tries hard, lawyerlike ("I take up the history of events as they befell under my own observation, like a witness in a court"; Stevenson 1889: 19), to reestablish reality as his main concern and aim ("The full truth of this odd matter is what the world has long been looking for"; 9) and to reduce his text to a reliable copy (it is "an authentic memoir," and "evidence"; 9). But obeying Stevenson's injunction, "Death to the optic nerve" (*Ltrs* 8: 193), the first page of Mackellar's manuscript is saturated with heterogeneous texts that blindly and recklessly invent reality. In fact, the real story of the Duries appears as a mere literary fertilizer. Indeed, it has already been many times told, used, and bent to the rules of several literary genres: romanticized in a couple of rhymes that Mackellar cannot help quoting; "defaced by legends" (10); registered in history books ("Authentic history besides is filled with their exploits" [10]); and disfigured in local folk's tales ("[Patey Macmorland] had more ill tales upon his tongue than ever I heard the match of" [19]). Reality is colonized by these grafted parasites, it disappears behind the palimpsest and becomes a mere pre-text to constant rewriting.[7] In Stevenson's stories, the boxes, chests, or safes in which the lawyers hope to contain the texts invariably prove to be telescopic reflexive boxes: several enclosures falling from Utterson's envelope, a map and a logbook escaping from the chest in *Treasure Island* (themselves resulting in two more pieces of writing, Jim's and the Doctor's manuscripts), and then, accelerating the process, "a prodigious accumulation of old-papers and old tin boxes" liberated from Mr. Thomson's safe in the preface to *The Master of Ballantrae*, thus constituting an endless reservoir of texts, only one of them being exploited, and thus triggering a new profusion of inner texts. Such a process once more seems to be copied from the "Story of the Young Man with the Cream Tarts," as if the story were an intratextual model of development. Indeed, the Suicide Club is appropriately situated in Box Court (Stevenson 1878: 56), and the house there is just as telescopic as Stevenson's texts: it keeps opening in on itself, containing folding doors that lead to one another, to embedded rooms (the cabinet, then folding doors and a closet, then a smoking room, then another set of folding doors, and then the playing room, but that proves to be another door, "Death's Private Door") each of which in turn are called "ante-chambers" (40). In the same way as there is no escape from this "Box House," there is no escape from the text in Stevenson's stories: *Strange Case* opens with a *mise-en-abîme* narration followed by Jekyll's manuscript will and ends with Jekyll's threatened, and thus shortened, incomplete manuscript (and will quite magically give

birth, after it is over, to many new versions); *The Master of Ballantrae* too
ends with a text within the text, that remarkably enough (though it is a
conclusive epitaph) is notably ambiguous and thus fails to have the final
word, as if things were left unsaid.

But it is with the Captain's multifarious "bundle of papers" in *Treasure
Island* that I would like to end this study, to argue that it constitutes the
alternative treasure,[8] an experiment in an ideal literary form. "The last
thing" (Stevenson 1883: 22) in the chest is a telescopic bundle, a confined
and obviously ill text that needs to be set free by the doctor: "The bundle
was sewn together, and the doctor had to get out his instrument case, and
cut the stitches with his medical scissors. It contained two things—a book
and a sealed paper" (32). At the end of the delivery, some kind of par-
thenogenesis seems to have happened: the bundle "looking like papers"
has been divided into two, and the proliferating process triggered. There
is now the heterogeneous logbook and the "sealed paper," which, unpicked
too, will give birth to the prolific map, a multidimensional text-surface
that will in turn generate two more texts, Jim's and the Doctor's manuscripts. To the modern reader, it is striking how these two elements, the
logbook and the map, come as modern intruders into literary tradition,
and anachronically remind the modern reader of Deleuze's ideal literary
rhizome:

> On the first page there were only some scraps of writing, such as a man
> with a pen in his hand might make for idleness or practice. One was the
> same as the tattoo mark, "Billy Bones his fancy;" then there was "Mr W.
> Bones, mate." "No more rum." "Off Palm Key he got itt;" and some other
> snatches, mostly single words and unintelligible. . . .
>
> "Not much instruction there," said Dr Livesey, as he passed on.
>
> The next ten or twelve pages were filled with a curious series of entries.
> There was a date at one end of the line and at the other a sum of money, as
> in common account-books; but instead of explanatory writing, only a vary-
> ing number of crosses between the two.
>
> "I can't make heads or tail of this," said Dr Livesey. . . .
>
> There was little else in the volume but a few bearings of places noted in
> the blank leaves towards the end. (32–33)

In this text that resists interpretation, the three major principles of the
rhizome are highlighted, namely the principles of "connexion and hetero-
geneousness," of "multiplicité" and of "ruptures a-signifiantes" [meaningless

breaks] (Deleuze 1980: 13–20). Indeed, the book consists in a juxtaposition of multiple fragments ("scraps of writing"), it breaks the linear, diachronic tradition, it is essentially discontinuous. There is no central unit acting as mainspring, no transcendence, no hierarchical system, no solution given from above. As the Doctor remarks, it is not meant for instruction, it is not meant to fix reality in a signification; fanciful, it develops in an anarchistic way, it is full of deviations, blank spaces, random monosyllables that are like textual buds, and open what Deleuze calls "deterritorialization lines," pushing the text out of its usual ways, expanding it, forcing the reader to venture multiple interpretations of reality. It is the very opposite of James's description of Zola's *Vérité*: "*Vérité* marks the rigid straightness of course from point to point. He [Zola] had seen his horizon and his fixed goal from the first, and no cross-scent, no new distance, no blue gap in the hill to right or to left ever tempted him to stray" (James 1903: 405). As opposed to a mechanic and linear text, Stevenson prefers a form that is incidental: the text becomes a surface to be explored in all directions, with no beginning and no ending, with no compulsory direction, disordered, dynamic. The logbook, inscribing in a very Deleuzian way the link between writing and exploring, is discontinuous, each section relates to others through virtual connections, which are there for the reader to imagine. Toward the end of the logbook, the blank pages gradually take over the text, and the single words, "bearings of places," interspersed and nearly intruding islands of meaning in between the blank spaces, are like invitations to travel. The blank pages open the text, they materialize and picture the multiplicity of virtual ways that are for the reader to devise. The text, against authoritative verticality, is successfully flattened, it becomes level with itself, it becomes the opaque surface Stevenson was after, as his literary correspondence with James shows.[9] In fact, the logbook truly becomes a map, with its still unexplored zones of "undifferentiation" or "indiscernability" that invite the reader to deviate, to cross in between the traditional routes, and invent his own unreferenced ways. It illustrates the fact that for Stevenson as for Deleuze: "Ecrire n'a rien à voir avec signifier, mais avec arpenter, cartographier, même des contrées à venir" [Writing has nothing to do with signifying. It has to do with surveying, mapping, even realms that are yet to come] (Deleuze 1980: 11).

NOTES

1. The original is "Man is not truly one . . . "
2. The preface to *The Master of Ballantrae* has a very troubled publication story

itself and even risked becoming itself another buried or censored text. It was written along with the first two chapters (Swearingen 1980: 119), as we know because on January 2, 1888, RLS asked his lawyer and friend, Charles Baxter, to compose M'Briar's "indorsation" for the cover of Mackellar's bundle of papers in an eighteenth-century style (*Ltrs* 6: 99). At that point in time, RLS was proceeding to a revision of the initial ninety-two pages. When *Ballantrae* was about to be published, however, he decided to omit the preface, because, as he later told Baxter, "I . . . condemned the idea as being a little too like Scott" (*Ltrs* 8: 290). When preparing the Edinburgh Edition, however, he changed his mind again and wanted to put the preface back in its original position, but Colvin refused. RLS insisted, but when, seven months later he died, as Ernest Mehew dryly puts it, Colvin "solved the problem by omitting the Preface" (*Ltrs* 8: 345 and n10), which was first published four years later in an appendix to the very last volume of the Edition.

3. This reminds the reader of Henry James's denunciation of naturalism through the sterile and morbid image of the pyramid: "The pyramid had been planned, and the site staked out" (James 1903: 406).

4. "Fate has put it in my power to honour your arrival with something really original by way of dessert" (Stevenson 1898: 6) The same trick is played in *Treasure Island*, where the Captain's manuscript is another literary mille-feuilles for dessert, which can only be leafed through after the pigeon-pie has been eaten.

5. For the 1889 Scribner's edition and the posthumous Edinburgh Edition, Stevenson insisted on unnumbered chapter titles for *Ballantrae*, as he had used for *Strange Case of Dr. Jekyll and Mr. Hyde*, thus reinforcing the impression of a collection of documents.

6. In *Strange Case of Dr. Jekyll and Mr. Hyde*, such textual emergency is even more acute, as Jekyll's text, after being delayed for two-thirds of the total narrative, runs the constant risk of being destroyed, so each word is like a textual reprieve: "Should the throes of change take me in the act of writing it, Hyde will tear it in pieces" (Stevenson 1886: 97). Jekyll's text is here like a talisman, for a while it makes Jekyll literally Hyde-proof, before his final surrender.

7. In fact, it is obvious that Mackellar soon loses sight of his referential duty toward reality and rather adopts a reflexive position: the real challenge is to imitate his literary rivals, not reality, and to write the authoritative version "that the world has long been waiting for, and public curiosity is sure to welcome" (Stevenson 1889: 9).

8. Indeed, these textual discoveries amount to treasure hunts. Jim comes closer to the table on which the bundle of documents is being opened "to enjoy the sport of the search" (Stevenson 1883: 32), while Mr. Thomson has "instituted a hunt through all the M'Brair repositories" (Stevenson 1898: 7).

9. James underlined Stevenson's "love of a literary surface" (James 1888: 259). Stevenson himself praised James for his short story "The Marriages" because he achieved the creation of this literary surface: "yours is so neat and bright and of so exquisite a surface" (*Ltrs* 7: 292).

REFERENCES

Barthes, Roland. 1970. *S/Z*. Paris: Seuil.
Deleuze, Gilles et Felix Guattari. 1980. *Mille Plateaux*. Paris: Les Editions de Minuit.

Gard, Roger, ed. 1987. *Henry James, The Critical Muse: Selected Literary Criticism.* Harmondsworth: Penguin Books.

James, Henry. 1888. Robert Louis Stevenson. In Gard 1987.

———. 1903. Emile Zola. In Gard 1987.

Jankélévitch, Vladimir. 1998. *Philosophie morale.* Paris: Flammarion.

Naugrette, Jean-Pierre. 1987. *Robert Louis Stevenson: L'aventure et son double.* Paris: Presses de l'Ecole Normale Supérieure.

Rivière, Jacques. 1913. *Le roman d'aventure.* 2000. Paris: Editions des Syrtes.

Stevenson, Robert Louis. 1878. "The Suicide Club." In *The Complete Short Stories of Robert Louis Stevenson.* Ed. Charles Neider. 1998. New York: Da Capo Press.

———. 1883. *Treasure Island.* Ed. Emma Letley. 1985. Oxford: Oxford University Press.

———. 1886. *Strange Case of Dr Jekyll and Mr Hyde.* In *The Strange Case of Dr Jekyll and Mr Hyde and Other Stories.* Ed. Jenni Calder. 1979. Harmondsworth: Penguin.

———. 1889. *The Master of Ballantrae.* Ed. Adrian Poole. 1996. Harmondsworth: Penguin.

———. 1898. Preface [to *The Master of Ballantrae*]. Edinburgh Edition. Vol. 28. In Stevenson 1889.

Swearingen, Roger G. 1980. *The Prose Writings of Robert Louis Stevenson, A Guide.* Hamden, CT: Archon Books; London: Macmillan.

Zola, Emile. 1881. Les romanciers naturalistes. In *Œuvres complètes.* Vol. 11. 1968. Paris: Tchou.

Trading Texts

Negotiations of the Professional and the Popular in the Case of Treasure Island

GLENDA NORQUAY

In many of his letters and essays Stevenson engages with the idea of writing as a trade: what impact does the need to earn a living through his craft have on a writer's work?[1] A further concern is the ways in which texts are traded: what distinguishes serious artistic endeavor from popular fiction aimed at the commercial market, and how might the circulation of a text through that market affect its status? And what exchanges might occur between such different forms of writing? Stevenson's concerns about authenticity and seriousness were highly representative of his time with its concerns over the increasing professionalization of the author and the resultant reconfiguration of aesthetics, but also particular and characteristic in their subtle negotiations of such tensions. A paratextual exploration of *Treasure Island* shows how Stevenson as author traded texts to establish his own literary authority and reveals how his work became part of contemporaneous debates on the nature of artistic production.

The story of *Treasure Island's* creation is well known: on vacation in Braemar, kept inside with his stepson Lloyd Osbourne in a period of bad weather, Stevenson produces a treasure map at Lloyd's request, then begins a yarn to accompany it. While reading the tale to the boy and to his own father, the household receives a visitor, Dr. Japp, who listens to the story and is so impressed that he carries away the manuscript and passes it on to his friend Mr. Henderson, the editor of *Young Folks.*[2] In *Young Folks* it is subsequently published.[3]

In 1900, six years after Stevenson's death, a curious spat takes place in the pages of *The Academy*. Stevenson's friend (and the inspiration, of course, for Long John Silver), W. E. Henley, writes for the *North American Review* an article later reported in *The Academy*, which suggests that the "gold" of *Treasure Island* was not fully appreciated by its readers, so much as it was recognized by other writers who realized its value and therefore made it "currency" by debasing it through imitation in their own popular fictions: "He had paid in gold and his gold was not recognized as current coin until it was turned into copper. The currency was debased? Of course it was . . . it was turned into copper" (Henley 1900). The tale when first published was not a great commercial success, but other writers recognized its worth and—through their imitations—a wider public learned to become more responsive to Stevenson's novel. The reading public, Henley suggests, might be compared to a set of Japanese boxes: "one inside the other, the larger containing the lesser throughout the series," and this is why "a good writer . . . is very often felt to some extent a great way outside the limits of the particular public which happens to be his" (Henley 1900). Musing upon his own particular example of this phenomenon—the publication of *Treasure Island*—Henley speculates about the fate of the *Young Folks* editor, James Henderson, whom he believes might be dead.

The Academy's plea for information on this subject elicits a response the following week from Robert Leighton, an editor of *Young Folks* in 1885, who confirms Henley's point that *Treasure Island* was not a great commercial success, helpfully notes that James Henderson *is* still alive, but then immediately complicates the picture by stating that Mr. Henderson (introduced to Stevenson by their mutual friend Dr. Japp) "offered to take a story from the young Scotsman, and, as indicating the kind of story he desired for *Young Folks*, he gave to Stevenson copies of the paper containing a serial by Charles E. Pearce—a treasure-hunting story entitled 'Billy Bo's'n'" (Leighton 1900: 189). Leighton continues: "In his 'My First Book' article in the *Idler*, Stevenson seems to suggest that 'Treasure Island' was already formed and planned in his mind prior to the time at which it was thought of as a serial for *Young Folks*; but there is evidence that in 'Billy Bo's'n' he found and adopted many suggestions and incidents for his own narrative." Leighton's version of events, suggesting that Stevenson was inspired by a "popular" story, quite reverses Henley's reading of *Treasure Island* as encouraging weaker imitators who then educate public taste into an appreciation of the novel—which Henley sees as quite properly belonging to the realm of art. Leighton's account, by contrast, suggests that the "gold" of *Treasure Island* emerges in fact from a debased "currency."

His assertion provokes an immediate response. First, and perhaps predictably, Stevenson's friend Sidney Colvin writes to the journal protesting against this version of events and enclosing an account by Dr. Japp, "in his own words," of the production of *Treasure Island,* which confirms Stevenson's version. Colvin argues that "*Treasure Island* was written absolutely for the sake of writing it, and in conformity with the ideas suggested by the map which R.L.S. had elaborately drawn and coloured . . . so that the statement that he found and adopted many incidents from 'Billy Bo's'n' is thus wholly met and disposed of" (Japp 1900: 210). The main thrust in Japp's account of the process of placing *Treasure Island* with *Young Folks* is to stress the importance of his personal connection and friendship with both Stevenson and Henderson, in direct contrast to the emphasis on the commercial context and the hierarchies of editors and writers that emerge from Leighton's letter. He also stresses Stevenson's "originality" in contrast to Leighton's depiction of Stevenson as an apprentice, who is not only guided by Henderson but needs to be shown the dubious literary merits of "Billy Bo's'n" as a model.

Colvin's intervention is followed a week later by a letter from James Henderson (Henderson 1900: 237–38), supporting Japp and endorsing his statement that Henderson's first meeting with Stevenson took place *after* the proofs had been corrected. The voice of the (clearly living and therefore suitably authenticated) Henderson appears to have put an end to the dispute, and the demon raised by Leighton is safely put back within its own set of Japanese boxes.

The speed and vehemence with which Leighton's suggestion is disposed of suggests that this whole contretemps raises difficult questions about relationships between popular fiction and original art, between the commercial and the pleasurable dimension of literature, between writing as a "trade" and writing as an act of creative inspiration. Moreover, the alacrity with which Stevenson's friends sprang to his defense after his death demonstrated their own awareness that he occupied a particularly precarious position in relation to such issues. Yet, as was often the case, with Stevenson's defenders, they also underestimated his own complicated and complicating role within these debates. The postpublication spat over *Treasure Island* is but one aspect of the novel's location within a complicated paratextual process of exchange.

In his image of "gold," namely, artistic quality, passing unrecognized until it was transformed into copper, thus turned into "currency" and debased through imitation, Henley establishes a dichotomy between "art," expressed in familiar terms of purity of form and originality of content, and the "trade," the economic exchange, of writing. The subsequent argument in *The Academy* over "Billy Bo's'n" reveals how much is at stake here, how much is invested in the need to prove Stevenson was not influenced by a popular text: that his work was original. Stevenson, moreover, has to be kept separate from the commercial processes of publication that function within a recognizable economy of exchange and imitation, an economy that legitimizes both mass production and plagiarism. The debate operates then with the classic demarcations of high and low by which art is defined. Henley's metaphor of coinage allows him to work with a recognizable polarization of the authentically unique (pure gold, artistically shaped for the maker's pleasure) and the inauthentically repetitive (the copper, mass-produced, circulating as currency) as normative categories in the separation of high and low culture. The contribution by Stevenson's other defenders, which prove that Stevenson produced the novel in an "unfettered" context for his own pleasure rather than with any eye to a commercial market, likewise works with familiar terms. As John Frow notes of contemporary popular culture: "the terms in which the emancipation and universalization of the category of art come to be cast are those of a distinction between works founded in freedom and internal necessity, on the one hand, and in unfreedom and external economic necessity on the other" (Frow 1995: 18). Pleasure remains a problematic issue for Stevenson and more could be written on the dynamic between the pleasure of creation and the textual provision of pleasure,[4] but it is Stevenson's maneuverings around the opposition of originality and imitation that are most interesting in the case of *Treasure Island.*

Apart from the abhorrence with which the suggestion that "Billy Bo's'n" may have been an influence on *Treasure Island* is met, what is most striking about the correspondence in *The Academy* is the way in which Stevenson's essay, "My First Book", is invoked as a source of authority. This compelling narrative, first published in *The Idler* and written a considerable time after the creation of *Treasure Island,* has been subsequently questioned on some details (Katz 1998: xxix–xxxiii). In addition, it can also be read as demonstrating Stevenson's own ambivalent and ambiguous take on this business of popular fiction and originality.

In his account of the creation of *Treasure Island* Stevenson can be seen as working within two very different aesthetic modes, two different regimes of value.[5] In his narrative he creates a romantic picture of coming to Pitlochry "in the fated year," transferring to Braemar on health grounds and sharing his cottage with a schoolboy home for the holidays. "And now admire the finger of predestination" he dramatically admonishes: the map is duly drawn, the story famously begun, "on a chill September morning" (Stevenson 1894: xxiv, xxv, xxvi). Chance therefore dictates the course of events; inspiration is inevitable and almost beyond his control. This is the version Japp and Colvin embrace, this is the part of the essay they recall. It is at this point in the essay, however, that the retrospective and analytic nature of Stevenson's narrative takes over; he cannot remember, he says, having sat now to write a story with more complacency but, in looking back, he has to embark upon: "a painful chapter" for "stolen waters are proverbially sweet." There follows a confession of his dismay at later discovering the sources that had influenced him in the writing of the tale: some are fairly minor—the parrot taken from *Robinson Crusoe,* the stockade from *Masterman Ready.* Others are more painful to discover: rereading Washington Irving's *Tales of a Traveler* he recognizes the source material for Billy Bones. Yet, although he goes on to itemize traces of Johnson's *Buccaneers,* Poe, Defoe, and Kingsley's *At Last,* at the time of writing, he informs us, ownership was assured: "[I]t seemed to belong to me like my right eye" (Stevenson 1883: xxvii). The essay, therefore, while acknowledging possible sources of plagiarism and repetition of published material, also makes claims for the apparent originality and innocence of the writer. *Treasure Island* is still, he suggests, different from these sources and arose from individual inspiration: "cultural value" therefore is indeed being calculated in terms of opposition to other texts, set apart by its breaking of expectations, by the way it complicates rather than simplifies—defined by the familiar strategies deployed to separate high culture from the popular. Yet, simultaneously, Stevenson provides an alternative reading, one that securely locates the text in a pattern of familiarity and repetition, the very source of "popular" pleasures. *Treasure Island* is categorized not only as dependent upon a range of other well-known tales, and therefore firmly within an identifiably popular genre, but also as distinctive and "original," again not only by this narrative of inspirational processes and innocent plagiarism but also through the metaperspective revealed in the author's ability to review his own influences. This latter element places him in a "high" literary context, while also claiming his familiarity with the "low" of his sources. While Stevenson with this double-voiced discourse may seem to situate his text within two different regimes of value, a hierarchy is clearly operating in which the inevitability of his "high" cultural instincts are asserted, at the same time his "low" cultural sources are contained and their influence diffused through the process of sophisticated acknowledgment.

Not that his sources really are that "low." Much lower, of course, are the other tales of piracy and adventure upon the high seas that Stevenson would have had access to through *Cassell's Family Paper* and in the works of certain other "Popular Authors" whom he talks about in his 1888 essay of that name. Although these authors are not mentioned in his reflection on the creation of *Treasure Island,* it is worth exploring further processes of exchange that may be discerned between the essay "Popular Authors" and his novel.

Written while he was trapped in the wilderness of Saranac Lake, the essay "Popular Authors" was part of a series commissioned by *Scribner's Magazine*. Although produced through economic necessity, the writing of this particular essay gave Stevenson a range of pleasures, as it became both a process of recollection and reconstruction of his childhood reading. Calling from his isolation for books half-remembered from his youth, he could reenact the pleasures of immersion in those tales that had thrilled him as a boy. The essay, however, also becomes a highly sophisticated and wickedly parodic exploration of the nature of literary hierarchies and the demands of the literary marketplace. Stevenson's discourse is again double-voiced: as a writer he articulates the dynamics of the marketplace but presents himself above such ephemeral hacks as Bracebridge Hemming; as a reader he is both the passionate reenactor of his early enthusiasms and an older and wiser critic of them.

In relation to *Treasure Island,* however, and this business of originality and imitation, the essay presents further complications. One of the novels that Stevenson discusses in the essay is *Tom Holt's Log* by the prolific novelist W. Stephens Hayward. Stevenson opens the essay with an anecdote about an emigrant meeting up with a sailor, late at night on the deck of an Atlantic liner. Which book, he inquires of the hand, most gives a true picture of a sailor's life? "'Well,' returns the other, with great deliberation and emphasis, 'there is *one*; that is *just* a sailor's life. You know all about it if you know that'" (Stevenson 1888a: 162). The book is then revealed as *Tom Holt's Log*. This is the story that will send a young boy to sea; indeed, even once he has experienced life at sea and learned the bitterness of its reality, a part of him will still structure his longings in the terms of his youthful reading, as the essay continues: "And he does go to sea. He lives surrounded by the fact, and does not observe it. He cannot realize, he cannot make a tale of his own life; which crumbles in discrete impressions even as he lives it, and slips between the fingers of his memory like sand. It is not this that he considers in his rare hours of rumination, but that other life, which was all lit up for him by the humble talent of a Hayward—that other life which, God knows, perhaps he still believes that he is leading—the life of Tom Holt" (Stevenson 1888a: 173).

In his reference to *Tom Holt's Log*, Stevenson's double-voiced discourse is once again based upon occlusion and omission, trading texts in such a way as to again reinforce his own cultural authority. For although *Tom Holt's Log* is absent from Stevenson's litany of sea stories that relate to *Treasure Island*, the text is similar in several respects: it is a first-person narrative, with early sections of the book written from memory and the remainder compiled from a daily journal, with insertions of ship's logbook material. The tale is, of course, only one of many nineteenth-century yarns in which a young boy narrates a series of extraordinary sea adventures, and it includes a striking parallel with *Treasure Island* in the moment at which Tom Holt finds himself alone at sea, when everyone else has been swept off the boat and drowned in a waterspout storm. Like Jim, taking control of the *Hispaniola* after the fight with Israel Hands, he becomes master of all he surveys: "No other eye than mine saw the bosom of the great blue ocean; from the ship, far away to the horizon, rising and falling with a slow solemn swell, or with the waves crested with foam—I was alone" (Hayward 1868: 1). So in this essay we find mention of a book that Stevenson had certainly read and might well have influenced his imagining on *Treasure Island* but is absent from his own account of its sources.[6] This may make us begin to suspect that in his essay in *The Idler*, there is a careful process of selection going on in the acknowledgment of sources, in the playful admissions of plagiarism.

Tom Holt's Log is also an extremely interesting choice within the overall context of "Popular Authors" because it is much more explicitly reflective upon the textual creation of desire than Stevenson allows, even though he is himself reflecting on the nature of literary longings. It is also more knowing about its own status as fiction than he suggests, for even in *Tom Holt's Log* we find a degree of self-referentiality. As a boy, Tom struggles with his mother's restrictions on his choice of reading—reading material that will shape his choice of career.[7] While depicting Tom's amazing adventures during his life at sea, the novel permits the maternal voice to warn against the fantasy fulfillment offered by such narratives:

> By degrees there grew in my breast an ardent longing to see more of the world than was contained within our island. But when I spoke of such a wish, my mother always replied discouragingly, and, so to say, threw cold water on the idea, declaring that the books I had read gave highly coloured

and untrue accounts of the lives of those men whom I looked upon as fortunate heroes, and that the hardships and mishaps they endured more than compensated for the fame they gained and the pleasures of exploring foreign countries.

I was a dutiful son, and did not always attempt to argue with my mother. But nevertheless the thoughts which reading about the adventures of others had instilled into my breast were not driven away, and as I grew in years the desire to travel and see the world increased. (Hayward 1868: 3–4)

So, this supposedly simplistic yarn is, like several others of its genre, a text that explicitly articulates the nature of narrative desire or at least acknowledges the shaping influence of early reading in structuring fantasies. Yet in "Popular Authors" it is portrayed as a novel with which the naive reader might (indeed did) identify but to which the sophisticated author can adopt a patronizing evaluation. In order to present himself as a discerning consumer of such reading pleasures, Stevenson has to exclude the novel's own gestures toward the narrative creation of desire and the dangerous pleasures of seeking fulfillment through the word. Moreover, the text he dismisses through such an approach may well have been an influence on his own *Treasure Island*, even though he does not include it in his list of its sources.

If "My First Book" allows Stevenson to recognize the commercial and intertextual context in which he operates but at the same time lays claim to the uniqueness and originality necessary for the "artist," achieved in part through the process of excluding less desirable texts from the narrative of composition, in similar fashion "Popular Authors" situates him within that commercial context but also elevates him above it through processes of exclusion and simplification. In this respect Stevenson is extremely successful (if perhaps somewhat disingenuous) in negotiating the opposition between the unique and the repetitive and also in sustaining his position as professional writer but one with artistic integrity. There is, however, a greater strain evident in the demands of accommodating mass appeal, mass production, and artistic creation when it comes to the idea of pleasure, around which so many contradictions appear to crystallize.

Many years later Lloyd Osbourne and Stevenson are again marooned together, their boat is stuck in Apenema in the South Seas; to pass the time they again concoct a tale. This tale becomes *The Wrecker*, perhaps Stevenson's most interesting exploration of the relationship between trade and art, and a novel preoccupied with questions of taste and authenticity.[8]

The Wrecker too shows Stevenson's discourse as double-voiced as he gestures toward the thriller form that the tale takes, yet conveys his own repulsion at "the appearance of insincerity and shallowness of tone" associated with such fiction (Stevenson 1892: 405). Again his literary maneuvering involves a declaration of popular influences and a simultaneous affirmation of his distance from them.

Ironically, this novel too is prefaced in the Tusitala Edition by a little narrative—from Lloyd Osbourne—about its creation, which again stresses the simple and unmotivated pleasures of production: "It was exhilarating to work with Stevenson," he writes, "he was so appreciative, so humorous—brought such gaiety, *camaraderie*, and goodwill to our joint task. We never had a single disagreement as the book ran its course; it was a pastime, not a task, and I'm sure no reader ever enjoyed it as much as we did" (Stevenson 1892: ix). Osbourne positions himself and Stevenson as leisured seekers after pleasure: the book was not written for material gain, only to entertain the writers; pleasure is to be found in the unfettered nature of the pursuit. As Henley struggled to free Stevenson from links to the commercial context and establish his artistic originality, so Osbourne strives to maintain the writing process as pastime not trade. As was usual with Stevenson's friends and defenders, they were policing borders that had already been crossed, maintaining fences that Stevenson himself had long since slipped through.

NOTES

1. See, for example, Stevenson 1881, 1888b, 1915. For the professionalization of authorship see Keating 1989, MacDonald 1997, Sutherland 1995.

2. For accounts of the composition and publication of the text, see Japp 1905, Furnas 1951, and Katz 1998.

3. For an analysis of the significance of this form of publication, see Pierce 1998.

4. For a related discussion of pleasure see Arata, "Stevenson, Morris, and the Value of Idleness," in this volume.

5. Frow 1995 (ch. 4) has a particularly helpful discussion of the concept of "regimes of value."

6. Interestingly, Stevenson spends far less time talking about this novel than he does about another novel by the same author, *The Twenty Captains or the Diamond Necklace.*

7. Hayward of course is not alone in warning against the dangers of reading and the lure of adventure. For a detailed discussion of this element in R. M. Ballantyne, see McCulloch 2000.

8. For a recent discussion of the relationship between art theory and economics in relation to the novel, see Gray 2002.

REFERENCES

Colvin, Sidney. 1900. [Letter.] *The Academy* (10 March): 209–10.

Frow, John. 1995. *Cultural Studies and Cultural Value*. Oxford: Clarendon Press.

Furnas, J. C. 1951. *Voyage to Windward, The Life of Robert Louis Stevenson*. New York: William Sloane.

Gray, William. 2002. Stevenson's "Auld Alliance": France, Art Theory and the Breath of Money. *The Wrecker. Scottish Studies Review* 3 (2): 54–65.

Hayward, William Stephens. 1868. *Tom Holt's Log: A Tale of the Deep Sea*. London: C. H. Clarke.

Henderson, James. 1900. *The Academy* (March 17): 237.

Henley, W. E. 1900. Some Novels of 1899. *North American Review*. February. Reported in *The Academy* (February 24): 156.

Japp, Alexander. 1900. *The Academy* (March 10): 209–10.

———. 1905. *Robert Louis Stevenson, A Record, An Estimate and a Memorial*. London: T. Werner Laurie.

Katz, Wendy. 1998. Introduction to *Treasure Island*, by Robert Louis Stevenson. Ed. Wendy Katz. Edinburgh: Edinburgh University Press.

Keating, Peter. 1989. *The Haunted Study: A Social History of the English Novel 1875–1914*. London: Secker & Warburg.

Leighton, Robert. 1900. Stevenson's Beginnings. *The Academy* (March 3): 189.

McCulloch, Fiona. 2000. The Broken Telescope: Misrepresentation in *The Coral Island*. *Children's Literature Association Quarterly* 25 (3): 137–45.

MacDonald, Peter D. 1997. *British Literary Culture and Publishing Practice 1880–1914*. Cambridge: Cambridge University Press.

Norquay, Glenda, ed. 1999. *R. L. Stevenson on Fiction: An Anthology of Literary and Critical Essays*. Edinburgh: Edinburgh University Press.

Pierce, Jason A. 1998. The Belle Lettrist and the People's Publisher: or, the Context of *Treasure Island's* First-Form Publication. *Victorian Periodicals Review* 31 (4): 356–68.

Stevenson, Robert Louis. 1881. "The Morality of the Profession of Letters." *Fortnightly Review* 157: 513–20. In Norquay 1999, 40–50.

——— [as "Capt. Geo. North"]. 1881–1882. "Treasure Island; or the Mutiny of the Hispaniola." *Young Folks* 19–20 (October 1881–January 1882).

———. 1883. *Treasure Island*. Tusitala Edition. Vol. 2.

———. 1888a. "Popular Authors." *Scribner's Magazine* (July 4): 122–28. Also appears in Norquay 1999. 161–73.

———. 1888b. "Letter to a Young Gentleman Who Proposes to Embrace the Career of Art." *Scribner's Magazine* (September 4): 377–81. In Norquay 1999. 174–82.

———. 1892. *The Wrecker*. Tusitala Edition. Vol. 12.

———. 1894. "My First Book—Treasure Island." *The Idler* 6:2–11. Tusitala Edition 2:xxiii–xxxi.

———. 1915. "On the Choice of a Profession." *Scribner's Magazine* 57 (January): 66–69. Tusitala Edition 28:12–19.

Sutherland, John. 1995. *Victorian Fiction: Writers, Publishers, Readers*. London: Macmillan.

Swearingen, Roger G. 1980. *The Prose Writings of Robert Louis Stevenson, A Guide*. Hamden, CT: Archon Books; London: Macmillan.

Stevenson and Popular Entertainment

STEPHEN DONOVAN

Like our own, the late-Victorian public was fixated with popular entertainment. As the Scottish lawyer and man of letters Alexander Innes Shand
explained in *Blackwood's Magazine* in August 1879: "[T]he ferment of
thought, the restless craving for intellectual excitement of some kind, have
been stimulated; till now, in the last quarter of the nineteenth century, we
are being driven along at high-pressure pace; and it is impossible for any
one who is recalcitrant to stop himself" (Shand 1879: 238–39). Shand's
hyperbole was not unwarranted. These years saw the rise of the music-hall,
of organized leisure travel, of mass sports and royal spectacles, of a capi-
talized newspaper and magazine press, as well as revolutionary innovations
in visual and audio technology (Bailey 1998). "Like us," notes Matthew
Sweet, "the Victorians loved staring at things with their mouths open"
(Sweet 2001: 4). For literary historians, the late nineteenth century marks
the definitive transition to an era of mass sales and new audiences, of periodical serialization and syndication, of celebrity authors and agents, and
of modern marketing methods. In the vanguard of its popular new genres
were the imperial romance, the detective story, and the sci-fi fantasy.

Stevensonians need little reminding of the importance of these factors
for Stevenson's own literary project and its reception. In this I reconsider
how Stevenson treats this subject in the context of contemporary views of
popular entertainment as a cultural and social *problem*. In particular, I
reconstruct the case (or cases) that Stevenson, it seems to me, is implicitly
making for popular entertainment as a meaningful and valuable activity.

Although my primary concern is not be the direct impact of various forms of popular entertainment on Stevenson's writing, their influence is clearly discernible throughout his work as a rich source of analogies, settings, and experiences. Consider photography, for example: in "The Manse," he describes how "memories, like undeveloped negatives, lay dormant in [my grandfather's] mind" (Stevenson 1887: 65); and in "Talk and Talkers," he compares his cousin Bob to a "shaken kaleidoscope" (Stevenson 1882a, 85). Stevenson's literary identity, as a substantial body of secondary literature now attests, was constituted by very different impulses and contradictory experiences, and the reception of his work, in turn, was tied to the shifting tastes of a markedly heterogeneous readership. In his treatment of popular entertainment, I propose, his status as a writer of boundaries appears most clearly, ranging as it does across the fields of imagination and commodification, childhood and maturity, as well as the class and national politics of popular and mass culture.

Stevenson's status as a popular writer has always been fraught with tension. In his own lifetime, the tension drew its force, at least in part, from the steady growth of various forms of popular entertainment, a growth that paralleled the extension of the franchise in Britain and a rise in real earnings and leisure time, as well as a series of flashpoints of social unrest and high-profile investigations into the problems attendant upon rapid urbanization. Rightly or wrongly, popular entertainment and popular culture appeared to many observers as not merely objects of capitalist modernization but also catalysts of sudden convulsions in the body politic, the motive force of an ongoing transformation of the social landscape. Thus in an essay titled "On a Possible Popular Culture" that appeared in the *Contemporary Review* in July 1881, Thomas Wright ("The Journeyman Engineer") portrayed Britain as facing an historic challenge to invent for the working class a wholesome and integrated culture capable of withstanding the evils of the pub and debased titillation of organs such as the *Police Gazette*. In his concluding words Wright laid a weighty cultural imperative upon the nation's authors, calling on them to forge a "higher, healthier, simpler culture . . . the culture to be wrought by bringing the masses of the people to a knowledge of the boundless treasures that lie open to them in the glorious literature of their own country . . . . [to] make men more valuable to themselves and to society; better men, better citizens, ay, and even better workmen" (Wright 1881: 43–44).

Sentiments of this kind characterize numerous other contributions to the debate during these years. Walter Montague Gattie lamented the baneful

effect on women of ephemeral literature and popular sport, and urged pragmatism: "[W]e have extended the literary franchise, and those who would
succeed must learn to pander to the new electorate" (Gattie 1889: 321).
Francis Hitchman took a similarly jaded view, declaring that "In a lane
not far from Fleet Street there is a complete factory of the literature of
rascaldom—a literature which has done much to people our prisons, our
reformatories, and our Colonies, with scapegraces and ne'er-do-wells"
(Hitchman 1890: 153). Hitchman closed his jeremiad with a grim caveat:
"Let us beware lest the unclean spirit [of working-class ignorance] returns
with seven other spirits more wicked than himself, and turn the class we
have made our masters into the agents for the overthrow of society" (170).
This point was reiterated by Hugh Chisholm, who called for a program-
matic campaign against cheap sensationalist literature, what he colorfully
described as "the murder-mongering 'penny dreadful'" (Chisholm 1895:
765), an allusion to a recent matricide trial in which the coroner had urged
the suppression of "sensational literature of a demoralizing tendency"
(Chisholm 1895: 768). Tellingly, interventions in the debate during these
years mostly refrained from proposing Christian morality tales of the Religious Tract Society stripe as the solution to this crisis of popular entertainment. The task, in essence, was to instill a degree of conformity without
being seen to do so.

The instrumentality with which social commentators regarded popular
entertainment, and which Oscar Wilde would soon be languidly satirizing,
is particularly striking. One apocryphal anecdote has it that Cecil Rhodes
once lent a copy of *Treasure Island* (1883) to a friend with the elliptical
comment, "Very instructive." The mind boggles at what Rhodes could
have meant by this—a vision of buried gold, perhaps, like that which
prompted him to order the troops of his British South Africa Company to
invade Mashonaland in 1890—but his choice of the term "instructive"
raises unnerving possibilities. Moreover, as the target of these competing
discourses—of, let us say, moral didacticism and artistic purism—popularity became an increasingly suspect quality. The reception of Stevenson's
work often took place within this contested framework, from the cam-
paigners for sanitized literature who sought a popular fiction that was
socially cohesive to the conservative avant-gardistes of the Henley circle,
who welcomed what they viewed as Stevenson's robust masculinity and
patriotism in an era of social leveling and cultural emasculation. Indeed,
in his disdain for Stevenson, Joseph Conrad effectively had it both ways,
referring dismissively in a letter to James Pinker of January 1902 to the

"airy R. L. Stevenson who considered his art a prostitute and the artist as no better than one" (Karl and Davies 1983, vol. 2: 371), yet telling Alfred Knopf in 1913 that "When it comes to popularity I stand much nearer the public mind than Stevenson" (vol. 5: 257). Even *Punch*, in its parody of the "Jekyll and Hyde" sensation on 6 February 1886, caricatured Stevenson as a writer bent upon driving a shrewd financial bargain: "And now, after piecing all this together, if you can't see the whole thing at a glance, I am very sorry for you, and can help you no further. The fact is, I have got to the end of my '141 pages for a shilling.' I might have made myself into four or five people instead of two,—who are quite enough for the money" (Maixner 1981: 210).

The new climate of popular entertainment involved more than just a surge in the marketing and sales of mass publications. Malcolm Bradbury has suggested that during this period its influence may be detected in changes in the English language itself, a result of what he calls "the invisible uses of journalism . . . the columns of *Answers* and *Tit-Bits*, where in the encapsulated sentence and the brief paragraph experience was being redefined" (Bradbury 1971: 32). Stevenson's work was thoroughly imbricated with this new culture and, in particular, with what Bradbury describes as "a mood of imaginative unease" among writers (6). Whatever their debt to Poe, we can see Stevenson's "Suicide Club" short stories of 1878 as unwitting documents of the emergence of a recognizably modern, *Tit-Bits*-style universe of bizarre stunts and paragraph-length human interest items, just as his choice of title for *The New Arabian Nights* in 1882 anticipates the popular success of Richard Burton's scandalous retranslation of the classic three years later. And, again, the *Strange Case of Dr. Jekyll and Mr. Hyde* (1886) and *The Wrong Box* (1889) serve as sophisticated meditations upon the late-Victorian media sensation, notable near-contemporary examples of which include W. T. Stead's exposé of child prostitution in 1885, the Cleveland Street rent-boy scandal of 1889, and the Whitechapel murders of 1888 (Walkowitz 1992; Curtis 2001).

As a way of coming afresh at Stevenson's relationship to popular entertainment, it may be useful to draw a comparison with a classic artistic treatment of this theme: Pieter Brueghel's *Children's Games* (1560). For a long time, the received wisdom was that Brueghel's painting simply offered viewers a visually delightful panorama of a huge range of Flemish children's games, a kind of juvenile equivalent of the sketches of peasant culture that the artist had earlier drawn surreptitiously under his cloak. To be sure, more than seventy such games have been identified. In the same way, Stevenson, too, can be seen as a recorder of various popular cultures, including extinct or endangered species like the worthy horticulturalist affectionately described in "An Old Scots Gardener" (1871). More recently, however, art historians have drawn attention to the tremendous serious-ness of Brueghel's children at play: of a hundred and fifty, no more than five are smiling. Their earnestness, together with their physical domina-tion of the entire landscape, reinforces the impression that Brueghel's sub-ject is also adult life with its own role-playing, competitiveness, and violent conflict. Seen in close-up, the rubicund faces and awkward poses of Brueg-hel's children bespeak a complex inner world of desires and anxieties. On this view, popular entertainments bridge the boundaries between child-hood and adulthood, playful individual expression and codified social organization.

A review of Stevenson's treatment of juvenile and adult popular enter-tainment in his nonfiction reveals a similarly nuanced attitude toward the social character of imagination and performance. Consider his well-known "A Penny Plain and Twopence Coloured," in which he offered an encom-ium to "that national monument" Skelt's Juvenile Drama, the classic Vic-torian toy theater (Stevenson 1884: 114). In the essay, Stevenson moves from autobiographical anecdotes about buying Skelt cutouts and play-scripts on Leith Walk, to a philosophical meditation on the special appeal of an artifice whose characters and settings all struck him as having near-mythic power. "Skeltery," he announces solemnly, "is a quality of much art" (118), and, in a famous passage, goes on to explain that "out of this cut-and-dry, dull, swaggering, obtrusive, and infantile art, I seem to have learned the very spirit of my life's enjoyment; met there the shadows of the characters I was to read about and love in a late future . . . [and] acquired a gallery of scenes and characters with which, in the silent theatre of the brain, I might enact all novels and romances" (120).

Now, modern-day enthusiasts frequently portray mid-Victorian toy theater in warmly nostalgic terms as an artifact of a prelapsarian world of childhood based upon collective entertainment and blissfully ignorant of consumerism. On the surface, Stevenson's homage to Skelt's—itself now a touchstone text for such enthusiasts—certainly seems to underpin this view. And yet a mock-heroic tone throughout the essay alerts us to the presence of his underlying irony. Whatever it actually means, the state-ment "England, when at last I came to visit it, was only Skelt made evi-dent" (119) can hardly have been intended as a national compliment. Somewhat unpredictably, Stevenson also recalls the "summit" of his pleasure as being "[t]he purchase and the first half-hour at home" with a new item, and while conceding that coloring in the figures might have contained some pleasure, points out that, as for actually putting on a performance: "You might, indeed, set up a scene or two to look at; but to cut the figures out was simply sacrilege; nor could any child twice court the tedium, the worry, and the long-drawn disenchantment of an actual performance. Two days after the purchase the honey had been sucked. Parents used to complain. . . . Then was the time to turn to the back of the play-book and to study that enticing double file of names" (117). The names are, of course, the advertisements for the others in the series. It is an arresting image: not only does the young Stevenson reject the proper use of the theater for which it has been devised (by adults), he even confesses to relishing the moment of deferred consumption. This is not to contradict Jenni Calder's point that the essay confirms the uniqueness of Stevenson's desire to preserve childhood's "border territory between fantasy and reality" (Calder 1980: 37). But it does suggest that his refusal to conform socially could even extend to a celebration of some of the very aspects of popular entertainment—namely, its commercialism and discursive instability— that so discomforted late-Victorian commentators.

As is well known, Stevenson's visit to Menton in the winter of 1873–74 has a liminal significance in his personal and literary lives. On this, his first solo foreign trip, he met Andrew Lang, spent time with Sydney Colvin, tried opium, and decisively committed himself to professional writing, the first important fruit of which would be his celebrated essay "Ordered South." In short, as Louis Stott notes, "RLS grew up in Menton" (Stott 1994: 33). One remarkable feature of Stevenson's time at the Hotel Mirabeau in Menton was the intense friendship he struck up with three young girls—"my children," he called them (*Ltrs* 1: 433)—a friendship that would most likely have been prohibited in our own more cynical age. Sitting rather curiously alongside Stevenson's concurrent decision to "grow up" and become a writer, his relationship with these children reveals much about his attitude toward popular entertainment at this crucial juncture in his career.

Initially, Stevenson's attentions were focused upon little Mary (May) Johnson, the eight-year-old daughter of a American couple, whom he described as "the most charming of little girls," adding "Both Colvin and I have planned an abduction already" (*Ltrs* 1: 424). His letters of this time detail a number of charming incidents of role-playing and harmonious misrule: "Marie, the American girl, . . . is grace itself, and comes leaping and dancing simply like a wave—like nothing else; and who yesterday was Queen out of the Epiphany cake and chose Robinet (the French painter) as her *favori* with the most pretty confusion possible" (*Ltrs* 1: 428). And again: "The little Russian kid . . . and her sister (*aet.* 8) and May Johnson (*aet.* 8) are the delight of my life. Last night I saw them all dancing—O it was jolly; kids are what is the matter with me" (*Ltrs* 1: 429). He explained to Frances Sitwell that he had written a letter to May Johnson containing a poem: "I lost a Philippine to little May Johnson last night; so today I sent her a rubbishing doll's toilet and a little note with it. . . . She has just been here to thank me, and has left me very happy. Children are certainly too good to be true" (*Ltrs* 1: 437).

This "little note" is not collected in Booth and Mehew's *Letters of Robert Louis Stevenson* and appears to have been lost to Stevensonians. However, May Johnson kept her precious souvenir and, thirty years later, sent it to the editors of *The South African Magazine*, a short-lived Cape Town journal, who gratefully reprinted it in facsimile (Figures 1 and 2) in the October 1906 number as follows:

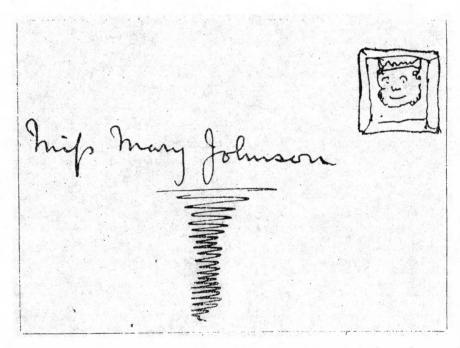

FIGURES 1 & 2. Stevenson's verse letter to May Johnson. Reproduced from *The South African Magazine*, October 1906 (original untraced).

To Mary Johnson

Children happy all day through
Can make others happy too.
So, dear child, the sight of you
Makes me glad— whate'er you do.

—

Keep these lines and some fine day,
Dear, when you are far away,
Older, taller, strong and well,
Grown a stately demoiselle,
It may make you glad to know
You gave pleasure long ago

—

It may make you glad to see
That your childhood, fair and free,
Here, beside the southern sea,
Was a pure delight to me

—

And, in the meantime, play with your toys and
the ugly little dog, and do not trouble your little
head about the meaning of my bad verses. You
will be ill some day like me, and then you will
know all that they mean. and you will be glad
to see them.

Mentone
January 13th 1874   Robert Louis Stevenson

To Mary Johnson

Children happy all day through
Can make others happy too.
So, dear child, the sight of you
Makes me glad whate'er you do

Keep these lines and some fine day,
Dear, when you are far away,
Older, taller, strong and well,
Grown a stately demoiselle,
It may make you glad to know
You gave pleasure long ago

It may make you glad to see
How your childhood, fair and free,
Here, beside the southern sea,
Was a pure delight to me

And, in the meantime, play with your toys and the ugly little dog, and do
not trouble your little head about the meaning of my bad verses. You will be
ill some day like me, and then you will know all that they mean, and you
will be glad to see them.

Mentone
January 13th 1874   *Robert Louis Stevenson*

Neither great literature nor weighty subject matter, this is nonetheless an
interesting item. Most obviously, it is a rare example of a Stevenson letter
that traverses the boundary from adult writer to child reader: in a sense,
he is literally addressing his future readership here. In addition, it reveals
Stevenson as meditating on a kind of long-term retrospective vision not
only at the moment when he launched his career but also as he revisited a
key scene from his own childhood. The poem itself, while perhaps deserving of Stevenson's self-depreciation, imagines the future as a foreign country where "far away" is necessarily also "older"—in much the same way as
he seeks in *A Child's Garden of Verse* (1885), as Anne Colley has shown, to
create an imaginative topography of childhood (Colley 1998: 107–23).
Indeed, in its theme and style it anticipates a number of later poems, particularly "To My Name-Child":

Some day soon this rhyming volume, if you learn with proper speed,
Little Louis Sanchez, will be given you to read. [. . .]
While you thought of nothing, and were still too young to play,
Foreign people thought of you in places far away. (Stevenson 1885: 54)

Finally, "Children happy all day through" would appear to be Stevenson's
first poem for a child.

More than one reviewer of Stevenson's poetry criticized him for mis-
takenly ascribing adult perspectives to child readers. And yet, as this little
carpe diem verse suggests, the truth of the matter is more complex. What
Stevenson is performing here is a kind of multilayered ritual: on the one
hand, he socializes the child by introducing her to the conventions of
adulthood through a parallel, imaginary reality; on the other, he holds out
to this young reader a freedom in which the playing of a role becomes an
act of assuming—and perhaps even usurping—authority. Hence the Philippine game, the mock-flirtatious tone, and, most importantly, the nice
role-reversal by which Stevenson, so often caricatured as a children's enter-
tainer, presents himself as having been entertained by a child.

If the treatment of popular entertainment in Stevenson's *oeuvre* deserves
more extensive analysis than the present context can permit, it is clear that
a great many practices and cultural artifacts might be usefully reevaluated
under this rubric, from the scene in *The Black Arrow* in which Dick Shel-
ton passes off the tales of Ali Baba as his own experiences in order to
beguile his dull-witted captors, to the scene in *David Balfour* in which Pre-
stongrange tests David's mettle through a mock interrogation that he later
describes as a "stage play." In *The Wrecker*, in turn, readers are supplied
with inside accounts of the worlds of newspaper publishing, lecture tour
boosting, and day-trip excursions, while Stevenson's demystification of the
supernatural in the dénouement of "The Beach at Falesá" surely resembles
nothing so much as a colonial corollary to the thrilling spectacular entertainments with which late-Victorian audiences were intimately familiar
(Booth 1981). Stevenson uses incidents such as these to achieve very specific narratological and thematic effects, as when Captain Davis sings to
the Polynesians for his breakfast in *The Ebb-Tide*, a vignette that confers
upon him an obvious pathos even as his choice of songs—"Home, Sweet
Home," "The Beautiful Land," and "Fifteen Dollars in the Pocket" (Stevenson 1894: 20)—supplies an oblique echo to the novella's satire on
colonization. In *Kidnapped*, too, David is alerted to the menace of his

uncle by a memory of "some ballad I had heard folk singing" (Stevenson 1886: 27), while the piping duel between Alan Breck and Robin Oig presents popular entertainment as a unique kind of space in which the past speaks to the present and the alien becomes the known.

Particularly intriguing is Stevenson's predilection for foregrounding moments of staging, role-play, and performance in which a youthful protagonist, rather than merely observing the action, actively directs it. In *Kidnapped*, when David recounts his and Alan's heroic stand against the crew who come at them through door and skylight, he takes pains to describe the spatial layout in detail. The result is staginess, not in the sense of crude melodrama, but rather of Skeltery, a moment that not only works in the reader's imagination but that can be translated almost directly to the stage (or, better still, the screen). The same logic governs numerous other moments in Stevenson and is immortalized in Ralph Steadman's wonderful illustration of Jim anxiously eavesdropping from inside the apple barrel in *Treasure Island*. This is Skelt's theater with the child at center stage. As Glenda Norquay notes, for Stevenson the internal dynamics of play made it of value in itself, and not only as it imitated adult roles. I would go further still and propose that staging and performativity occupied a central place in his theory of human consciousness, as evidenced by his description of children as enjoying "a delightful dress-rehearsal of experience" (Stevenson 1896: 237) or his luminous image of "the silent theatre of the brain" (Stevenson 1884: 120), a metaphor found also in his discussion of "the warm, phantasmagoric chamber of [the] brain" (Stevenson 1888a: 186).

Where a growing number of his contemporaries sought to denigrate popular entertainment as, among other things, mere infantile gratification, Stevenson can be seen as provocatively arguing for its importance on these very grounds, that is to say, because popular entertainment gave expression to what he recognized as the psychological depth of children's imagination. Naturally, he was not alone in taking children's play seriously: we need think only of Lewis Carroll, J. M. Barrie, or Robert Baden-Powell on the subject. But in his emphasis on the connection between children's play and popular entertainment, Stevenson anticipated the more radical directions that would be taken by later writers such as Joyce and even Freud for whom childhood experiences set an indelible mark upon every aspect of adult emotional and intellectual life. Tales of melodrama, insists Stevenson in "Popular Authors," "were not true to what men see . . . [but] to what the readers dreamed. . . . [They] supply to the shop-girl and the shoe black vendor vesture cut to the pattern of their naked fancies" (Stevenson

1888b: 31). As a lexicon of experience and a repertoire of meaningful social interactions, popular entertainment opened up new horizons for Stevenson's own creative art, what he defined as "the realisation and the apotheosis of the day-dreams of common men" (Stevenson 1882b: 136), or more simply—as he told Mary Johnson beside a southern sea in January 1874— "pure delight."

REFERENCES

Bailey, Peter. 1998. *Popular Culture and Performance in the Victorian City*. Cambridge: Cambridge University Press.

Booth, Michael. 1981. *Victorian Spectacular Theatre, 1850–1910*. London: Routledge.

Bradbury, Malcolm. 1971. *The Social Context of Modern English Literature*. Oxford: Blackwell.

Calder, Jenni. 1980. *Robert Louis Stevenson: A Life Study*. London: Hamish Hamilton.

Chisholm, Hugh. 1895. How to Counteract the "Penny Dreadful." *Fortnightly Review* 64 o.s. (November): 765–75.

Colley, Ann C. 1998. *Nostalgia and Recollection in Victorian Culture*. Basingstoke, UK: Macmillan.

Curtis, L. Perry. 2001. *Jack the Ripper and the London Press*. New Haven, CT: Yale University Press.

Gattie, Walter Montagu. 1889. What English People Read. *Fortnightly Review* 52 o.s. (September): 307–21.

Hitchman, Francis. 1890. Penny Fiction. *Quarterly Review* 171 (July): 150–71.

Karl, Frederick and Laurence Davies, eds. 1983–. *The Collected Letters of Joseph Conrad*. Cambridge: Cambridge University Press.

Maixner, Paul. 1981. *Robert Louis Stevenson: The Critical Heritage*. London: Routledge.

Shand, A. Innes. 1879. Contemporary Literature: Readers. *Blackwood's Magazine* 126 (August): 235–56.

Stevenson, Robert Louis. 1882a. "Talk and Talkers." *Cornhill Magazine* (April). South Seas Edition. Vol. 13.

———. 1882b. "A Gossip on Romance." *Longman's Magazine* (November). South Seas Edition. Vol. 13. 21–34.

———. 1884. "A Penny Plain and Twopence Coloured." *The Magazine of Art* (April). South Seas Edition. Vol. 13. 114–121.

———. 1885. *A Child's Garden of Verses*. London: Longmans, Green & Co.; New York: Scribner's.

———. 1886. *Kidnapped*. London: Cassell; New York: Scribner's. South Seas Edition. Vol. 11.

———. 1887. "The Manse." *Scribner's Magazine* (May 1887). South Seas Edition. Vol. 13. 59–65.

———. 1888a. "The Lantern Bearers." *Scribner's Magazine* (February). South Seas Edition. Vol. 13. 175–187.

———. 1888b. "Popular Authors." *Scribner's Magazine* (July). Tusitala Edition. Vol. 28. 21–34.

————— (with Lloyd Osbourne). 1894. *The Ebb-Tide. A Trio and a Quartette.* London: Heinemann; Chicago: Stone & Kimball. South Seas Edition. Vol. 14.

—————. 1896. "Rosa Quo Locorum." Edinburgh Edition. Vol. 21. South Seas Edition. Vol. 13. 237–245.

—————. 1906. "Verse [Hitherto Unpublished]." *The South African Magazine* (Cape Town) 1 (6) (October): 733–37.

Stott, Louis. 1994. *Robert Louis Stevenson and France.* Milton of Aberfoyle: Creag Darach Publications.

Sweet, Matthew. 2001. *Inventing the Victorians.* London: Faber.

Walkowitz, Judith.1992. *City of Dreadful Delight: Narratives of Sexual Danger in Late-Victorian London.* Chicago: University of Chicago Press.

Wright, Thomas. 1881. On a Possible Popular Culture. *Contemporary Review* 40 (July): 25–44.

Tontines, Tontine Insurance, and Commercial Culture

Stevenson and Osbourne's The Wrong Box

GORDON HIRSCH

In 1887 while they were staying at Saranac Lake in upstate New York, Robert Louis Stevenson encouraged his nineteen-year-old stepson Lloyd Osbourne to type away at the humorous book first called *The Finsbury Tontine*, then *A Game of Bluff,* and eventually *The Wrong Box.* In his letters Stevenson called the work-in-progress "so damned funny and absurd . . ., the merest farce, an Arabian Night on the scale of a novel" (early March 1888; *Ltrs* 6: 125), as well as "a sort of insane police story" (ca. March 6, 1889; *Ltrs* 6: 259). It is also a story about the catastrophic decline of a family business and that family's desperate effort to recover its investment. And it is, as Stevenson noted, "a Tontine story" (*Ltrs* 6: 259)—a tontine being a speculative annuity based on the longevity of a designated individual. The surviving members of a tontine group are paid an annual income that increases as other members of the group die. Although popular in the eighteenth and early nineteenth centuries, by 1887 the tontine was pretty much a thing of the past; "tontine dividend" life insurance policies, however, had become extremely popular in the United States and Britain, and these policies embodied some of the speculative principles of the earlier tontines, including a gamble on longevity. Tontine insurance policies had become familiar emblems of many of the least desirable aspects of Victorian commercial culture: its greed, its preference for speculation over saving, its willingness to take advantage of the many and the vulnerable while enriching the few, and its substitution of a cash nexus for values of family and community.

In their comic novel, Stevenson and Osbourne focus on the idea of the tontine as a counterweight to the catastrophic decline of a family business. They depict high-stakes risk and skullduggery, portray a family struggling to keep its business afloat, call attention to the replacement of family feeling by a cash nexus, and anatomize the way crimes are contemplated or committed for the sake of an inheritance. In *The Wrong Box,* the tontine idea evokes the suspect values of Victorian commercial culture and is even more directly relevant to this than we might suppose from the text itself, which whimsically presents the tontine at the outset as a historical curiosity ("its fine, sportsmanlike character endeared it to our grandfathers"; Stevenson and Osbourne 1889: 7). Indeed, a very real contemporary manifestation of that idea, tontine life insurance, is the specter haunting the book.

In 1652, Lorenzo Tonti developed his scheme for sponsorship by the French state of a life annuity. According to his original "tontine" scheme, a group of individuals would each subscribe a specific amount, without regard to age or gender, and each year the interest produced would be divided among the subscribers remaining alive, until the death of the last nominee, when the principal would be surrendered to the state. Tontines thus were a speculation on an individual's longevity, producing predictable and notorious results. The last survivor of one of the French tontines, Charlotte Barbier, was the subject of much publicity; at the age of ninety-six she was enjoying—if that is the right word—an income of 73,500 livres derived from her original subscription of only 300 livres (O'Donnell 1936: 162). Nor was her case unusual; the last survivor of many tontines was frequently a nonagenarian with a fabulous income.[1]

Life insurance antedates the tontine. Early life insurance was associated with marine insurance; the lives of voyagers were insured to pay either their heirs, or, more usually, their creditors. Originally, then, life insurance involved a limited-term speculation or a hedge for creditors against a speculative loan. Until passage of the Gambling Act of 1774, in fact, insurance could be written as a pure wager on the lives of public men like Sir Robert Walpole or George II. The act required for the first time that the person purchasing a policy have some "insurable interest" in the insured (Zelizer 1979: 71).

In the eighteenth century, forms of more conventional life insurance developed as well as tontine schemes. The Amicable Society for a Perpetual Insurance Office was granted a charter in Britain in 1706. It insured lives "perpetually" rather than only for a specific term of years, though, since actuarial statistics were not yet widely understood, it assessed the same premium for all ages within the range it accepted, twelve to forty-five years. A charter for the Society for Equitable Assurances for Lives and Survivorships was presented in 1757, proposing the more "equitable" system of assigning insurance costs based on the age of the insured, which permitted the company to assess level annual premiums throughout an individual's life (Raynes 1950: 126–30). The historian Lorraine J. Daston (1987: 255) cites the Equitable's reliance on mortality statistics and the mathematics of probability as evidence of a new "rationality" in insurance practice, another move away from speculation.

Toward the end of the eighteenth century and early in the nineteenth, new companies were founded on the actuarial principles established by the Equitable, and they began to issue policies designed to emphasize protection for the surviving families of the insured (Raynes 1950: 139; Stone 1942: 34–36; Daston 1987: 225). Provincial life insurers were established throughout Britain in the nineteenth century, particularly in Scotland. Cornelius Walford (1887: 499), the best known of the nineteenth-century historians of insurance, lists fifteen life insurance companies founded in Scotland between 1815 and 1846, mostly in Edinburgh, the hometown of Robert Louis Stevenson. Edinburgh-based Scottish Widows was the first company to develop a system of branch offices throughout the United Kingdom, and it was the first British company to employ a system of sales agents. Another Edinburgh insurer, the Standard Life Assurance Company, became one of the largest underwriters in Britain by mid century (Treble 1976: 124).

A mania in the establishment of new insurance companies followed passage of the Joint-Stock Companies Act of 1844: "Of 900 companies of all kinds registered during the years 1844–56, a remarkable 195 were insurance companies" (Trebilcock 1985: 597). Because of this explosive growth and the paucity of governmental regulations, frauds and failures proliferated. One of the most notorious was the failure of the West Middlesex, one of the inspirations for Dickens's corrupt Anglo-Bengalee Disinterested Loan and Life Assurance Company in *Martin Chuzzlewit* (1843). Outside the world of fiction, the historian Clive Trebilcock (1985: 572) notes that of the 219 insurance companies founded between 1843 and 1870 in Britain, "no fewer than 170 collapsed."

Similar luxuriant growth and its concomitant problems occurred in the United States as well. Between 1865 and 1870, 107 new American life insurance companies were formed through the sale of stock, and by 1904 they controlled a billion dollars of assets and had two million policy-holders (Keller 1963: 8, 14).

One American innovation had a great impact on the international insurance market. Life insurance companies traditionally build up a conservative "surplus" from favorable mortality rates, from interest on reserves that exceeds the assumptions used to set premium levels, or from lapsed policies (Cox and Storr-Best 1962: 15–16). In 1867, however, Henry Hyde, the head of New York's Equitable Life, persuaded the New York legislature to permit his company to retain rather than to remit the surplus to policyholders as annual dividends, as was customary, thus enabling the company to seek additional investment return on this "tontine fund." The company might retain these "deferred dividends" or "tontine dividends" for five-, ten-, fifteen-, or twenty-year periods, depending on the contract. Insured individuals who *died* within the tontine period would receive only the face amount of the death benefit stipulated by the policy, without any return of the accumulated surplus or profits—earnings achieved from the investment of the reserves and the surplus. Those policies that *lapsed* due to failure to pay the premium at any point through the tontine period would have no "surrender value" at all. The surplus and profits from dead or lapsed policyholders would accrue entirely to the benefit of those who survived and continued to pay their premiums throughout the tontine period. In this way, tontine life insurance policies resembled the original tontines: survivors would gain the most, by sharing in the distribution of the surplus and profits generated by other policyholders who had died or lapsed in their payments before the end of the tontine period.

Hyde's original tontine fund idea was immensely popular and successful for New York's Equitable, and most other American companies fell in line. American life insurance companies offered their tontine policies in Britain, and British companies followed suit. Tontine insurance policies were marketed successfully because agents, pursuing large commissions, promised huge investment returns from the retained dividends (North 1962: 243). Tontine surpluses did in fact increase the companies' size and soundness as well as providing a large, stable pool for capital investment (Keller 1963: 62–63). On the other hand, holders who let their insurance lapse or who died before the deferred dividends were distributed might well feel that the Equitable and its brethren had treated them inequitably. Furthermore, the huge surpluses accumulated by the companies became "an inducement to managerial extravagance and irresponsibility" (Keller 1963: 63).

Some rival companies and executives attacked Hyde's Equitable in anonymous circulars and in the press for favoring its richest customers, those least likely to let their policies lapse. Pamphlets appeared, such as the anonymous *Tontine: What It Is; How It Works*, which attacked tontine insurance (1882: 8–9): "Tontine, we say, is a bet that the insured will not for any reason, whether failure in business or carelessness or fraud of an agent, fail to pay his premium for a period of ten, fifteen, or twenty years. Like all bets it is an attempt to take other people's money for nothing, on the turn of an unknown contingency. . . . All the extra profits must come by dividing up the money of unfortunate people who have been persuaded to make the bet and have lost. The poor people, the people who have failed in business, the people who most need the money they have put into insurance, they lose it all, and those who need it least, divide up what they have robbed their unlucky neighbors of." As if exemplifying the then-prevalent doctrine of Social Darwinism, the wealthy and more careful (or more fortunate) did indeed benefit at the expense of their brethren. The modern economic historians, Ransom and Sutch, ran a simulation of the 1871 Equitable tontine fund and discovered that "59 percent of the survivor's dollar return was produced by the accumulation of his own deposits, 12 percent was transferred from those who died, and 30 percent was contributed by those who lapsed" (1987, 387). Colonel Jacob Greene, president of Connecticut Mutual publicly attacked the American firms that had adopted various tontine policy schemes, which he described as "pure gambling" (Zelizer 1979: 88). Those firms responded in kind: "In 1885 the pages of the New York *Tribune* contained numerous letters from the presidents of the big three [American life insurance firms] on the one hand and Greene on the other" (North 1962: 250). Tontine insurance thus raised vividly questions that had lain at the heart of debates about insurance for centuries: Was insurance basically about gambling and chance, or was it founded on mathematical probability for the purpose of protection and prudence? Was its purpose self-enrichment (as in the purchase of life annuities for oneself) and possible gain at the expense of others (as in the case of tontine insurance), or was its proper aim the protection of one's family against a sharp drop in their standard of living?[2]

By the 1880s it was becoming clear that tontine policyholders who died or let their policies lapse were aggrieved; not only that, but even surviving policy holders were receiving smaller dividends than prospectuses and agents had originally promised, giving rise to considerable public outcry (Hendrick 1907: 208–11; Keller 1963: 57–58; O'Donnell 1936: 559–62). There were tontine investigations in New York in 1877 and in Ohio in 1885 (Cooper 1972: 17).[3] The culmination of these stirrings was a broad inquiry into life insurance in 1905 by a committee of the New York State Legislature chaired by Senator William W. Armstrong. According to Ransom and Sutch (1987: 389–90), the Armstrong "investigation revealed institutional and personal corruption on a shocking scale. The tontine surpluses were apparently a temptation difficult for some executives to resist." As a result of these hearings and subsequent legislation in which New York State led the way, a number of insurance practices were changed and tontine dividend policies banned. Henceforth accounts would have to be reckoned and surpluses distributed annually. Ransom and Sutch estimate, however, that by the time of these 1905 hearings about 64 percent of all life insurance in force in the United States was of the tontine dividend sort (1987: 385), and North contrasts the twentyfold growth of insurance in force for four tontine companies with the mere doubling of insurance in force for five annual dividend companies during the time period 1868 to 1905 (1962: 240). A contemporary article in a British insurance journal offers a broad survey of the "Varieties of Life Insurance" at the turn of the century and notes the ubiquity of tontine insurance, citing examples in the United States, Scotland, and England (Fox 1905: 81, 92). Sales of tontine life insurance policies dwindled rapidly, however, after the Armstrong Committee's investigation.

Although the kind of pure, speculative gamble of the tontine lay in the past by 1887, when Stevenson and Osbourne set to work, it nevertheless had played a role in the development of the life insurance industry. Furthermore, both the term itself and the idea of rewarding longevity at the expense of those fallen along the wayside were reintroduced with the heavy promotion of tontine dividend life insurance policies by the burgeoning financial services industry in America and Britain.

Though *The Wrong Box* is broadly satirical—taking music, literary genres and conventions, aesthetics, politics, and learning as objects of satire—the book focuses above all on the decline of a small family business and its replacement by a commercial culture of speculation and greedy competition, for which the tontine is the emblem. Two brothers, Joseph and Masterman Finsbury, are the last surviving members of a tontine worth £116,000. Children when their father, a well-to-do merchant, subscribed an initial £1,000, the brothers have now both reached their seventies. One paradigmatic aspect of this particular tontine is volunteered in the account of its inception: when it was created, a "war" and "battle-royal" erupted between Joseph and another tontine member who kicked Joseph's shins (Stevenson and Osbourne 1889: 8). That this competition is a rather nasty, zero-sum game even the young nominees recognize.

In adulthood, Joseph Finsbury has acquired the charge of two orphan nephews, Morris and John, sons of a deceased younger brother, and he has invested their parental inheritance in his leather business. Through his neglect, however, the business has failed to prosper: "Even by making over to his two wards every penny he had in the world, there would still be a deficit of seven thousand eight hundred pounds" in their inheritance (11). Once worth £100,000, the business now receives derisory buyout offers in the range of £4,000. As Joseph laments, "there is nothing in the whole field of commerce more surprising than the fluctuations of the leather market. Its sensitiveness may be described as morbid" (107–8).

One of these two nephews, Morris, is particularly outraged at his uncle's running the business into the ground, calling him "my fraudulent trustee": "I was robbed of this money while I was an orphan, a mere child, at a Commercial Academy" (178–79). Morris has "threatened his uncle with all the terrors of the law," and forced him to sign over all that he possesses, including both his contingent interest in the tontine and the leather business, though "Joseph's name was still over the door [and] it was he who still signed the cheques" for the firm (11–12). So far as Morris is concerned, his uncle has now become "a rather gambling stock in which he had invested heavily; and he spared no pains in nursing the security" (12). He takes care of Joseph not because Joseph is his uncle but because he is "his living investment" (13), a "Golden Goose" (18), a relation who must be "taken out and brought home in custody, like an infant with a nurse" (14). Uncle Joseph, in turn, feels himself "a captive in the halls of his own leather business" (13) and his nephew's economic hostage. In a significant metaphor, Morris takes upon himself "the cares and delights of empire"— i.e. absolute control over his family—and Joseph becomes his "slave" (11). For his part, Joseph regards "his nephew with something very near akin to hatred" (12). Their journeys *to* the leather business are "dreary enough, for there was no pretence of family feeling. . . . But the way there was nothing to the journey back; for the mere sight of the place of business, as well as every detail of its transactions, was enough to poison life for any Finsbury" (12). As the narrator wryly remarks, "in a large, dreary house in John Street, Bloomsbury, [they] dwelt together: a family in appearance, in reality a financial association" (11). Cash nexus defines this Victorian family.

Morris will thus do everything he can to safeguard his uncle Joseph's health, in order that Joseph may win the tontine and restore the lost inheritance. Unfortunately, a railroad accident occurs as the family, quarrelsome as ever, returns from vacation in the purer air of Bournemouth, and a faceless corpse dressed just like Uncle Joseph is discovered near the wreck by the nephews, who assume it to be their uncle. The plot of the story is concerned, initially, with attempts by the nephews to hide the stranger's body so as to preserve Joseph's eligibility for the tontine. The corpse, while being shipped by train to London in a water barrel, is sent astray when the address label on the barrel is exchanged for the label on a gigantic packing case containing a colossal Italian statue of Hercules, which is being smuggled into the country. The divagations of the corpse now drive the plot; as recipients of this unwelcome item, fearing that they may be arrested for murder, try to pass it off on unsuspecting others. The recognition slowly dawns on Morris Finsbury that, putting the tontine aside, he will eventually require the corpse in order to establish his uncle's death and assume full control over the leather business, so he tries to recover that which he had first tried to hide. For the sake of the tontine, the body and the fact of Uncle Joseph's death must remain hidden; for the sake of the leather business, however, the body must be recovered and produced. In the peripatetic corpse, Stevenson and Osbourne find a perfect symbol for bourgeois ambivalence toward family and inheritance. Joseph's "body" becomes a macabre kind of familial capital: repugnant yet desirable; spurned and hidden away, yet ultimately sought; initially subject to the nephews' control, yet finally uncontrollable. From the first, Uncle Joseph played a largely material role in the family constellation. As a supposed corpse, he is now totally reified, an inheritance. Sent into a bizarre kind of financial circulation, he is repeatedly palmed off on unaware recipients, like a bad coin.

In this complex plot of tontine, family business, and circulating corpse, nearly every crime of the traditional police novel is invoked: forgery (twice), blackmail (twice), conspiracy, murder, swindle, and theft. Venal physicians who might be bribed to postdate a death certificate are repeatedly mentioned. Partly the book traces, in the words of one of its earlier titles, "a game of bluff" in which Morris struggles with his cousin, the attorney Michael Finsbury, son of Masterman, for supremacy. At different points in the narrative, both Morris and Michael propose compromise and a sharing of the tontine proceeds, but both proposals are rejected in favor of a winner-take-all contest. Just as tontine life insurance revealed the greed and gambling instinct underlying the respectable insurance culture, the Stevenson-Osbourne novel lays bare a struggle within the family over inheritance.

Most of the middle-class male characters in this novel, in fact, feel similarly hard-pressed financially and ambivalent about the predominant commercial values and professional culture. Young men struggling to earn a living, establish their careers, or retain some modicum of respectability in their professions populate the book. For instance, the smuggled statue of Hercules, for which the corpse is exchanged, is originally addressed to William Dent Pitman, who is characterized as "a distinguished artist . . . , highly distinguished by his ill-success" (72). "Though he was never thought to have the smallest modicum of talent," the young Pitman had been sent to study art in Paris and Rome, "supplied by a fond parent who went subsequently bankrupt in consequence of a fall in corsets" (73). Pitman now earns his meager living by teaching in a seminary for young ladies, and throughout the novel he is terrified lest his employers discover him in any of the desperate measures into which he is led in a frantic effort to dispose of the corpse. Because of this vulnerability to disgrace, Pitman turns to his attorney, Michael Finsbury, who plays upon Pitman's anxieties chiefly, it seems, in order to amuse himself.

Michael Finsbury turns all his business affairs into fun. He delights in fantastic disguises (including at one point wearing whiskers, spectacles, and a deerstalker hat), repeatedly goes off on drinking bouts, and devises the wild scheme to pack the unwelcome corpse inside a Broadwood piano and send it on to Gideon Forsyth, another attorney manqué. It is Michael who speaks the novel's most reverberant line, "Nothing like a little judicious levity" (82), and whose "prevailing jocularity" (155) is repeatedly confirmed. Gaining the upper hand over his cousin Morris, Michael is able to set things more or less to rights at the end of the book. A reader who brings traditional, moralistic expectations might wonder, though, whether Michael is likely to benefit unfairly from the financial arrangement he imposes upon his cousins, Morris and John, at the novel's end, whereby they receive the leather business and a check for the balance of their inheritances, while Michael will get the tontine fortune, regardless of whether his father Masterman or Uncle Joseph dies first. Michael's shrewd insouciance carries the day.

Nor is it exclusively the young men who dream of riches, or an artist's or novelist's life, or simply of escape from the unappealing workaday world of business and the professions. Uncle Joseph Finsbury himself inhabits a dreamworld, "a heaven of populous lecture-halls and endless oratory" in which he lectures to a rapt audience (44). Ironically, given his failure at business, his lectures most often settle upon economic topics. He speaks on "How to Live Cheerfully on Forty Pounds a Year" (9), on "Life Insurance Regarded in its Relation to the Masses" (9), on Lorenzo Tonti himself (45), on the cost of living in London (105), and on the comparative costs of living in various other lands (40–41). He lectures bankers on the principles of banking (71), as well as telling carriers how they should drive (37). It is significant that—in a book so obsessed with money, earning a living (or not), inheritances, and winning a tontine through fraud and skullduggery—Joseph should so persistently be drawn toward lectures that lead to his being described in the text as "the economist," or, in the original manuscript, as an "old bore with a smattering of political economy" (41, 193). Moreover, the inclusion of "Life Insurance" on the list of Joseph's favorite topics points to the authors' awareness that the idea of the tontine has been subsumed in the late nineteenth century under tontine life insurance.

In the relationship between Joseph and his nephews, Stevenson and Osbourne play out in a comic vein a narrative in which crimes are contemplated or committed for the sake of acquiring an inheritance—more particularly, for the sake of a tontine annuity. Committing murder or fraud in order to gain the proceeds of a tontine or insurance policy will, of course, continue to be the stuff of mystery and detective fiction from the Victorian era on, feeding into the double indemnity crimes of Hollywood film noir. One might even note that the spirit of the tontine lives on in the "reality television" program *Survivor*, where individuals try to manipulate the votes of others in their artificially constituted group in an effort to capture the survivor's million-dollar prize. For all its lightheartedness, Stevenson and Osbourne's novel does seem to have identified social and economic practices that have remained quite significant in Anglo-American culture from late Victorian times to the present.

There is a biographical subtext in *The Wrong Box* that is worth noting as well. Lloyd Osbourne, a child of Fanny Osbourne and her first husband, was the stepson of Robert Louis Stevenson. By the time the nineteen-year-old Osbourne began to peck away at his typewriter to draft this story, Stevenson had become a famous and sought-after author following the success of the *Strange Case of Dr. Jekyll and Mr. Hyde* (1886). Osbourne himself (1924, 76–77) described the manifestations of Stevenson's overnight success that were so apparent upon their arrival in New York on 7 September 1887: "When we stepped off our old cattle-boat, the *Ludgate Hill*, in which we had taken nineteen days to cross the Atlantic, it was to find himself famous. Hordes of reporters met him; the lobby of his hotel buzzed with callers; he was head-lined in all the papers—interviewed, photographed, lionized—his coming a veritable sensation." If Lloyd Osbourne had any "Golden Goose" equivalent to the fictional Uncle Joseph Finsbury, it would have been his stepfather.

Osbourne's dependency on his stepfather is evident from Stevenson's letter of instructions to his friend and attorney Charles Baxter (September 1, 1890; *Ltrs* 6: 417) about how to handle Osbourne's one-fifth share of the publisher's payment for *The Wrong Box*: "Turn the whole money for *The Wrong Box* into my account, and debit the estate with one third of it as a loan from Lloyd at three per cent. This, in the case of my demise, will keep his coin out of the general average business; in the meantime it keeps him from spending it, and stores it up against a time when he may want it dam [*sic*] bad."

Osbourne continued in his easygoing and spendthrift ways after Stevenson's death in 1894, deriving both fame and fortune from the connection with his stepfather. The biographer Frank McLynn (1993: 512) casts a particularly censorious light on Lloyd: "When Fanny died in 1914 . . . [Osbourne] had finally achieved his life's ambition of moneyed ease and idleness. . . . For the rest of his life he existed as *flâneur*, dilettante and drone, being well-known at the Lambs Club in New York and the nightspots of Paris. He died in California in 1947."

Lloyd Osbourne had no need of a tontine to make him wealthy. *His* Uncle Joseph carried his own particular brand of *literary* life insurance.

NOTES

1. In *The Wrong Box*, the tontine nominees Masterman and Joseph Finsbury are both said to be in their seventies; Masterman lives "in absolute seclusion" and his mind is "in abeyance" (8, 178). Stevenson and Osbourne comment wryly on "the peculiar poetry and even humor" of tontine schemes, under which "the proceeds are fluttered for a moment in the face of the last survivor, who is probably deaf, so that he cannot even hear of his success—and who is certainly dying, so that he might just as well have lost" (7).

2. Another novel, simply titled *Tontine*, was published in London four years before Stevenson and Osbourne began work on their book and explicitly links the traditional tontine with tontine insurance by alluding to the very public controversies associated with the latter and insisting on the ethical problems common to both (Barnett 1883: 432–33): "Every species of lottery is popular. The spirit of gambling, to which human nature is prone, if encouraged in the least, easily degenerates into a base and uncontrollable passion. I have lately been reading those controversies in the papers, on the application of this [tontine] principle of yours by life-assurance companies, in distributing their surplus profits, and I entirely disapprove of such a course."

3. American insurance companies are regulated by the states, not the federal government.

REFERENCES

Barnett, Matilda J. 1883. *Tontine.* London: Pitman.

Cooper, Robert W. 1972. *An Historical Analysis of the Tontine Principle.* Homewood, IL: Huebner Foundation.

Cox, P. R. and R. H. Storr-Best. 1962. *Surplus in British Life Assurance.* Cambridge: Cambridge University Press.

Daston, Lorraine J. 1987. The Domestication of Risk: Mathematical Probability and Insurance 1650–1830. In *The Probabilistic Revolution.* Ed. Lorenz Krüger, Lorraine J. Daston, and Michael Heidelberger. Vol. 1: *Ideas in History.* Cambridge, MA: MIT Press. 237–60.

Fox, Morris. 1905. Varieties of Life Insurance. *Journal of the Federation of Insurance Institutes of Great Britain and Ireland* 8: 75–97.

Hendrick, Burton J. 1907. *The Story of Life Insurance.* New York: McClure, Phillips.

Keller, Morton. 1963. *The Life Insurance Enterprise: 1885–1910.* Cambridge, MA: Harvard University Press.

McLynn, Frank. 1993. *Robert Louis Stevenson: A Biography.* London: Hutchinson.

North, Douglass. 1962. Capital Accumulation in Life Insurance between the Civil War and the Investigation of 1905. In *Men in Business: Essays in the Historical Role of the Entrepreneur.* Ed. William Miller. New York: Harper. 238–53.

O'Donnell, Terrence. 1936. *History of Life Insurance in its Formative Years.* Chicago: American Conservation Company.

Osbourne, Lloyd. 1924. *An Intimate Portrait of R. L. S.* New York: Scribner's.

Ransom, Roger L., and Richard Sutch. 1987. Tontine Insurance and the Armstrong Investigation: A Case of Stifled Innovation, 1868–1905. *Journal of Economic History* 47: 379–90.

Raynes, Harold E. 1950. *A History of British Insurance.* London: Pitman.

Stevenson, Robert Louis and Lloyd Osbourne. 1889. *The Wrong Box.* Ed. Ernest Mehew. 1989. London: Nonesuch.

Stone, Mildred F. 1942. *A Short History of Life Insurance.* Indianapolis, Ind.: Insurance Research Service.

Tontine: What It Is; How It Works. 1882. New York: Franklin Ford.

Treble, James H. 1976. The Performance of the Standard Life Assurance Company in the Ordinary Life Market in Scotland 1850–75. In *Scottish Themes.* Ed. John Butt and J. T. Ward. Edinburgh: Scottish Academic Press. 124–40.

Trebilcock, Clive. 1985. *Phoenix Assurance and the Development of British Insurance, 1782–1870.* Vol. 1. Cambridge: Cambridge University Press.

Walford, Cornelius. 1887. History of Life Insurance in the United Kingdom: Part 6, 1844 to 1870. *Journal of the Institute of Actuaries* 26: 436–65.

Zelizer, Viviana A. Rotman. 1979. *Morals and Markets: The Development of Life Insurance in the United States.* New York: Columbia University Press.

PART II

Scotland and the South Seas

The Master of Ballantrae,
or the Writing of Frost and Stone

JEAN-PIERRE NAUGRETTE

Stevenson began *The Master of Ballantrae* during the winter of 1887–88 while staying with his family at Saranac, "a hill and forest country on the Canadian border of New York state" (*Ltrs* 6: 32). While Fanny was chronically out of health and soon preferred to leave and visit family and friends, Stevenson found the below zero temperatures "delightful" and even "healthful" to him, a kind of American Davos in the wilderness. This climate also spurred his literary inspiration. In the "Genesis of The Master of Ballantrae" written as a preface to the novel, he connects the "stringent cold of the Canadian border" and the process of writing: "It was winter; the night was very dark; the air extraordinary clear and cold, and sweet with the purity of forests. From a good way below, the river was to be heard contending with ice and boulders. . . . For the making of a story here were fine conditions. . . . On such a fine frosty night, with no wind and the thermometer below zero, the brain works with much vivacity" (Stevenson 1889: xxiii).[1] Such words as "cold," "ice" and "frosty" related to weather conditions are here associated with "clear" and "fine," adjectives that also apply to Stevenson's own prose.

It will be argued here that the correlation between landscape and fictional representation is not merely a matter of represented setting, like the Adirondacks and the Canadian border present in the last two chapters of the novel. What is eventually at stake is the process of writing itself as exemplified by Mackellar's narrative, at the end of which the narrator emerges as a writer of epitaphs: from cold to stone, a Stevensonian image of writing.

Winter's Tale and *Winterreise*

The novel is aptly subtitled *A Winter's Tale*, and it is true that winter, with
its recurrent climatic correlatives like "frost," "cold," "ice" and "snow," is
so present in the text that the other seasons seem written off. The key
events take place indeed during winter:

> Mackellar's arrival in Durrisdeer in 1748, "in the cold end of December, in a
> mighty dry day of frost" (13), is fully described and thus overshadows the
> brief reference to the marriage between Henry and Alison that took place a
> few months earlier on June 1—an event which, by definition, Mackellar was
> unable to attend.
>
> The scene of the duel between the two brothers, "on the night of
> February 27th, 1757," is preceded by a weather report: "It was unseasonable
> weather, a cast back into winter: windless, bitter cold, the world all white
> with rime, the sky low and grey: the sea black and silent like a quarry-hole"
> (90). The duel is thus set against a "very pretty, wintry, frosty landscape":
> "there was no breath stirring; a windless stricture of frost had bound the air"
> (92, 95).
>
> The return of the Master after his reported death takes place in late March
> or early April, 1764: "It was a cold, sunny morning, with a thick white frost"
> (137). Secundra Dass is first introduced into the novel as already complaining
> of cold (150).
>
> In the last chapters set in the American wilderness, Mackellar complains
> of being bitten by the "stringency of frost" (205). The final scene where Dass
> tries to resurrect the Master is dominated by "the extremity of frost", hence
> his failure: "'Too cold,' said he, 'good way in India, no good here.'" (227, 233)

This prevailing climatic mood endows the novel with an overall tone of
sadness and melancholy. This is the most obvious relevance of the Shake-
spearian subtitle and intertext, echoed by Mackellar's opening words about
the Master, which write the title of the play into Stevenson's text: "I sailed
with him on his last voyage almost alone; I made one upon that winter's
journey of which so many tales have gone abroad" (1). If, according to
Mamillius in the play, "A sad tale's best for winter" (2.1.25) then the novel
is a sad tale indeed, the overwhelming cold being quite naturally an image
of death (Amalric 1994: 123).

As Winterreise, this "winter's journey" also sheds a more romantic light
on Mackellar's narration and character. His underlying melancholy strain

or "humor" is best expressed at the end of chapter 8, where he describes his forthcoming journey with the Master as "ill-omened": while "hearkening to the turmoil of the gale," he imagines a dire "perspective of consequences" (158) that will haunt him down till the end. At the beginning of chapter 9, "the house of Durrisdeer" appears "like a place dedicate to melancholy." When leaving his ancestral home for good, James Durie sings "Wandering Willie," "the saddest of our country tunes" (159), but Stevenson quotes from his own poem "To the Tune of Wandering Willie," known to Charles Baxter (*Ltrs* 6: 222) but only later to be published in *Songs of Travel* (1895): a clear diegetic impossibility, a metaleptic frame-breaking, an intertextual abyme (Naugrette 1990: 106). The first poem of this collection, "The Vagabond," is explicitly written in the Schubertian mode ("To an air of Schubert" is the subtitle) (Smith 1971: 245),[2] and indeed, Mackellar sounds like a melancholy graduate student saddened by the prospect of leaving Durrisdeer: home-leaving is a leitmotiv of Schubert's *Winterreise* (1826), where the vocal narrator of Wilhelm Müller's poems laments over his leaving behind the house of his beloved (2: "Die Wetterfahne," [The Weather-Vane]), or vainly traces her footsteps on the snow (4: "Erstarrung," [Numbness]). Mackellar regrets both past and future, never to be happy in the present time, as if he were suffering from a post-Kantian, Romantic "exilic" sentiment, as Steiner puts it (1984: 15). When Lord Henry, Alison, and the rest of the family sneak out of Durrisdeer in order to escape from "The Enemy in the House," Mackellar paradoxically describes their leave-taking as a kind of inverted exile: "It seemed that we who remained at home were the true exiles" (Stevenson 1889: 151).

Images of Stone: A Study in Petrification

Two female characters are described, right from the first chapter, as flinging either coin or stone: first, Alison flinging "that piece of gold which had just sent her lover to the wars in the great painted window," then "one trollop, who had had a child to the Master" (5, 10), flinging a stone at Mr. Henry, at a time when James is reported dead after the Jacobite defeat of Culloden. Two opposed figures, and yet a similar gesture, a first hint that female characters seem endowed with the power of stoning or petrifying males. While James, at this early stage, is viewed by the country folk as a wild character, Henry is a "skinflint" (10), a first image of petrification. Alison behaves toward him with "cold kindness" (22–23), an oxymoron that characterizes their frozen relationship, derived as it is from what

Mackellar calls "this tragedy" (2), a word echoed by Stevenson in a famous letter to Henry James (*Ltrs* 6: 105). Mackellar, too, seems to be on the "grave" side: "I remarked you for a young man of a solid gravity of character," Colonel Burke says in his letter to him (Stevenson 1889: 68). In contrast, James is first introduced into the novel as lacking "gravity," characterized by "levity" (2, 5): "I go my way with inevitable motion," he will later declare on his first return from the dead (72), as if his center of gravity were of a slippery kind. After he has sung his song, the whole assembly—Mackellar included—sit silent, holding their breath while the singer is the first to move (83). While the Master—who is always on the move and pops in when least expected—appears like une force qui va, the rest of the family tend to solidify and petrify "like changelings" (72).[3] The stone and stricture motif is thus gradually transposed from a literal onto a more metaphoric plane. Frost and stone are not just props of the tragedy, but recurrent images—similes and metaphors—that undergo a specific symbolic treatment.

Alison's case is different from the rest of the family, though. The images used by Mackellar here suggest transformation and plasticity. On first hearing the news, after the duel, that James is dead, she seems to be deep down in her grave: "it was as though she had lain buried under a hill and sought to move that burthen" (100). Soon, however, she will recover her motion. When she sees the sword lying on the ground, she picks it up and thrusts it "to the hilt into the frozen ground" (106). This is "one of my inconceivable blunders," as Stevenson will admit to Schwob (*Ltrs* 7: 69). Yet it may also be explained as a meaningful choice.

1. It may be viewed as an internal echo of the coin being flung into the family shield. Alison appears as a domineering figure, an image of female wrath potentially able to paralyze or "stonify" men. Her gesture is typically masculine, an echo of irritated Henry earlier driving "his knife up to the hilt" (65). Mackellar seems quite helpless here.

2. It can be seen as a recurrent, obsessive Stevensonian image. Again, we move from a frosty, literal atmosphere of stricture to a more metaphorical plane, a transport or crossing of countries, boundaries, and texts. In *The Ebb-Tide*, the figurehead of the ship "on top of the beach" is successively described as (a) "a woman of exorbitant stature and as white as snow . . . beckoning with uplifted arm," later identified as "a piece of naval sculpture" (Stevenson 1894: 239): a woman turned into a statue; (b) "a defiant deity" with "her formidable arm apparently hurling something,

whether shell or missile" (Stevenson 1894: 249): a statue turned into a woman; (c) a whipping-post or totem, which the helpless and subdued Davis frantically clutches behind him when fired at by Attwater, who is then compared to a red Indian (297). This simile, together with the "white as snow" image, also connects *The Ebb-Tide* and the last chapters of *The Master of Ballantrae*.[4] The figurehead is thus a "formidable" female "figure," whose plastic and apparently contradictory polarities— invitation, aggression, punishment—correspond to a gradual weakening of male strength: "God knowsI am not so hard as I appear" (106), Mackellar rather pitifully laments after Alison has powerfully thrust the sword: the writer's "blunder," or perhaps the character's strength, a sign of her "exorbitant stature" although her role seems rather minor and subdued in the story?

3. If we relate the image of "buried" Alison wakening up to life to that of the statue of Hermione coming down from her pedestal in the last act of *The Winter's Tale*, we can observe a singular similitude of attitudes and effects. In both cases, male spectators are turned into stone: "I am asham'd: does not the stone rebuke me / For being more stone than it?" (5.3.37–38) wonders Leontes who asks the "dear stone" to "chide" him after "grave" Paulina has drawn the curtain. When Burke first brings news about the Master, Mrs. Henry is described by Mackellar as springing up "standing with a mechanical motion" (25), as if she were a walking statue, while Henry is unable to speak. A similar effect is produced when Mackellar returns to the castle after the discovery of the sword,[5] and finds Mr. Henry "like a man of stone" who cannot be "moved" by his wife (107).

The same image is used by Dr. Jekyll about Mr. Hyde, whom he describes as "relentless like a man of stone" (Stevenson 1886: 86). This recurrent simile suggests that Henry, not James, is the Mr. Hyde of the tale. This is borne out by the use of initials in the two novels. "H. J." stand for Henry Jekyll—as they appear at the bottom of the letter sent to Dr. Lanyon—but, as Richard Dury aptly suggests (1993: 59), since Henry Jekyll "has a set of initials which includes" both Hyde and Jekyll, they also stand for Hyde/Jekyll. On the other hand, "H. J." also stand for Henry and James Durie who appear as "H. D." and "J. D." in the final epitaph,[6] which again places "Henry" and "Hyde" in the same structural position. Yet one must make a chiasmic distinction between character and image here: Henry's character changes for the worse, but his petrified image does not. James' character is on the whole stable, while his image undergoes a change.

Stevenson's obvious and devious use of references suggests a splitting of characters into sundry images. As Henry's character degrades and drifts into a Scottish Mr. Hyde, Mackellar is transformed into a potential Leontes who is bent on bringing about the ruin of his rival—the Master. After all, it is only through his own jealous eyes that the wooing of Alison/Hermione by James/Polixenes is perceived: while talking apparently in Henry's name, he is led gradually to his own conclusions about this "bond of union between the lady and the Master" (84).[7] In contrast, Alison and himself returning to the shrubbery "hand in hand" (106) after the duel also suggest an intimacy between two lovers. The character of Leontes in Shakespeare's play is in fact shared out between Henry, the potential betrayed husband,[8] and the meddling house-steward who, as a homodiegetic narrator, chooses, uses, and manipulates images and references: all those stone and grave images are his, like so many bricks built into the text.

Like Alison, James undergoes a textual transformation that also points to the plasticity of his image: he and Alison are the plastic couple par excellence. In chapter 7, he is compared by Burke to "an image in a pagoda" (135) while sitting "cross-legged, after the Oriental manner" (134). If taken seriously—and not as one of his numerous tricks—this static attitude and his refusal to speak to his old fellow-soldier may be read as a sign of wisdom regained,[9] or the prospective end of adventure understood as greedy treasure hunt. The "inevitable motion" of the beginning has given way to a "stricture" that, like the figurehead in the sand, tolls the knell of adventure per se and introduces a new quest-pattern with religious and political issues. As Richard Ambrosini shows, James's speech to Mackellar about his being "the least king of naked negroes in the African desert" (174–75) announces Kurtz and *Heart of Darkness* (Ambrosini 2001: 325).[10] James Durie, Attwater, but also Long John Silver are potential idols, "chieftains," kings or tyrants that have to be worshipped or followed, overthrown or "deposed" (in Silver's case, when given the black spot), a political and colonial motif treated at the same period by Kipling in "The Man Who Would Be King" (1888).

In the final American sequence of *The Master of Ballantrae*, the wintry mood reigns supreme. Frozen landscape, "agony of cold," "stringency" or "extremity of frost" (Stevenson 1889: 197, 205, 227), while human figures turn into stone. Mackellar describes Henry as "cold as stone" in relation with the *quantum mutatus ab illo* motif (201) also reminiscent of *Jekyll and Hyde*. While the Master in his flight is sitting "his arms folded and his back to a huge stone" like Davis against the white figurehead, his scalped companions and rivals gradually pave the warpath "whose every stage was

mile-stoned with a mutilated corpse" (210, 219). In the final scene, the
sounds of Secundra's attempts to unbury the Master turn Henry into
stone, while the sight of Secundra "deep in the grave of his late Master"
strikes all the spectators "into pillars of stone" (228, 229).

Compared with the previous wintry scene with Alison, the effect of this
general petrification on Mackellar is much more ambivalent this time.
While in the first scene the image was that of male weakness, not to say
impotence, the final one turns the house-steward into a more active force,
someone who is able to "raise up" Henry (232): The very ambivalence of
the sentence ("and when I raised him up, he was a corpse") suggests a tem-
poral, if not causal correlation between the two clauses, as if "raising up"
did not mean trying to revive, but already to sculpt a funeral monument.
The same verb—"raised this stone"—will be used to describe the erection
of the monumental epitaph of the two rival brothers (234).

In his study of "Medusa's Head" (1922), Freud argues that the horror
created by the sight of the decapitated head of Medusa as a symbol of
female genitals, and of the snakes squirming on her head,[11] has to do, on
the male part, with the fear of castration proportionate to "a multiplication
of penis symbols": "The sight of the Medusa's head makes the spectator
stiff with terror, turns him to stone." But he also adds that this petrification paradoxically stiffens him like an erection: a "transformation of affect"
that enables the spectator to sublimate his fear of castration into a "consolation" (Freud 1922: 273).

This "transformation of affect" seems to be at work in the two distinct,
yet related scenes of the duel and the opening of the Master's grave.

1. After the duel, Mackellar is awestruck by Alison who thrusts the sword
   into the frozen ground. The female figure is endowed here with a potential phallic force, which changes the spectator into a weak, impotent
   onlooker of this superhuman, exorbitant feat. Commenting on the myth
   of Oedipus and its structural variants, Lévi-Strauss notices that the Sphinx
   is often assimilated in archaic representations to a female monster "with
   an inversion of sign" who first terrifies, then rapes the young men she
   meets. In that respect, the Sphinx can be related to the "child-protruding
   woman" of the Hopi Indians, a "phallic mother" who provokes both terror and erection among her male companions (Lévi-Strauss 1958: 238 n1).
   Significantly, the very first image Mackellar gets of Mrs. Henry is that of a
   pregnant woman who is "very far gone, Miss Katherine being due in
   about six weeks" (Stevenson 1889: 14).

2. If we accept that James and Alison, like Macbeth and Lady Macbeth, share inverted polarities, then James, when he emerges from his grave, may embody Medusa in his turn. While Henry and Mackellar are already "pillars of stone" (229) and held "in a horror not before experienced," "the disclosure of the man's eyes" brings about Henry's fall to the ground, and death. This is reminiscent of the sight of Medusa's head striking horror, petrification, and death into the male spectators: his brow, "contorted with an agony of pain and effort" (232), may conjure up an image of snakes. If we follow Lévi-Strauss (1962: 141), the haunting detail of the Master's teeth showing in his beard can also be read as a revival of the archaic vagina dentata or toothed vagina motif, another male fear of castration. But if "the week-old corpse" of the Master looks "for a moment" in Mackellar's face, it is for a moment only. This "display of life," he next explains, he has not witnessed until the end since he has averted his eyes as soon as Henry fell to the ground, a gesture that has probably saved him in the same way as Perseus managed to cut off Medusa's head by gazing at its reflection in his mirrorlike shield, thus averting his eyes from the awesome sight. Here, the petrifying vision is deflected by Henry's death and the report of the other witnesses, a kind of narrative shield. Again, what matters in this scene is not its realistic probability but its symbolic impact: Henry is no more likely to drop dead at this sight than Alison to thrust the sword into the frozen ground.

3. While Henry falls dead and thus prompts Mackellar to avert his gaze, it is his house-steward and unlikely Doppelgänger who emerges as the one who will be able, with Alison's symbolic help this time, to "raise this stone" dedicated to the two fraternal enemies. Again, two characters share out polarities: while Henry takes on himself the petrification of death, Mackellar undergoes a "transformation of affect," which brings about a symbolic display of the pen(is). Mackellar's subdued, repressed and awestruck feelings for Alison find a "consolation" in the contiguity of stone (Stevenson 1889: 234):

> THE PIETY OF HIS WIFE AND ONE OLD
> SERVANT RAISED THIS STONE
> TO BOTH

The intimacy with Alison is thus made possible and sublimated by the inscription. Mackellar seems to have grown out of his chronic feeling of exile and gotten closer to her,[12] while becoming a writer in his own right. As opposed to Dass, Mackellar does not stand out as a Resurrection Man, nor a potential resurrecting man like the Master, but as a res-erecting man, a potent stone-raiser, and as such a *mise-en-abyme* portrait of the artist as one who chisels and cuts out his prose into a monument.

Portrait of the Artist as an Engraver: on Epitaphic Writing

The image of the epitaph is typically Stevensonian, as evidenced by his "Requiem," where the pun on "grave" as tomb and "grave" as engrave is the verbal equivalent of the *mise-en-abyme* of the whole: it is a requiem about a requiem, a poem about a poem that will be eventually engraved on Stevenson's grave in Samoa. It is no coincidence if along with his "Moral Emblems" and "Moral Tales" he titled a series of poems "The Graver and the Pen," while he himself provided the corresponding woodcuts: the two activities are presented as "The ambidextrous Kings of Art," "Two muses like two maiden aunts, / The engraving and the singing muse" (Smith 1971: 427). His first paper was published "under the harmless anagram of L. S. Stoneven" (*Ltrs* 6: 47), as if "stone" were (even) written into his name. His fellow writers and admirers have often compared his style to the art of engraving or cutting. In the original opening paragraph of "Black Jack" (*Soldiers Three*, 1888), Kipling says of Stevenson that he "makes most delicate inlay work in black and white" (Page 1989: 71). Schwob quotes the famous blunder of the sword being thrust into the frozen ground but vindicates the "puissance d'impression" generated by those "images plus fortes que les images réelles" (Schwob 1894: 580, 582). In the second chapter of his book, Chesterton also mentions Alison's impossible thrust as typical of Stevenson's love for sharp edges and cutting actions, and defends the first blundering version as more significant. In a letter to Stevenson, Henry James called *The Master of Ballantrae* "a pure and hard crystal," "a work of ineffable and exquisite art" (Edel 1980, vol. 3: 273). An image of the writer as stone-cutter and polisher.[13]

Hence perhaps Stevenson's fascination with epitaphs, not as mere literary motifs but as a mode of writing which might be called "epitaphic."[14] In a letter to Colvin about *The Ebb-Tide* being "done" at last (*Ltrs* 8: 91), he includes Huish's epitaph, an echo of the Duries' grave. This shows that Stevenson was not so much interested in truth meant as adherence to the actions of the external world, as in the truth of telling, the exactness of the sentence, of the sensation, of the gesture, as Pavese puts it in his 1950 article for *l'Unità*, which may explain why Alison's momentous gesture rings symbolically true, although literally false. Beyond the haunting leitmotiv of frost and cold as part of Mackellar's *Winter's Tale* or *Winterreise*, *Bal-lantrae* best mirrors the emergence of Stevensonian writing as epitaph, as the introductory words of *Weir of Hermiston* will confirm, where "the chisel of Old Mortality" is associated with "that lonely gravestone," and "the facts of the story" compared to "the bones of a giant buried there and half dug up" (Stevenson 1896: 193), an echo of the Master's "emergent countenance" (232). Quite symptomatically, many Stevensonian situations are thus wintry scenes where the dramatic art of the writer is capable of cutting out its hard edges: this goes for "The Sire de Malétroit's Door," "A Lodging for the Night," "The Pavilion on the Links," "The Body Snatcher," chapter 2 of *Treasure Island*, or his ballad "Christmas at Sea." Stevenson's careful chiseling of dedications can thus be read as a mode of epitaphic writing, of writing on stone.[15] Around 1887–88, perhaps Stevenson does constitute the aesthetic link between Thomas Hardy's obsession with stonecutting mentioned by Proust in *La Prisonnière* (1923: 376–77)[16] and Mallarmé's conception of symbolist writing as chiseling and "tombeau,"[17] or tombstone as the very touchstone of modern writing.

NOTES

1. "The Genesis of The Master of Ballantrae" is an incomplete draft preface writ-ten in late 1893, first published in 1896 in the Edinburgh Edition, 21: 297–302).

2. Stevenson was keen on Schubert's songs when he wrote *The Master of Ballantrae*: see his letters to Charles Scribner and Fanny dated 10 October 1887 (*Ltrs* 6: 28). That the novel is also about singing is evidenced by the compared gifts and performances of James, a "master-singer" (159–60) and Henry, who has "no gift of music" (200–201).

3. See Schiller's play *Die Räuber* (*The Robbers*, 1781), also a story of fraternal rivalry: at the beginning (1.1), Franz von Moor describes himself as "der kalte, trockne, hölz-erne Franz" ("cold, dry, wooden Franz"), as opposed to the fiery spirit or evil genius of his exiled, outlawed brother Karl, whose tombstone in the wilderness will stand out as a "monument," while Franz predicts that he will die at home, forgotten.

4. In May 1887, Stevenson had written "Ticonderoga," a ballad about a Scottish feud transposed into the American setting and context of the Indian wars, a structure taken up in *The Master of Ballantrae*.

5. Carried by Alison, "a strange burthen for that woman" (Stevenson 1889: 107).

6. Both Naugrette (1987: 105; 1990: 35 n42) and Dury (1993: 59 n3) comment on Stevenson's potential pun on Henry/James. Naugrette argues that the reader is led to make the link between Henry/James, thereby acting out a postmortem reunion be-tween the two brothers.

7. "Bond" is a recurrent image in *Strange Case*: see Naugrette (1987: 58–59).

8. In "Some Character-Types Met with in Psycho-Analytic Work" (1916), Freud mentions Ludwig Jekel's study of Macbeth and Lady Macbeth as the splitting of a

single individual into two distinct characters: each of them, in turn, takes on values and polarities normally belonging to the other (Freud, Standard Edition, Vol. 14).

9. See Marlow at the beginning of *Heart of Darkness*: "he had the pose of a Buddha preaching in European clothes and without a lotus-flower" (1902, 9). Also see Kipling's Purun Baghat in *The Second Jungle Book*.

10. Also compare "He bury, he not dead" (Stevenson 1889: 231) with the famous "Mistah Kurtz—he dead" (Conrad 1902: 118).

11. See P. B. Shelley's poem "On the Medusa of Leonardo da Vinci in the Florentine Gallery" (1819). The novel is dedicated to Sir Percy and Lady Shelley, whom Stevenson and Fanny had often visited while staying in Bournemouth. Fanny mentions the presence, in Boscombe Manor, of "a bust of Mary Wollstonecraft done from a death mask, over which Louis raves" (*Ltrs* 5: 121). It might be argued that this "whole stone craft" is to be found in *The Master of Ballantrae*.

12. Which was also Stevenson's: see a letter to Schwob dated 7 July 1894 (*Ltrs* 8: 316) and the "old, consistent exile" referred to as the "editor" in the preface to *The Master of Ballantrae* (*xix*).

13. Writing *The Master of Ballantrae* is contemporary with Saint-Gaudens making a medallion of the author (*Ltrs* 6: 88). Later, Stevenson will praise "the artistic merits of the God-like sculptor" (*Ltrs* 8: 318).

14. Which may be derived from Sir Walter Scott: see the last sentence of *The Bride of Lamermoor*, where marble monument, tomb and epitaph are mentioned, but not the inscription itself.

15. Sir Percy Shelley died in December 1889, a few months only after the novel was published: "I am so glad Sir Percy saw The Master; I little thought what a strange second sense, BRD would come to bear," Stevenson wrote in February 1891 to Lady Shelley, also providing a suggestion for an inscription in verse on a Shelley Memorial (*Ltrs* 7: 89–90). In retrospect, this uncanny dedication sounds like a farewell epitaph, while Stevenson and Lady Shelley seem busy erecting a Shelley monument in the same way as Mackellar and Alison erect a Durie tombstone.

16. The strange image of "the sea black and silent like a quarry-hole" (Stevenson 1889: 90) sounds as if taken from Hardy: in "A Humble Remonstrance," Stevenson voices his admiration for *A Pair of Blue Eyes*, also quoted approvingly by Proust in *La Prisonnière*.

17. See his "Médaillons" and "Tombeaux" series. Both Proust and Mallarmé were admirers of Stevenson. In *Le Temps retrouvé*, Swann mentions Stevenson as a major writer, equal to the greatest (1927: 716). Mallarmé wrote a short text of praise (7 December 1896) to the members of a Stevenson Memorial Committee for the erection of a Stevenson Monument or Memorial in Edinburgh (1945: 879–80).

REFERENCES

Amalric, Jean-Claude. 1994. The Master of Ballantrae: Un conte d'hiver? *Cahiers Victoriens & Edouardiens* 40: 119–25.

Ambrosini, Richard. 2001. *R. L. Stevenson:Lla poetica del romanzo*. Rome: Bulzoni Editore.

Chesterton, Gilbert Keith. 1927. *Robert Louis Stevenson.* London: Hodder & Stoughton.

Conrad, Joseph. 1902. *Heart of Darkness.* 1981. New York: Bantam.

Dury, Richard. 1993. *The Annotated Dr Jekyll and Mr Hyde.* Milano: Guerini Studio.

Edel, Leon, ed. 1980. *Letters of Henry James.* Vol. 3: 1883–95. Cambridge, MA: Harvard University Press.

Freud, Sigmund. 1922. Medusa's Head (Das Medusenhaupt). In *The Standard Edition of the Complete Psychological Works of Sigmund Freud,* vol. 18. 1955. Trans. and ed. by James Strachey. London: The Hogarth Press.

Lévi-Strauss, Claude. 1958. *Anthropologie Structurale.* Paris: Plon.

——. 1962. *La Pensée Sauvage.* Paris: Plon.

Mallarmé, Stéphane. 1896. Sur Robert-Louis Stevenson. In *Œuvres complètes*, vol. 2. 1979. Paris: Gallimard (La Pléiade). 879–80.

Naugrette, Jean-Pierre. 1983. Les aventures du roman: en dérivant de Ballantrae. *Critique* 89 (No. 432): 365–78. In Naugrette 1990. 25–55.

——. 1987. *Robert Louis Stevenson: L'aventure et son double.* Paris: Presses de l'École Normale Supérieure.

——. 1989. Ballades à Ballantrae. *Bulletin de la Société de Stylistique Anglaise* 11. In Naugrette 1990. 103–36.

——. 1990. *Lectures aventureuses.* La Garenne-Colombes: Editions de l'Espace Européen.

Page, Norman. 1984. *A Kipling Companion.* London: Macmillan Papermac.

Pavese, Cesare. 1950. Robert Louis Stevenson. In *La letteratura americana e altri saggi.* Ed. Italo Calvino. Torino: Einaudi, 1953. Trans. J.-B- Para. 1994. Raconter à bride abattue. *Europe* 779: 12–14.

Proust, Marcel. 1923. *La Prisonnière.* In Proust 1954. Vol. 3.

——. 1927. *Le Temps retrouvé.* In Proust 1954. Vol. 3.

——. 1954. *À la recherche du temps perdu.* Paris: Gallimard-La Pléiade.

Schwob, Marcel. 1894. Robert Louis Stevenson. In *Marcel Schwob.* Ed. Alexandre Gefen. 2002. *Œuvres.* Paris: Belles Lettres. 580–82.

Steiner, George. 1984. *Antigones.* Oxford: Oxford University Press.

Smith, Janet Adam, ed. 1971. *Robert Louis Stevenson—Collected Poems.* 2nd ed. London: Hart-Davis.

Stevenson, Robert Louis. 1886. *Strange Case of Dr. Jekyll and Mr. Hyde.* In *The Strange Case of Dr Jekyll and Mr Hyde and Other Stories.* Ed. Jenni Calder. 1979. Harmondsworth: Penguin.

——. 1889. *The Master of Ballantrae.* Tusitala Edition. Vol. 10.

——. 1896. *Weir of Hermiston.* 1984. London: Dent.

Quarreling with the Father

LUISA VILLA

Questions of authorization of the individual subject in the Victorian age have been haunting me for a long time: particularly while studying late-nineteenth-century fiction I have repeatedly been struck by the peculiar position of the individual situated at a historical junction when, on the one hand, he or she appears to be fully legitimized, and on the other the scope for individuality to develop and achieve self-realization seems to be shrinking (Villa 1997). Indeed, the pressure of cultural and economic imperatives that enjoin social conformity, and the curbing of the most pronounced aspects of self-assertion by means of internalized norms rather than by an appeal to outmoded notions of authority based on hierarchy and coercion, played a crucial role in the very same democratic transformation of British society that, at the same time, stood for freedom from traditional constraints. Full democratization was indeed a long way off in the 1870s, when the young Robert Louis Stevenson started his literary career, but there is no doubt that to avant-garde writers of the late Victorian generation the perplexities generated by such contradictory imperatives were part and parcel of their experience of modernity. Given the nature of social and cultural trends that authorized a vertiginous unmooring of the self from well-established conformities and social pieties while enforcing new measures for the standardized containment of individual subjects, it is no surprise that many imaginative writers among those placed, like Stevenson, on this turbulent border of modernity reacted to such a veritable double bind by developing and expressing a degree of ambivalence toward social transformation.

In view of such conceptual premises, it was perhaps inevitable that the one critical contribution to the father-son relationship in Stevenson that I found most helpful in tackling my subject should be Steven Mintz's chapter on the Stevensons in his valuable book on the Victorian family. Mintz—who is an historian—has little to say as to Stevenson's literary production, but his reading of the biographical material provides an invaluable framework for any reassessment of Stevenson's fictional harping on fathers and father substitutes. The problems faced by the Stevensons in working through the intergenerational transition are, to Mintz, fairly typical of their social class at the time: the field of religion, for instance— apparently free from "base and selfish motives" (Mintz 1983: 89)—was often subconsciously chosen by the Victorians as a comparatively "safe" arena onto which to displace and disguise more personal and thorny bones of contention; mild consequences of the bitter and soul-rending crises between son and father were far from uncommon, and such domestic quarrels hardly ever resulted in radical breaks within Victorian families. And with compromise more common than ultimate disruption, such rebellions seem to have been a somewhat standardized element in the son's negotiation of a degree of personal independence compatible with the reassertion of intergenerational continuities.

One of the most interesting points made by Mintz, however, has to do with ambivalent attitudes toward economic and professional success. According to Mintz, the erosion of the ideological-religious basis of the patriarchal family implied that paternal authority was increasingly "rooted in emotional bonds and money" (Mintz 1983: 61). This in turn called for new complex ways of establishing the son's capacity for (economic and emotional) independence while preserving his allegiance to the family and its values. On the one hand, the very pressure put by Victorian fathers on their sons—to pursue an economically rewarding profession—clashed with their desire to secure their children's emotional subordination. On the other hand, the sons' desire to achieve professional success, though perfectly in line with the bourgeois expectations of their fathers, was ultimately guilt-ridden since the very same achievement of economic independence was bound to weaken domestic bonds. Thus Stevenson's qualms about his own intense, meretricious interest in cash (as in his famous letter to Gosse: "We are whores . . . whores of the mind, selling to the public the amusements of our fireside as the whore sells the pleasures of her bed,"

Ltrs 5: 171) are both a reflex of the late-Victorian man of letters' unease at the mass-marketability of his books, and a consequence of his own conflictual quest for financial and moral independence.

There was at least one further reason for Stevenson's ambivalent attitude toward the erosion of the father's authority, which does not actually fall within the scope of Mintz's study but is surely as relevant to the peculiar Stevensonian mix. It has to do with Stevenson's own brand of avant-gardism, which in the late-Victorian field of literary production was definitely marked by a strong polemical antagonism toward everything that stood for middle-class domesticity in the Victorian novelistic tradition. There was indeed something aggressively misogynistic in the literary party he joined with his statements on the art of fiction—since he himself was among the most prominent to denounce "the haunting and truly spectral unreality" of the English realists, and to declare his "incredulous wonder" at their typical "hero's constancy under the submerging tide of dulness, and how he bears up with his gibbering sweetheart, endures the chatter of idiot girls, and stands by his whole unfeatured wilderness of an existence, instead of seeking relief in drink or foreign travel" (Stevenson 1888: 234). As critics of the *fin de siècle* have repeatedly underscored, to side with "King Romance" (Showalter 1991, ch. 5) meant to share and legitimize a number of gender assumptions that ultimately had to do with the marginalization of women writers (Tuchman 1989) and with the decline of the "feminine" moral authority that had presided over much Victorian mainstream fiction (Armstrong 1987). Thus, the avant-garde's desire to dislodge itself from the constraining molds of the past problematically conflicted with the emphatic gender inflection of professionalism and its ideology: to sons rebellious against paternal dominance, literary authority was nevertheless gendered male. Indeed, it was so with a (polemical? defensive?) emphasis unknown to the previous generation.

In a sense, then, the Oedipal scenario mobilized by Stevenson and his relationship to his father—such as emerges, most notably, from Jean-Pierre Naugrette's *L'aventure et son double* (1987)—seems to be largely overdetermined by powerful cultural scripts wherein, for instance, the son's attempts to develop his own gift as a professional writer were bound to be experienced as eroding his own emotional dependence on his family, ultimately undermining the father's own patriarchal status. And since the fall of the fathers anticipates and portends the fall of the sons-as-fathers (the fall of the sons, that is, who dream to replace their fathers as patriarchs, sharing with them the privileges of fin de siècle professionalism), fear as

well as guilt accompany success, and resentment at the father's domineering role strangely mixes with resentment at his pathetic vulnerability. As
William Veeder (1988: 110) put it, in his memorable reading of *Dr. Jekyll
and Mr. Hyde*: "Stevenson hates fathers for being overbearing, but he hates
them still more for being weak."

The problematic connection, in Stevenson, of personal self-affirmation
with the perception of the father's (mental, moral, professional) weakness
has been recently underscored by Hilary Beatty, in her "Father and Son:
The Origins of Strange Case of Dr. Jekyll and Mr. Hyde." Beatty's essay
seems to derive much of its strength from her drawing our attention to the
one unmitigated "failure" in Thomas Stevenson's distinguished career as
lighthouse and harbor engineer. This occurred at the end of 1872, when "a
tremendous storm . . . washed away the entire harbor of Wick and inval-
idated a life's study of the force of the waves" (Beatty 2001: 329). Latent personal and family tensions seem to have aggressively erupted in the aftermath
of the traumatic event that undermined Thomas's professional self-reliance
in his war waged against the hazards of navigation and the powers of the
sea.[1] Scarcely a month later the famous quarrel between son and father
over questions of religious belief broke out, ushering in Thomas's severe
depression, perhaps the first symptom of his future slow mental decline.
The young Robert Louis had long been testing the limits of his father's
tolerance, consciously "lingering about the landmark to pass which is to
sour his half-hearted patience into petty persecution" (October 1872, *Ltrs*
1: 225): it might well be that evidence of the father's weakness opened up
a space for self-affirmation, which the son tried *guiltily* to profit from.
Thus, potentially emancipatory clarifications and self-assertions turned sour
and rebounded back onto themselves: guilt and fear make independence
hard to bear, shaping and constraining both life and the imagination.

Given the rich mythical resonance of the imagery associated with the
civil engineer's profession and by this "chief disaster" (Stevenson 1887: 212)
in his life, it is no surprise that storms at sea should represent one crucial
set of images and situations by which Stevenson's fiction might be conceived as working through the Oedipal knot of ambivalent feelings in the
father-son relationship. Waters (streams, floods, turbulent seas) are traditionally associated with women, and particularly with dangerous, unruly,
and seductive feminine forces, thus becoming—as Klaus Theweleit's *Male
Fantasies* impressively underscores—a crucial metaphor for all that, in the
swelling turmoil of democratic modernity, threatens to disrupt the established
patriarchal order.[2] Hence, the failure of fathers to build barriers against

oceans, and the sinking of ship's crews into tempestuous seas almost inevitably come to represent an (incestuous) collapse of the masculine self into (feminine) shapelessness, a suspension of ethical norms, a wholesale breakdown of civilization. Such might ultimately be the consequences of revolutionary modernity—the age of treacherous modernist sons, with their irreverent attitudes toward traditional structures of authority, domestic and otherwise.

Sea storms are, indeed, a recurring feature in Stevenson's fiction, and they do occur at significant junctures in narratives as diverse as *The Black Arrow*, *Kidnapped*, *The Wrecker*, and *The Master of Ballantrae*. Although the "fear of the awesome power of the sea" might well be "traceable to a Calvinistic upbringing, which tended to see gigantic forces of nature as the agents of supernatural intervention" (McLynn 1993: 194, 195), and although ships tossed about by winds and waves are a quasi-obligatory component in a good adventure story, there is at least one sea storm in Stevenson that brings to light the intensely charged cathexis, and psychological complexity, of this narrative *topos*. Such is the storm that furnishes the pivotal episode in "The Merry Men" (1882). In this visionary reworking of troubling personal material, Stevenson recasts as father, daughter, and nephew the characters of the original Oedipal triangle, with its perplexing tangle of love and hate, emulation and rivalry.[3] The younger man's successful engagement of Mary Ellen's affections, his (largely unacknowledged) elation at such a triumph over the Oedipal rival, his impatient desire to dispel the lingering faithfulness she has to her father, might be taken to furnish the regressive emotional setting for the narration. The setting proper is a Scottish isle that Jenny Calder (1980: 81–82) identifies as Earraid—the same featured in *Kidnapped*—where the young Robert Louis had spent three weeks in 1870 at the time when it was being used as a base for the construction of Dhu Hearteach lighthouse, one of most daring feats of engineering accomplished by the Stevensons. The site, then, had very strong associations with Thomas and his professional vocation, which probably account for the hallowed atmosphere surrounding the events narrated and emblematized by the island's fictional name (Aros Jay = "the House of God"), and by the wrecked vessels *Christiania* (or "Christ-Anna") and *Espirito Santo* ("Holy Ghost"). Here, traditional pieties and superstitions should enhance, rather than weaken, patriarchal authority, and it seems hardly possible that the bulwarks of conscience should give in to the violence of archaic antagonisms and obscene selfish greeds. But very much as the delirious Gordon Darnaway (the narrator's uncle and father of Mary Ellen) in the story is excited into moral transgression by the awareness of its sinfulness ("if it wasna sin, I dinna ken that I would care for it"; Stevenson 1882: 407), Stevenson's text seems to indulge a sacrilegious pleasure in unmasking and debunking a stern, religious patriarch, subjecting him to a fatal oral regression, whereby waters inside and outside conspire, and the father's sympathy with the indomitable ocean waxes in conjunction with the mounting alcoholic dilution of his blood.[4]

Even a superficial knowledge of the author's biography allows the reader to perceive an additional ironic twist in a fictional arrangement by which a distinguished lighthouse engineer, whose profession was to make navigation safe, is turned into a drunken lunatic exulting in the power of sea gales to sink ships and kill human lives. The upright Thomas—who always refused to profit economically from his many inventions[5]—is here perfidiously portrayed as a subhuman wretch, "panting like a dog" for the spoils of shipwrecks. This negative distortion of the father's image shows how some of the emotional contents of the son's experience *vis à vis* the father's loss of mastery come to be displaced onto the older man. In "The Merry Men" the young man's unholy joy at the father's failure to keep the seas at bay is excluded from direct representation, and it surfaces as projected onto the father figure dutifully demonized. The same applies to the irrational, murderous burst of violence, a recurrent component in Stevensonian plotting, directed here off scene by Gordon Darnaway against the surviving mariner of the *Christiania*. This provides one significant example of Stevenson's tendency to shift onto his fictional fathers and father substitutes the burden of guilt and transgression that pertains primarily to the younger man's own involvement in the Oedipal quagmire. Following a displacing/disguising strategy fairly standard in dream censorship, the sins of the Stevensonian son come to be represented as the sins of the father.

It might be useful to underscore that such shifting of negative (emotional) contents from son to father is accompanied by an analogous shifting of positive (ethical) contents from father to son. Indeed, the latter provides the central motive in the moral growth of the fictional narrator, who in the course of the events learns to feel and express his piety toward the victims of sea storms. The young man who reaches Aros Jay at the beginning of the story is indeed coveting the submerged treasure of the Spanish galleon and, "being a fellow of a mechanical turn" (i.e. being endowed with some of the father's engineering skills), he has been "plotting how to weigh that good ship up again with all her ingots, ounces, and doubloons, and bring back the house of Darnaway to its long-forgotten dignity and wealth" (Stevenson 1882: 369). As Jean-Pierre Naugrette (1987: 189) points out, the discovery of a houseful of incongruously luxurious objects looted by his uncle from the *Christiania* seems to represent the magical realization of the nephew's own greed, which will be chastised and cured, mainly through the spectacle of his uncle's moral and mental degeneration, and the "strange judgment of God's" that will bring his life to an end. The narrator's acquisition of commendable moral qualities of self-restraint, human sympathy, and moderation (traditional precepts of paternal wisdom, whose task is to curb the young man's hubris of success and self-assertion, and to secure his satisfactory socialization) frames and ultimately re-contains the subversive *mise en scène* of Gordon Darnaway's derangement. Thus the furiously aggressive fantasy that debunks and disfigures the image of the father and makes "The Merry Men" such a haunting piece of fiction hardly touches the essence of conventional patriarchal values that, through the tremendous vicissitudes narrated, are relegitimized and dutifully passed on to the younger generation.

"The Merry Men," with its poignant representation of the quarrel with the father and the strategies it deploys in order to effect its discursive containment, offers a range of interesting suggestions as to the inner logics superintending Stevensonian plots and characterizations. It foregrounds, above all, Stevenson's penchant for criminal, weak, devious, unreliable father figures, opposed to honest young people. From *New Arabian Nights*, where innocent youths get repeatedly involved in the immoral and criminal calculations of older men (and women), to *Treasure Island*, where the most intensely cathected adult male is the astute "paternal" pirate Long John Silver; from the "Sire de Malétroit's Door," where the cynical brutality of the Sire is juxtaposed to the crystal-clear honesty of Denis and Blanche, to the "Pavilion on the Links," where the father is a fraudulent banker and a traitor, whereas his daughter and her future husband figure as upright and courageous young folks; from *Kidnapped* to *Catriona*, with their gallery of treacherously hostile uncles, mercenary skippers, ambiguous Lord Advocates and cowardly clan chieftains—Stevenson does seem to go out of his way to underscore the moral unreliability of the older generation as compared to the sane moral fiber of their sons and (occasionally) daughters. It is interesting to notice that one of the clearest exceptions to the rule is situated at the beginning of Stevenson's career as a writer of fiction, in "A Lodging for the Night," which confronts the shifty and frankly criminal young Villon with a stern, respectable, and hospitable elderly knight who gives him food and shelter as well as a fatherly lecture. This story shows how this plotting option—being more immediately biographical—was readily available to Stevenson but failed somehow to exert a steady appeal on his imagination. It could be argued that criminal father surrogates were more attractive than stern legalistic ones because they allowed anger to be expressed while leaving the structures of patriarchal authority unchallenged, together with the traditional set of values whereon positive masculinity gets defined (honor, sincerity, moral and physical courage, and a gentlemanly behavior toward women and underlings). Thus, quarreling with criminal father surrogates prevented the full radicalization of private quarrels into public ones.

It is true, however, that Stevenson never gave up the attempt to balance his father-son relationships more fairly: there are stories where the blame clearly falls on the representative of the younger generation ("Markheim," for instance), as well as stories where nobody is really guilty or really innocent ("The Misadventures of John Nicholson"), and obviously there are stories (such as *Dr. Jekyll and Mr. Hyde*, or *Ballantrae*) where the conflict does not ostensibly occur across the generation gap. But it seems to me that it is only in the later works that there is a pronounced swerve toward a different configuration of the quarrel with the father, wherein the son frankly inclines to side with the criminal, and the quarrel ends up by undermining the criteria by which good and evil get defined. The upshot of this seems to be the pronounced political radicalism of *The Ebb-Tide*, with the polemics against exploitative imperialism incarnated in the piously legalistic "paternal" Attwater. In *Weir of Hermiston* Stevenson appears to be moving in the same direction. In this tantalizingly unfinished novel, he seems to be really striving to give back to the father what belonged to him (the wielding of the law, the professional expertise, and unimpeached honesty) and to the son his due: his generational complicity with the forces of revolutionary modernity (represented by a new more humanitarian ethos), his (inevitable) disloyalty to the parent, his weaknesses, his passions, his rivalries, even his homicidal outbursts. Concomitantly, the very existence of an overarching ethical frame of reference is called into question: when there seems to be no consensus as to how loyalty to traditional values could be made compatible with self-respect and self-determination, then quarreling with the father seems bound to lose its "ritualistic" character; its consequence will be an irremediable break of social cohesion and family bonds, rather than the cultural continuity through marginal adjustment that Steven Mintz so persuasively describes.

The second set of suggestions has to do with the way "The Merry Men" focuses on the problems of intergenerational transition. Here the splitting of good and bad and the doubling of self fairly explicitly occur across the generation gap—showing very clearly Stevenson's tendency to shift the psychological burden of transgression from son onto father. Stevenson seems to be both pleased by the ease with which fathers and sons can be made to exchange their roles this way, and disturbed by the dishonesty of this ruse. No doubt his imagination is very much taken by the fictional possibilities and ethical implications thereof. He is fascinated by the reversal of conventional Oedipal roles: in Jekyll and Hyde, for instance, the rebellious passion that energizes the plot is not represented as the hubris of a treacherous Oedipal son dreaming of replacing his father—it is, as William Veeder (1988: 148) points out, the desire of the middle-aged man who wants to make himself his own son. In *The Dynamiter*, two villains harbor similar unholy desires (the sinister Dr. Grierson in the "Story of the Destroying Angel," and the voodoo priestess Madame Mendizabal in "The Story of the Fair Cuban"); interference with genealogical legitimacy, a connected crime, figures prominently in *The Black Arrow, Kidnapped*, and (in a comical vein) in *The Wrong Box*; and the whole tragic destiny of the Durie family narrated in *The Master of Ballantrae* springs from the impious whim of an elder son to usurp the position of his younger brother. Conventional roles are again strangely reversed, though the story shows how this reversal is far from stable: the rights of the new head of the house of Durrisdeer will be perpetually questioned by the ever-returning Master. Likewise, the younger Hyde will soon try to usurp Jekyll's paternal position of control and mastery, and David Balfour will return to question the rights of his avaricious uncle.

More generally, Stevenson's fiction seems to thrive on suddenly exchanged positions between fathers and sons—on adults who descend to "bairnly conduct," or are suddenly reduced to beg "after the manner of a schoolboy" (Stevenson 1889: 207, 162), as well as on sons who stand up to and lecture their elders and betters. It thrives on sudden narrative twists where positions of domination and positions of subjection get suddenly reversed. It thrives on the fluidity of affects, their displacements, and their uncanny tendency to reverse—"To fight or make friends?" (Stevenson 1889: 38), as the Master of Ballantrae says, leaving the choice which way to go to the inscrutability of chance. It thrives—as Stevenson's readers have repeatedly noted—on ethical ambiguity and on dramatic oscillations between extremes of badness and goodness; above all, it thrives on the tendency to blur the generation gap, dramatizing the conflict between son and father as sibling rivalry between the self and its double. It is my contention here that the son's (guilty) pleasure at the confusion of roles between sons and fathers probably accounts for the irrepressible compulsion (the gusto, one might say) with which Stevenson, who was an only child, kept on fictionally courting the idea of a brother and was apparently much attracted by older women who could provide him with what was crucially missing in his original family arrangement: a sibling of his own.

There is, in other words, a distinctive, forbidden pleasure inherent in such fictional exchanges, reversals, and confusions of roles, a pleasure that, it seems to me, is a crucial ingredient in the modernist romancer's vocation. Indeed, the very attraction Stevenson felt for the romance form, which could captivate children and adults alike, seems to chime with the idea of a pleasurable interference with the genealogical order of things. As Stevenson conceived it, romance was a genre that could effect a collapse of generational differences, where the old become young again and the young (like the enterprising Jim Hawkins) have their chance to fight with their elders on equal terms and even win the game. The image of Robert Louis, his elderly father—who "caught fire at once with all the romance and childishness of his original nature" (Stevenson 1893: 280)—and his stepson merrily cooperating at the *Treasure Island* project seems to authorize such an interpretation of Stevenson's penchant for the narrative of adventure. This is not meant to rule out other explanations for this preference. What I wish to point out is the specific libidinal cathexis sustaining his theoretical commitment to a type of novel that (as he wrote in his "Humble Remonstrance") allows the (male) reader "to be submerged by the tale as by a billow" (Stevenson 1884: 196), leaving judgments, laws, and invidious distinctions aside and freely (and safely) flirting with the watery maternal element—with its disruptive fury, as well as with its subversive fluidity.

NOTES

1. Significantly, there is no trace of the episode in the letters written by Stevenson at the time, which is probably why his biographers have never taken it much into account. Later, however, he will appear to be aware of the impact it had had on his father (Stevenson 1887). Beatty's source is Bathurst's book on the Stevensons (Bathurst 1999: 230–31). Both Bathurst and Mair (1978: 206–7) have consulted the archives of the firm; and Mair speaks of "scores of letters, ranging in tone from the defensive to the apologetic . . . sent to Wick Town Council." As for Thomas's own reaction, in the 1874 edition of his *The Design and Construction of Harbours* (Stevenson 1874: 45–48), he added a detailed account of the "incredible" events of 1872. In the plates section he also published a photograph of the ruined breakwater taken in the immediate

aftermath of the storm. The breakwater was rebuilt by the firm and destroyed again by the waves in 1877, leaving the distinguished engineer baffled and dismayed. Thus, in the 1886 edition, a further paragraph was added to the account: "Extraordinary as this may appear, it was surpassed in 1877, when another concrete mass, which had been substituted for the one that was moved, was in like manner carried away, though it contained 1500 cubic yards of cement rubble, the weight of which was about 2600 tons" (Stevenson 1886: 52).

2. Marianne DeKoven (1991) has shown the relevance of Theweleit's insights for the study of such early modernist texts as *The Awakening*, or *The Nigger of the "Narcissus"*. Jean-Pierre Naugrette (1987: 155–90) comments on Stevenson's tendency to project onto images of waves, tides and seas, the image of the mother.

3. The relevance of the Oedipal plot in Stevenson's fiction (and particularly of its Hamlet variant, which figures the uncle as a necessary mediator in the father-son relationship) has been underscored by Naugrette (1987: 45–54).

4. Among Stevenson's scholars, it is—to my knowledge—William Veeder (1988: 128 ff), who has most interestingly commented on the crucial role played by oral regression in Stevenson's fiction, underscoring the oral/maternal connotations of wine and potion consumption in *Dr. Jekyll and Mr. Hyde*.

5. R. L. Stevenson himself underscores the lighthouse Stevensons' selfless devotion to their profession: "[T]hey regarded their original work as something due already to the nation, and none of them has ever taken out a patent. It is another cause of the comparative obscurity of the name: for a patent not only brings in money, but infallibly spreads reputation" (Stevenson 1887: 213).

REFERENCES

Armstrong, Nancy. 1987. *Desire and Domestic Fiction*. Oxford: Oxford University Press.

Bathurst, Bella. 1999. *The Lighthouse Stevensons: The Extraordinary Story of the Building of the Scottish Lighthouses by the Ancestors of R. L. Stevenson*. London: HarperCollins.

Beatty, Hilary J. 2001. Father and Son: The Origins of Strange Case of Dr. Jekyll and Mr. Hyde. *The Psychoanalytic Study of the Child* 56: 317–60.

Calder, Jenny. 1980. *Robert Louis Stevenson: A Life Study*. London: Hamish Hamilton.

DeKoven, Marianne. 1991. *Rich and Strange: Gender, History and Modernism*. Princeton, NJ: Princeton University Press.

Mair, Craig. 1978. *A Star for Seamen: The Stevenson Family of Engineers*. London: John Murray.

McLynn, Frank. 1993. *Robert Louis Stevenson: A Biography*. London: Pimlico.

Mintz, Steven. 1983. *A Prison of Expectations: The Family in Victorian Culture*. New York: New York University Press.

Naugrette, Jean-Pierre. 1987. *Robert Louis Stevenson: L'aventure et son double*. Paris: Presses de l'Ecole Normale Supérieur.

Showalter, Elaine. 1991. *Sexual Anarchy: Gender and Culture at the "Fin de Siècle."* London: Bloomsbury.

Stevenson, Robert Louis. 1882. "The Merry Men." In *The Complete Short Stories of Robert Louis Stevenson*. Ed. Charles Neider. 1969. New York: Da Capo Press.

————. 1884. "A Humble Remonstrance." In Stevenson 1988.

————. 1887. "Thomas Stevenson, Civil Engineer." In Stevenson 1988.

————. 1888. "The Lantern-Bearers." In Stevenson 1988.

————. 1889. *The Master of Ballantrae.* Ed. Claire Harman. 1992. London: Everyman's Library.

————. 1893. My First Book—*Treasure Island.* In Stevenson 1988.

————. 1988. *The Lantern-Bearers and Other Essays.* Ed. Jeremy Treglown. London: Chatto & Windus; New York: Cooper Square Press.

Stevenson, Thomas. 1874. 2nd edition. *The Design and Construction of Harbours: A Treatise of Maritime Engineering.* Edinburgh: Adam and Charles Black.

————. 1886. 3rd edition. *The Design and Construction of Harbours: A Treatise of Maritime Engineering.* Edinburgh: Adam and Charles Black.

Theweleit, Klaus. 1977. *Männerphantasien,* Bd. 1: *Frauen, Fluten, Körper, Geschichte.* English translation: *Male Fantasies.* Vol. 1: *Women, Floods, Bodies, History.* Trans. Chris Turner. 1987. Cambridge: Polity Press.

Tuchman, Gaye with Nina Fortin. 1898. *Edging Women Out: Victorian Publishers, Novelists and Social Change.* London: Routledge.

Veeder, William. 1988. Children of the Night: Stevenson and Patriarchy. In *Dr. Jekyll and Mr. Hyde after One Hundred Years.* Ed. William Veeder and Gordon Hirsh. Chicago: University of Chicago Press. 107–60.

Villa, Luisa. 1997. *Figure del risentimento. Aspetti della costruzione del soggetto nella narrativa inglese ai margini della "decadenza."* Pisa: ETS.

Figures in a Landscape

Scott, Stevenson, and
Routes to the Past

JENNI CALDER

Scott and Stevenson both wrote "road novels," fiction that takes its characters on actual and metaphorical journeys through Scotland as a means of drawing together disparate cultures and conflicting histories. Journeys are rooted deep in Scottish literary traditions, and the palpable diversity in the structure of the land, MacDiarmid's "multiform" Scotland, has been a distinguishing feature of the Scottish literary imagination as it has of the narrative of Scotland's past. Scott and Stevenson both draw on this rich tradition, consistently exposing their characters to new landscapes and alien environments. How their protagonists respond to the "other" is organic to experience and plot; and is a crucial connection between past and present. Otherness in space is a means of invoking otherness in time.

The half century between Scott's last fiction and Stevenson's first saw the economic, social and industrial consequences of the technological revolution that was well established before Scott's death. As a result of agricultural improvement and the large-scale uncovering of the earth that came with increasing industrial activity, the past was simultaneously overlaid and exposed as never before. Humankind's interference with the natural world accelerated, while, stimulated by an awareness of imminent loss, interest in a preindustrial environment intensified.

Scott's evocations in his poetry of Highland and Border terrain and his conjuring of a mythic history out of mountains, lochs, and ruins, caught the mood exactly. These were real places through which he offered the reader a connection with both nature and the past. Landscape provided dimensions in time as well as space. Scott achieved this because he was still in touch with a preindustrial experience. And the Highland landscape, though widely affected by human activity, did not suffer the same industrial incursions as that of Scotland's central belt. Stevenson, for all his immersion in environments of the past, did not and could not share the intimate connection that was Scott's, except in urban Edinburgh. The seventy years between the publication of *Waverley* and *Kidnapped* had transformed Scots into a predominantly urban people and inevitably distanced the urban Scot from wild country.

In looking at the response to landscape of the two writers, I want to suggest some ways it provides in each a route to the past: in Scott's *Rob Roy* (1818), *Waverley* (1814) and *Redgauntlet* (1824), which between them span the period from before the 1715 Jacobite Rising to 1765; and in Stevenson's *Kidnapped* (1886), *Catriona* (1891) and *The Master of Ballantrae* (1889), which share the Jacobite context although the timescale is more concentrated.

When Edward Waverley makes his journey into the Perthshire Highlands, he has the benefit of a halfway house. The house and parks of Baron Bradwardine are south of the Highland Line, but it is through him that Waverley first learns about the Highlands and their inhabitants. He reflects on the strangeness of it all, as he glimpses a life that is untamed and untouched by his assumptions about social order. "It seemed like a dream to Waverley that these deeds of violence should be familiar to men's minds, and currently talked of, as falling within the common order of things, and happening daily in the immediate neighbourhood, without his having crossed the seas, and while he was yet in the otherwise well-ordered island of Great Britain" (Scott 1814: 72–73).

Already attracted by "the dusky barrier of mountains," Waverley considers an "excursion" into this foreign territory (73). The word suggests a recreational trip, not a military or commercial expedition but a journey to view exotic terrain and its native inhabitants. When Waverley and Evan Dhu reach the pass between Lowland and Highland, the hint of danger only adds to the adventure:

> the path, which was extremely steep and rugged, winded up a chasm between two tremendous rocks, following the passage which a foaming stream, that brawled far below, appeared to have worn for itself in the course of ages. A few slanting beams of the sun, which was now setting, reached the water in its darksome bed, and shewed it partially, chafed by an hundred

rocks, and broken by an hundred falls. The descent from the path to the stream was a mere precipice, with here and there projecting fragments of granite, or a scathed tree, which had warped its twisted roots into the fissures of the rock.

This landscape is ancient, harsh, and dynamic. The drama is generated by human as well as natural history, for the pass, as Evan Dhu explains, was defended by "ten of the clan Donnochie against a hundred of the low country carls" and contains the graves of the slain (76). Scott is telling us, on several levels, that landscape and history are inextricably linked.

In unknown territory where only Highlanders can detect the trail, Waverley reflects not on risk but on romance: "what a fund of circumstances for the exercise of a romantic imagination, and all enhanced by the solemn feeling of uncertainty at least, if not of danger." Waverley is not a reliable witness, but Scott makes very clear the nature of his unreliability, his romantic ingenuousness. The reader is aware, if Waverley is not, that the precipitous path has taken us on a journey in time as well as space. We have entered the habitat of a race adapted to the wild: when the path disappears into "murky darkness," Waverley's guide "seemed to trace it by instinct, without the hesitation of a moment" (78).

This sense of human life organic to the landscape is amplified. Wilderness is populated by a Gaelic-speaking wild people, in outlandish dress and with fearsome weapons, who belong to another age. They dine on stolen cattle; their movements are incomprehensible; their consumption of whisky is prodigal without "the usual baneful effects either upon the brain or the constitution" (82). The essentials of their survival, food, drink, the tartan they wear, are the products of the land. The Highlanders' belief in their right to the property of others confirms a vanished ethos that appears integral to their oneness with the environment. As Evan Dhu puts it, "to take a tree from the forest, a salmon from the river, a deer from the hill, or a cow from the Lowland strath, is what no Highlander need ever think shame upon" (85). As we see again in *Rob Roy*, the theft of cattle can be accomplished successfully only by those who know the terrain and its covert tracks and hidden glens.

Waverley is eased gently into this new and even in 1745 anachronistic world. He has guides and intermediaries, and meets with sufficient sophistication of manners to reassure him and to allow the superficial romance to predominate. The landscape itself is an emblem of this. It is both dangerous and attractive, alien and inspiring. Waverley is drawn into a fight that is not his own, and ultimately he walks away from it unscathed. An old, heroic, primitive way of life has been destroyed; in case we have missed the point, Scott drives it home in his final chapter, titled "A Postscript, which should have been a Preface." The novel ends where Waverley's adventure began, within sight of the Highland hills, but now there is a memento on the wall of Tully-Veolan, "a large and spirited painting, representing Fergus Mac-Ivor and Waverley in their Highland dress, the scene a wild, rocky, and mountainous pass, down which the clan were descending in the background" (338). Waverley, married to Rose Bradwardine, is set to inherit an estate that, in spite of, or indeed because of, the Jacobite disturbances, has been replenished and improved. The painting, like the novel itself, safely contains an event that profoundly threatened the stability of the nation. The landscape is tamed but still serves, in reality and through its representation (in Scott's novels as well as in pictures), as a connection with the past.

Although written later, chronologically *Rob Roy* comes first, set before the earlier Jacobite rising of 1715. While *Waverley* provides a convenient model for Scott's subsequent fiction, *Rob Roy* is a starker, more complex, and more historically illuminating novel. His use of landscape as a route to the past is less compromising and less compromised. While Edward Waverley approaches the Highlands primed for romance, Frank Osbaldistone is less susceptible. He claims to be "a citizen of the world" and regards the Scots "as a race hostile by nature to the more southern inhabitants of this realm" (Scott 1818: 103, 106). At the same time, he is a self-confessed lover of nature and sees romance in wilderness. But he meets his first Highlanders not in the mountains but on the streets of Glasgow, a city on the brink of huge economic success following the Union of 1707:

> Hordes of wild, shaggy, dwarfish cattle and ponies, conducted by Highlanders as wild, as shaggy, and sometimes as dwarfish, as the animals they had in charge, often traversed the streets of Glasgow. Strangers gazed with surprise on the antique and fantastic dress, and listened to the unknown and dissonant sounds of their language, while the mountaineers, armed even while engaged in this peaceful occupation with musket and pistol, sword, dagger, and target stared with astonishment on the articles of luxury of which they knew not the use, and with an avidity which seemed somewhat alarming on the articles which they knew and valued. It is always with unwillingness that the Highlander quits his deserts, and at this early period it was like tearing a pine from its rock, to plant him elsewhere. (238)

The Highlanders, wrenched from their natural territory, are "antique," belonging to a former age. Soon we will approach their antiquity and exoticism through the landscape itself.

The essential intermediary in *Rob Roy* is Bailie Nicol Jarvie, who guides the expedition north (and this is an expedition, rather than an excursion) and interprets the landscape. He is pragmatic when it comes to the economic possibilities of the Highlands—at the end of the novel he proposes draining Loch Lomond for development purposes, a suggestion that has a horribly twenty-first-century ring to it—but has little time for the people. They are lawless, untrustworthy, and with an alien code of behavior. As they progress north the scene becomes "wild and open," a vista of "hopeless barrenness" (309), neither fertile nor picturesque, but the character of the landscape changes when they cross the River Forth, an actual and symbolic boundary between Lowland and Highland. "'That's the Forth,' said the Bailie, with an air of reverence, which I have observed the Scotch usually pay to their distinguished rivers. The Clyde, the Tweed, the Forth, the Spey, are usually named by those who dwell on their banks with a sort of respect and pride, and I have known duels occasioned by any word of disparagement. I cannot say I have the least quarrel with this sort of harmless enthusiasm. I received my friend's communication with the importance which he seemed to think appertained to it. In fact, I was not a little pleased, after so long and dull a journey, to approach a region which promised to engage the imagination" (314).

Frank Osbaldistone is detached, unaware of the very real significance of the River Forth, but not blind to the moonlit and evocative scene. They cross the river by "an old-fashioned stone bridge, very high and very narrow" (316), as if to emphasize the archaic nature of the territory they are entering, and as they ride into the Clachan of Aberfoyle it becomes evident that this territory is not only archaic but primitive. Hovels of stone, mud, and turf, and the meager material possessions of the inhabitants suggest a crude poverty. But this material culture is organic to the territory. The landscape that appeals to Frank's imagination is the same landscape that houses, feeds, and clothes its inhabitants. It is the environment itself that is the link between incomer Frank and the country that is doubly "other." It is manifestly the past to the reader, but it is also a time warp in the eyes of Frank and the Bailie. This way of life is on the way out.

Yet Scott demonstrates that this same environment produces a vibrant, if in some eyes barbaric, culture. The following day Frank emerges from the "smoky, smothering atmosphere of the Highland hut" into an apparently benign scene of "natural romance and beauty." The loch is "lightly curled into tiny waves by the breath of the morning breeze, each glittering in its course under the influence of the sunbeams . . . High hills, rocks, and banks, waving with natural forests of birch and oak, formed the borders of this enchanting sheet of water; and, as their leaves rustled to the wind and twinkled in the sun, gave to the depth of solitude a sort of life and vivacity. Man alone seemed to be placed in a state of inferiority, in a scene where all the ordinary features of nature were raised and exalted" (338).

Frank is deceived on two counts: in his identification of an unthreatening romantic landscape, and in his relegation of humankind's place in it. Soon he and the Bailie, now traveling with a troop of English soldiers, meet hostile Highlanders: "the path, instead of keeping the water's edge, scaled the promontory by one or two rapid zigzags, carried in a broken track along the precipitous face of a slaty grey rock, which would otherwise have been absolutely inaccessible. On the top of this rock, only to be approached by a road so broken, so narrow, and so precarious, the corporal declared he had seen the bonnets and long-barrelled guns of several mountaineers." The landscape contains and fosters a very human menace. The Highlanders' symbiosis with the terrain is reinforced by the commanding appearance of Helen MacGregor, her face "imprinted with deep lines by exposure to rough weather" with "strong, harsh and expressive" features, evoking an analogy with the rock itself. Her sonorous invective against the redcoats—"Ye have left me and mine neither house nor hold, blanket nor bedding, cattle to feed us, or flocks to clothe us"—extends this, and in the subsequent skirmish the Highlanders' affinity with the terrain gives them an easy victory (343, 344). This episode, visually and rhetorically, is powerfully suggestive of the clash between incomers and Native Americans—a mainstay of the Western. The analogy is not as far-fetched as it might seem, as Scott himself in his introduction describes Rob Roy as having "the wild virtues, the subtle policy, and unrestrained licence of an American Indian" (17).

The drowning of Morris, the hostage, confirms the Lowlanders' worst fears of the Highlanders as barbaric, but it also demonstrates their alliance with nature: it is the waters of the loch that put an end to Morris, just as it is the River Forth at the Fords of Frew that enables Rob to escape. Nature is on his side: "the river was rendered inaccessible by the steepness of its banks, or the thickets of alders, poplars, and birch, which, overhanging its banks, prevented the approach of horsemen" (373). The troopers don't know how to deal with these quite ordinary features of a Highland landscape.

Frank succumbs, despite the violence, to the spectacle of the river and the hills silvered by moonlight. This maintains his role in connecting not only pragmatism and romance but the present—and the future even, as anticipated by the Bailie—and an outdated way of life. "My foot is on my native heath, and my name is MacGregor," declares Rob Roy, invoking "kin, clan, country, wife, and bairns" (383). To guarantee our understanding of the intimate relationship between Highland life and Highland landscape, Rob's almost valedictory comment is "my heart would sink, and my arm would shrink and wither like fern in the frost, were I to lose sight of my native hills" (398). Finally this Highland journey takes the party to a waterfall where they hear "the wild notes of the bagpipes, which lost their natural discord from being mingled with dashing sound of the cascade" (402). Highland nature and Highland culture are at one, but it is that very oneness that makes the entire culture vulnerable. Sever the connection and, as Rob himself makes clear, a whole way of life disintegrates. This, of course, was exactly what happened. The landscape became the possession of the tourist rather than the native, and Scott himself helped it to happen.

Scott clearly intended to provide a narrative of historical interpretation, to guide his readers through a delineated terrain, and to generate a connection with key episodes and characters of the past, real and fictional. Stevenson's intentions are different. He turns to the past in order to find paradigms for the present, and often these are of a very personal nature. It is not historical narrative that interests him, so much as a cognitive unfolding of personality located in the past. And by the time he was writing, roads and railroads had made the Highland landscape familiar to many.

In *Kidnapped*, David Balfour does not have the benefit of a gradual preamble to foreign territory. He is flung into an environment that takes him totally by surprise. When Highlander and Jacobite Alan Breck Stewart bursts on the scene, we know that David is a Presbyterian and a Whig and largely ignorant of Scotland beyond the boundaries of the inland Borders parish of his birth. This is the ignorance of a Scot, not the ignorance of Scott's heroes from the other side of the Border. David gains from Alan Breck "some knowledge of that wild Highland country, on which I was so soon to land," just as Waverley does from Bradwardine, and adds, with an irony that will emerge only later: "In those days, so close on the back of the great rebellion, it was needful a man should know what he was doing when he went upon the heather" (Stevenson 1886: 71). Alan himself is a product of this alien culture and landscape, not an intermediary, and unlike

Edward Waverley or Frank Osbaldistone, David Balfour has no predisposition in favor of the picturesque.

Kidnapped's Highland landscape is unambiguously hostile. Even with the survival skills of the native inhabitants and without the incursions of an occupying army, existence is precarious. David is a country boy, but the gentle rural scene he leaves at the start of the novel is no preparation for his precipitate landfall on barren rock. On the *Covenant* Alan had nonchalantly painted a picture of bare Highland hillsides and heather but also of solidarity and mutual support. On Erraid David finds none of that, and quickly discovers that it is he who is alien. He has no means of understanding the environment—"I had never seen a place so desert and desolate"—and soon he envisages "starving on an isle at the extreme end of the wild Highlands" (83). His inability to relate to the landscape means he cannot locate himself.

When he finally crosses to Mull he finds it "rugged and trackless . . . being all bog, and briar, and big stone," with people "grubbing in little miserable fields that would not keep a cat" (94). Stevenson gives us no set-piece descriptions, no commanding evocations of moor and mountain. Yet the terrain traversed by David is a felt landscape, literally felt by his feet and his hands and knees as he struggles through it, metaphorically and psychologically felt as he registers its overwhelming difference. He experiences the Highland landscape more intimately than either Waverley or Osbaldistone.

Throughout, his response is relentlessly negative. The inn at Kinlochaline "the most beggarly vile place . . . full of smoke, vermin, and silent Highlanders," the mountains "high, rough and barren, very black and gloomy in the shadow of the clouds" (108). After the murder of the Red Fox it only gets worse, for now David is a fugitive and reluctantly dependent on the natives for his safety as well as his subsistence: "we're in the Hielands, David; and I tell ye to run, take my word and run. Nae doubt it's a hard thing to skulk and starve in the heather, but it's harder yet to lie shackled in a red-coat prison," instructs Alan (117–18).

The mountain wilderness is without any compensating visual impact. The need to travel by night further interferes with David's perception of where he is. Stevenson's portrayal of landscape is topographical, not picturesque. Landscape determines the movements of his protagonists and is as much the enemy as the redcoats, with all human life diminished by the scale of it. The signs of human habitation are hardly visible, and although this suggests a symbiosis between human activity and environment similar to that found in Scott, in fact it emphasizes vulnerability. "Cluny's Cage" on Ben Alder, an improvised structure of branches, earth, and moss that "half hung, half stood in that steep, hillside thicket, like a wasp's nest in a green hawthorn" becomes an emblem of instability, as well as the scene of anxiety and discord (151).

From Ben Alder, David and Alan make their way south through the territory of nightmare, both literally (as David has a fever) and figuratively. They are traveling by night, through

> eerie mountains and among the well-heads of wild rivers; often buried in mist, almost continually blown and rained upon. . . . By day, we lay and slept in the drenching heather; by night; incessantly clambered upon breakneck hills and among rude crags. We often wandered; we were often so involved in fog, that we must lie quiet until it lightened . . . This was a dreadful time . . . the rain driving sharp in my face or running down my back in icy trickles; the mist enfolding us like as in a gloomy chamber—or perhaps, if the wind blew, falling suddenly apart and showing us the gulf of some dark valley where the streams were crying aloud. (162)

This country and climate are hostile to Highlander and Lowlander alike, obscure and obscured, and that the two of them are by this stage not on speaking terms confirms their isolation from each other as well as from the terrain. It is clear from the last chapters of *Kidnapped,* and reinforced by *Catriona,* where David needs a guide to make his fruitless ride to Inveraray, that the Highlands will remain alien territory to David as he makes his way in the professional world of Scotland's capital. His marriage to a Highland wife does not change this, and although his friendship with Alan survives and he drinks to "the king over the water," this is personal, not political. Unlike Waverley, David's disconnection from the Highlands is complete. He cannot occupy a Lowland space within sight of the Highland hills.

Stevenson is as well tuned as Scott to the historical and cultural dimensions of the landscape and of course was quite aware of the territory that had been mapped by his predecessor. But by the 1880s the relationship of human activity to landscape had changed, and both men were implicated in the process. Scott incessantly improved Abbotsford and its estate at the same time as he collected antiquarian material and deliberately echoed and evoked anachronistic styles and modes. Stevenson's family contributed, through a range of civil engineering works, to the modernization of Scotland, and made their own imprint on the landscape. But Stevenson's

native habitat was urban, however historic, and he had more distance to
cover to connect with the historical meaning of the environment.

In *Redgauntlet* and *The Master of Ballantrae*, the Jacobite narrative moves
to the southwest and the Solway Firth. The scale of the environment is
very different from the bold masses of Highland rock and mountain, but
in both novels the landscape has an intrinsic resonance. It is border country, on many levels. It is close to England and to Ireland. It is open to
Europe and to America. Both novels are patterned with psychological and
emotional borders, involving family relationships, political allegiances,
and masquerades. In *Redgauntlet* quicksands and unpredictable tides reinforce uncertainty; this is a landscape that eludes clear definition. Yet there
is the same organic and by implication primitive relationship between
human activity and the terrain that we find elsewhere in Scott: the horsemen spearing salmon on Solway sands are a good example. Darsie Latimer
traverses an uncultivated and desolate countryside, and compares it unfa-
vorably with the view of Cumberland across the Border, "crossed and inter-
sected by ten thousand lines of trees growing in hedge-rows, shaded with
groves and woods of considerable extent, animated by hamlets and villas,
from which thin clouds of smoke already gave sign of human life and human
industry" (Scott 1824: 41). The anachronistic Herries, relic of an outdated
conflict, belongs to the primitive, undeveloped landscape of Scotland. The
future rests with the tamed, controlled countryside of England.

Latimer, a less guided traveler than most of Scott's heroes, rides south,
not north, and the landscape and life he encounters are directly interpreted through his letters to his friend Alan Fairford, rooted in the very
particular milieu of Edinburgh's legal profession. Like Latimer, Ephraim
Mackellar is also an urban professional who makes a journey to the southwest and is the main vehicle of the narrative. The nature of the environment emerges only slowly and erratically. Mackellar's interest in landscape
is confined to its more pleasant aspects, but inevitably something much
less benign impinges on his tale.

The duel between the Durie brothers takes place in a shrubbery, an
obscured, intermediate territory, with the candles providing a light more
sinister than illuminating: "as we went forth in the shine of the candles,
the blackness was like a roof over our heads . . . The cold of the night fell
about me like a bucket of water" (Stevenson 1889: 78). When Mackellar
returns to the scene of the duel he finds a scene of intrusion and dislocation: "One of the candles was overthrown, and that taper quenched. The

other burned steadily by itself, and made a broad space of light upon the frosted ground. All within that circle seemed, by the force of contrast and the overhanging blackness, brighter than by day. And there was the blood-stain in the midst; and a little farther off Mr Henry's sword, the pommel of which was of silver; but of the body, not a trace. . . . The ground was so hard, it told no story" (86). Landscape is reduced to an intimate arena now strewn with the evidence of violence. Nature and the terrain have been imposed on but not conquered. The dark, the cold and the ground (so hard "it told no story") are independent of human action, and the theatricality of the scene heightens the disjunction.

When Mackellar eventually escorts James Durie on his departure from Scotland, they leave in mist and take "a road over moorish hills, where was no sound but the crying of moor-fowl in the wet heather and the pouring of the swollen burns. Sometimes I would doze off in slumber, when I would find myself plunged at once in some foul and ominous nightmare" (129–30). As in *Kidnapped*, a hostile and obscured landscape becomes the territory of fevered dreams.

There is another landscape integral to the story, the savage and malevolent North American wilderness where human motives and actions are stripped naked, and moral judgments become impossible. "He's not of this world," says Henry of his brother James, who he believes has come back from the dead and will again (179). But in a sense James is of the world they all now temporarily inhabit, a world that none of them can control or comprehend. Literally, he has been subsumed by the landscape, buried alive. The harsh physical environment contains and completes the process of mutual destruction that the two brothers embarked on in the psychologically and emotionally dislocated territory of Scotland. The climax is particularly stark, because the American landscape is disengaged, indifferent, even while it has colluded in violence. The brothers and their associates are intruders in a terrain that offers no natural connections and no history. They are on a route to nowhere, in time or space. The survivors can only withdraw, as David Balfour withdraws. The difference is that in the mid-eighteenth century the historical meaning of the North American landscape has not yet fully materialized, while the Highland landscape's history is perceived as contained by the past.

Scott's protagonists journey through landscapes that live in the past and where the past lives. Scott peoples this territory with characters who are genuinely indigenous, whose language, culture, and customs are organic to the environment. Ultimately, they recede into distance in time, but not before they have been firmly rooted in space. Scott's explorers are then able to take up a neutral position, maintaining a link with the past but unequivocally allying themselves with the future. Stevenson's protagonists are also travelers, but they don't so much open up Scotland as remind us just how readily time and change estrange us from both the landscape and the past. Alan Breck lives in exile and will never again scramble through the heather. Nor will David. The Durie brothers die on foreign soil and leave their disconnected history in the hands of an unreliable custodian, the narrator Mackellar. The landscape does not aid interpretation; the frozen ground yields no clues.

REFERENCES

Scott, Walter. 1818. *Rob Roy*. 1985. London and Glasgow: Collins.
———. 1814. *Waverley*. 1986. Oxford: Oxford University Press.
Stevenson, R. L. 1886. *Kidnapped*. 1986. Edinburgh: Chambers.
———. 1889. *The Master of Ballantrae*. 1976. London: J. M. Dent & Sons.

Burking the Scottish Body

*Robert Louis Stevenson and the
Resurrection Men*

CAROLINE MCCRACKEN-FLESHER

Robert Louis Stevenson's tale "The Body Snatcher," written in 1881, is just one in a series of Scottish stories that reaches before and after the nineteenth century, revealing the degree to which Scotland is haunted by the horrible reality of the corpse that walks.[1] This chapter focuses on the peculiarly Scottish anxieties that animate the tale and make it, in the language of the day, a "crawler," a text that moves the skin and creeps through culture, crossing the boundary into British sensibility.

"The Body Snatcher" derives from a distinctly Scottish source. Patrick Scott recognizes this tale of body-snatching that evolves into complicity in murder as "overtly derivative, retelling the horrendous tale of those notorious Edinburgh entrepreneurs, Burke and Hare" (Scott 1999: 113). Stevenson builds from the 1828 scandal shared by the murderers and their customer, Dr. Knox the Anatomist. Fettes and Macfarlane receive bodies for "Mr. K— [who] was then at the top of his vogue" (Stevenson 1884: 412). Like Knox, K— "enjoyed a popularity due partly to his own talent and address, partly to the incapacity of his rival, the university professor"; he is a "meteorically famous man . . . a *bon vivant* as well as an accomplished teacher; he liked a sly allusion no less than a careful preparation [a body readied for dissection]" (412).

The implied model was so clear that Knox's onetime pupil, now Professor John Goodsir, immediately sprang to the doctor's defense. He objected: "It will be said, of course, that the *Body Snatcher* is only a piece of fiction. A pleasant piece of fiction, certainly, to attach the stigma of cold-blooded deliberate murder to the name and memory of a man who has relatives and friends and admirers amongst the few still living of his many thousands of pupils" (Rae 1964: 150). Goodsir asked: "Was it out of delicate consideration for their feelings that Mr Stevenson made use of the K—, when he well knew that he might just as well have written KNOX." Of course, Goodsir's intervention only serves to remove any doubt about the model for Stevenson's character (Scott 1999: 124).

More interestingly, Goodsir draws our attention to Stevenson's choice to focus not on the murderers—who obviously deserve the scalpel of the narrative—but on the dissecting doctor.[2] He insists: "It would have lessened the flesh creeping effect of Mr Stevenson's sensational piece of fiction had he made himself acquainted with the true facts of the case. That the accusation against poor Dr Knox never amounted to more than mere vulgar *fama clamosa*. That the Crown Law Officers failed in eliciting one tittle of evidence upon which to found a case against him. That a Committee of leading Edinburgh citizens spared no pains for many days in weighing all the evidence, and in their Report entirely cleared and exonerated Knox from either knowledge of, or participation in, the Burke and Hare atrocities" (Rae 1964: 150). For Goodsir the doctor's status should put him beyond vulgar accusation and to suspect him is to put oneself on a different—less educated, suspect—side of society, in opposition to the "Crown Law Officers," the "leading Edinburgh citizens" who (Goodsir claims with less-than-perfect accuracy) made a distinction between Knox and his associates. To Goodsir, the issue is the "social" versus what is "other." But the former, associated through Knox with the body and corpse, is now inevitably contaminated with the rejected other. Respectable Edinburgh fixated on the unruly body, the corpse purveyed—and perhaps represented—by Dr. Knox. Thus, the disturbing resurrections, murders, dissections, and corporeal hauntings of Stevenson's "The Body Snatcher" bring to the fore elite Scotland's worries about identity.

This social obsession with the corpse in inappropriate circulation was peculiar to Scotland and reaches beyond this period.[3] Scots have inscribed their anxieties in texts from James Hogg's *The Private Memoirs and Confessions of a Justified Sinner* (1824) to Alasdair Gray's *Poor Things* (1992), and more recently in Christopher Wallace's *The Resurrection Club* (1999), Ian Rankin's *Resurrection Men* (2001), and Alan Warner's *Morvern Callar* (1995) and *These Demented Lands* (1997).

For Scotland, the bodily circulation of the deceased manifests old, deep, and ongoing concerns about cultural otherness. The late medieval and early modern interdependence between the regal "body politic" and "body natural" permeated Scottish mythologies of governance (Fradenburg 1991). Then with the 1603 union of crowns, the northern body politic found itself strangely housed cheek-by-jowl with that of England in the body natural of James VI and I. The 1707 merging of the two bodies politic in one parliament was often represented in contemporary debates as an equally problematic bonding into "one flesh" by marriage (Manning 2002: ch.1). In both cases, union constituted Scotland as inevitably the other in an unequal partnership. As a result, the former distinction of body politic and body natural was mapped onto the two still distinct nations, with the "body natural" assigned to Scotland. And that body was in no healthy state. Lacking representation as a body that was politic, Scotland seemed a walking corpse.

Cairns Craig has analyzed the ways in which the Scot oddly embodied through death represents cultural degradation (Craig 1996: ch. 2). Carol McGuirk and Douglas Mack have considered how Scots persistently disturb their heroic dead—specifically Robert Burns—in order to revivify current nationality (McGuirk 1994; Mack 1996). This chapter focuses on Scots' recognition, development, and circulation of otherness to give a value to not just Scottishness but also Britishness. The central figure in this exchange is the body that problematizes circulation both politic and natural—the corpse that walks.

Post-Union Scotland needed to find a body that was politic. Constituted as the bodily other—Sawney, the naked highlander, and so on—Scots had trouble achieving value through the market of reputation and money that was increasingly located in England. A number of late- eighteenth-century satirical prints (now in British Library collections) give us an insight into the situation: "Progress of a Scotsman," for instance, tracks a bare-assed Scotsman through various menial but opportunistic roles until he becomes a (suspected) Lord (Duffy 1986: fig. 98). During the eighteenth and nineteenth centuries, Scots circulated south and, perversely, climbed socially as bodily others and cultural outcasts (Fry 1992; Colley 1992). Soldiers, politicians, doctors—skilled operators at the margins of culture—for Britons they suppressed the difference that supposedly undoes community by placing themselves within society as markers of its boundary.

By 1826, however, opportunity seemed to have deserted the Scottish body politic. To protect English banks, Westminster sought to extend into Scotland legislation, which neglected current Scottish practice. This seemed to confirm Scots as secondary in the context of Union.[4] The circulations of English legislation to the north and Scottish bodies south produced the

Scots as lesser beings. Significantly, to Walter Scott they transformed the living body of Scotland into a cadaver, subject to dissection by junior English students. In his three protest letters written through the persona of "Malachi Malagrowther," Scott presents the nation as lying under the mandate *Fiat experimentum in corpore vili*—Experiment on this vile body (Scott 1826: 11).[5]

Dr. Knox constituted a problematic crux for this complex of ideas. Knox seems in some respects the prototypical Scot on the make (Roughead 1921: 78–80). Middle class, Knox climbed the ranks of meritocracy through his medical training. The discipline's most energetic researcher and popular teacher, he swelled his anatomy classes to a remarkable 504 students by 1828. But the doctor's public authority depended on easy access to cadavers for himself and those he taught. It was Knox's pressure on the market that raised prices and stimulated Burke and Hare to murder (Roughead 1921: 79–80). Indeed early in the very year that saw the activities of Burke and Hare, Knox had drafted a letter to Home Secretary Robert Peel, expressing concern that his supply was uncertain, often interrupted, and subject to legal impediment. At the same time his (apparently unsent) letter hedges his protest with an appeal for reserve: "I have ever been an advocate for the making of these matters as little public as possible" (Rae 1964: 62–3). "The Echo of Surgeon's Square" (*sic*) quotes Paterson, Knox's museum-keeper and sometime receiver of bodies, that "I had positive orders from the Doctor not to interfere at all with these men," and notes that Burke and Hare becoming troublesome, Knox directed Paterson to serve as intermediary—"he not being altogether over anxious of such visitors" (*Letter to the Lord Advocate* 1829: 7–8). Knox maintained his status by closing his eyes to the disgusting intrusions upon and illicit circulations of the very real but no longer social bodies that produced it.

Thus when the Burke and Hare scandal broke, Knox stayed mute. He did not speak of his work; he did not acknowledge any meaningful connection between himself and the murderers. Despite the fact that fresh and probably murdered corpses were what they constantly supplied, and as a doctor of ability this should have been clear to him, he insisted on his ignorance of the murderers' exploits. When pressured to respond, he did so in ways that tried to open a gulf between the politic doctor, and a fully othered Burke and Hare. A month and a half after Burke's execution, Knox presented himself (in a letter to the *Caledonian Mercury*) as a mere passive actor who risks "being imposed upon by those who furnish the material of their science to anatomical teachers" (Rae 1964: 98–99).

His establishment "happened" to be the one with which the murderers "chiefly dealt." He refers to his "situation," his "misfortune." It is "popular prejudice" that operates against him.

This last term, crucially, cuts away Knox's critics together with Burke and Hare. When an angry mob surged around his lecture hall, Knox addressed his students: "Gentlemen, . . . Do not be alarmed! . . . The assailants of our peace . . . are too cowardly in act to confront such a phalanxed body of gentlemen as I see before me. How little I regard these ruffians you may well judge" (Rae 1964: 92). Those who question Knox, who reveal his connection with the grotesquely natural body in the form of the executed Burke or his murdered and now dissected subjects, are themselves "ruffians." Knox "expected the excitement to subside, and that the better classes would never believe in so dire a motive as his connivance with criminal acts of fearful enormity, much less his associating with monsters of the deepest dye of infamy" (Lonsdale 1870: 80). The issue is association. The audience is "the better classes," and Burke and Hare are criminal monsters. To a man focused on his status, the murderers are, interestingly, "infamous." His critics Knox aligns with the murderers as manifesting the grotesque body natural in its divorce from the social. He insists that they are the vulgar bodily other opposed to a body politic represented by the doctor with his class of "gentlemen."

Unfortunately, Knox's detractors included those who were most certainly members of the official and legitimate community. For them, the cut between society and the other sliced a different way. If Knox tried to associate himself with Edinburgh's intellectual and social elite, they worked to distance the doctor. Perhaps predictably, the newspapers denied Knox the luxuries of silence and blindness, pushing him to recognize himself as the site of otherness. The *Caledonian Mercury* of 27 December 1828 stressed: "The conviction of Burke alone will not satisfy either the law or the country" (Rae 1964: 85). Two days later it persisted, invoking the polity against the particular: "All the anatomical teachers . . . and others who use cadavera for their classes . . . ought to be examined as to the manner in which they are accustomed to receive their subjects. And, in particular, the students and assistants . . . of one gentleman, whose name has unfortunately been too much mixed up with the late proceedings, ought to undergo an examination. . . . The present impression on the minds of the people is, that one gentleman stands in the same relation to Burke and Hare that the murderers of Banquo did to Macbeth. This impression . . . should induce him to demand an inquiry" (Rae 1964: 85).

For *Blackwood's*, "Christopher North" (John Wilson) similarly challenged Knox's blindness. He declared the doctor "the most unsuspicious and generous of surgeons that ever gave a bounty on the dead for the benefit of the living" (Wilson 1829: 383). Knox's carefully fenced activities, practiced by "gentlemen," are revealed as insistent otherness: "The system established and acted on in the dissecting-rooms of that anatomist is manifestly of the most savage, brutal, and dreadful character" (387). Knox's phalanx of gentlemen, cheering him against the mob, themselves have uttered a "savage yell within those blood-stained walls," and their voice "is no more to the voice of the public than so much squeaking and grunting in a pig-sty during a storm of thunder" (388). "The Ettrick Shepherd" (a ventriloquized James Hogg) marks the realignment of society and other across the activities and now the body of the unfortunate Knox: "Some writers, I see," he says, "blame the magistrates o' Edinburgh, and some the polish, and some the London Parliament House, for a' thae murders—but I canna help blamin', especially, Burke and Hare—and neist to them Dr Knox and his assistants" (389). The politic gentlemen of the press required Knox to speak his otherness. North declares: "Dr Knox stands arraigned at the bar of the public, his accuser being—Human Nature. . . . He is ordered to open his mouth and speak, or be for ever dumb." And Tickler bursts out, "Does he dare to presume to command all mankind to be mute on such a series of dreadful transactions!" (388).

Walter Scott understood the need for dissection so far that he concluded to Maria Edgeworth on 4 February 1829: "an unprejudiced person would have no objection to the idea of his own remains undergoing dissection, if their being exposed to scientific research could be of the least service to humanity" (Grierson 1932–37, vol. 11: 125). Yet he, too, separated Knox from the social order and preferred him to acknowledge his im/politic body. He told Edgeworth: "*Here* is a doctor who is able to take down the whole clock-work of the human frame, and may in time find some way of repairing and putting it together again; and *there* is Burke with the body [of his] murdered countrywoman on his back, and her blood on his hands, asking his price from the learned carcass-butcher" (128). "I cannot imagine," he added to his son on 11 January 1829, "[that he] can be exculpated." And Scott refused Knox the opportunity to maintain his discourse of professional surfaces. When Knox wished to deliver an address on dissections to the Royal Society, Scott (president since 1820) successfully opposed it, for "it is very bad taste [for Knox] to push himself forward just now" (Anderson 1998: 565). A few days later, asked to serve on a committee of "Mr. Knox's friends" to investigate "his late traffick with the West port," Scott refused "to lend a hand to whitewash this much to be suspected individual. . . . [H]e shall ride off on no back of mine" (571). Knox was expected to "make a defence" (566), and his refusal to engage the big issue distanced him even farther from society. His respectable surface itself came to image the othered body that problematized the Scottish body politic in a British context.

By trying to separate himself from the bodily otherness that produced his social being, Knox made visible that which he tried to hide. 1828 society was anxious to distance itself from Knox because his medical and criminal associations revealed not just the otherness of the body but also its uncanny movement that allowed the construction of the politic self. Sixteen years later, a student who would successfully integrate the personal and the political to become Sir Benjamin Ward Richardson, marked the curious disturbance in identity Knox forced on Scots: when Knox again taught in Scotland, in 1844, Glaswegians noted his presence and "would stare with all their eyes, and probably would turn away trying to conceal themselves as quietly, as if they had seen the devil" (Rae 1964: 131–32). For Scots, Knox's troubles revealed the constant cutting between self and other that gives the illusion of social being. His insistence on his continued public role prevented the amputation of otherness by the admission of guilt and by the social exclusion that should result. Instead, Knox manifested a wound through which otherness seeped into daily life. The doctor, with his never-buried corpses and professional success made it hard for Scots to avoid the knowledge that money and status were threatened by but also derived from the circulation of otherness. Knox's subjects enacted and he himself signified the worrisome reality that the uncanny Scottish body walks most energetically when Scots seek to advance through British systems.

Robert Louis Stevenson picked up this cultural complex, playing it across two mobile Scottish bodies and into England where they now circulate. "The Body Snatcher" (1884) at first establishes a society not unlike those favored by H. G. Wells and elsewhere in Stevenson. But in place of Wells's scientist, newspaper man, philosopher, or Conrad's Director of Companies and Accountant, Stevenson gives us an older group with perhaps a different cultural meaning. The George at Debenham, a pub that by its name and location seems to signify stability, order, Britishness, contains its landlord but also the undertaker, the degraded doctor, and the uncharacterized "myself." The landlord and undertaker mark the bounds of life, its inclusive, homey hospitality, and unhomey exile. The narrator's talent is to "[worm] out a story"—to control the discourse of the local by setting its margins (Stevenson 1884: 411). Fettes is the representative Scot: a doctor, a man of property, of education, an alcoholic. He stands apparently confined within this society—"by a mere continuance of living [he] had grown to be an adopted townsman" (405). But like Knox, Fettes constitutes the wound in the self-satisfied body politic that, here, is British culture.

At first, Fettes seems quite the reverse of the Scot circulating successfully in England. He is the town drunk. His "old, crapulous, disreputable vices, were all things of course in Debenham" (405): "He drank rum—five glasses regularly every evening; and for the greater portion of his nightly visit to the George sat, with his glass in his right hand, in a state of melancholy alcoholic saturation. We called him the Doctor, for he was supposed to have some special knowledge of medicine" (405). But more, Fettes "made no deductions" (407); he deliberately asked himself no questions about what he saw. Against his own diagnostic training, Dr. Fettes resists the mental movement that is analysis. Caught within stereotypes, static in his demeanor, he appears to represent the loss to Scottish subjectivity in its circulation south.

Strangely, this manifestation of delimited Scottishness appears even more completely in the hale and hearty Wolfe Macfarlane. Macfarlane is the official body of medicine, thoroughly recognized by this respectable English town: " 'He's come,' said the landlord. . . . 'He?' said I. 'Who?—not the doctor?' 'Himself,' replied our host" (406). Like Knox's most successful pupil, the William Fergusson who became Serjeant Surgeon to the Queen and president of the Royal College of Surgeons, Macfarlane is "in England . . . a celebrated physician who performs excellent surgery on the bodies of those that have enough money to meet his price" (Egan 1970: 11). Macfarlane is a professional and social triumph. Similar to Scotland's soldiers and her exported politicians, he manages England's deviance and profits therefrom. But Macfarlane, too, is delimited into a creature of surfaces. The narrator tells us: "Dr. Macfarlane was alert and vigorous. His white hair set off his pale and placid, although energetic, countenance. He was richly dressed in the finest of broadcloth and the whitest of linen, with a great gold watchchain, and studs and spectacles of the same precious material. He wore a broad-folded tie, white and speckled with lilac, and he carried on his arm a comfortable driving-coat of fur. There was no doubt but he became his years, breathing, as he did, of wealth and consideration" (408). Stevenson stresses that Macfarlane offers "a surprising contrast to . . . our parlour sot—bald, dirty, pimpled, and robed in his old camlet cloak" (408). But he too is a mere heap of clothes.

Macfarlane breathes "wealth and consideration"—not life. In fact, to one another, Macfarlane and Fettes each constitute the body that walks. Roused by Macfarlane's name, "Fettes became instantly sober." The narrator recalls: "We were all startled by the transformation, as if a man had risen from the dead" (406). When they meet, and Fettes names "Toddy Macfarlane!" "The London man almost staggered" (409–10). "'Fettes!' he said, 'you!' 'Ay,' said the other, 'me! Did you think I was dead too?'"

Each man effectively has buried himself in order to circulate in England —Macfarlane as the social success in the body politic, Fettes as its unfortunate failure. Brought together, however, they manifest an otherness brought out in Scotland by its professional involvement with England, and also free that same otherness within English culture. After their encounter and departure, it is the landlord, undertaker, and narrator who remain at the fireside, deducing in a way resisted by Fettes and Macfarlane, but that ultimately will reveal to England the social costs lurking in Scots who succeed as mere stereotypes. "Each man, before we parted," says the narrator, "had his theory that he was bound to prove" (411). The story he subsequently extracts from Fettes implicates not just Fettes but the teller himself, and points toward a national and British tale.

Together, Fettes and Macfarlane managed Mr. K—'s dissecting rooms. The younger Fettes is led by Macfarlane from complicity in body-snatching, to blinking at murder. Then Macfarlane is humiliated in front of Fettes by the mysterious Gray. Gray's name links him with those who finally exposed Burke and Hare, and his demeanor links him to the murders. One night, Macfarlane produces this man's corpse. It is suspiciously dead and never interred, and Macfarlane pressures the callow Fettes to accept it on the usual body-snatching terms. The discourse is crucial. K—'s policy is to "Ask no questions . . . for conscience' sake" (414). Macfarlane, another ambitious Scot, prefers "not to recognise" the first suspicious body (417). He insists upon this as a politic "man of the world" and trains Fettes in his avowed principles. When he deposits Gray's corpse, requires payment, and then splits the proceeds with his naïve accomplice, he plays on Fettes's ambition, talking to him again as "a man of the world" (421). This world, he declares, is peopled by "two squads . . . the lions and the lambs. If you're a lamb, you'll come to lie upon these [dissecting] tables. . . . [I]f you're a lion, you'll live and drive a horse like me, like K—, like all the world with any wit or courage" (422). Fettes accepts the body. The dissection that is supposed to bring understanding and thus support society is transformed into a "dreadful process of disguise" for both cadaver and social-climbing

Scot (423). And Fettes "began to plume himself upon his courage" (423). "I was an ass till I knew you," he declares to Macfarlane, "You and K— between you . . . you'll make a man of me" (426). Scots like K—, Macfarlane, and now Fettes circulate into social success and through the body politic at the price of death and silence.

But as the story goes on to make clear, suppression of the other transforms the social self that this suppression is supposed to protect and define. We have seen Fettes and Macfarlane disguised into stereotypes and mere surfaces by their circulation south and into the British body politic. Yet before their eruption into England, they already have been re-created by their silences into what they would deny. Complicit in Gray's murder, Fettes steps into the victim's monetary relationship with Macfarlane. Applauded by his partner for his politic behavior, Fettes boasts, "'Well, and why not? . . . It was no affair of mine. There was nothing to gain on the one side but disturbance, and on the other I could count on your gratitude, don't you see?' And he slapped his pocket till the gold pieces rang" (426). Not surprisingly, "Macfarlane somehow felt a certain touch of alarm at these unpleasant words." The attempt to enter the body politic at the cost of the body natural actually deploys Scotland's grotesque otherness.

Fettes's and Macfarlane's climactic visit to the rural graveyard merely confirms a narrative dynamic that questions and problematizes that of the nation, both Scottish and British. At dead of night, they resurrect a once-respectable woman who is now manifested as taboo through the death that exiles the body from social circulation. As the two set off for Edinburgh, the woman's corpse claims uncanny affinity with each: "it bumped from side to side; and now the head would be laid, as if in confidence, upon their shoulders" (429). The boundary between bodies politic and those excessively natural dissolves. When, terrified, they stop to inspect the corpse and confirm and delimit it as that of their excavated female subject, "The light fell very clear upon the dark, well-moulded features and smooth-shaven cheeks of a too-familiar countenance, often beheld in dreams of both of these young men. A wild yell rang up into the night; each leaped from his own side into the roadway; the lamp fell, broke, and was extinguished; and the horse, terrified by this unusual commotion, bounded and went off toward Edinburgh at a gallop, bearing along with it, sole occupant of the gig, the body of the dead and long-dissected Gray" (430). The circulation of Scots in the British body politic is possible only by the suppression of their otherness. But suppression deadens the circulating Scot, and thus paradoxically resurrects his affinity with the other. And since the Scot circulates south, the otherness that is Scottishness bears its taint and trouble only first to Edinburgh. Lacking any narrative intervention, the gig rolls crazily toward the city, through the story, and into the snug lounge of the George at Debenham. The Scottish body politic is always and already "burked," made away with silently in its own construction. Yet Scottish silence bodies forth its uncanniness through "myself," the English narrator now implicated as other by his naïve articulation of a northern tale.

Oddly, Robert Louis Stevenson disliked his own story. Although it was written in June and July 1881 (Swearingen 1980: 60), he withheld it from publication until the end of 1884 when he was under pressure to produce a Christmas tale for the *Pall Mall Gazette*. As early as June 1881, he told W. E. Henley he had had taken "a scunner" at it (i.e. felt nauseated by it; *Ltrs* 3: 200). He laid it aside, he wrote to Sidney Colvin on 3 July, "in a justifiable disgust, the tale being horrid" (*Ltrs* 3: 204). How horrid was it? Too horrid, it seems, for a Scot who not only was attempting to enter British systems of literary circulation, but also—after circulating his suffering body through the system of British doctors—was contemplating a return to Scotland. In June 1881, a Stevenson exiled by ill health and an opposition to respectable Edinburgh values sought election to the Edinburgh University Chair of History and Constitutional Law (*Ltrs* 3: 196). In late May 1881, Henley, after being present when Stevenson underwent a medical examination, reported that his lungs were basically all right but that "his nerves are all to pieces" (*Ltrs* 3: 183). Disturbed in mind and body, Robert Louis Stevenson sought a belated coherence within Scottish culture. But perhaps in this context, even for the counterculture RLS, his Scottish body too obviously revealed itself as other for social and personal comfort.

NOTES

1. Oliver S. Buckton notes how often the trope of the revenant appears in Stevenson's work and sees it as part of an occluded narrative of Victorian homosexuality (Buckton 2000: 23).

2. Scott argues that the tale's focus on the medical students emphasizes its critique of late-Victorian professionalism (Scott 1999: 119).

3. Interestingly, the English and Irish also suffered scandals of body-snatching and murder for the purposes of dissection, but these did not produce the same social concern. See for example Hubert Cole, 1964, *Things for the Surgeon: A History of the Resurrection Men* (London: Heinemann). Also Norman Adams, 1972, *Dead and Buried: the Horrible History of Bodysnatching* (Aberdeen: Impulse Books).

4. *The Parliamentary Debates,* vols. 14 and 15 (London: Hansard, 1826).

5. For a fuller analysis of the grotesque body in these letters, see McCracken-Flesher 1995/96.

REFERENCES

Anderson, W. E. K., ed. 1998. *Journal of Sir Walter Scott.* Edinburgh: Canongate.

Buckton, Oliver S. 2000. Reanimating Stevenson's Corpus. *Nineteenth-Century Literature* 55 (1): 22–58.

Colley, Linda. 1992. *Britons: Forging the Nation 1707–1837.* New Haven, CT: Yale University Press.

Craig, Cairns. 1996. *Out of History: Narrative Paradigms in Scottish and English Culture.* Edinburgh: Polygon.

Duffy, Michael. 1986. *The English Satirical Print 1600–1832: The Englishman and the Foreigner.* Cambridge: Chadwick-Healey.

Egan, Joseph J. 1970. Grave Sites and Moral Death: A Reëxamination of Stevenson's "The Body Snatcher." *English Literature in Transition* 13 (1): 9–15.

Fradenburg, Louise Olga. *City, Marriage, Tournament: Arts of Rule in Late Medieval Scotland.* 1991. Madison: University of Wisconsin Press.

Fry, Michael. 1992. *The Dundas Despotism.* Edinburgh: Edinburgh University Press.

Grierson, H. J. C., ed. 1932–37. *The Letters of Sir Walter Scott.* Repr. Vol. 11. New York: AMS.

Letter to the Lord Advocate, disclosing the accomplices, secrets, and other facts relative to the Late Murders. 1829. Edinburgh: np.

Lonsdale, Henry. 1870. *A Sketch of the Life and Writings of Robert Knox the Anatomist.* London: Macmillan.

Mack, Douglas. 1996. The Body in the Opened Grave: Robert Burns and Robert Wringhim. *Studies in Hogg and His World* 7: 70–79.

Manning, Susan. 2002. *Fragments of Union: Making Connections in Scottish and American Writing.* Houndmills, UK: Palgrave.

McCracken-Flesher, Caroline. 1995/96. Speaking the Colonized Subject in Walter Scott's *Malachi Malagrowther Letters. Studies in Scottish Literature* 29: 73–84.

McGuirk, Carol. 1994. Burns and Nostalgia. In *Burns Now,* ed. Kenneth Simpson. Edinburgh: Canongate Academic.

North, Christopher [John Wilson]. 1829. Noctes Ambrosianae No. XLI. *Blackwood's Edinburgh Magazine* 25 (150) (March 1829): 371–400.

Rae, Isobel. 1964. *Knox the Anatomist.* Edinburgh: Oliver and Boyd.

Roughead, William. 1921. *Burke and Hare.* Toronto: Canada Law Book Company.

Scott, Patrick. 1999. Anatomizing Professionalism: Medicine, Authorship, and R. L. Stevenson's "The Body Snatcher." *Victorians Institute Journal* 27: 113–30.

Scott, Walter. 1826. *Thoughts on the Proposed Change of Currency. . . .* In *Sir Walter Scott's Thoughts on the Proposed Change of Currency.* 1972. New York: Barnes & Noble.

Stevenson, Robert Louis. 1884. "The Body Snatcher." *Pall Mall Gazette* (Christmas Extra). Thistle Edition, second issue. Vol. 8. 405–30.

Swearingen, Roger G. 1980. *The Prose Writings of Robert Louis Stevenson, A Guide.* Hamden, CT: Archon Books; London: Macmillan.

Stevenson's Unfinished Autopsy of the Other

ILARIA B. SBORGI

In 1850, Robert Knox published *The Races of Men,* in which he argued that race is "everything" in human history. Twenty years earlier, when he was an anatomy professor in Edinburgh, Knox had been implicated in the Burke and Hare scandal, accused of buying murdered bodies for his anatomy classes. Robert Louis Stevenson alludes to this scandal in his short story, "The Body Snatcher," referring to Knox as "K—," the extramural "teacher of anatomy" whom he designates by this letter, as "his name was subsequently too well known" (Stevenson 1884: 78). Anatomy, autopsy, mystery, the supernatural, but also, though indirectly, anthropology and race are woven together in a text that blends fiction, local history, and folklore. Here, I propose a cross-reading of this Scottish story through Stevenson's *Strange Case of Dr. Jekyll and Mr. Hyde* and his Polynesian novella, "The Beach of Falesá." These three texts, apparently so different from one another, share a similar narrative structure: their open endings dramatize the narrative process itself, its strategies of containment, and that which is left out for the narrative to be cohesive and complete,[1] a residue that inevitably returns. This "return of the repressed,"[2] brings to the fore a number of issues brewing in the literary and cultural context of Stevenson's writing (the jingoism of imperial culture, the "other side" of scientific progress, the encounter with native cultures, the consolidation of the middle-class and its professions, the debate on realism and the novel), but also stages a significant feature of Stevenson's work: its probing the boundaries of representation.[3]

Gray's Anatomy

In 1807, the University of Edinburgh established a Department of Legal Medicine, responding to the long-felt need of preparing doctors for this kind of specialization. Shortly after, the Edinburgh medical school numbered among its students scientists whose work would soon become famous in other related disciplines—the above mentioned Robert Knox, the ethnologist James Cowles Prichard,[4] and Charles Darwin. Stevenson's story, "The Body Snatcher," is set in Edinburgh and features medical students attending Knox's extramural school of anatomy during the Burke and Hare murders (1827–28). Knox was then very popular and his lectures were crammed with students. His constant need of fresh bodies to be dissected in the classroom and the fact that his assistants paid for them in cash and asked no questions, induced many to consider him the patron of the Burke and Hare crimes.

Patrick Scott (1999: 114) sees Stevenson's retelling of the story as a critique of "Victorian professionalism's smugness and self-delusion." Stevenson's critical strategy in "The Body Snatcher," Scott argues, "is to redirect blame for Edinburgh's most famous murders, from criminality to respectability" (115). Rather than focusing on the murderers or the victims, Stevenson centers his story on Dr. Knox's anatomical assistants. The protagonists are two budding professionals, Fettes and Macfarlane, responsible for supplying K—'s lectures with corpses and for supervising students in the dissecting rooms.

One early November morning, Fettes identifies "the sad merchandise" brought to him by his usual providers: "I know her I tell you . . . She was alive and hearty yesterday" (Stevenson 1884: 80). Once alone, he is seized by a fit of panic: what would happen if K—'s students also recognized Jane Galbraith? Yet, when he seeks for the advice of his immediate superior, Wolfe Macfarlane, the latter convinces him to keep quiet. This episode functions as a prelude to their murderous complicity. When Macfarlane kills Gray—the stranger who exercised "a very remarkable control" over him—and gets rid of his body by bringing it to K—'s classroom, his argument is indisputable: "Mr. Gray is the continuation of Miss Galbraith; you can't begin and then stop; if you begin, you must keep on beginning" (85).

Gray's body is thus bought by Fettes and dissected by K—'s students. Ironically, Patrick Scott notes, Stevenson names the corpse after the standard first-year medical textbook, *Gray's Anatomy* (1858). In "The Body Snatcher" the alive Mr. Gray makes only a brief appearance. His mysterious influence over Macfarlane is the cause of his death, yet, just before he disappears, his looks and manners are carefully described: "This was a small man, very pale and dark, with coal-black eyes. The cut of his features gave a promise of intellect and refinement which was but feebly realised in his manners, for he proved, upon a nearer acquaintance, coarse, vulgar, and stupid" (82).

Gray's description echoes, and at the same time contrasts with, the discourse of contemporary criminology that claimed a connection between criminal behavior and physical appearance. In 1876, only a few years before the publication of "The Body Snatcher" (1884), the Italian doctor Cesare Lombroso published *L'uomo delinquente* in which he argued that criminals are a distinct physical and biological type, and that they can therefore be identified by observing certain physical traits. At the time of Stevenson's writing, although Lombroso's ideas were not yet widely circulated in England, "theories of degeneration and the view of crime as a throwback to an earlier, more primitive phase of human development were prevalent" (Danahay 1999: 21).[5]

If we look at the table of contents of *l'uomo delinquente,* we will see that there is a major section dedicated to the anatomy and anthropometry of criminal bodies, studied in each of their parts. With respect to Lombroso's criminology, Mr. Gray's appearance is similarly dissected. We are given his stature, his complexion, the color of his eyes. Yet what follows is a sequence of contradictory terms. If the first part of Gray's description seems to correspond to the physical traits of Lombroso's criminal (he is "small" and "dark"), the following segment suggests the opposite ("the cut of his features gave a promise of intellect and refinement"). Gray also looks as if he could be intelligent and refined. The word "promise" underlines the ambiguity of his appearance. On the one hand it conveys a sense of positive expectation; on the other it implies the uncertainty of something that is not yet realized, and, in Gray's case, never will be. His manners are not refined but "coarse, vulgar, and stupid." Gray looks like a criminal and yet could be a gentleman; he looks like a gentleman and yet acts like a brute. Interestingly, this seems to anticipate Stevenson's double par excellence.

The Anatomical Theater

In his introduction to Stevenson's *Tales of Terror,* Robert Mighall (2002: xv) argues that "The Body Snatcher" prefigures the concerns that Stevenson would later develop in Jekyll and Hyde. Mighall's analysis focuses on the analogies between the protagonists of the two stories. Similarly to Henry Jekyll, Fettes and Macfarlane are professional men who lead "double lives." The apparent dichotomy between their "daylight respectability and nocturnal transgression" (Mighall 2002: xvii), however, is presented ironically. For his "day's work," Fettes "indemnified himself by nights of roaring blackguardly enjoyment" (Stevenson 1884: 79). This ironic twist, I believe, aptly depicts the character's "cold, light, and selfish" personality but also reminds us that "part of his 'service' to his employer involves supplying the corpses upon which the anatomy school depended" (Mighall 2002: xvi).[6] The difference between daylight activities and nocturnal vices, professional distinction and "blackguardly excess" collapses in the "hours before winter dawn" when, "after a night of turbulent pleasures," Fettes "would be called out of bed . . . by the unclean and desperate interlopers who supplied the table" of the dissecting room (Stevenson 1884: 78).

Yet rather than focusing on these professional gentlemen let us look at their foes, and compare the above-mentioned description of Mr. Gray with the nondescription of Mr. Hyde. In *Strange Case,* Hyde's appearance exceeds vision. We never actually see him; rather, we perceive him through the characters who meet him. Hyde is "particularly small, and particularly wicked looking" (Stevenson 1886: 118). He emanates a "haunting sense of unexpressed deformity" (121), but no one is capable of saying what makes him look so horrible. Only Jekyll gives a more detailed account. First of all, he tells us what it *feels like* to be Hyde: "I was conscious of a heady recklessness, a current of disordered sensual images. . . . I knew myself, at the first breath of this new life, to be more wicked, tenfold more wicked, sold a slave to my original evil" (160). In addition, Jekyll provides a few more details to Hyde's indefinite appearance: his hands are "corded and hairy," he gnashes his teeth (172, 173).[7]

Both Hyde and Gray are identified with their bodies. In "The Body Snatcher" Gray features chiefly as a corpse, the object of anatomical dissection. In *Strange Case,* Hyde is repeatedly associated with brutal physicality. Moreover, their bodies are located in similar spaces. Gray is destined for K—'s dissecting rooms, Hyde is repeatedly seen entering Jekyll's home from the laboratory's back door. And, significantly, this laboratory was formerly an "anatomical theatre." The doctor, Stevenson writes, "had bought the house from the heirs of a celebrated surgeon; and his own tastes being rather chemical than anatomical, had changed the destination of the block" (122).[8]

In their respective theaters, Gray and Hyde are *anatomized* by scientific discourse, and in particular by theories of criminal degeneration. Cesare

Lombroso believed that propensity toward crime was the result of atavism, a reversion to a more primitive state of human development, and that such evolutionary "throwbacks" were "born criminals," the most violent criminals in society.[9] Gray's appearance, as we have seen, has affinities with Lombroso's criminology but also seems to complicate its equation between physical traits and criminal behavior. Edward Hyde, on the other hand, seems to confirm it. "Evil," Jekyll writes in his statement of the case, "had left on that body an imprint of deformity and decay" (161). Throughout the story, Hyde is perceived by the other characters as "hardly human," "ape-like," "something troglodytic." This terminology also echoes Victorian fears of biological degeneration and racial decline, sparked by Darwin's evolutionary theory.[10] Hyde's behavior, David Punter (1979: 241) suggests, can be read as "an urban version of 'going native,'" a threatening regression to a savage, primitive state.[11]

Stephen Arata (1996: 33–53) gives an interesting reading of Hyde's "degeneracy." From the first publication of Stevenson's novel "readers have noted the similarities between Lombroso's criminal and the atavistic Mr. Hyde" (34). The Italian doctor's descriptions of criminal deviance corresponded to long-standing prejudices of the British middle class, which equated criminality with the working classes. However, if we consider degenerationism as class discourse, "we need to look up as well as down." For theorists such as Lombroso and Max Nordau,[12] degeneration was also endemic to the decadent aristocracy and the "cultured aesthetes" (Arata 1996: 35).[13] This sheds a peculiar light on the "ape-like" Mr. Hyde, who, for his proximity to the refined Henry Jekyll, could also be seen as a representation of the decadent aesthete, his rooms in Soho being furnished "with luxury and good taste" (Stevenson 1886: 121). Arata's analysis thus carefully proceeds to show how Stevenson's text gradually transforms Hyde from a *savage* criminal into a criminal *gentleman*. Throughout the story, Jekyll's friends despise Hyde and at the same time recognize him as one of "their own."[14] Hyde is not just ape-like but also a "sedulous ape," capable of imitating Jekyll and living in his world. Most critical accounts of the novel "have with good reason focused on the social and psychological pressures that lead Jekyll to become Hyde. Yet Stevenson is also concerned with the reverse transformation. That is, the novel details the pressures which move Hyde closer to Jekyll" (Arata 1996: 39).

Mr. Gray's promising looks and poor manners seem to anticipate both Jekyll and Hyde. The "cut" of his features recalls Dr. Jekyll's semblance of refinement. His pallor and dwarfish dimensions, combined with the adjective "'dark'"—which seems to refer to his complexion but could also indicate the color of his hair—and his "coal-black eyes," evoke Edward Hyde.[15] At the same time however, Gray could be seen to embody their reciprocal transformations into each other. The sequence of binary oppositions that characterize his ambiguous appearance could be read as a sign of the gradual fluidity by which Jekyll becomes Hyde and Hyde becomes Jekyll. Or, more precisely, Hyde becomes Jekyll and Jekyll becomes Hyde. For if we read Gray's description in relation to Utterson's memories of the young Dr. Jekyll ("He was wild when he was young . . . Ay it must be that; the ghost of some old sin"; Stevenson 1886: 109), the series of transformations recounted in *Strange Case* seems to have a different beginning, or perhaps no beginning at all. The fixation of these metamorphoses into one character and one body, Mr. Gray's, suggests the impossibility of distinguishing between the two, and preludes to the strangeness of a no longer univocal (and unequivocal) self.[16]

In the Pacific

"The Beach of Falesá" is quite a different story. Set in the South Pacific on a fictional island, it recounts the rivalry between two traders, Wiltshire and Case, for the monopoly of commerce with the natives. The narrative is told in the first person by Wiltshire, befriended upon his arrival by Case and convinced by him to marry a native woman, Uma. This proves to be insidious advice, for Uma is "tabooed," that is, a proscribed person with whom the other islanders are forbidden to interact. A few months earlier, Case had spread a negative report on her so as to isolate her and have her all to himself, but Uma had refused him. When Wiltshire comes along he thus decides to use her against his rival in order to neutralize his business. To convince Uma, Case tells her that Wiltshire wants her even though she is tabooed. Yet Wiltshire and Uma uncover his treacherous machinations. Case has used village politics and local superstitions for his own ends. The only way for Wiltshire to counter his rival's influence over the village is to uncover the superstitions he has created, starting with "Tiapolo," the devil, and a mysterious cave in the jungle.

In her reading of "The Beach of Falesá," Roslyn Jolly (1999: 463) views Stevenson's Polynesian novella as a "generic hybrid" that disrupts the "conventional polarization of the domestic and the exotic in the Victorians' fictional mapping of their world, and challenges notions of racial as well as fictional purity." The "moral center" of the tale is the protagonist's

"commitment to a mixed-race marriage and family" (Jolly 1999: 463).
Wiltshire and Uma's marriage challenges the European taboo of miscegenation. Their children are racially hybrid—a hybridity, Jolly observes, that
reflects and is reflected by the text's mixing of different literary genres.
Through his marriage, Wiltshire's colonial adventure gradually becomes a
domestic tale. His language blends with Uma's pidgin English, his family
life gradually prevails over his rivalry with Case and at the same time provides its solution. The marriage between Wiltshire and Uma "initiates a
series of transgressions, both generic and ideological, whereby the story
calls into question the boundaries that separate romance and realism, adventure and domesticity, masculinity and femininity, white skin and brown"
(Jolly 1999: 482).

Throughout Wiltshire's narrative, racial differences are repeatedly fore-
grounded. The corrupted Captain Randall, "squatting on the floor native
fashion, fat and pale, naked to the waist, grey as a badger, and his eyes set
with drink" (Stevenson 1892: 8) seems to belong to a Victorian study on
degeneration. His regression to a primitive state, however, stands in sharp
contrast with the natives themselves, repeatedly associated with animals,
nature, and innocence, as in a study of Victorian anthropology.[17] Corruption is represented by white colonists, whereas the islanders are seen as
children. The paternalism of these anthropological views is strong and yet
Britain's civilizing mission seems far away. Uma's bearing at her mock
wedding is that of a countess—"no even mate for a poor trader like myself," Wiltshire comments (12). His imagery, Jolly notes (1999: 481), "substitutes differences of class for differences of race, with the result that
expected hierarchies are inverted." This doesn't dismantle his racist views,
nor do his views cancel his insights, rather, "insight and blindness coexist
side by side." Wiltshire and Uma's racially hybrid children embody the
complexity of this coexistence.

The Return of the Repressed

If the setting and content of "The Body Snatcher," "The Beach of Falesá"
and *Strange Case of Dr. Jekyll and Mr. Hyde* are remarkably different, all
three are characterized by a narrative structure that highlights its residue,
that which each story has tried to eliminate but could not. In "The Body
Snatcher," it is the body of the murdered Gray, which returns to Fettes and
Macfarlane in a country graveyard where they go to steal the cadaver of a
woman.[18] Just as they are about to open the coffin, Macfarlane accidentally

hits the lamp with a stone, and they have to finish their business in the dark. Going back to town, their gig jumps "among the deep ruts," the dogs howl as they go by, and the "thing" between them keeps falling "now upon one and now upon the other," giving them "creeping" chills. Fettes begins to fear "that some unnatural miracle had been accomplished, that some nameless change had befallen the dead body" (Stevenson 1884: 90). His colleague has similar fears, and they stop the horse to look at the contents of their big sack, only to discover the remains of the man Macfarlane has murdered. The story ends thus: "A wild yell rang up in the night; each leaped from his own side into the roadway; the lamp fell, broke, and was extinguished; and the horse, terrified by this unusual commotion, bounded and went off toward Edinburgh at a gallop, bearing along with it, sole occupant of the gig, the body of the dead and long-dissected Gray" (91).

Just as the rest of the story, this final scene is permeated by a gothic atmosphere (cf. Mighall 2002a). It is dark and the only light is that of a lamp, which goes out twice. We don't know who yelled. It could have been either of the men, and yet both jump off the gig. We don't know if they made a mistake, if they got the wrong body, or if something supernatural happened as they were stealing it away. We don't know what happens to the body, we are left with the sound of a horse galloping away in the dark. An open ending, as confirmed by the story's beginning when Fettes encounters Macfarlane after many years and asks him, "Have you seen it again?" (Stevenson 1884: 76).

In "The Beach of Falesá" Wiltshire concludes his first-person narrative with a rhetorical yet pressing question. "I'd like to know where I'm to find the whites?" he asks, worried about finding white men who would marry his half-caste daughters (71). His children are of a mixed race, and Wiltshire knows that they are much better off on a Polynesian island than in a "white man's country." Yet what bothers him most are the girls because he does not want them to marry native men. Hence the question and its summing up of Wiltshire's racial and domestic contradictions. There is nobody that thinks less of half-castes than he does, and yet these are his kids; to stay with them he gives up his dream of opening a public house in England. Again, it is the return of the repressed in the shape of the other's body, but this time it is a colored body. The issue of racial miscegenation is at stake throughout the narrative, and at the same time it is constantly repressed by Wiltshire who cannot reconcile his sentiments for Uma with his low esteem of her race. His marriage with her does not change his racist views of the natives, even though his sentiments prevail on such views. Yet with his daughters the issue of miscegenation comes up again,[19] he cannot remove it from his life, and it cannot be resolved within the story's narrative framework. The final question leaves the story open, Wiltshire's racism may be uncovered and undermined, but the issue of race continues with his children.

In a parallel reading of these open endings, a number of issues are brought to the fore. As in *Strange Case of Dr. Jekyll and Mr. Hyde,* the theme of the return of the repressed is actualized not only by the content but also in the narrative structures of these stories. Their open endings underline and magnify the inevitable reiteration of this return.[20] The body of the other (Hyde, Gray, Wiltshire and Uma's children), can be removed but not deleted. It leaves a trace within the self that struggles to get rid of it. In the case of Jekyll and Hyde, it is that which remains of the struggle: Hyde is found in the cabinet, Jekyll is nowhere to be seen. Moreover, the discourse of science is used to cut up the other's body in the anatomical theater of Victorian ideology: Hyde's body is analyzed, separated, and distinguished from that of Jekyll as in Lombroso's criminology; Gray's is disassembled by K—'s students as in a lesson of anatomy; Wiltshire and Uma's children are divided into two races, as in a study of evolutionary anthropology. Yet in all three cases, the "autopsy" performed on these bodies remains unfinished. The three texts cannot complete their analysis, they fall short of the other's perspective, a lack that is reiterated by their narrative strategies and devices. The other may be ignored but the materiality of his/her body inevitably reappears within the text, confronting the self's vision and the very notion of boundary.[21]

In his study of *fin-de-siècle* degeneration theories, Stephen Arata (1996: 19–20) notes that if "the degenerate subject was himself a text to be read . . . degeneration theory made apparent, often unwittingly, the troubling multivalence of bodily signs." Only a "professional scrutiny" could unravel texts that were so "notoriously hard to interpret." This "encouraged certain aggressive forms of reading," which were accompanied by "equally aggressive modes of writing," or "strong representations," whose aim was to make visible "what cannot be easily perceived" (Arata 1996: 21). The bodies of Gray, Hyde, and Wiltshire and Uma's racially hybrid children, cannot be deciphered nor textually contained. They resist interpretation (and representation), or rather, represent textual undecidability,[22] challenging the very possibility of making things "easily perceived."

Barry Menikoff observes that Stevenson's stories "often end abruptly," yet the inconclusiveness of their endings is both "dramatic and symbolic—the

completion of the action on one level, and its subversion on the other."
For Stevenson, Menikoff writes, "uncertainty and ambiguity are not only
part of our language but conditions of our existence" (1993: 37). Moreover,
if "strong representations," as Arata (1996: 22) points out, "were centrally
concerned with revealing character," a territory "traditionally covered by
the realist novel," Mr. Gray, Mr. Hyde, and the Wiltshire children could
also be read as examples of Stevenson's challenge to the fixity and arbi-
trariness of norms and categories—be they a reflection of middle-class values or of the literary dominance of realist fiction.[23] In portraying these
undecidable bodies and their disruptive effects on narrative closure, Stevenson, I believe, brings to the fore the nonrepresentability of the other,
thus representing otherness paradoxically—to begin with, the otherness of
(his) writing.

NOTES

1. On the concept of narrative "containment strategies" see Jameson 1981.

2. The concept comes from Freud, according to whom human civilization, and in
parallel the child's introduction to society, are based on the repression of primitive
instincts and desires. In Freudian terminology, the "uncanny" (cf. "Das Unheimliche,"
1919) is a manifestation of the return of the repressed, the revelation of what is secret
and concealed.

3. This paper, originally presented at the "R. L. Stevenson: Writer of Boundaries"
conference, has been rewritten since, benefiting from the intellectual nourishment of
the other conference papers. Since it would be very difficult to acknowledge all my
debts, I wish to thank collectively all the other conference participants for contributing with their analyses, insights, comments, and lovely conversations to my study of
Stevenson's work.

4. Also famous for his influential work on moral insanity, *Treatise on Insanity* (1835).

5. The idea of degeneration was a major cultural paradigm of the Victorian *fin de
siècle* supported by a wide range of scientific approaches: from criminology to evolutionary anthropology, medicine, sociology, physics, psychology, psychiatry, and sexol-
ogy. See also Arata 1996 (11–32) and Mighall 2002b (145–61).

6. Commenting on this passage, Mighall (2002: 169 n9) suggests that "Fettes resembles Jekyll in these details, and may have been something of a trial run for this
more famous physician."

7. In his edition of *Strange Case* Martin A. Danahay publishes an extract from Darwin's *The Expression of the Emotions in Man and Animals* (1872) and highlights the
"similarities between Darwin's descriptions and Mr. Hyde's behaviour," in particular
his "savage" snarl (1999: 160).

8. Dury (1993: 122 n4) sees the laboratory as an "unheimlich space," and notes that
"Jekyll is here associated with dissection, the destruction of the single whole."

9. "Atavism." *Glossary. Terms of Criminology.* http://www.crimetheory.com/glossary.
htm (March 2003).

10. Edwin Ray Lankester, one of Darwin's followers, argued that "we are subject to general laws of evolution, and are as likely to degenerate as to progress" (Lankester 1880: 59–60). In Stevenson's short story, "Olalla" (1885), the protagonist's description of her family's degeneration strikingly resembles Lankester's words: "Man has risen; if he has sprung from the brutes, he can descend again to the same level" (Stevenson 1885: 127).

11. While supporting imperial claims such as Britain's "civilizing mission," British evolutionary anthropology confronted Victorian society with the otherness of natives, their alleged inferiority and primitiveness. After the mid-Victorian years "the British found it increasingly difficult to think of themselves as inevitably progressive; they began worrying instead about the degeneration of their institutions, their culture, their racial 'stock'" (Brantlinger 1988: 230).

12. Nordau (1892) claimed that degenerates were not always criminals but often authors and artists.

13. Olalla's family is an example of aristocratic degeneration.

14. See Jane Rago's chapter, "*Dr. Jekyll and Mr. Hyde:* A 'Men's Narrative' of Hysteria and Containment," in this volume. Rago views Hyde as both integrated within and disruptive of Jekyll's homosocial professional world.

15. Throughout the story, Hyde is repeatedly associated with darkness, both physical and moral: he is dusky and hairy; he has "black" secrets. At a first glance, Olalla's brother, Felipe, resembles Hyde and Gray for his small stature and "dusky hue" (Stevenson 1885: 98), yet his characterization is not marked by the same ambiguity. Felipe is "animal-like" but there is no sense that he could pass for a gentleman.

16. Dury (1993: 40–41) notes similar internally contradictory descriptions in *Dr. Jekyll and Mr. Hyde* of Utterson, Jekyll, Carew, and Hyde's housekeeper.

17. Stevenson's anthropological views were influenced by Edward Tylor, one of the prominent figures of late Victorian anthropology. In his book, *Primitive Culture* (1871), Tylor equated native cultures with primitive stages of Western civilization. On Stevenson's relation to British evolutionary anthropology see Ambrosini (2001) and Julia Reid's chapter, "Stevenson, Romance, and Evolutionary Psychology," in this volume. Reid's analysis highlights Stevenson's interest in contemporary evolutionary theories but also his originality with respect to the idea of evolutionary progress.

18. See Caroline McCracken-Flesher's chapter, "Burking the Scottish Body," in this volume. McCracken-Flesher also sees "The Body Snatcher" as a representation of the return of the repressed. In her analysis, Gray's corpse and, in the end, Fettes himself, represent the buried otherness of Scottish national identity.

19. Marina Warner (1996) notes how Wiltshire and Uma's daughters are marked by race, whereas their brother has the opportunity to go to Auckland for his education. This reflects the nature/culture polarity that excludes women from socioeconomic alliances—in this case, from the construction of whiteness and its privileges.

20. Oliver Buckton (2000) looks at the central role of the "reanimated" corpse in *The Wrong Box, Treasure Island, The Master of Ballantrae,* and *The Ebb-Tide,* and its "contaminating effects" on narrative closure. Buckton links the inevitable return of the unruly corpse to unspeakable homoerotic desires, but also to the disruption of the agenda of nineteenth-century realist fiction. For further discussion on narrative strategies of containment and the forestalling of narrative closure see Peter Brooks (1984).

21. On the liminality of Stevenson's writing and its textual boundary-crossings, see Richard Ambrosini's chapter, "The Four Boundary-Crossings of R. L. Stevenson," in this volume.

22. I adopt this term from Barbara Johnson's *A World of Difference*. Johnson links textual undecidability with Barthes' notion of the "writerly," i.e. a "hypothetical state of textual resistance" to "ideological norms of meaning" (Johnson 1987: 26). Undecidability is thus not a form of textual entropy leading inevitably to lack of meaning (and interpretation), but "the place where a new passage through otherness can be opened up" (Johnson 1987: 31).

23. See Stevenson's essays, "A Gossip on Romance" (1882), "A Note on Realism" (1883), "A Humble Remonstrance" (1884), all reprinted in Norquay (1999).

REFERENCES

Ambrosini, Richard. 2001. *R. L. Stevenson: La poetica del romanzo*. Rome: Bulzoni Editore.

Arata, Stephen. 1996. *Fictions of Loss in the Victorian Fin de Siècle*. Cambridge: Cambridge University Press.

Brantlinger, Patrick. 1988. *Rule of Darkness. British Literature and Imperialism, 1830–1914*. Ithaca, NY: Cornell University Press.

Brooks, Peter. 1984. *Reading for the Plot*. New York: Knopf.

Buckton, Oliver S. 2000. Reanimating Stevenson's Corpus. *Nineteenth-Century Literature* 55 (1): 22–58.

Danahay, Martin A. 1999. Introd. to *The Strange Case of Dr Jekyll and Mr Hyde*, by Robert Louis Stevenson. Ed. Martin A. Danahay. Peterborough, Canada: Broadview Press.

Dury, Richard, ed. 1993. *The Annotated Dr Jekyll and Mr Hyde*. Milan: Guerini Studio.

Jameson, Fredric. 1981. *The Political Unconscious: Narrative as a Socially Symbolic Act*. Ithaca, NY: Cornell University Press.

Johnson, Barbara. 1987. *A World of Difference*. Baltimore: The Johns Hopkins University Press.

Jolly, Roslyn. 1999. Stevenson's "Sterling Domestic Fiction," "The Beach of Falesá." *Review of English Studies* 50 (200): 463–82.

Knox, Robert. 1850. *The Races of Men: A Philosophical Inquiry into the Influence of Race Over the Destinies of Nations*. London: Henry Renshaw.

Lankester, Edwin Ray. 1880. *Degeneration: A Chapter in Darwinism*. London: Macmillan.

Lombroso, Cesare. 1876. *L'uomo delinquente*. Milan: Hoepli.

Menikoff, Barry. 1993. Introduction. In *Tales from the Prince of Storytellers*, by Robert Louis Stevenson. Ed. Barry Menikoff. Evanston, IL: Northwestern University Press.

Mighall, Robert. 2002a. Introduction. In Stevenson. 2002.

———. 2002b. Diagnosing Jekyll: The Scientific Context to Dr Jekyll's Experiment and Mr Hyde's Embodiment. In Stevenson. 2002.

Norquay, Glenda. 1999. Introd. to *R. L. Stevenson On Fiction*. Ed. Glenda Norquay. Edinburgh: Edinburgh University Press.

Punter, David. 1979. *The Literature of Terror: A History of Gothic Fictions from 1765 to the Present Day*. London: Longman.

Scott, Patrick. 1999. Anatomizing Professionalism: Medicine, Authorship, and R. L. Stevenson's "The Body Snatcher." *Victorians Institute Journal* 27: 113–30.

Stevenson, Robert Louis. 1884. "The Body Snatcher." In Stevenson 2002. 73–91.

———. 1885. "Olalla." In Stevenson 2002. 95–134.

———. 1886. *Strange Case of Dr. Jekyll and Mr. Hyde.* In Dury 1993.

———. 1892. "The Beach of Falesá." In Stevenson 1996. 3–71.

———. 1996. *South Sea Tales.* Ed. Roslyn Jolly. Oxford: Oxford University Press.

———. 2002. *The Strange Case of Dr Jekyll and Mr Hyde and Other Tales of Terror.* Ed. Robert Mighall. London: Penguin Books.

Tylor, Edward B. 1871. *Primitive Culture: Researches into the Development of Mythology, Philosophy, Religion, Art, and Custom.* 2 vols. London: John Murray.

Warner, Marina. 1996. Siren, hyphen; or, the maid beguiled: R. L. Stevenson's "The Beach of Falesá." In *A Talent(ed) Digger: Creations, Cameos and Essays in Honour of Anna Rutherford,* ed. Hena Maes-Jelinek, Gordon Collier. and Geoffrey Davis. Amsterdam: Rodopi.

Voices of the Scottish Empire

MANFRED MALZAHN

Among the diverse representations of imperialism in late nineteenth-century literature, one image in Robert Louis Stevenson's "The Isle of Voices" is surely a contender for maximum symbolic suggestiveness. The short story describes a beach infested with a cacophony of speech, produced by a sorcerers' league of nations whose members remain entirely invisible and largely incomprehensible to the native inhabitants of an island where foreign wizards turn leaves into dollars. In spite of the tale's fantastic nature, its gist is hardly at odds with Stevenson's nonfictional accounts of the South Seas. As other writers likewise recognized, the essentially surreal nature of imperial enterprise and its results called for means of artistic expression that went beyond the bounds of Victorian realism.

Scottishness could be of distinct advantage in this respect, for the blending of the bland with the quaint, the mundane with the fantastic, and the commonplace with the grotesque had a long standing in the Scottish literary tradition. Moreover, a Scottish author's look at Empire was likely to combine an inside with an outside perspective: a duality rooted in the more than proportional participation of Scots in British imperial ventures on the one hand, and the abortiveness of previous Scottish attempts at colonization on the other. If there was in any sense a Scottish Empire, as the title of a recent book by Michael Fry suggests, it had no visible bodily contours on a map where Scotland itself bore the same color as England. If a politically disembodied Scotland remained distinct from and distinguishable to the rest of the world, its chief mode of existence was that of a collective voice, given public utterance by individuals such as Burns, Scott, or indeed Stevenson.

It is perhaps notable, then, that readers will find Scottish sounds conspicuously unspecified in the above-mentioned colonial mélange of "all tongues of the earth" (Stevenson 1893: 179) on the Isle of Voices, whereas French, Dutch, Russian, Tamil, and Chinese are singled out by name. It is even more noteworthy, though, that readers of Stevenson's South Sea fiction in general will look in vain for Scots among its major characters. When Scottish voices are heard, they tend to appear as marginal or accidental. A prime example is a letter from Clydeside whose homey and "quite conventional" (Stevenson 1892c: 15) tones ring out from a dead man's chest on the half-submerged brig *Flying Scud* in *The Wrecker*. An anonymous "Glasgow voice" features in the frame narration of this novel (4, 5), while Edinburgh provides an episodic touch of local color to the main narrative, whose American-born protagonist is glad to escape from the "somewhat dreary house" (37) of his Edinburgh relations. All told, Stevenson's fictional South Seas may well strike us as a virtually Scot-free setting.

This discrepancy between Imperial reality and its literary reflection is perhaps best explained in such psychological terms as repression or displacement, and I would suggest that reference be made not only to individual but also to Scottish national psychology. Scottish involvement in colonial rule clashed with a Scottish complex in which, by Stevenson's lifetime, Burns's fiery rants about equality and brotherhood of men had become just as essential constituents as the popular egalitarian saw, "We're a' Jock Tamson's bairns," loosely translatable as "We are all children of Father Phallus." However, the "politically aloof" stance of leading eighteenth-century thinkers (Calder 1981: 682) had paved the way for a neutralization of the Scottish Enlightenment's radical intellect, by means of a bigamous marriage of convenience to sentimentalism and commercialism. Scottish thought, feeling, and behavior could thus at the same time cohabit and betray each other quite merrily.

The nineteenth-century Scottish psychogram, which I have thus begun to sketch, would not be complete without a representation of that special alliance between Tory sentiment and unorthodox ideas that could generate rebelliousness in conservative quarters. If Stevenson's liberal reputation coexisted peacefully with his essential identity as a Tory who was "much more logically conservative than we generally credit him with being" (Harvie 1981: 112), then we can see in him the contradictory but logical product of a culture in whose artistic imagination or popular mythology the figures of Bonnie Prince Charlie, John Knox, Lenin, and Christ may appear aligned with each other, to stand united against all kinds of Philistines and Pharisees.

To Stevenson, the Reverend Dr. Hyde of Honolulu, whom he lambasted for hypocritically finding fault with Father Damien's self-sacrifice in a leper colony while living in safety and ease himself, surely ranked among the latter. Yet, members of a group that Stevenson in "Father Damien" apostrophized as "a sect—I believe my sect, and that in which my ancestors laboured" (Stevenson 1890b: 338), could do quite differently in similar conditions. Consider the following description of the tiny Hawaiian island Niihau, bought in 1863 from a native king by the widow Elizabeth Sinclair from Glasgow, and managed in her spirit ever since, "on three happily compatible principles. It is a pastoral estate, carrying 15,000 cattle, 7000 sheep and a stud of Arabian horses. It is a Calvinist community, with the Sabbath strictly observed, drinking forbidden and smoking discouraged. It otherwise consciously preserves Hawaii's traditional way of life, obliterated elsewhere. The people, 12 families numbering more than 200, farm and fish as their ancestors did. Their language is Hawaiian. Tourists are banned" (Fry 2001: 235).

Here, apparently, is proof of a resilient Scottish myth that has been summed up as the tenet "Our empire would have been a nice empire" (Easton 1991: 261). In the article from which this slogan is taken, however, the epigrammatic neatness of the formula serves merely to set up a clear target for debunking before the author duly proceeds to adduce substantial evidence against the contention. The conclusion is that Scots of any creed could be as greedy and unscrupulous as any other colonialist, and that individual exceptions were just that. Even the Pacific-Platonic paradise described above is likely to evoke mixed feelings: Stevenson, while busy creating his own Scoto-imperial microcosm in Samoa, would certainly not have found all aspects of life on Niihau equally to his liking. In his South Sea fiction, elements of utopianism are embedded in a more ambiguous and ironic vision, which at the same time engenders and defies attempts to brand his work as either pro- or anticolonial.

The most obvious case in point is certainly the story "The Beach of Falesá," which has received widely divergent ratings on the political correctness scale. A history of such disparate critical reactions has been given by Katherine Linehan, who herself reads the tale as a "critique of colonialism" that "incorporates a remarkable dimension of feminist insight into the parallel workings of racial and sexual domination"; almost in the same breath, however, she points out her desire "to emphasize how much care is needed in reaching conclusions about the social views transmitted in the story" (Linehan 1990: 407). If this makes the critical stance look ambivalent, then such ambivalence is arguably more appropriate than any one-sided labeling of the text or the author as either colonialist or anticolonialist. Both inferences would seem to me undue simplifications that ignore contradictory elements in the plot as well as in the narrative structure.

The plot intertwines the fates of three main characters, two English traders called Case and Wiltshire, and a Polynesian woman called Uma, whom Wiltshire marries twice: first in a farcical ceremony that dupes her by a travesty of legal form, and the second time for real, in atonement for the former deception. In the given historical context, the second of these marriages appears a lot more unusual than the first. White men without white women would find ways to satisfy their needs, and women of the South Sea islands had at one point in the eighteenth century even been considered as an exportable commodity, in a kind of mail-order scheme aimed at redressing a gender imbalance in the Australian colonies, where the lack of females prevented quite a few soldiers from setting up that widespread "warped colonial version of the household" (Rees 2002: 41), which substituted a consort conveniently referred to as "wife" for a legally wedded spouse.

If Wiltshire is thus a follower of custom in negotiating a local comfort woman, he soon finds that his sense of fairness militates against the personal deception involved. "My conscience smote me when we joined hands" (Stevenson 1892a: 17), says the narrator about the mock wedding that Uma takes seriously; nonetheless, he also testifies to other pangs of conscience caused by the discovery that his feelings for his wife interfere with the standards of behavior he had deemed proper for a man in his position: "To speak to her kindly was about more than I was fit for; I had made my vow I would never let on to weakness with a native, and I had nothing for it but to stop" (21).

This conflict between a morally sound and a socially deformed voice of conscience is not the only feature of the story that invites a comparison with Mark Twain's *The Adventures of Huckleberry Finn*, a book Stevenson praised in an 1885 letter to J. A. Symonds as "the whole story of a healthy boy's dealings with his conscience, incredibly well done" (*Ltrs* 5: 80). The Huck who states "It was fifteen minutes before I could work myself up to go and humble myself to a nigger" (Twain 1884: 72) is similar to the Wiltshire who calls upon the aid of a missionary with the words "I want you

to help me make it up to a person I've deceived" (53). Both characters
show that they are capable of rising above the prejudices of their respective group; but both also remain trapped in those prejudices and in the
language that expresses them. Huck still uses the term "nigger" like Wiltshire uses the term "Kanaka." All that the two have apparently learned
is to make exceptions, as Wiltshire shows when at the very end of his
account, he talks about the daughters Uma bore him: "They're only half-
castes, of course, and there's nobody thinks less of half-castes than I do;
but they're mine, and about all I've got" (106).

In both stories, the ending is a final challenge to the reader, and there
are two different ways of misreacting. One is to elevate the protagonist to
the status of an enlightened reformer, rebel, or revolutionary, who has
rejected racist ideology outright. This is clearly nonsensical in the light of
evidence such as that quoted above; and there is plenty more to prove
John Wiltshire's kinship to Huckleberry Finn who, as I have argued elsewhere, "remains recognizably a product as well as an integral part of his
surroundings" (Malzahn 1998: 169). The other extreme, however, is equally
untenable: to take the protagonist's apparent relapse for an invalidation of
all he has said and done before. If Huck and Wiltshire have done justice
to their essential humanity in the course of the events, the reader is finally
called upon to test the scope of his or her own by giving due credit to the
act itself—regardless of the agent's lasting imperfection—or even more so
in full view of it. Someone who does good because he knows it to be good
may after all be less deserving of praise than someone who does good in
spite of a false consciousness telling him that it is bad.

I would hence suggest to see the resolution of "The Beach of Falesá,"
like the final section of *Huckleberry Finn,* as an ending that mars the pro-
pagandistic value of the tale at the same time as saving its artistic integrity, by setting up a complex structure in which reader responses are first
elicited and then obstructed or sabotaged by contradictory injunctions.
The result is a double bind: if the reader gets at all emotionally involved,
then he or she has been led to an identification with the narrator that is
subverted by the ending. This makes both Twain's novel and Stevenson's
story a good example of the true work of art that pleases to attract, and
irks to affect. Such aesthetic sequentiality has been cast in more metaphysical terms by V. S. Naipaul, who is reported to have said that "good
writing canceled out what had existed before. Even the second half of
a book canceled out the first half, and each book canceled out the previous one and existed as a reincarnation of the earlier work" (Theroux 1998:

157). One only needs to add that both selves inform each other simultaneously as well as sequentially, in order to grasp the anachronistic tension especially in first-person narration, where the new and the old self vie for control.

In setting up just such a paradoxical structure within the framework of a short story, Stevenson's "The Beach of Falesá" gives us an ironic inversion of the Scottish incongruity between egalitarian theory and discriminatory practice; it shows an Englishman who can think wrong and act right, and thus could well have been addressed with words said to Oscar Wilde's Lord Henry in *The Picture of Dorian Gray*: "You never say a moral thing, and you never do a wrong one" (Wilde 1891: 20). This is of course a blatantly erroneous assessment of Wilde's English aristocrat and his fatal speech acts, but it might indeed serve to sum up Stevenson's English punter, whose racist clichés are delivered as obsessively as Lord Henry's nihilistic witticisms. However, Wiltshire's bigoted patter may drone over, but it never completely drowns out the voice of his heart. This is partly due to narrative technique; in the third-person narration of *Dorian Gray*, Lord Henry's inner voice remains a mystery to the reader, while with the first-person narrators Wiltshire and Huck Finn, the inner and the outer voice are seen to work against each other in a contrast that in turn works against complete reader identification with the protagonist, and against the reduction of the tale to a simple moral.

The distancing of the reader from the character thus invited is bound to incite questions regarding the distance between character and author. Obviously, Stevenson is at the very least as remote from Wiltshire as Sam Clemens or even Mark Twain are from Huck Finn. Nonetheless, Stevenson's choice of narrator in "The Beach of Falesá" has a very personal significance, for the author can here be seen as crossing a boundary not only in the sense of an "attempt to reach inside the mind of an alien personality" (Hammond 1984: 90) but through entry into the consciousness of a character who incarnates at least one of his very own prejudices. In other stories, Englishmen of Wiltshire's type give occasion for fairly unmixed feelings, ranging from a passing contempt to an intense disgust at that epitome of loathsomeness, the Londoner Huish in *The Ebb-Tide*.

In nonfictional writings, too, Stevenson has left no doubt that the very last thing he wanted to hear in the South Seas was a Cockney voice with its metropolitan-proletarian cockiness. While a Kipling might portray such demotic irreverence of England's lower orders in a sympathetic manner, Stevenson tends to pick up on the negative effect of sneers and jeers:

In the South Seas, for instance, contains a passage dwelling on a "sense of kinship" between Polynesians and Scots, and terminating in the assertion that "the presence of one Cockney titterer will cause a whole party to walk in clouds of darkness" (Stevenson 1896: 15). In his view, courtesy toward the islanders should govern European behavior on their territory, as an expression of respect for what he characterizes as the native population's "fairness and simplicity" (Stevenson 1892b: 69). Stevenson, in short, found the Wiltshires of this world hard to take, especially in a South Sea context. The writing of the story thus seems to have been a conscious or unconscious self-examination of Stevenson's capacity to do what Wiltshire does in the story: to cut through layers of bias to the individual worth at a human being's core. At least in this respect, Uma is to Wiltshire what Wiltshire is to Stevenson.

If, however, in "The Beach of Falesá" Wiltshire and Stevenson show a similar readiness to let personal appreciation override generic disrelish, then they will by the same token also show comparable limitations to their broadmindedness. For this deduction, there is indeed some interesting intertextual evidence. Wiltshire's aforementioned suspicion of half-castes parallels the authorial stance toward Mac, a minor character in *The Wrecker*. As "a north of Ireland man, between Scotch and Irish" (Stevenson 1892c: 194), he is difficult to fathom for his shipmates on *The Currency Lass*: "his passions, angry and otherwise, were on a different sail-plan from his neighbours'; and there were possibilities of good and evil in that hybrid Celt beyond their prophecy" (206). The formidable Attwater, in *The Ebb-Tide*, is described as a different kind of hybrid with an equally ambivalent nature: his "complexion, naturally dark, had been tanned in the island to a hue hardly distinguishable from that of a Tahitian; only his manners and movements, and the living force that dwelt within him, like fire in flint, betrayed the European" (Stevenson 1894: 290).

Attwater, the prototype of Conrad's Kurtz, is not merely a civilized man gone savage; his is the savage face of civilization, as well as the barbaric face of religion. Both of these are belied by the voice of a man who, according to the protagonist Herrick, "laughs like God" (334). Attwater himself stops short of claims to be the deity, but he does pose as a divinely inspired voice in the wilderness, where the belief in his mission sustains him. Others will scream like wounded animals, or stammer like terrified infants; Attwater remarks on this with disdain, while he carries on talking in the stentorian tones of a hellfire-and-brimstone preacher: "I never gave a cry like yours. Hay! It came from a bad conscience! Ah, man, that poor diving-dress of self-conceit is sadly tattered! To-day, if ye will hear my voice. To-day, now, while the sun sets, and here in this burying-place of brown innocents, fall on your knees and cast your sins and sorrows on the Redeemer" (311). As Huish's attempt to destroy Attwater's face with vitriol fails, the sermons and the atrocities go on in the same oxymoronic symbiosis.

In the context outlined above, this fictional creation of a Scottish writer surely asks for a Scottish reading. While being as dangerous as Duncan Mackiegh, the blind catechist in *Kidnapped*, Attwater combines the non-chalant verbosity of Wilde's English aristocrats, expressed in one-liners such as "One isn't a fatalist for nothing" (367), with the grim earnestness and the biblical rhetoric of Scott's Covenanters. It is thus certainly legiti-mate to see here yet one more form of hybrid mixture as being branded "explosive." Mackiegh is likewise a compound creature, whose villainy is a deviation from the norm of behavior that David Balfour finds in the Highlands. In the pattern of the novel, this links an imported creed with departures from a chivalric and tribal code of conduct. When David Bal-four violates this code by berating his hosts because they play cards for money, he comes to realize the incongruity: "And indeed it must be owned that both my scruples and the words in which I declared them, smacked somewhat of the Covenanter, and were little in their place among wild Highland Jacobites" (Stevenson 1886: 334).

The association between Highlanders and South Sea islanders in Ste-venson's mind can hardly escape any reader of his oeuvre at large, but if he was perhaps "prone to overplay parallels between Samoan ways and those of Highland clans" (Furnas 1981: 135), the juxtaposition highlights the blend of an idealizing with a condescending perspective. It has been argued that "there is nothing in the South Sea Island stories to counter the view that, for Stevenson, the natives were simple, passive, incapable of effective resistance" (Gilmour 1983: 192). This is devious logic based on unwarranted ideological expectations of literature, and blatant misread-ings of literary text: the contention, for example, that Stevenson pays "no attention to Wiltshire as a white man with racist tendencies" (Gilmour 1983: 191) must seem patently absurd in the light of the foregoing analysis.

As regards the grain of truth in the general accusation, one would have to consider that the post-1745 Highlanders of *Kidnapped* and *Catriona* are likewise the victims of history, or the anachronistic remnants of a doomed heroic age, whose death-throes produced commensurately final and futile efforts to "save an unsavable clan" (Stevenson 1890a: 242). These words are from Stevenson's South Sea poem "The Feast of Famine," and it is in narrative poetry that Stevenson commemorates the warlike past of the South Sea people. The ballad I quoted contains another oblique image of colonial conquest, telling of the destruction of one island clan by another, whose warriors come "with death and fire in their hand" (242). However, the parallel and dichotomic alignments existing in Stevenson's worldview allow nations, cultures, and tribes to stand as ciphers for one another in his imaginative writing, as well as generating nonfictional similes such as: "The rank and file of the white nationalities dared each other, and sometimes fell to on the street like rival clansmen" (Stevenson 1892b: 130).

Stevenson's imaginative world thus appears to be a metamorphic one in which any permutation is possible: as Edinburgh can take on the shape of Dr. Jekyll's London, South Sea wizards can stand in lieu of European colonialists, and an English trader can be taken for a representation of his Scottish author. Likewise, Scotland, which Stevenson in a letter to Sidney Colvin in August 1893 called "the blessed, beastly place" (*Ltrs* 8: 159), can surface as the "lovely and detested scene" of *The Ebb-Tide* (Stevenson 1894: 197). The shape of the figure depends on the coloring that the Protean voice of the storyteller assumes, in filling a narrative space with creatures of his own creation. The Scottish Empire of his mind is neither a utopian model nor a dystopian critique; rather, it is an attempt to give a body or a face to a baffling and multifaceted reality. In the resulting ambivalence of its literary products, this attempt is not altogether irrelevant to the judgment that Stevenson passed on colonial fact: "the nearest we can come towards understanding is to appreciate the cloud of ambiguity in which all parties grope" (Stevenson 1896: 218–19).

Nonetheless, we can sense even underneath all the ethnic and aesthetic obfuscation of Stevenson the artist a fundamentally straightforward ethical and practical stance of Stevenson the man. As William J. Scheick has noted, the writing that grew out of Stevenson's perception of the scene around him implies a judgment not only upon what he observes but upon the observer himself as a living part of the tableau. Scheick reads "The Isle of Voices" as a warning of material and artistic selfishness: "no man should be a self-centered island of greed and . . . no art should try to be a self-centered island of aestheticism devoid of ethical influence on human behavior" (Scheick 1992: 148). This moves Stevenson's art dangerously close to Victorian orthodoxy, and it is thus a conclusion from which I would try to dissuade any thinking undergraduate. Yet I am ready to agree that Stevenson himself is present in this story, too: for after all, was he not trying to convert the leaves of impressions he gathered in the South Seas and imprinted onto the leaves of his books into the money he needed to keep his Samoan chiefdom going?

In another respect, too, Keola's magical moneymaking forays in "The Bottle Imp" correspond to authorial flights of fancy, requiring ever-new departures from the material here and now in the interest of perpetuating it, with the fear that one departure too many may cut the traveler off from the home fire he tries to feed. Both colonial and literary enterprise depend on the willingness of individuals to take that risk, and literary exile doubles it. The disembodied voice of Empire must thus carry at least an undertone of anxiety about its status and influence: Keola, for instance, knows that "white men are like children and only believe their own stories" (Stevenson 1893: 168–69). Consequently, the voice of the bodiless Scottish Empire can hardly be expected to engage in plain moralizing. The absence of moralizing, though, has to the best of my knowledge never prevented any work of art from raising or examining serious moral issues, nor indeed any person from being moral and acting morally.

REFERENCES

Calder, Angus. 1981. *Revolutionary Empire. The Rise of the English-Speaking Empires from the Fifteenth Century to the 1780s.* London: Jonathan Cape.

Calder, Jenni, ed. 1981. *Stevenson and Victorian Scotland.* Edinburgh: Edinburgh University Press.

Easton, Norman. 1991. The Empire that Never Was. In *The End of a Regime? Scottish-South African Writing Against Apartheid.* Ed. Brian Filling and Susan Stuart. Aberdeen: Aberdeen University Press. 261–70.

Fry, Michael. 2001. *The Scottish Empire.* East Lothian, Scotland: Tuckwell Press; Edinburgh: Birlinn.

Furnas, J. C. 1981. Stevenson and Exile. In Calder 1981, 126–41.

Gilmour, Peter. 1983. Robert Louis Stevenson: Forms of Evasion. In *Robert Louis Stevenson.* Ed. Andrew Noble. Vision Press: London; Totowa, NJ: Barnes & Noble.

Hammond, J. R. 1984. *A Robert Louis Stevenson Companion. A Guide to the Novels, Essays, and Short Stories.* New York: Macmillan.

Harvie, Christopher. 1981. The Politics of Stevenson. In Calder 1981. 126–41.

Linehan, Katherine Bailey. 1990. Taking Up With Kanakas: Stevenson's Complex Social Criticism in "The Beach of Falesá." *English Literature in Transition* 33 (4): 407–22.

Malzahn, Manfred. 1998. "It All Happened Right Out of the Books": Romantic Imagination at Work in *The Adventures of Huckleberry Finn.* In *Romanticism and Wild Places: Essays In Memory of Paul Edwards.* Ed. Paul Hullah. Edinburgh: Quadriga. 165–75.

Rees, Siân. 2002. *The Floating Brothel: The Extraordinary True Story of an Eighteenth-Century Ship and Its Cargo of Female Convicts.* London: Review.

Scheick, William J. 1992. The Ethos of Stevenson's "The Isle of Voices." *Studies in Scottish Literature* 27: 143–49.

Stevenson, Robert Louis. 1886. *Kidnapped*. Edinburgh Edition. Vol. 12.

————. 1890a. "The Feast of Famine." *Ballads*. Edinburgh Edition. Vol. 14. 217–242.

————. 1890b. "Father Damien: An Open Letter to the Reverend Doctor Hyde of Honolulu from Robert Louis Stevenson." Edinburgh Edition. Vol. 11. 335–55.

————. 1892a. "The Beach of Falesá." Edinburgh Edition. Vol. 19. 153–285.

————. 1892b. *A Footnote to History: Eight Years of Trouble in Samoa*. Edinburgh Edition. Vol. 25.

———— (with Lloyd Osbourne). 1892c. *The Wrecker*. Edinburgh Edition. Vol. 17.

————. 1893. "The Isle of Voices." Edinburgh Edition. Vol. 19. 153–285.

———— (with Lloyd Osbourne). 1894. *The Ebb-Tide*. Edinburgh Edition. Vol. 19.

————. 1896. *In the South Seas*. Edinburgh Edition. Vol. 20.

Theroux, Paul. 1998. *Sir Vidia's Shadow. A Friendship Across Five Continents*. London: Hamish Hamilton.

Twain, Mark. 1884. Ed. Sculley Bradley et al. 1977. *Adventures of Huckleberry Finn: An Authoritative Text, Backgrounds and Sources, Criticism*. 2nd edition. New York: Norton.

Wilde, Oscar. 1891. *The Picture of Dorian Gray*. In *The Works of Oscar Wilde*. 2000. Leicester: Abbeydale Press.

Stevenson and the Property of Language

Narrative, Value, Modernity

ROBBIE B. H. GOH

"If you adopt an art to be your trade, weed your mind at the outset of all desire of money," Stevenson declares (1888b: 181). He is possibly exaggerating for dramatic or rhetorical purposes: he seems to violate his own totalizing injunction on numerous occasions, judging by his frequent mentions of the pecuniary pressures and considerations surrounding his own writing. More than this, many of his works foreground or begin with various kinds of financial transactions—inheritance and its thwarted or deferred fulfillment, economic competition, penury as a threat to art and to one's moral character, and other such scenarios—that become crucial to the furthering of the plot.

Stevenson's own career and life seem to exhibit a dualistic attitude to money. Menikoff (1984a: 94) observes that "as mercenary as [Stevenson] appears in his correspondence with McClure, Scribner's, and Cassell, he nonetheless retained an integrity, almost an innocence, about the process of artistic creation." This artistic "innocence" often manifests itself as a sense of the special moral and social duty of the writer, one that somehow had to transcend the baseness of everyday life: The writer should "tell of the kind and wholesome and beautiful elements of our life; he should tell unsparingly of the evil and sorrow of the present, to move us with instances; he should tell of wise and good people in the past, to excite us by example; and of these he should tell soberly and truthfully, not glossing faults, that we may neither grow discouraged with ourselves nor exacting to our neighbours. So the body of contemporary literature, ephemeral and feeble in itself, touches in the minds of men the springs of thought and kindness, and supports them . . . on the way to what is true and right" (Stevenson 1881: 46).

In all this, the writer is somehow to steer clear of the motivation of "profit," which only leads to "a slovenly, base, untrue, and empty literature" (41). Yet in Stevenson's quasi-autobiographical account of the writing process, "A Chapter on Dreams," he acknowledges that the process of writing is very much a "business," in which the writer's "financial worries" and his "eye to the bank-book" are in large part responsible for transforming his private dream-content into the polished and consumable product of "a considerate story" (Stevenson 1888a: 131, 135).

Stevenson's narratives are the site in which he plays out the dualities of both a financial and literary nature, working out ambivalent feelings toward the necessity of money (and of earning it through popular modes of writing) on the one hand, and a repugnance of money and its corrupting influences (contrasting with a moral ideal of literature) on the other. Many of Stevenson's narratives reflect these concerns, and among these "The Bottle Imp," *Treasure Island*, and *Kidnapped* have recently attracted scholarly analysis of the interpenetrations of textuality, ethics, and finances (McLaughlin 1996; Wood 1998; Sorensen 2000). These studies have emphasized the ways in which Stevenson's "ambiguous aesthetic" works toward "actively deconstructing binaries" of aristocratic morality vs. "nongentlemanly" expedience, valuable "gold" standards vs. corrupt "silver" ones, precommercial sign systems vs. commercialized "textualization[s] of value" (Wood 1998: 61–62; Sorensen 2000: 281). In such narratives, Stevenson is seen as negotiating between opposing literary and financial value systems, such that "domestic romance . . . becomes inseparable" from "consequences" and "profit and loss"; and the criteria for evaluating "serious" literature also accommodate the need for writing to "furnish a living wage" (McLaughlin 1996: 178; Wood 1998: 79).

There is clearly a close relationship between language and money, two of the principle media of modern society—although not the relationship of a simple homology. Sorensen (2000: 292) emphasizes the historical and contextual particularities of both linguistic and monetary systems; language is not only functionally different from money in that it is capable of "generating money," but it is also true that "different languages have different values" in the unequal polities and economies of different regions. Thus problematized, the relationship between language and money cannot merely be that of analogous equivalence; and accordingly, Stevenson's literary project cannot rest on the acknowledgment and demonstration of "the overwhelming reality of the market" (Wood 1998: 76). Stevenson's acute awareness of the material conditions governing linguistic and financial exchange was very much rooted in the politics of place, in the unequal cultural transactions between fringe and dominant positions (the Highlands, the Pacific islands, natives, itinerant traders, laborers, and artists on the one hand; and the Lowland cities, European commercial networks, white men, owners of capital and property on the other). He was interested, not in the sweeping equivalences ultimately effected by the market but rather in the processes of negotiation and transformation involved in linguistic as well as financial exchange. His acceptance of the ubiquitous nature of the market was tempered by an acute awareness of the boundaries of individual cultures, values, beliefs, and dominant narratives; commerce motivated transactions across these boundaries but did not automatically or mechanically guarantee their success. Languages and narratives were not only a model of exchange but also an important tool of that exchange, and played a significant part in guaranteeing relative success or failure.

Stevenson's account of political and cultural contact (between advanced and less-advanced societies) thus followed the model of commercial exchange, in which both sides were indelibly marked and transformed by the process: if the producer has to suit his product to the tastes and judgments of the consuming public, he also in various ways influences and shapes their tastes and behavior. This co-determining relationship fitted Stevenson's own sense of the author's interaction with the literary market: On the one hand a seller who had to "live by his writing," the author was in many ways also a preceptor, moral influence, and guide: he expresses "a whole experience and a theory of life," contributes in some positive way to "the sum of sentiments and appreciations which goes by the name of Public Opinion or Public Feeling," and in so doing, renders a "service to the public" (Stevenson 1881: 43–44, 47, 49). Stevenson's theory of the literary market thus cuts right across the generic boundaries of "high" and "low" writing by focusing on the very practical consideration of communicative reach: If a debased and amoral form of commercial writing was valueless, a truly elitist and rarified mode of writing was not serviceable either, because however high its moral tone might be, it could not influence the public if it was not read. Hence his lament about the "rare utterances of good men," which (while potentially an "antidote" to the ill influence of bad writers) "[lie] unread upon the shelf" (44).

Stevenson's reluctant and cautious laissez-faireism, which he records in his critique of socialism in "The Day After Tomorrow,"[1] together with his emphasis on discourse as both a model for and instrument of modern commercial society, places him in a Scottish tradition of social thought stemming from thinkers like Adam Smith and (to a lesser extent) David Hume. As much as Smith defended free commerce from the monopolistic ambitions and interventions of rulers and nations, he was aware of the possibilities of inequality and abuse. As a moral guide to the self-interestedness of commercial transactions, Smith offers the principle of an "impartial spectator": "In the race for wealth, and honours, and preferments," the individual may strive as hard as he can, commensurate with the "indulgence of the spectators"; the moral limits of commercial competition are strained where the individual does something to lose this "indulgence" (Smith 1759: 183). It is this possibility of exchanging positions through imaginative sympathy that guarantees fair play: for Smith, moral judgments require the possibility of the spectator entering into the place of the agent "by the imagination," and "changing places in fancy" with the latter (Smith 1759: 2, 3). For Smith, too, literary and dramatic discourses were the appropriate paradigms for such exchanges, as he elaborates in his *Lectures on Rhetoric and Belles Lettres*: "When the sentiment of the speaker is expressed in a neat, clear, plain and clever manner, and the passion or affection he is possessed of and intends, by sympathy, to communicate to his hearer, is plain and cleverly hit off, then and then only the expression has all the force and beauty that language can give it" (Smith 1748: 127).

Such textual interactions require accommodations from both sides if a successful meeting of values is to occur; the communication of "sympathy" requires control and clearness on the part of the writers, just as it requires imagination and engagement in readers. Where the writer or agent is unable to moderate his passions, he loses the sympathetic engagement of the reader or spectator: thus Smith insists that an individual who experiences some extremely violent passion must "flatten . . . the sharpness of its natural tone" if he is to communicate it effectively to others and expect them to give their sympathies (Smith 1759: 38).

Notions of "harmonious" and "agreeable" accommodations run throughout Smith's account of language and polite letters, even extending to phonetic shifts in the English language ("the melody of sound") as speakers and listeners gradually adjust speech toward producing more pleasing sounds (Smith 1748: 15–16, 21). In this he differs significantly from his contemporary theorist of commercial society, David Hume, who while agreeing that "intercourse of sentiments . . . in society and conversation" played a role in forming "some general unalterable [moral] standard," also thought that "the heart takes not part entirely with those general notions" (Hume 1772: 229). More skeptical about the extent to which the individual submitted his behavior to the court of public opinion, Hume's poetics accordingly stressed a "sublimity," an authorial "force of imagination" that was to carry the reader's (passive and acquiescent) sensibilities (Hume 1777: 433). In reading and criticism, he emphasizes the role of the "great judges" of literary worth in influencing the tastes and opinion of "the public" (Hume 1777: 433). This corresponds with the emphasis he places on the "good policy of the magistrate" in stimulating industry, discouraging vicious luxury, and thus guaranteeing the moral tone of commercial society (Hume 1752: 40). In contrast, Smith's theory of commercial society, like his poetics, relied on the accommodations made by individuals in the course of everyday transactions that collectively forged the consensual values and standards required for social harmony.

Stevenson's views on the complex morality and geopolitics of financial exchange, and on the role of language in these contexts, are allegorized in "The Beach of Falesá", a work that foregrounds various kinds of financial transactions but has not been the subject of close reading on those terms. The protagonist of the piece, Wiltshire, a white trader who is caught in the horns of a moral, ethnological, and commercial dilemma, is arguably a proxy through whom Stevenson works out his complex views of cultural contact and the market. In the process, Stevenson demonstrates that the art of "retailing"—not merely the isolation of a smaller piece of goods for sale and consumption ("retaille"), but also the packaging of a unit of narrative for similar purposes[2]—is a central process of the emerging global market and its society.

Wiltshire's mercantilist career closely parallels his ethnological, cultural, and linguistic encounters. In the opening chapter of the tale, he is inserted simultaneously into a new job and shop ("station"), a new society with a peculiar set of social relations and rituals, a new domestic arrangement (involving a fake marriage to a native woman), and a new set of market conditions. Language is the agency through which he is placed in these various settings: it is Case's deceptions that have ruined Wiltshire's trade on Falesá (and that of his predecessors), and acting as translator he also brokers the marriage between Wiltshire and Uma.Case, the arch-merchant who exploits linguistic differences as well as he plays on market differentials, capitalizes on Wiltshire's lack of "the native" tongue to foist on him a marriage with an "excommunicated" girl, which then also effectively cuts Wiltshire off from trade with the islanders (Stevenson 1893: 119, 145).

Case simultaneously exploits Uma's lack of English to maneuver her into position: He only pretends to tell Wiltshire about the excommunication, and calms his anxieties about "the word marriage" by supplying a sham wedding service "read from . . . an odd volume of a novel" (141, 120, 123).

Case's cunning and manipulative actions later in the story are prefigured in his linguistic flexibility near the beginning: "He could speak when he chose fit for a drawing room; and when he chose he could blaspheme worse than a Yankee boatswain and talk smut to sicken a kanaka" (117). Unlike others who butcher the name of the French priest Father Galuchet (as "Galoshes"), Case "always gave it the French quirk" (132). His close association with the "negro" Black Jack, and his marriage to a Samoan woman, no less than his easy interactions with the Falesá islanders, make him appear the spokesperson for racial and cultural integration. This familiarity with local conditions, customs, and languages seems initially to be part of his strength as a trader, who after all is in the business of relationships and social interactions. In contrast, Wiltshire appears almost bigoted and reactionary in his commentary on the "strange idea" that the islanders count Black Jack (or for that matter "a Chinese"!) as "a white man" (120), and has no thought of marrying a native woman until Case plants the idea in his head.

Yet in the course of the narrative, Case's cultural and linguistic flexibility is shown to be symptomatic of a lack of inherent values, a moral and social rootlessness that allows him to mimic and simulate different positions. His past and origins are a mystery ("No man knew his country," 117), and he is described in terms of contrary or opposite attributes: apparently of "good family," he is yet "accomplished" in vulgar card and magic tricks; a "lion" in courage, he is ratlike in "cunning" (117). Essentially motile and lacking stable attributes, Case is the embodiment of a ruthless and unprincipled opportunism: "The way he thought would pay best at the moment, that was Case's way; and it always seemed to come natural and like as if he was born to it" (117).

This depiction of Case also corresponds to Stevenson's indictment of unscrupulous financial adventurers in other writings. Francis Villon in "A Lodging for the Night" is a type: He sees an acquaintance murdered and receives a share of his purse, takes the last of a dead woman's money from her frozen hand, attempts to burgle a nobleman's house only to find the owner at home, and then brazenly accepts the owner's hospitality while quarreling with and insulting him, all in a night's work (Stevenson 1877). Dr. Desprez in "The Treasure of Franchard," Wolfe Macfarlane in "The

Body-Snatcher," and Long John Silver in *Treasure Island* are also variations on this theme. All capitalize on their facility with language to deceive or browbeat opponents for their own financial advantage: Silver in *Treasure Island*, for example, is "all for argyment" and uses language to position himself advantageously throughout all his changes in loyalties and circumstances (Stevenson 1883: 176).

Case also embodies the diabolical, Mephistophelean quality of the unscrupulous commercial adventurer. He is associated with magic and devils, and creates a secure hideaway for himself by giving out that it is the place of devils. Characteristically, he uses the agency of language to foster this diabolical air, preying on native beliefs to create "all sorts of stories" of his being able to "speak with the dead and give them orders," and of his being "Tiapolo" (Stevenson 1893: 161). This devilish quality is not gratuitous but is once again closely associated with trade: Case uses such narratives and tricks in order to further his mercantile ambitions, as when he convinces the natives that one of his competitors, old Underhill, who is stricken with a palsy and can only blink one eye, is "now a devil" and must be buried alive (154). Case may be said to both worship money and proselytize on its behalf; like an antimissionary, he battles the religious influence of Tarleton in order literally to "profit" in part by undermining the "native contributions to the mission," and in part by establishing his superior spiritual authority over the natives (155). His diabolical sermons and tricks convert the natives to the belief in his status as an anti-Christ—the "son" of Tiapolo, as Uma puts it (161). He even manages to convert the native pastor, Namu, by seducing him with trade goods until he is "deep in Case's debt" (154). Again, this bears comparison with the supernatural agency of money and profit in other Stevenson tales: thus the bottle imp, which seduces with the promise of all manner of material and bodily good but (mimicking the form and function of money itself) attaches itself to the possessor (and thus might be said to possess him) by a curious monetary logic that resembles the devaluating effect of inflation on money. Likewise in "The Isle of Voices," the origin of all money is explained as the magical harvesting of shells from the isle—a dangerous process that seduces Keola and finally entraps the wizard Kalamake himself, and which the missionary at the end of the story likens to "coining false money" or counterfeiting (Stevenson 1893b: 495).

Yet Case comes to a spectacularly bad end, reserved for those of Stevenson's characters (the hapless money-harvesters in "The Isle of Voices," the Boatswain in "The Bottle Imp," Pew and other ruthless buccaneers in

Treasure Island) who blindly allow money to rule their lives—whose lives become homologous to the destabilizing and dehumanizing logic of profit and the market. There is a strong sense of his being hoist by his own petard in the end: In marrying off Uma to Wiltshire (which he intends as part of a complex plan to keep Uma in view while ruining Wiltshire's trade by associating him with the banned woman), he succeeds only in creating a marriage that strengthens his rival and saves the latter's life (when Uma risks her life to bring warning to Wiltshire). While Case treats Uma as an object (of his earlier desire, and then as an ostensible gift-commodity and a real counter in his secret stratagems), Wiltshire is "much moved" by her situation and character, and it is this emotional relationship that assists him in triumphing over Case in the end. Case's attitude to native women in general is commodifying—"you can have your pick of the lot for a plug of tobacco," he opines (120)—and this attitude informs even his "one good point," his relationship with his Samoan wife. In contrast to Uma's active and involved role in Wiltshire's life and career, the Samoan woman never appears or acts in the events of the story, does not come to Case's assistance in his quarrel with Wiltshire, and is not even named. She is mentioned only for the one use she has, which is to be the repository of Case's worldly wealth when he dies, and thus the means of his cheating Randall and Black Jack too. The fact that she then sells out Case's establishment and goods to Wiltshire is as much a corroboration of Case's unsentimental mercantilism (and an indication of her unsentimental, functional relationship with him) as it is poetic justice on Case.

Wiltshire, Case's nemesis, offers a contrasting commercial morality. Wiltshire is certainly no saint, with his unrepentant racial and cultural superiority, his propensity for violence, his pride, and his own commercial ambitions. Yet in the course of the narrative, he is shown to negotiate these egocentric views and beliefs in relation to others around him who possess quite different values. When he first meets the missionary Tarleton, Wiltshire is prompted to declare that "I don't hold with missions," and that "I think you and the likes of you do a sight of harm" (149). Yet at the end of the story, he allows Tarleton to prevail upon him to "deal fairly with the natives," to the extent that this makes him "bothered about [his] balances" (186). This is despite the fact that he is convinced that all traders "have queerish balances" and that the natives "water their copra in a proportion; so that it's fair all round";[3] Wiltshire keeps his word to Tarleton for as long as he remains on Falesá, as a compact reached between two men of very different aims and value systems.

This willingness to negotiate a fair exchange between his own values and those of the local people and place is characteristic of Wiltshire's career throughout the story. While lacking Case's easy (and irresponsible) command of native and other languages, he evinces a fundamental interest in the words and narratives of others. He listens attentively to the priest Galuchet's discourse in French and native, and while comprehending little, pieces together enough (in part by remembering one significant native word, "fussy-ocky" or to "make dead," whose meaning he checks with Uma) to become wary of Case (131). Wiltshire is one of the few people who takes Galuchet with any seriousness (Case has motives for deriding him and destroying his credibility, Uma repeats the gossip about the priest that Case propagates, and others apparently laugh him off with the mocking sobriquet "Father Galoshes"); and while he then refers to Case for Galuchet's story and standing, and is inclined to think the warning about Case poisoning Adams "only talk," his attention to the priest's garbled discourse is the beginning of his ultimate wisdom about Case and the situation in Falesá. Wiltshire's interest in language is also seen in the fact that he very soon picks up enough native words to reach some kind of social exchange with the natives: "And as I had begun to pick up native, and most of them had a word or two of English, I began to hold little odds and ends of conversation, not to much purpose, to be sure, but they took off the worst of the feeling" (160).

It is in the course of struggling through the different origins and semantic fields of native words like "aitu" and "tiapolo" that he comes the better to understand Case's schemes and stratagems (162). While he scornfully declares "I don't value native talk a fourpenny piece," and it is largely his feeling of white superiority to the superstitious nature of the natives that enables him to uncover the mystery of Case's hideaway, Wiltshire is nevertheless very much a collector of native supernatural tales and cautionary narratives. This balancing of white skeptical scorn of natives, with a degree of open-minded interest and acceptance, allows Wiltshire not only to trade in information until he pieces the true story together but also cautions him to proceed "mighty carefully," which may be the saving of his life (166).

Of course, it is in his marriage to Uma that Wiltshire's ethical character is most clearly seen. Wiltshire's attitude to Uma moves from a passive acquiescence in her exploitation to a deep affection that is the basis of a marital partnership. Their marriage contract itself, which Wiltshire calls a "dandy piece of literature" (150), is the occasion for a relationship of mutual trust and dependence not unlike that of reader and author: Wiltshire asks Uma to surrender her *faux* certificate, written by Case but cherished unbeknownst by her; this trust enables him to replace that false narrative with a true one, a proper marriage conducted by Tarleton through which Wiltshire gives her "the proper name of a man's wife" (151). Unlike the exploitative pseudo-marriage encouraged by Case, this true marriage requires give and take on both sides, and Wiltshire's maritime metaphor for this—to be "spliced"—is not inappropriate, since it signifies a coming together (of two individual ropes) for a common purpose (to form a stronger functional unit) in which the individual elements are still distinct. Despite their ordeal, and their affection and cooperation that helps them survive it, Wiltshire and Uma retain many of their individual characteristics at the end: Uma is generous to a fault, and built generously as well, which Wiltshire accepts as being "natural in kanakas" (186). Wiltshire, while abandoning his ethnocentric ambitions (to return to England and open a public house) and accepting that he is "stuck here" in the islands, does not entirely give up his awareness of racial and cultural divisions, even though his own daughters problematize his assumptions: "They're only half castes of course; I know that as well as you do, and there's nobody thinks less of half castes than I do; but they're mine, and about all I've got; I can't reconcile my mind to their taking up with kanakas, and I'd like to know where I'm to find them whites?" (186).

Paradoxically, differences (in individual values, cultures, racial traits, and financial positions) are for Stevenson and moral commercialists the sign of fair trade and of the efficacy of the market. The half-caste children of the next generation do not represent the end of racial and cultural differences and their attendant problems, but their continuation and the continued need for mediating transactions.

While Stevenson has no simplistic answers or idealistic views of modernity, stories like "The Beach of Falesá" reveal his belief that "it is only by trying to understand others that we can get our own hearts understood," in a continual process that he calls both a "commerce" and a "battle for the truth" (1879: 97, 99). Many of his stories indeed depict the failure of intercourse: from the brutal boatswain's outright refusal to negotiate and trade with Keawe in "The Bottle Imp" ("I don't value any of your talk," Stevenson 1891: 23), to the lengthy discourse between Francis Villon and the Lord of Brisetout in "A Lodging for the Night," in which both fail to see the validity in the other's arguments (Stevenson 1877: 397). Yet this acceptance of the limits of social and commercial intercourse differs from the modernist "disenchantment" that Edward Said (1993: 226–27) describes and attributes to writers like James Joyce, Henry James, Joseph Conrad, and others. If high modernism might be described as a conviction of the totality of language and culture—one is reminded of Yeats' angry acknowledgement of his imprisonment, "I owe my soul . . . to the English language in which I think, speak, and write" (Yeats 1938: 519)—Stevenson qualifies this by insisting on the possibilities of negotiated, differentiated positions, and thus holds out some hope (however fragile) for the dignified plurality of cultures and social positions. This in turn defines the moral role of the author, as one who trades in the pleasure of retailing stories, but who in this trade is also bound by the need to edify readers as to "what is true and right" (Stevenson 1881: 46)—for Stevenson, neither an idealistic nor a disenchanted morality, but a practical and commercialist one rooted in the very nature of narrative, imaginative, and social exchanges.

NOTES

1. In which he laments that "*laissez-faire* declines in favour; our legislation grows authoritative, grows philanthropical, bristles with new duties and new penalties" (Stevenson 1887: 202).

2. Stevenson employs the simile in "The Body-Snatcher," where Fettes, the dealer in cadavers, displays a similar facility in social and narratological terms: "He had talent of a kind, the talent that picks up swiftly what it hears and readily retails it for its own" (Stevenson 1884: 504).

3. In "Authors and Publishers," Stevenson compares the relationship between authors and publishers to that between Pacific islanders and traders, epitomized in an island chief's saying, "You cheat me a little, no cheat too much" (Stevenson 1988a: 263). This seems to mark the limits of Stevenson's tolerance of commercial competition, and Wiltshire is once again a representative of this.

REFERENCES

Hume, David. 1752. Of Money. In *David Hume: Writings on Economics*. Ed. Eugene Rotwein. 1955. Edinburgh: Thomas Nelson and Sons.

———. 1772. *Enquiries Concerning Human Understanding and Concerning the Principles of Morals*. Ed. L. A. Selby-Bigge. 1975. Oxford: Oxford University Press.

———. 1777. *Essays Moral, Political and Literary*. Ed. T. H. Green and T. H. Grose. 1875. London: Longmans, Green & Co.

McLaughlin, Kevin. 1996. The Financial Imp: Ethics and Finance in Nineteenth-Century Fiction. *Novel: A Forum on Fiction* 29 (2): 165–83.

Menikoff, Barry. 1984a. A Study in Victorian Publishing. In Menikoff 1984b. 1–98.

———. 1984b. *Robert Louis Stevenson and "The Beach of Falesá": A Study in Victorian Publishing*. Ed. Barry Menikoff. Stanford, CA: Stanford University Press.

Norquay, Glenda, ed. 1999. *R. L. Stevenson on Fiction: An Anthology of Literary and Critical Essays*. Edinburgh: Edinburgh University Press.

Said, Edward. 1993. *Culture and Imperialism*. London: Chatto & Windus.

Smith, Adam. 1748. *Lectures on Rhetoric and Belles Lettres*. Ed. J. C. Bryce. 1983. Oxford: Clarendon Press.

———. 1759. *The Theory of Moral Sentiments*. London: A. Millar.

Sorensen, Janet. 2000. "Belts of Gold" and "Twenty-Pounders": Robert Louis Stevenson's Textualized Economies. *Criticism* 42 (3): 279–97.

Stevenson, Robert Louis. 1877. "A Lodging for the Night." In Stevenson 1923. 3–23.

———. 1879. "The Truth of Intercourse." In Stevenson 1988b. 93–99.

———. 1881. "The Morality of the Profession of Letters." In Norquay 1999. 40–50.

———. 1883. *Treasure Island*. 1994. London: Penguin.

———. 1884. "The Body Snatcher." In Stevenson 1923. 497–519.

———. 1887. "The Day After Tomorrow." In Stevenson 1988b. 202–10.

———. 1888a. "A Chapter on Dreams." In Norquay 1999. 126–38.

———. 1888b. "Letter to a Young Gentleman Who Proposes to Embrace the Career of Art". In Norquay 1999. 174–82.

———. 1891. "The Bottle Imp." In Stevenson 1923. 367–97.

———. 1893a. "The Beach of Falesá." In Menikoff 1984b. 115–86.

———. 1893b. "The Isle of Voices." In Stevenson 1923. 475–95.

———. 1923. *The Short Stories of Robert Louis Stevenson*. New York: Charles Scribner's Sons.

———. 1988a. "Authors and Publishers." In Stevenson 1988b. 259–64.

———. 1988b. *The Lantern-Bearers and Other Essays*. Ed. Jeremy Treglown. London: Chatto & Windus.

Wood, Naomi J. 1998. Gold Standards and Silver Subversions: Treasure Island and the Romance of Money. *Children's Literature* 26: 61–85.

Yeats, W. B. 1938. A General Introduction for my Work. In *Essays and Introductions*. 1961. London: Macmillan.

Light, Darkness, and Shadow

Stevenson in the South Seas

ANN C. COLLEY

According to the accounts of Stevenson's missionary acquaintances, the Polynesians gave precedence to the moon over the sun and counted by nights, not by days. The fluctuating moon and its varying play of light and shadow against a background of darkness structured their understanding of the passing of time.[1] As if this orientation influenced the perspective of Westerners who sailed to the islands, foreign residents and travelers to the South Seas tended to situate themselves according to the ways in which light—from whatever source—illuminated the pitch-black night. Stevenson was no exception, for in the South Seas his writing, his photographic images, and his sense of place relied upon the manner in which the occasional lamp lights a trackless darkness, how a flash camera reveals a segment of a night dance, or the way a magic lantern's glow casts shadows across church rafters. From Stevenson's point of view, darkness serves as the foundation of seeing.

In his South Seas writing Stevenson positions both himself and his reader in a landscape oriented by lights shining in the darkness. As if he were still the child admiring the lamps that mapped the city of Edinburgh or the young boy carrying a bull's-eye lantern so he could illuminate the black night of a Scottish fishing village ("The Lantern Bearers"), Stevenson continues to follow the glow of lanterns or the sight of a young moon on his nocturnal journeys through the islands. These luminous points of reference shine not only upon the dense thickets and rough roads of the islands' interiors but also upon the "wild, ill-charted and unlighted seas" that lie about their shores (*Ltrs* 7: 212). In a sense, his coming to the South

Seas led him back to the landscape of his childhood where the stars, the oil and gas lamps still held dominion, and where the "old mild lustre" of the lantern illuminated the dark by degrees and not all at once (Stevenson 1878: 192). Now in the South Seas his lamp's rays overspread his manuscript pages, to reappear as scattered beams glowing in a green thicket (Stevenson 1892b: 15), as the street lamps' trembling reflections on the waters of the port (Stevenson 1894: 123), and as distant lights from fires and torches of many fishers moving on the reef (Stevenson 1892a: 61).

In a way, Stevenson's appreciation for the sight of a light penetrating the darkness forms the very letters of his prose. In the opening passages of *In the South Seas*, when he describes his first sighting of the Marquesas, it is as if his words, like hieroglyphic silhouettes, emerge from the appearance of a "radiating centre of brightness" within the disappearing gloom of night (Stevenson 1896a: 6). The ensuing contrast brings into view the black lines of the horizon upon which stands a "morning bank" as "black as ink" and reveals a prospect in which the dark peaks or needles of Va-pu show themselves in outline against the first rays of the sun (6). One of Stevenson's photographs displays the mountains appearing to write upon the sky, and one of his pencil sketches done on board the *Casco* illustrates how the contrast of strong, black lines upon a white sheet of paper creates a kind of vocabulary with which to delineate and realize what he sees. These images give Stevenson the lines, the ink, and the letters with which to mark his arrival and to proceed. His ideas and words emerge, bit by bit, as the dawn allows the landscape slowly to take shape "in the attenuating darkness" (6). The prospect of light against darkness helps him describe what he has never seen before and to articulate what at that moment was "a virginity of sense" (6). On his subsequent journeys through the islands, he is never content to rest in the full whitewashed blaze of day but returns, as if to refurbish his vocabulary, into a landscape where he remarks on "the hour of the dusk, when the fire blazes, and . . . the lamp glints . . . between the pillars of the house" (15), and where the fronds of the palm trees "stand out dark upon the distance, glisten against the sun, and flash like silver fountains in the assault of the wind" (78).

Stevenson's fiction and imagination thrive upon the alternating, uneven dispersal of light and darkness. His characters seem to step out of the shadows onto the brightness of the page. Like the native women in *The Wrecker* who "came by twos and threes out of the darkness" (Stevenson 1892b: 15) and into the glow of the scattered lights, his characters emerge as if from oblivion onto the brilliant text.[2] Their succession of illuminated faces stirs his fancy and stimulates Stevenson to explore the mystery of what surrounds them. Stevenson continues what he had done before and perpetuates a style in which intermittent light is prominent. Just as when he had placed his characters in the half-lit streets and drawing rooms of London, positioning Mr. Utterson, who waits for a sighting of Mr. Hyde, under the gas lamps that draw "a regular pattern of light and shadow" (Stevenson 1886: 15), now, in the South Seas, he must enter areas where the unknown, the hidden, the unseen, the unarticulated press upon the edge of a sun's beam, or a moon's ray, or where a shining lamp punctures a dark place. As a result, his stories like "The Beach of Falesá" move from the full brightness of the morning to where the lantern, the candles, the torches, and matches punctuate the nocturnal landscape and reveal silhouettes of incomplete meaning. The story shifts from the sun-baked beach to the dark interior of the forest. The narrative's backdrop of contrasting light and darkness carries on what already had been essential to *Dr. Jekyll and Mr. Hyde*, where most of the action plays on a shadowy set occasionally illuminated by a flame from a fire, the glimmer of a gas lamp, or the rays of the moon, and where Hyde prowls at night. Stevenson's style, especially in the first part, written from Mr. Utterson's point of view, represents this fragmented or partially lit perspective. Stevenson writes Mr. Utterson's narrative so that it progresses through fits and starts, and moves through disconnected details. Any evidence that could give Mr. Utterson a more complete view is obscured by the night or the dark shadows of the action.

Stevenson's South-Sea letters and journals also portray episodes of inter-rupted darkness and discontinuous light in which metonymic figures and fragments replace the full, inclusive prospect. They describe the strange effects made by lanterns placed at intervals within the big shadowy halls at Vailima; the lamplight bursting through the crannies in the walls, and the spectacle of natives dancing by the light of a dying fire that made it "just possible" to see the nearest dancers and catch a glimpse of their shoulders "polished in the glow" (Stevenson NLS MS 9893). On the Gilbert Islands he follows the progress of a sunset when the shadows thicken to create a succession of luminous images, each splintered by darkness until the day is gone. Within Stevenson's metonymic field of vision, these partial images often seem to succeed one another like slides in a magic lantern show. Like the scrolls of lighted pictures that run through Mr. Utterson's mind when he recalls, at night in bed, what Mr. Enfield has told him about a Mr. Hyde, they come, one by one, between intervals of darkness, until night or sleep overtakes all.

Because Stevenson had an enduring infatuation with patterns of light and darkness and because he lived in a world of intermittent visibility, he was naturally drawn toward light's protean attendant, the shadow. As in *A Child's Garden of Verses*, where the child watches his shadow go "in and out" ("My Shadow") and waits boldly for its crooked presence to crawl in corners and march "along up the stair" ("Shadow March"), Stevenson in the South Seas watches huge gorges "sinking into shadow" and traces "crude shadows in the sand" (Stevenson 1896a: 77, 135). When night comes (evening is "that hour before the shadows," 174), he stalks these shadows and rides through treacherous and disquieting nocturnal landscapes where the moving light of a lantern tosses about a "curious whirl of shadows" (*Ltrs* 8: 373) or where the dense shade of the tree makes the way confusing. In Stevenson's imagination, shadows are what animate their source. They extend, enlarge, and give movement to the object itself as well as to its surroundings. They infuse what they represent with life, dimension, and possibility. In so doing, they negatively confirm the myth of the woman without a shadow who remains no more than a sterile body (Barthes 1980: 110).

In a sense shadows are the primary images, for they narrate the spirit of their origin and the shape they represent. And, like Fanny's shadow portraits of Ori a Ori, they are what gives substance to a person and character. In 1888, when the Stevensons were more than two months the guests of Ori a Ori (otherwise known as Teriitera) in Tahiti, Fanny, whom the chief called Jaffini Tuta (the maker of shadows), made silhouettes of him by "taking the shadow of his head on the wall, with the help of a lamp, drawing the outline and then filling it in with India ink" (M. Stevenson 1903: 242). These were the images that the Stevensons were to take away with them as a memento of their journey, and the silhouettes that Fanny made of themselves were also what they left behind, an impulse that suggests that it is the shadows when captured in a such a manner that permits one to remember, not the actual thing itself. In her pocket diaries, Margaret Stevenson noted that they "bequeathed their shadows in memoriam" (M. Stevenson B 7304). Paradoxically, for something strangely insubstantial and elusive, shadows are what the mind retains.

As if he were catching shadows of scenes and imprinting them as in the Samoan myth on the water, Stevenson assiduously pursued photography.[3] Photography was part of his fascination with the intermittent light and shadows that helped articulate the life around him. By exposing the blackened photographic plate to the sun, the moon, and to the sudden glare of exploding flash powder, he and members of his family illuminated segments of their new life.[4] These pictures, such as the photos of dancers in Butar-itari and in Apemama, capture their subjects and their shadows as well as the silhouettes of the onlookers. Like the child's shadow in *A Child's Garden of Verses*, dark phantoms of the dancers' arms haunt the speak-house walls. They loom larger than life to register the subjective experience of his subjects' movement and presence.

Beginning with the first voyage on board the yacht *Casco*, photography was to be a significant accompaniment on Stevenson's various journeys around the islands. Supply lists at the back of Lloyd Osbourne's diary reveal the seriousness with which they considered the photographic projects, for the photographic equipment was not only cumbersome (on one voyage they took along twelve hundred photographic plates) but also was listed second after "Mackintosh" and stood significantly ahead of such items as "6 bottles of brandy, laudanum, plaid, presents, tobacco, money, and clothes" (Osbourne B 7278). In their enthusiasm, they carried not only conventional cameras but also flash equipment and a detective camera with which Lloyd Osbourne hoped to catch what was not usually permit-ted to come to light.

The photographs were to be used as illustrations for Stevenson's writing about the South Seas. He considered them a necessary complement to his writing. They were a means of legitimizing or illuminating his words and of giving his readers a more genuine image to consider. He wanted to cor-rect the inaccurate, generic photographs frequently selected from banks of images that were generally available in books about the South Seas and often had little to do with the texts. In this respect, Stevenson was in the tradition of some missionaries and a number of anthropologists who went about with cameras collecting shots of new tribes and scenery, in the belief that the camera was the most accurate means by which to portray a visi-ble object.[5] Like them, he considered that records made in writing were helped out by the camera. As a result, as if verifying the idea of the mutu-ally authorizing relationship between fiction and photography (cf. Arm-strong 2000), the pages of Stevenson's fiction often seem to develop from a photographic negative. One of the most vivid examples of this phe-nomenon occurs in the opening of *In the South Seas*. As I have mentioned earlier, in these initial paragraphs Stevenson lets his readers follow his own eyes as he watches the landscape's particulars slowly come to light in the dissolving darkness. When he writes these opening passages, he is in the dark room of night and watching the shores gradually take their shape through the rising morning light.

Stevenson's fascination with lighting up the darkness also found its expression when he arranged for his own magic lantern shows in which he could project "that great bright eye of light" upon a darkened room (*Ltrs* 7: 372). On the voyage of the *Equator* there seem to have been only three recorded magic lantern exhibitions, two in a Butaritari church before an audience of three hundred, and one in Apemama. Stevenson's exhibition followed the standard missionary order: First there were slides of wild animals, and then a group of humorous images, and finally, true to missionary fashion, he ended with a group of gospel pictures. What is most significant about the magic lantern exhibitions is that instead of watching his own lantern slides, Stevenson turned toward the peripheral play of light, darkness, and shadow that repeatedly took hold of his imagination. He turned his eyes from the screen and focused upon the passing singers emerging from the night. He was fascinated by the ways in which the lightening and darkening of the church arrested their movements, and how one by one they broke away to watch the images and then regrouped to disappear down a dark road (Stevenson 1896a: 198). The troupe's defection from the performance was also Stevenson's. Rather than looking at the pictures, he concentrated on how the rays of light struck the cook's face, revealed a ghostlike vision of Strong (Stevenson HM 2412), and created shadows in the hollow of the roof.

Stevenson knew, though, that the light he shed upon the islands and the peoples he visited was by no means complete. As much as he attempted to collect data, take photographs, interview those who had been residing there longer than he, learn the various languages, observe as best he could, and compile lists of such medical details as the use of abortifacient herbs in the vagina, he found it impossible to grasp the variety and the complexity of what was before him. No matter how diligently he read, listened, and watched, he could do little more than offer a partial, imperfect representation of his experiences. As a result, his *In the South Seas* is essentially a collage of illuminated spaces and images surrounded by areas of obscurity and dogged by shifting shadows of meaning and understanding. The resulting text honors the unknown, the unseen, and the unspoken as well as episodes of insight. The heterogeneous chapter titles suggest the incompleteness and the discontinuity of knowledge and perception. Complete illumination is neither possible nor desirable. Reading *In the South Seas* and looking at his snapshots that he intended to accompany it helps one better understand that, for Stevenson, darkness is the foundation of seeing and knowing. The text allows one to realize that generally, in

Stevenson, as in the photographic negative, it is the dark, obscure moment that brings to view an event, a sighting, a consequence. Without the dark, light is without significance. In Stevenson, light is really incidental to darkness. As in *Dr. Jekyll and Mr. Hyde*, character, event, and revelation cannot exist without the background of night or shadow.

By illuminating segments of the Polynesian world for others to read and to see, Stevenson not only completed and transformed his "Creek Island, or Adventures in the South Seas" that he had begun at the age of twelve, into a Pacific reality but also became the lamplighter of his *A Child's Garden of Verses*, fulfilling the desire of the child who had promised, "But I, when I am stronger and can choose what I'm to do, / O Leerie, I'll go round at night and light the lamps with you" ("The Lamplighter"). With his observations and images Stevenson, like his forefathers, built his texts as if they were lighthouses whose intermittent beams shone upon uncharted isles and seas. His words guide his readers through the unknown. As the lenses of his understanding turn and the text proceeds, what was not visible emerges from "the yawning blackness," and, as the hours "keep running," the images disappear back into shadow and invisibility (Stevenson HM 2394). These alternations convey Stevenson's sense that a full, resplendent, all-encompassing brilliance is not necessarily desirable; that the recording of experience, if it is to be close to subjective truth, must be full of interruption. It was, perhaps, his recognition of this truth that motivated Stevenson, as a young man, to write his prize-winning essay, "On a New Form of Intermittent Light for Lighthouses" (1871) and to describe how the intermittent beam illuminates for a moment what will soon become invisible and fall back into the darkness of the sea at night.

When in Samoa, Stevenson described the toil of this Scottish great-grandfather, Thomas Smith, in his incomplete *Records of a Family of Engineers*: "The seas into which his labours carried the new engineer were still scarce charted, the coasts still dark . . . the isles in which he must sojourn were still partly savage. He must toss much in boats; he must often adventure on horseback by the dubious bridle-track through unfrequented wilderness; he must sometimes plant his lighthouse in the very camp of wreckers" (Stevenson 1896b: 165). A century later, in the South Seas, Stevenson also rooted himself among wrecks and traveled among the partly savage. Paradoxically, even though Stevenson was miles and years away from his past and from his predecessors' profession, in building lighthouses out of his prose he brought his life full circle, back to where his ancestors had been and back to where, as a young boy, he had accompanied his father on his tour of the lighthouses and the islands off the Scottish coast. His continuing awareness of the way light, darkness, and shadow alternate is testimony to that return. His orientation and sense of place was also theirs. His images of intermittent light, whether represented in words or on photographic plates, renewed and carried on what had been undertaken by earlier generations. In the end his metaphor of lighting up the darkness recalled a precedent already entrenched in Stevenson's perception of his world.

NOTES

1. Two London Missionary Society missionaries, the Reverend T. Powell and the Reverend G. Pratt, explained that the Polynesians, "like the Gauls and other ancient nations, gave precedence to the moon, and counted by nights, not by days. The sun, they say, is 'changeless' like a statue, and every day is very much like another, whereas the moon changes, and they can reckon by its phases" (Powell & Pratt 1890: 213 n7).

2. One cannot help but be reminded here of Stevenson's account of his dreams in which he speaks of his characters in them as being independent of himself—as being the work of goblins. (Stevenson 1888: 229–52).

3. One of Stevenson's South Sea missionary acquaintances, the Reverend George Turner, recounts a Samoan myth about a lady who "caught the shadows" and imprinted them on the water (Turner 1884: 101).

4. Stevenson was never the primary photographer. In fact, it seems that he lacked confidence in his technical skills and thought his negatives inferior. In his mind they resembled "a province of chaos and old night in which you might dimly perceive fleecy spots of twilight, representing nothing" (*Ltrs* 8: 319). For this reason, he usually took Lloyd along and placed the main photographic responsibilities in his stepson's hands. In a December 1889 letter to Charles Baxter, for instance, he informed his friend that "Tomorrow I go up the coast with Mr. Clarke, one of the London Society Missionaries in a boat to examine schools . . . Lloyd comes to photograph" (*Ltrs* 7: 346–47). Stevenson did, however, continue to show an interest in identifying subjects and composing the photographic shots. For a period Stevenson also relied upon Belle's husband, Joe Strong, who was an excellent photographer.

5. For an example of the importance of the camera for nineteenth-century anthropologists, see Thurn 1893.

REFERENCES

Armstrong, Nancy. 2000. *Fiction in the Age of Photography: The Legacy of British Realism.* Cambridge, MA: Harvard University Press.

Barthes, Roland A. 1980. *La Chambre Claire: Note sur la photographie.* English translation: *Camera Lucida: Reflections on Photography.* Trans. Richard Howard. 1981. New York: Hill & Wang.

Osbourne, Lloyd. B 7278. *Diary, 1889.* The Beinecke Rare Book and Manuscript Library, Yale University.

Powell, T. & G. Pratt. 1890. Some Folk-Songs and Myths from Samoa. *Journal of the Royal Society of New South Wales* 24.

Stevenson, Margaret. B 7304. *Diary, 1853–1897*. The Beinecke Rare Book and Manuscript Library, Yale University.

———. 1903. *From Saranac to the Marquesas and Beyond. Some Letters Written by Mrs. M. I. Stevenson to Miss Jane Whyte Balfour during 1881–1888*. Ed. Marie Clothilde Balfour. New York: Charles Scribner's Sons.

Stevenson, Robert Louis. HM 2394. "In the Lightroom." Huntington Library. San Marino, CA.

———. NLS MS 9893. "Journal in Tutuila." National Library of Scotland. Edinburgh.

———. 1878. "A Plea for Gas Lamps." In *Virginibus Puerisque and Other Papers*. 1905. London: Chatto & Windus. 187–193.

———. 1885. *A Child's Garden of Verses*. 1969. New York: Airmont Publishing Company.

———. 1886. *Strange Case of Dr. Jekyll and Mr. Hyde*. 1985. Toronto: Bantam Books.

———. 1888. "A Chapter on Dreams." In *Across the Plains with Other Memories and Essays*. 1896. New York: Charles Scribner's Sons. 229–252.

———. 1892a. "The Beach of Falesá." In Stevenson 1996. 3–71.

——— (with Lloyd Osbourne). 1892b. *The Wrecker*. 1913. New York: Charles Scribner's Sons.

——— (with Lloyd Osbourne). 1894. *The Ebb-Tide: A Trio and a Quartette*. In Stevenson 1996.

———. 1896a. *In the South Seas*. Ed. Neil Rennie. 1996. Harmondsworth: Penguin.

———. 1896b. *Records of a Family of Engineers*. Vailima Edition, vol. 5. 1912.

———. 1996. *South Sea Tales*. Ed. Roslyn Jolly. Oxford: Oxford University Press.

Thurn, E. F. 1893. Anthropological Uses of the Camera. *Journal of the Anthropological Institute* 22: 184–203.

Turner, George. 1884. *Samoa A Hundred Years Ago and Long Before, Together with Notes on the Cults and Custom of Twenty-three Other Islands in the Pacific*. London: Macmillan.

Violence in the South Seas

Stevenson, the Eye, and Desire

RALPH PARFECT

The subject of this paper, that of the eye as a focus of violence in Stevenson's South Seas writing, was first suggested by a remark of the French philosopher Georges Bataille (1897–1962). In an early essay simply titled "Oeil" (1929) Bataille alludes briefly to Stevenson's travel book *In the South Seas* (1896). Bataille's theme is the uncanny power of the eye to disturb our thought. As a contemporary of Dalí and Buñuel in the surrealist movement in Paris, he not unsurprisingly begins by discussing the unforgettable image from their film *Un chien andalou* of the same year (1929) of an eye being sliced open with a razor blade. What is less expected is that he links this image to Stevenson: "That a razor would cut open the dazzling eye of a young and charming woman—this is precisely what a young man would have admired to the point of madness, a young man watched by a small cat, a young man who by chance holding in his hand a coffee spoon, suddenly wanted to take an eye in that spoon. Obviously a singular desire on the part of a white, from whom the eyes of the cows, sheep and pigs that he eats have always been hidden. For the eye—as Stevenson exquisitely puts it, a cannibal delicacy—is, on our part, the object of such anxiety that we will never bite into it. The eye is even ranked high in horror, since it is, among other things, the eye of conscience" (Bataille 1929: 17).[1] Bataille's reference is almost certainly to that part of *In the South Seas* where Stevenson writes the following of lapsed cultural practices among Polynesians: "the eyes of the victim were formally offered to the chief: a delicacy to the leading guest" (Stevenson 1896: 70).

As is characteristic of Bataille's often richly suggestive writing, his juxtaposition of Stevenson and *Un chien andalou* calls other passages to mind, including other instances in Stevenson's work where the human eye becomes linked with violence. The young man taken with the sudden desire to take an eye in his spoon, to claim power over the eye, has affinities with two of Stevenson's characters who in different ways also attack the eye. First, from *Strange Case of Dr. Jekyll and Mr. Hyde*, there is Dr. Jekyll, whose alter ego Mr. Hyde is described at one point as "closer than an eye" (Stevenson 1886: 75). This figure of speech brings home not only Hyde's unbearable proximity to Jekyll but also his control of Jekyll's very perception and understanding. Jekyll's solution is the desperate one of suicide; only via his own death can the alien eye be put out and Hyde's power resisted. Second, there is Huish in *The Ebb-Tide*, who plots literally to throw vitriol into the eyes of the tyrannical Attwater. Attwater himself, who subdues this revolt using his own deadly violence, may recall for us Bataille's phrase, "the eye of conscience"; his role in the story is that of the stern, self-appointed, conscientious white man in the colonies. What could be more fitting than that Huish should try to blind him?

To explore further such links between the eye and violence in Stevenson's work, I shall look at three works where the connection is particularly prominent. All belong to Stevenson's South Seas writing: *The Ebb-Tide* (1894) and "The Beach of Falesá" (1892), and finally *In the South Seas* (1896). In examining the latter in particular, I shall also draw attention to the prominence of a third theme in which Stevenson and Bataille shared an interest, namely desire. As we shall see, both violence and the eye are to a certain extent the instruments of desire in Stevenson's work as in Bataille's.

The Ebb-Tide is a story greatly preoccupied with the power of the look, the violence of the gaze. As its motley trio of adventurers, Davis, Herrick, and Huish, sail closer to Attwater's settlement, looking acquires a murderous intensity, and the violence of their lustful gaze seems to be reflected back at them: "[I]f intensity of looking might have prevailed, they would have pierced the walls of houses; and there came to them, in these pregnant seconds, a sense of being watched and played with, and of a blow impending, that was hardly bearable" (Stevenson 1894: 191). Looking is associated here, as in Freud's work, with the desire for mastery. But through the projection of the adventurers' desperation onto the landscape around them—they have found the island just when drunken recklessness has driven them to the point of open hostility with one another—a hostile returning gaze is imagined, "a sense of being watched and played with," a contest for the mastery of the gaze.

A deadly power struggle does indeed develop on the island, and it repeatedly involves the eye. When the trio, having moored their ship, encounter the self-appointed overlord of the island, Attwater, they are immediately dazzled by the seemingly indomitable power focused in his eye: "It was only the eye that corrected this impression [of languor in his limbs]; an eye of an unusual mingled brilliance and softness, somber as coal and with lights that outshone the topaz; an eye of unimpaired health and virility; an eye that bid you beware of the man's devastating anger" (192). This virile gaze seems to assault the three men when Attwater looks at them with "a sudden weight of curiosity that was almost savage" (192). Yet there is also a haunting beauty in Attwater's eye, suggested when Stevenson describes its gleam as "topaz"-like. This combination of irresistibility and fearsomeness, what might be called a glamour (in the archaic meaning of a witch's spellbinding power), is equally well understood by Bataille when he writes: "It seems impossible, in fact, to judge the eye using any word other than seductive, since nothing is more attractive in the bodies of animals and men. But extreme seductiveness is probably at the boundary of horror" (Bataille 1929: 17). The eye's dual role as seducer and catalyst of violence that Bataille hints at in fact runs through the narrative of *The Ebb-Tide*. Partly via the attractiveness of his eye, Attwater "seduces," in the sense of winning over, both Herrick and Davis; he is helped in the first instance by his Oxonian charm, and in the second by his impressive disciplinary prowess. Both Herrick and Davis end up effectively his servants, trapped on the island under Attwater's watchful eye. Yet the violent climax of the tale makes the eye also the focus of horror. One ending for *The Ebb-Tide* contemplated by Stevenson was for Huish's attempted blinding of Attwater to succeed; instead, just as horrifically, Huish himself is destroyed when Attwater shoots the vitriol bottle in his hand. Huish's agonies, which have a disturbingly orgasmic tone, are related in a way that again draws attention to the eye: "For the twinkling of an eye the wretch was in hell's agonies, bathed in liquid flames, a screaming bedlamite; and then a second and more merciful bullet shot him dead" (Stevenson 1894: 247).

The phrase "twinkling of an eye" here has multiple meanings. That the eye should be mentioned as Huish dies is poetic justice, for he himself wished to "chuck this vitriol in [Attwater's] eyes" (241). In addition "twinkling of an eye" also suggests a gaze of desire, "a twinkle in the eye" signifying an awakening sexual interest: just as Huish's cough was a "cruel ecstasy" at an earlier point in the story (128), so too is the moment of death both sacred and orgasmic. Herrick's contemplation of murder is also described as an "orgasm" (208). Furthermore, since the controlling gaze here belongs to Attwater, "the twinkling of an eye" can be seen as his, the magician in control of the stage, as when he tortures Davis by sharp-shooting around him (an echo of the previous mention of Weber's opera *Der Freischütz,* a story in which magic bullets never miss their mark [129]).

In the ending that Stevenson opted for, with the death of Huish, the harshness of the Law of Hammurabi (an eye for an eye) is invoked, casting the four characters in a kind of quasi-biblical drama. The drama is also psychological. Blinding, as Freud has observed, is a form of symbolic cas-tration, and there are repeated references in this text to blinding, suggesting what may be at stake in the war of looks, namely an embattled masculin-ity (Freud 1919: 352). From the open sea, we are told, the reflections of "blinding copper suns, no bigger than sixpences, danced and stabbed them in the eyeballs" (242). This image of blinding, already multiple here, is multiplied throughout the story; the sun is a dominant presence, seem-ingly driving the three adventurers' madness and greed, and as they plot against Attwater its paradoxical links with darkness and death are also sug-gested when we are told that "the excess of light seemed to be changed into a sinister darkness" (242).

The battle for mastery of the gaze, under the sign of the all-powerful sun, is also a feature of "The Beach of Falesá," but here it is more explicit, becoming part of the deadly power struggle among whites and native islanders. The use of the eye as a sign of aggression is familiar in European folklore in traditions of "the Evil Eye," and Wiltshire tells us that Case had once craftily exploited this superstition (which evidently has resonances for a Pacific people) by telling the credulous islanders that the trader Vigours had the Evil Eye; at the behest of the compliant pastor Namu, the island-ers supposedly then began making the sign of the cross against Vigours, and eventually drove him from the island, as Case had desired (Stevenson 1892: 38).

It is not just whites who exploit the power of the eye, however. The Polynesians in the tale are repeatedly associated with the eye as a disturb-ing sign of their threatening exclusion and distancing (as interpreted by Wiltshire), deconstructing the apparent opposition between violent whites and peaceful natives. Wiltshire awakes the first morning in his new home to be confronted with a circle of natives staring at him. The violent asso-ciations of this gaze are suggested in several ways. Immediately it reminds

Wiltshire of a disturbing incident of domestic violence: "I have seen a house in a South Sea village thus surrounded, but then a trader was thrashing his wife inside, and she singing out" (14). This recollection prompts Wiltshire to an act of defiance that only increases the level of perceived threat: "I leaned my arms on the rail and stared back. Devil a wink they had in them! . . . they stared at me, dumb and sorrowful, with their bright eyes; and it came upon me things would not look much different if I were on the platform of the gallows, and these good folk had come to see me hanged" (15).

The dramatic impact of this scene is enhanced by the fact that it occurs at sunrise; this conjunction of the sun, the islanders' gaze, and recollected violence creates a cluster of images that will recur in this tale, as also in *The Ebb-Tide*. The sun, like the threatening gaze, is of course associated in many cultures' religious rituals with sacrifice. The link that the eye/sun/death image-cluster has with violence and sacrifice is repeated, albeit sardonically, in Wiltshire's narrative: "All day . . . the fools sat . . . waiting for the show, whatever that was—fire to come down from heaven, I suppose, and consume me, bones and baggage" (16). Although the starers eventually disperse, the stare returns; the following day, a Sunday, Wiltshire wanders into the local church to receive a still more abjective gaze from the native pastor, Case's helper, Namu: "Well, he looked up suddenly and caught my eye, and I give you my word, he staggered in the pulpit; his eyes bulged out of his head, his hand rose and pointed at me like as if against his will, and the sermon stopped right there" (21). In response to this ocular aggression, Wiltshire attempts to regain control of the gaze. Having already assaulted Case once to demonstrate his awareness of his enemy's identity, he threatens Case's associate Black Jack, using his own eye as a metaphorical weapon: "there was trouble in my eye, if anybody took the pains to look" (45).

In the end, however, the "magical" threatening gaze is part of the often-illusory visual world; the association of looking with illusion is made at the start of the tale, when Wiltshire first views the island with binoculars and experiences a violent disjunction in perception: "I took the glass; and the shores leaped nearer" (3). Violence, although often no more reliable, can be a means to dispel illusion. At a key moment in the story, Wiltshire recalls from his own childhood the efficacy of a flogging in demystifying a would-be schoolboy "sorcerer" of whom Case's antics have reminded him: "I remember a boy I was at school with at home who played the Case business. . . . And then it came in my mind how the master had once flogged that boy, and the surprise we were all in to see the sorcerer catch it and bum [cry] like anybody else" (55). Wiltshire goes on to use the all-powerful physical violence of a dynamite explosion to destroy Case's "altar," an altar whose power over the islanders is enhanced by eye-symbols: it incorporates a number of "carved and painted faces ugly to view, their eyes and teeth [made] of shell," and a "shining face" splashed with "luminous paint," which, in a kind of power-based emanation comparable to that of the gaze, pours out smoke (54–55). Case's associations with sacredness are mocked but also confirmed when it is decided to bury him "upon the field of glory, right in the hole where he had kept the smoking head" (69). The power of the eye, which Case once commanded via his tales of the Evil Eye and his carved faces with shells for eyes, is symbolically destroyed by an artificial sun, the fire of dynamite.

In both *The Ebb-Tide* and "The Beach of Falesá," then, there is a strong element of symbolic violence, focused around the image of the eye. The text that Bataille (mis)quoted on the eye as "cannibal delicacy" shows a congruent preoccupation with violence, albeit treated in less symbolic ways. *In the South Seas* is in part an attempt to recuperate what is valuable about the Polynesian cultures Stevenson encountered, including violent folklore and traditions, and to change the reader's perceptions about a misrepresented realm through writing that is informed by an energetic new interest in anthropology. In the chapter titled "Long-Pig—A Cannibal High Place" the ethics of cannibalism are interrogated using what is for Stevenson uncharacteristically academic language. Stevenson asks: "How shall we account for the universality of the practice over so vast an area, among people of such varying civilization, and with whatever intermixture, of such different blood?" (Stevenson 1896: 70). Fanny Stevenson for one protested at the new scientific or pseudoscientific direction that Louis had taken, writing to Sidney Colvin: "He has taken it into his Scotch Stevenson head . . . that his book must be a sort of scientific and historical impersonal thing" (qu. McLynn 1993: 334).

Fanny's fears were in fact somewhat groundless. Not only does Stevenson repeatedly garnish his observations in the text with personal reactions and reflections, particularly in his accounts of violence, he also places a consistent emphasis on desire in a such a way that it is not hard to see why Bataille, who has been called a philosopher of desire, might have approved. Stevenson was frank about his wish to collect violent stories: "When I desired any detail of savage custom, or of superstitious belief, I cast back in the story of my fathers, and fished for what I wanted with some trait of equal barbarism" (Stevenson 1896: 13). While the angling metaphors here project an image of the author as a vigorous pragmatist, casting for the matter that will ultimately feed him and his family, the word "desired" underlines the libidinal character of the search for violence. This character pertains to much of the searching or looking that goes on in this text. As Stevenson acknowledges in the first chapter, "An Island Landfall": "No part of the world exerts the same attractive power upon the visitor, and the task before me is to communicate to fireside travelers some sense of its seduction, and to describe the life . . . of many hundred thousand persons . . . as remote in thought and habit as Rob Roy and Barbarossa, the Apostles or the Caesars" (5–6).

The linking here of the libidinal language of "attractive power" and "seduction" with violent myths highlights a connection that remains implicit throughout the text. Narratives of violence become in a sense a substitute for narratives of sexuality. In spite of some glimpses of naked women in the text, Stevenson pays little attention to sexual themes, and when he does, it is to usually to pour cold water on the myth of the South Seas as a paradise of sexual license. The sexual adventurer, he significantly remarks at one point, is likely to end up "speared" by one of the woman's outraged relatives (199). Thus attention is steered quite explicitly away from sex to violence, focusing on one sensational set of myths in preference to another; the knowledge of violence is eroticized.

The writer, manipulating our readerly desires in this way, is open about his own voracious appetites. He is "an excited hearer," concerned to a certain extent that he might be an unreliable witness: "With my superstitious friend, the islander, I fear I am not wholly frank, often leading the way with stories of my own" (139). A lengthy episode involving an unintentional breach of etiquette on Stevenson's part inspires him to describe his almost sadistic enjoyment of the offended party's discomfort, using the language of gladiatorial combat: "I sat by and relished, and lustfully renewed his torments. *Ave Caesar*! Smothered in a corner, dormant but not dead, we have all the one touch of nature: an infant passion for the sand and blood of the arena" (249). Here again libidinal language—"relished," "lustfully," "passion"—is mixed with violent myth to create a heady concoction. The apparent cruelty here is diminished when we are told that the man offended by Stevenson's breach of etiquette is "a greedy man," but Stevenson too seems almost greedy here in the gratification of his aggressive instincts. In the chapter "Graveyard Stories," a lengthy chapter that presents grisly ghost stories from various islands, he sets up a hierarchy for tales of horror. Tahitian legends, he judges, are too bland, and to these he contrasts those of the Paumotuan islands, giving a gory example that revolves around "blood-gouts on the wall" (145).

It is rare in Stevenson's writing to find him offering a rationale for his attraction to violence; here in *In the South Seas*, however, a rationale is freely given. Having intervened in a dispute over the supply of alcohol to some very restless natives in the Gilbert Islands, Stevenson predicts a fight. Unsurprisingly, the prospect of violence arouses his ardor; unusually, it leads him also to rationalize his desire: "Scott talks moderately of looking forward to a time of fighting 'with a feeling that resembled pleasure.' The resemblance seems rather an identity. In modern life, contact is ended; man grows impatient of endless manoeuvres; and to approach the fact, to find ourselves where we can push our advantage home, and stand a fair risk, and see at last what we are made of, stirs the blood" (187). The appeal here to the notion of "contact" and the problem of its loss could of course be read more than one way; for the Victorians, it might apply as much to sexual contact as to aggressive confrontation. For Stevenson, violence is strongly associated with titillation.

In all three Stevenson texts I have looked at, the gratification of a lust for violent tales, in which we can "see what we are made of," is part of a libidinal economy. These tales are not only consumed by the author himself but also recycled as commodities for the reader's pleasure, and knowledge of violence is a kind of currency in this exchange. When Stevenson remarks that during his assiduous barter of the violent folklore of Scotland for that of the South Seas, "the black bull's head of Stirling procured me the legend of Rahero," the word "procured" draws attention to the fact that, for Stevenson at least, this is a commercial transaction (13). To "see what we are made of," as Bataille also thought, means for Stevenson acknowledging the power of the eye to seduce and to horrify—in short, to be an instrument of violence—and equally involves the recognition that violent transactions may be informed by powerful libidinal desires.

NOTE

1. "Car l'œil, d'après l'exquise expression de Stevenson, friandise cannibale, est de notre part l'objet d'une telle inquiétude que nous ne le mordrons jamais. L'œil occupe même un rang extrêmement élevé dans l'horreur étant entre autres l'œil de la conscience." Georges Bataille, *Œuvres complètes* (Paris: Gallimard, 1929/1970), 188.

REFERENCES

Bataille, Georges. 1929. Oeil—Friandise cannibale. In *Œuvres complètes,* vol. 1, 187–
    189. Paris: Gallimard, 1970–1988. English translation: Eye. In *Visions of Excess:*

Selected Writings, 1927–1939. Ed. Alan Stoekl. Minneapolis: University of Minnesota Press, 1996.

Freud, Sigmund. 1919. The "Uncanny" (Das Unheimliche). In *On Art and Literature.* Trans. James Strachey. Ed. Albert Dickson. 1990. The Penguin Freud Library, 14: 335–76. London: Penguin.

McLynn, Frank. 1993. *Robert Louis Stevenson: A Biography.* London: Hutchinson.

Stevenson, Robert Louis. 1886. *Strange Case of Dr. Jekyll and Mr. Hyde.* In *The Strange Case of Dr. Jekyll and Mr. Hyde and Weir of Hermiston.* Ed. Emma Letley. 1987. Oxford: Oxford University Press.

———. 1892. "The Beach of Falesá." In Stevenson 1996.

——— (with Lloyd Osbourne). 1894. *The Ebb-Tide: A Trio and a Quartette.* In Stevenson 1996.

———. 1896. *In the South Seas.* Ed. Neil Rennie. 1998. Harmondsworth: Penguin.

———. 1996. *South Sea Tales.* Ed. Roslyn Jolly. Oxford: Oxford University Press.

Cruising with Robert Louis Stevenson

The South Seas from Journal to Fiction

OLIVER S. BUCKTON

By the 1890s, Robert Louis Stevenson enjoyed international fame as the author of such masterpieces as *Strange Case of Dr. Jekyll and Mr. Hyde* (1886) and *Master of Ballantrae* (1889). Yet Stevenson suffered from a growing fear that his literary output was "inadequate," an anxiety that reached a crescendo during his cruises in the South Seas (from 1888) and residence on Samoa (from 1890), remote from what his friend Edmund Gosse termed the "literary atmosphere" of London (McLynn 1993: 408).[1] A significant source of this self-dissatisfaction was his failure to produce the *magnum opus* on the history, society, traditions, and culture of the South Seas that he had envisaged. "I am about waist-deep in my big book on the South Seas: *the* big book on the South Seas it ought to be, and shall," Stevenson wrote Marcel Schwob on 19 August 1890 (*Ltrs* 6: 401). Yet, daunted by the scale and complexity of this undertaking, Stevenson was compelled to scale down this project and find other outlets for his South Sea materials. The spontaneous and random propulsions of "cruising"—Stevenson's ideal mode of travel—were not propitious for the laborious production of a major volume of historical and anthropological analysis. Rather, cruising was conducive to the production of more informal texts such as journals and letters, which could be published in fragments, and the South Sea "yarns," being marketable commodities, would yield profit from further excursions in the South Seas.

Cruising, the antithesis of strain and labor, became a codeword for Stevenson's state of well-being, both physical and emotional, signifying travel without a specific destination or external compulsion, pursued for sensual pleasure, and rewarded by enticing encounters with new scenes.[2] In a letter to Sidney Colvin written in April 1890 while on board the *Janet Nicoll,* Stevenson made clear that it was not simply the South Seas climate that he needed but also the stimulation of cruising itself: "this life is the only one that suits me; so long as I cruise in the South Seas, I shall be well and happy . . . I mean that, so soon as I cease from cruising, the nerves are strained, the decline commences" (*Ltrs* 6: 388). I will argue that cruising also entailed a new practice of writing for Stevenson, a form of resistance to the pressures on him to commodify his experiences of the South Seas for consumption by distant readers. Stevenson continued to conceive of his nonfiction pieces on the South Seas as "chapters" of an imagined "big book," rather than occasional letters designed to convey the flavor of the South Seas to the casual reader. Writing Colvin in June 1889, Stevenson expresses his undaunted confidence that "By the time I am done with this cruise I shall have the material for a very singular book of travels: masses of strange stories and characters, cannibals, pirates, ancient legends, old Polynesian poetry, never was so generous a farrago" (*Ltrs* 6: 312).

The ambitious purpose for this "material" was undermined, however, by the commercial arrangement Stevenson had made with the American literary entrepreneur Sam McClure with whom, as early as March 1888, Stevenson had signed a contract to write a series of fifty "letters" from the South Seas. Planning to syndicate these letters in newspapers in Britain, the United States, Australia, and New Zealand, McClure wrote Stevenson (in May 1888) that he hoped to be able to get him $300 per letter (*Ltrs* 6: 192n), a sum Stevenson expected would defray the considerable expense of chartering the yacht *Casco* and crew: as he wrote Charles Baxter in May 1888, "the Casco letters may go towards repayment of the capital now borrowed. I shall think it unlucky if I cannot get from ten to fifteen hundred out of them" (*Ltrs* 6: 192).

As published in the New York *Sun,* the South Sea letters were subtitled "Letters from a Leisurely Traveller," evoking a context of ease and suggesting that the act of cruising was casual and pleasurable, rather than pursued for profit or with literary labor as its pretext (Stevenson 1891a).[3] Such an ambience of dilettante leisure was likely to alienate those Victorians who lived by the Protestant work ethic. Indeed, the initial response to these letters by British and American readers was discouraging, as the critics who had always doubted the wisdom of Stevenson's longterm "cruise" became more vocal. Colvin, rarely inclined to boost Stevenson's confidence, reported that *Black and White* wanted to cancel its publication of the letters because they were "too monotonous" (*Ltrs* 7: 157n). Stevenson angrily responded to Colvin's request for more personal details about his travels: "The Letters, it appears, are tedious; by God, they would be more tedious still if I wasted my time upon such infantile and sucking-bottle details. . . . The mistake is all through that I have told too much; I had not sufficient confidence in the reader, and have overfed him" (*Ltrs* 7: 157).

Gosse, relaying the "disappointment among the few who have read the approaching South Sea letters," ironically called into question Stevenson's opening assertion that cruising in the South Seas had restored his health: "The fact seems to me that it is very nice to live in Samoa, but not healthy to write there. Within a three-mile radius of Charing Cross is the literary atmosphere, I suspect" (Edmund Gosse, qu. McLynn 1993: 408). Of course, Gosse is referring not to physical disease but to a moral or intellectual malady, the chief symptom of which is inferior literature. Gosse clearly assumed that Stevenson did not begin to write the South Seas material until *after* he had decided to settle in Samoa (Gosse 1908): an assumption contradicted by the extensive (242 MS pages) "Journal of Two Visits to the South Seas" written by Stevenson throughout the first two cruises on the *Casco* and the *Equator*. The journal, now in the the Huntington Library, in effect presents a first draft of the work that eventually became *In the South Seas* and, I shall argue, furnished materials from which he would construct both his letters and his South Sea "yarns."

Stevenson's frustration at the fragmentation of his South Seas manuscript required by serial publication as letters was evident as he wrote Henry James in December of 1890: "what a strain is a long book! . . . And then think of writing a book of travels on the spot; when I am continually extending my information, revising my opinions, and seeing the most finely finished portions of my work come part by part in pieces" (*Ltrs* 7: 65–66). Stevenson's allusion to the impending disintegration of his textual body "part by part" during the process of serial publication articulates his anxiety that the magnum opus would be dismembered for what he described in a letter to his mother as the "grisly letters" (*Ltrs* 7: 68).[4]

The key to Stevenson's conception of his literary labor in the South Seas, however, is to be found in his defense of the letters—or rather, of the project of which they were a part—against Colvin's criticism: "*These letters were never meant and are not now meant to be other than a quarry of materials from which the book may be drawn*" (*Ltrs* 7: 115, original emphasis). By contrast to cruising, the industrious metaphor of "quarrying" materials for the purposes of constructing literary narratives (as his father's firm of engineers had quarried materials for the construction of lighthouses) depicts a more active role of authorship, reflective of Stevenson's admission that "I could have wished to be otherwise busy in this world. I ought to have been able to build lighthouses and write *David Balfours* too" (*Ltrs* 8: 235).[5] Clearly, Stevenson's desire to write a "big book" on the South Seas was spurred both by the output of his forefathers and by the vast amount of diverse material he had accumulated in his journal. The most mature fruit of Stevenson's cruises, however, was not the "book of travels"—which remained unexecuted, at least according to his original conception—but South Sea stories such as "The Beach of Falesá" and *The Ebb-Tide*. Stevenson creatively recycled images, episodes, encounters, and characters that had been initially recorded in the South Sea journal and then published in the South Sea letters—or in some cases had not been published at all—for use in the fictional narratives he somewhat dismissively termed his "South Sea Yarns." For the remainder of this essay I will examine key examples of such "quarrying" to show how the South Sea cruise furnished the constructive materials for new works of fiction, and suggest how Stevenson's use of these documentary materials radically reshaped his approach to fiction and brought a new relationship with his readers.

Acting on his conviction that "no part of the world exerts the same attractive power upon the visitor" as the South Seas, Stevenson recognized that "the task before me is to communicate to fireside travelers some sense of its seduction" (Stevenson 1896: 5). This desire to seek out and seduce the reader anticipates the critical practice of Roland Barthes, who deploys a similar metaphor to articulate the tension between distance and desire at work in textual production: "Écrire dans le plaisir m'assure-t-il—moi, écrivain—du plaisir de mon lecteur? Nullement. Le lecteur, il faut que je le cherche, (que je le 'drague'), sans savoir où il est. Un espace de la jouissance est alors créé. Ce n'est pas la 'personne' de l'autre qui m'est nécessaire, c'est l'espace" (Barthes 1973: 11) ["Does writing in pleasure guarantee—guarantee me, the writer—my reader's pleasure? Not at all. I must seek out this reader (must 'cruise' him) without knowing where he is. A site of bliss is then created. It is not the reader's 'person' that is necessary to me, it is this site" (1975: 4)]. Stevenson's cruise ship became his site of bliss, and served as the necessary transport (in both senses) to reach readers of his most powerful late works of fiction.

The first South Sea letter (published in *Black and White* on 6 February

1891), describing Stevenson's arrival in the Marquesas, began by inviting the reader vicariously to share an idyllic first encounter with the beauty of a Polynesian island: "The first experience can never be repeated. The first love, the first sunrise, the first South Sea island are memories apart and touched a virginity of sense" (1891b, 1: 23). Yet this passage, while conveying the "thrill of landfall heightened by the strangeness of the shores" also implies that Stevenson's paradise has already been lost—that the "virginity of sense" is no longer susceptible to such intense impressions. This blend of the seductive and the wistful notes is echoed in the opening of "The Beach of Falesá," where the island is first described by Wiltshire in an idealized, indeed eroticized language: "I saw that island first when it was neither night nor morning. The land breeze blew in our faces, and smelt strong of wild lime and vanilla. . . . Here was a fresh experience: even the tongue would be quite strange to me; and the look of these woods and mountains and the rare smell of them renewed my blood" (Stevenson 1892: 3).[6]

Of course, Wiltshire's blood is also renewed by the sight of Uma, the beautiful native woman, and his attraction and illicit marriage to her formed the most controversial aspect of the story. As has been richly documented by Menikoff (1984), Stevenson's narrative underwent severe editorial interference and, among other changes, Wiltshire's spurious marriage "contract" did not appear in the *Illustrated London News* serialization of the story. Yet the document had already been cited in "The Gilberts" section of *South Seas*: "All these women were legitimately married. It is true that the certificate of one, when she proudly showed it, proved to run thus, that she was 'married for one night' and her gracious partner was at liberty to 'send her to hell' the next morning' (Stevenson 1896: 200). Other episodes in the story are quarried from the cruises, as when the missionary Tarleton describes a horrifying incident in which one of Wiltshire's predecessors is buried alive at Case's instigation: "At last a grave was dug, and the living body buried at the far end of the village" (Stevenson 1892: 40). The incident was inspired by actual stories told to Stevenson and Fanny, which Fanny recorded in her journal, published in 1915 as *The Cruise of the "Janet Nichol"*: "A man who was paralysed on one side had a convulsion which caused spasmodic contractions on the other side. One of the sick man's family began at once to make a coffin. 'But the man's not dead,' said Mr Hird. 'Oh yes,' was the reply, 'He's dead enough; it's the third time he has done this, so we are going to bury him'" (1915: 64).[7]

The crucial text for assessing the contribution of the South Sea journal as a source for Stevenson's fictional art, however, is the final story published during his lifetime, *The Ebb-Tide*. As David Daiches observes, "Stevenson was aware that he was at a critical phase in his career as a writer, moving away from his earlier concepts of romance towards something more contemporary and more grimly realistic" (Daiches 1994: xxii). The complex literary treatment of the South Seas reaches its fruition in *The Ebb-Tide* rather than in the South Sea book that, as Robert Irwin Hillier remarks, "Stevenson had once hoped would be his masterpiece [but which] turned out to be the unrevised 'Letters' written for McClure published in book form . . . two years after his death" (Hillier 1989: 24–25). Yet other critics have seen in *The Ebb-Tide* the end of the line for Stevenson as a storyteller: "For *The Ebb-Tide*'s trio . . . a general failure of enterprise is signaled by the exhaustion of narrative possibility that marks their aleatory or shallow creative endeavours" (Smith 1998: 160).

Yet the story continues the theme of "island landfall," as the aptly named "New Island" is described from Herrick's idealizing point of view at the opening of Part II: The Quartette: "the isle—the undiscovered, the scarce-believed in—now lay before them and close aboard; and Herrick thought that never in his dreams had he beheld anything more strange and delicate. The beach was excellently white, the continuous barrier of trees inimitably green; the land perhaps ten feet high, the trees thirty more . . . so slender it seemed amidst the outrageous breakers, so frail and pretty, he would scarce have wondered to see it sink and disappear without a sound" (1894: 187–88). The narrator of *The Ebb-Tide* does not like Wiltshire transfer the seduction of the island onto a native woman but instead draws attention to a discarded object that serves as an emblem of the white man's colonization of the islands: "on the top of the beach and hard by the flagstaff, a woman of exorbitant stature and as white as snow was to be seen beckoning with uplifted arm. The second glance identified her as a piece of naval sculpture, the figure-head of a ship" (190). The most striking aspect of this figurehead, its whiteness, is itself identified as a symptom of disease—"its leprous whiteness reigned alone in that hamlet" (190)—that recalls the damning opening sentence of the novel: "Throughout the island world of the Pacific, scattered men of many European races and from almost every grade of society carry activity and disseminate disease" (123).

This figurehead—which reappears at key points in the story—is another object "quarried" from Stevenson's record of his cruise, in this case a visit made to the "pearl island" of Penrhyn. Stevenson and Fanny visited Penrhyn on 9–10 May, 1890, a visit not recorded in the South Sea letters but which Fanny describes in her journal: "From the first, I had been puzzled by a strange figure on the trader's veranda. When we were nearer I discovered it to be the figurehead of a wrecked ship, a very haughty lady in a magnificent costume. She held her head proudly in the air and had a fine, hooked nose" (F. Stevenson 1915: 55). Fanny goes on to describe the troubling influence of the figurehead on the natives of Penrhyn: "When the figurehead came ashore people were terribly alarmed by the appearance of the 'white lady.' The children are still frightened into submission by threats of being handed over to her" (56).

In Stevenson and Osbourne's story, the figurehead is linked—in its stature, its whiteness, and its menace—to the English colonialist William John Attwater who is invariably associated with white clothing, first appearing in his "white clothes, the full dress of the tropics" (Stevenson 1894: 191) and later identified on the shore by "his white clothes shining in the chequered dusk" (196).[8] A particular critical problem has developed around the character of Attwater, a curious merger between "copper-bottomed aristocrat" (197), evangelical missionary, and mercenary trader. Smith argues that "Stevenson represents in the figure of Attwater the dominance of evangelical discourse: a discourse which, in the later nineteenth-century Pacific, prospered through association with colonial policy" (Smith 1998: 162). Frank McLynn goes farther, identifying Attwater as a "terrifying figure . . . [a] monster who conflates the 'business' of profiteering with fundamentalist Christianity in the typical manner of the Victorians" (1994: 466) and suggesting another, autobiographical source: "At a deeper level Attwater is a barely disguised portrait of Thomas Stevenson and represents in hyperbolic form all that Louis most feared and despised in his father" (467). Yet critics have overlooked an equally important—and more immediate—source for Attwater's character in the South Sea journal.

In the climactic scene of the novel, Attwater uses the figurehead as part of a "cruel game," in which the bullet apparently meant for Davis causes "a spasmodic movement of the victim, and immediately above the middle of his forehead, a black hole marred the whiteness of the figurehead" (Stevenson 1894: 248). Two more shots and after the "third shot . . . [t]he cruel game of which he was the puppet was now clear to Davis; three times he had drunk of death, and he must look to drink of it seven times more before he was despatched" (248). This "cruel game" exposes the ideological complexity of Stevenson's quarrying of his South Sea material for use in the fiction, and establishes a source for Attwater in one of the most vivid characters Stevenson encountered on his travels in the South Seas: Tembinok, "The King of Apemama" in the Gilbert Islands. Neil Rennie has described the novelistic quality of this section of *In the South Seas*, terming it "an entertaining narrative [with] a powerful character around whom all the material naturally revolves" (Rennie 1996: xxx). Indeed, more text is devoted to Tembinok than to any other individual in the journal and letters—Stevenson introduces him as the "one great personage in the Gilberts," "the last tyrant, the last erect vestige of a dead society" (209). The parallels between Attwater and Tembinok are numerous. Tembinok rules his island with a Winchester rifle and tyrannizes over his subjects—for example, when his men are slow to build "Equator Town," the temporary residence for the Stevensons named after their schooner, Tembinok "rose, called for a Winchester, stepped without the royal palisade, and fired two shots in the air. A shot in the air is the first Apemama warning; it has the force of a proclamation in more loquacious countries" (219). Tembinok's method of punishing a disobedient subject directly parallels Attwater's "cruel game": "As soon as he was well within range, the travestied monarch fired the six shots over his head, at his feet, and on either hand of him: the second Apemama warning, startling in itself, fatal in significance, for the next time his majesty will aim to hit. I am told the king is a crack shot; that when he aims to kill the grave may be got ready; and when he aims to miss, misses by so near a margin that the culprit tastes six times the bitterness of death" (230).

In an intertextual moment in *The Ebb-Tide*, Attwater refers directly to his Gilbertian counterpart, telling Herrick of "an old king one knew in the western islands, who used to empty a Winchester all round a man, and stir his hair or nick a rag out of his clothes with every ball except the last; and that went plump between the eyes. It was pretty practice" (Stevenson 1894: 209). The explicit parallel is an example of colonial "mimicry," a practice that accounts for the disturbing resemblance between native king and English colonialist.

Tembinok is portrayed as a despotic native king, whose aggressive acquisitiveness mimics the Anglo-Americans' avarice, being "greedy of things new and foreign" and "possessed by the seven devils of the collector" (Stevenson 1896: 213). Attwater's materialism is still more sinister, what Herrick calls his "ten years' collection" (198) of pearls having been acquired at the cost of countless native lives. Attwater's evangelical zeal, far from moderating his profiteering, is its ideological engine: "I have had a business, and a colony, and a mission of my own. I was a man of the world before I was a Christian; I'm a man of the world still, and I made my mission pay" (204). Beneath the veneer of the English gentleman, Stevenson suggests, Attwater has "gone native," being repeatedly compared with native peoples—on his first appearance, the narrative states "A complexion, naturally dark, had been tanned in the island to a hue hardly distinguishable from that of a Tahitian" (192) and while aiming his rifle at Davis "Attwater smiled like a red Indian" (248).

Further physical and sartorial parallels emerge between the king and the trader. Both are physically imposing, indeed larger-than-life figures: Attwater is "a huge fellow, six feet four in height and of a build proportionately strong" (191) while Tembinok is remarkable for "his weighty body," and Stevenson comments, "His corpulence is now portable; you would call him lusty rather than fat" (Stevenson 1896: 211). In a passage later deleted from the South Sea journal, Stevenson describes how Tembinok greets the new arrivals in person: "The ship was no sooner at anchor, than a boat came out with Timpanok's [sic] ladder: and presently after, his majesty appears upon the scene himself and comes on board. . . . A big man, heavy with a somewhat elephantine gait, a bold, strong eye, a singular hooked/beaked profile, and a considerable mane of straight black hair: always elegantly dressed perhaps in green velveteen, perhaps in pajamas of cardinal red silk" (Stevenson HM 2412). Attwater's appearance is also immaculate, "dressed in white drill, exquisitely made; his scarf and tie were of tender-coloured silks" (Stevenson 1894: 192). Likewise, Attwater appears in person to welcome the crew of the *Farallone* (191). There is significant ambivalence, moreover, in this first appearance of Attwater, respecting his race. Appearing in the company of "brown oarsmen," Attwater's whiteness is signified by his clothing rather than his skin, as his face is "shaded."

Yet despite their elegant appearance, both men are brutal oppressors of their peoples: Stevenson describes Tembinok as "the only master, the only male, the sole dispenser of honours" who has shot one of his wives and then "exposed her body in an open box, and (to make the warning more memorable) suffered it to putrefy before the palace gate" (Stevenson 1896: 224). In the manuscript journal, Stevenson elaborates on the draconian disciplinary measures on Apemama: "The laws are strict and strictly but very justly enforced. No native must drink except with the King's leave, none go naked, none be abroad without a lantern between the hours of 9 and 4. Punishment is by fine, enforced by mortgage on crops, convict labour, and imprisonment on the insular prison. This last is considered highly dishonourable; and the convict sometimes escapes from his disgrace by suicide" (Stevenson HM 2412).

Attwater's claim that "I was making a new people here" (Stevenson 1894: 204) indicates his tendency to play God. Indeed, he narrates his own colonial version of divine punishment when "my justice had been made a fool of" (218) in which one native, whom he names Sullens, is falsely accused of breaking the rules, is punished, and later found "hanging in a cocoa-palm—I'm not botanist enough to tell you how—but it's the way, in nine cases out of ten, these natives commit suicide." Sullens's suicide, echoing the practice Stevenson records in his journal, results in Attwater sending the native he names Obsequiousness up a tree to retrieve the mutilated corpse and then shooting him dead so "they came to ground together" (219). Attwater's summary punishment of the native is a more extreme version of Tembinok's punishment of those who disobey him. In one episode from the journal, Stevenson narrates how he complained to Tembinok about a "mulatto cook" who had been assigned to help in the kitchen: "I put it carefully to the sovereign that he was too old and too lazy. 'I think he savy too much' observed the musing Timpanok. And the next I knew was that the cook cut me on the road; and the new man . . . informed Foo [Stevenson's cook, Ah Fu] in the kitchen that his majesty had fired all around the cook and frightened him to death" (Stevenson HM 2412). Herrick's passionate outrage at Attwater's atrocity ("It was a murder . . . a cold-hearted, bloody-minded murder! You monstrous being!"; Stevenson 1894: 219) is notably lacking in Stevenson's account of Tembinok. Indeed, "Stevenson, who was not immune from the appeal of the cult of the hero, admired the tyrant's rule rather than being appalled at the whimsical cruelty which accompanied it" (Hillier 1989: 21).

A more historical explanation would be that the substitution of Attwater for Tembinok doubtless reflects the transition of the Gilbert Islands, from native self-government to British control. In his "Editorial Note" to the 1896 Edinburgh edition of *The South Seas*—also published independently by Scribner's the same year—Sidney Colvin writes that the Gilberts, "at the time of his visit was under independent native government, but has since been annexed by Great Britain" and that the account of Tembinok therefore "derives additional interest from describing a state of manners and government which has now passed away" (Stevenson 1896: vi). As the Gilberts were annexed by Britain in 1892, Stevenson may have decided to represent this loss of independence or identity by turning the native king into an English colonial ruler, one whose only interest in the island is profit. Yet the most convincing reason for the transformation is that RLS saw his South Sea tales as quite different in purpose and status from his "documentary" writing about the region. To include a portrayal of a native king in one of his stories would have blurred the boundary between genres in a way Stevenson wished to avoid. In his desire to be "a serious chronicler of the Pacific" (McLynn 1993: 329), Stevenson made a sharp distinction between his "South Sea Book"—to which he dedicated his best literary labor—and the yarns that he was producing for popular consumption. Writing Colvin in September 1889 Stevenson set out his plans for his "South Sea Yarns," commenting: "strange ways of life, I think, they set forth: things that I can scarce touch upon, or even not at all, in my travel book" (*Ltrs* 6: 330).

Stevenson's cherished distinction between "yarn" and "book" broke down, however, during the serial publication of the "Letters" when his nonfictional observations on South Sea culture and society were juxtaposed with stories by Arthur Conan Doyle, Rudyard Kipling and indeed, Stevenson himself: in March and April, 1891, the serialization of *In the South Seas* was interrupted in *Black and White* for two weeks by the two-part publication of Stevenson's tale "The Bottle Imp." Stevenson came to recognize that the South Sea journal and letters could be "quarried" for more than a nonfictional work on the South Seas. These materials could also serve to revive Stevenson's interest in "romance," providing settings and characters for a new style of fiction. Stevenson's realization that his life in the South Seas demanded a new relationship with the reader is reflected in his assessment that "I must learn to address readers from the uttermost parts of the sea" (Stevenson 1896: 5), but he lamented to Colvin that in the South Sea letters "I have told too much" and "had not sufficient confidence in the reader, and have overfed him" (*Ltrs* 7, 157). Learning to "cruise" in Roland Barthes's sense of seducing the reader, Stevenson's insight was that he must dismember his corpus, and publish his literary remains in more appealing fragments, if he was to satisfy the voracious appetite of the voracious "fireside traveller" (Stevenson 1896: 5) who comprised his audience.

A more historical explanation would be that the substitution of Attwater for Tembinok doubtless reflects the transition of the Gilbert Islands, from native self-government to British control. In his "Editorial Note" to the 1896 Edinburgh edition of *The South Seas*—also published independently by Scribner's the same year—Sidney Colvin writes that the Gilberts, "at the time of his visit was under independent native government, but has since been annexed by Great Britain" and that that the account of Tembinoka therefore "derives additional interest from describing a state of manners and government which has now passed away" (Stevenson 1896: vi). As the Gilberts were annexed by Britain in 1892, Stevenson may have decided to represent this loss of independence or identity by turning the native King into an English colonial ruler, one whose only interest in the island is profit. Yet the most convincing reason for the transformation is that RLS saw his South Sea tales as quite different in purpose and status from his "documentary" writing about the region. To include a portrayal of a native king in one of his stories would have blurred the boundary between genres in a way Stevenson wished to avoid. In his desire to be "a serious chronicler of the Pacific" (McLynn 1993: 329), Stevenson made a sharp distinction between his "South Sea Book"—to which he dedicated his best literary labor—and the yarns that he was producing for popular consumption. Writing Colvin in September 1889 Stevenson set out his plans for his "South Sea Yarns," commenting: "strange ways of life, I think, they set forth: things that I can scarce touch upon, or even not at all, in my travel book" (*Ltrs* 6: 330).

Stevenson's cherished distinction between "yarn" and "book" broke down, however, during the serial publication of the "Letters" when his non-fictional observations on South Sea culture and society were juxta-posed with stories by Arthur Conan Doyle, Rudyard Kipling and indeed, Stevenson himself: in March and April, 1891, the serialization of *In the South Seas* was interrupted in *Black and White* for two weeks by the two-part publication of Stevenson's tale "The Bottle Imp." Stevenson came to recognize that the South Sea journal and letters could be "quarried" for more than a non-fictional work on the South Seas. These materials could also serve to revive Stevenson's interest in "romance," providing settings and characters for a new style of fiction. Stevenson's realization that his life in the South Seas demanded a new relationship with the reader is reflected in his assessment that "I must learn to address readers from the uttermost parts of the sea"(Stevenson 1896: 5), but he lamented to Colvin that in the South Sea letters "I have told too much" and "had not sufficient con-fidence in the reader, and have overfed him" (*Ltrs* 7, 157). Learning to "cruise" in Roland Barthes's sense of seducing the reader, Stevenson's insight was that he must dismember his corpus, and publish his literary remains in more appealing fragments, if he was to satisfy the voracious appetite of the voracious "fireside traveller" (Stevenson 1896: 5) who comprised his audience.

NOTES

1. In the first of his South Sea letters, Stevenson portrays himself as an invalid in search of health, "For nearly ten years my health had been declining; and for some while before I set forth upon my voyage, I believed I was come to the afterpiece of life and had only the nurse and undertaker to expect. It was suggested that I should try the South Seas" (1891b, 1: 23).

2. Stevenson's emphasis on the leisure of cruising, as well as the ease and stimulation of island life, was continuous with his earlier travel writings such as *An Inland Voyage* and *Travels with a Donkey*, which highlighted the casual and dilettante features of travel. Of his voyage by canoe along the canals of Belgium and France, he writes that "it was to be the most leisurely of progresses" (1878: 47) on which his canoe drifted randomly "like a leaf in the current" (51). In *Travels with a Donkey*, Stevenson asserted "I travel not to go anywhere, but to go. I travel for travel's sake. The great affair is to move" (1879: 163) and portrays his journey as motivated by casual desire rather than a solid purpose: "it was only a fancy; yet a fancy will sometimes be importunate" (189).

3. By contrast, the letters in *Black and White* were subtitled: *A Record of Three Cruises* suggesting a documentary purpose and organized itinerary, as opposed to the "leisurely traveler" of the New York *Sun*. This documentary quality to the letters was also enhanced by the high-quality, almost photographic illustrations in *Black and White*.

4. Stevenson "felt that the complex savagery and grandeur he was experiencing could inspire an epic masterpiece, which he would call *In the South Seas* and which would encompass history, ethnology, geology, and folklore, rather than the mere collection of observations and anecdotes on exotica McClure had hired him to write" (Hillier 1989: 34). McClure, unsurprisingly, objected that "the letters did not come as letters are supposed to come. They were not a correspondence from the South Seas, they were not dated and . . . in no way did the matter . . . fulfil the definition of the word 'letter' , as used in newspaper correspondence" (Stevenson 1896: xx–xxi).

5. In "Memoirs of an Islet" (1887) he recalls three weeks spent at such a "quarry" in the summer of 1870, during the construction of the Dhu Heartach lighthouse by his father's engineering firm.

6. There is an ongoing tension in Stevenson's South Seas writing between the pleasure and sensual stimulation of "cruising"—allowing for a distant and superficial or partial perception of the beauty of sea and islands—and the realities of labor, disease, exploitation, and conflict that descend on the "cruiser" when s/he disembarks and settles. In part this tension results from the contrast between myths and stereotypes of South Sea islanders as peace-loving "children," and the reality of civil war taking place at Samoa (dealt with in *A Footnote to History*, 1892), a work that unfortunately lies outside the immediate province of this essay).

7. The incident in "Falesá" is undoubtedly inspired by Ben Hird's anecdote, recorded by Fanny. However, it is interesting to note how fascinated Stevenson is by the idea of the living dead throughout his career. An early story, "The Body Snatcher," features a supposed corpse coming back to life at the end of the story. At the end of the *Master of Ballantrae* (1889), the Master is buried alive and returns to life, leading to the death of his brother (see Buckton 2000).

8. McLynn describes the white figurehead as "a symbol of hope . . . whose whiteness turns out on closer inspection to be 'leprous'" (1993: 466). However, the symbolism of the figurehead as hopeful is never, in my view, established.

REFERENCES

Barthes, Roland. 1973. *Le plaisir du texte*. Paris: Seuil. English translation: *The Pleasure of the Text*. Trans. Richard Miller. 1975. New York: Hill and Wang.

Buckton, Oliver. 2000. Reanimating Stevenson's Corpus. *Nineteenth-Century Literature* 55 (1): 22–58.

Daiches, David. 1994. Introduction. *The Ebb-Tide,* by Robert Louis Stevenson. London: Dent. xvii–xxvii.

Gosse, Edmund. 1908. *Biographical Notes on the Writings of Robert Louis Stevenson*. London: Chiswick Press (privately printed).

Hillier, Robert Irwin. 1989. *The South Seas Fiction of Robert Louis Stevenson*. New York: Peter Lang.

McLynn, Frank. 1993. *Robert Louis Stevenson : A Biography*. London: Pimlico.

Menikoff, Barry. 1994. *Robert Louis Stevenson and "The Beach of Falesá": A Study in Victorian Publishing*. Stanford, CA: Stanford University Press.

Rennie, Neil. 1996. Introduction. In Stevenson 1896/1996.

Smith, Vanessa. 1998. *Literary Culture and the Pacific: Nineteenth-Century Textual Encounters*. Cambridge: Cambridge University Press.

Stevenson, Fanny Van de Grift. 1915. *The Cruise of the "Janet Nichol" among the South Sea Islands*. New York: Scribner's.

Stevenson, Robert Louis. HM 2412. "Journal of Two Visits to the South Seas." Huntington Library. San Marino, CA.

———. 1878. *An Inland Voyage*. In *Travels with a Donkey in the Cévennes and Selected Travel Writings*. Ed. Emma Letley. 1992. New York: Oxford University Press.

———. 1879. *Travels with a Donkey in the Cévennes*. In *Travels with a Donkey in the Cévennes and Selected Travel Writings*. Ed. Emma Letley. 1992. New York: Oxford University Press.

———. 1887. "Memories of an Islet." In *Memories and Portraits*. 1898. New York: Charles Scribner's Sons.

———. 1891a. "The South Seas: Life Under the Equator, Letters from a Leisurely Traveller." [New York] *Sun*. February 1–December 13, 1891.

———. 1891b. "The South Seas: A Record of Three Cruises." *Black and White* 1–2 (London), 6 February–19 December, 1891.

———. 1892. "The Beach of Falesá." In *South Sea Tales*. Ed. Roslyn Jolly. 1996. Oxford: Oxford University Press.

——— (with Lloyd Osbourne). 1894. *The Ebb-Tide: A Trio and a Quartette*. In *South Sea Tales*. Ed. Roslyn Jolly. 1996. Oxford: Oxford University Press.

———. 1896. *In the South Seas*. Ed. Neil Rennie. 1996. New York: Penguin.

PART III

Evolutionary Psychology, Masculinity, and Dr. Jekyll and Mr. Hyde

Stevenson, Romance, and Evolutionary Psychology

JULIA REID

"The fortune of a tale lies not alone in the skill of him that writes," Stevenson wrote in 1887, "but as much, perhaps, in the inherited experience of him who reads; and when I hear with a particular thrill of things that I have never done or seen, it is one of that innumerable army of my ancestors rejoicing in past deeds" (Stevenson 1887a: 102). In this essay, "Pastoral," Stevenson scrutinized the pleasures of narrative and, shifting the focus provocatively from writer to reader, attributed these in part to the reader's "inherited experience," to a resurgence of unconscious, ancestral memories. The importance of heredity in literature was, indeed, a preoccupying interest for Stevenson. In essays written throughout the 1880s, he explored the unconscious roots both of artistic appreciation and of the creative imagination. These essays, after long critical neglect, have recently been given serious scholarly attention (Fielding 1996; Norquay 1999). Yet although Stevenson's emphasis on racial inheritance clearly allied him to the new science of evolutionary psychology, the engagement with evolutionary theories in these essays has remained largely unexplored. This chapter suggests that evolutionary psychology provided an important intellectual context for Stevenson's essays, underlying and shaping his interventions in literary debate throughout the 1880s. The chapter will explore Stevenson's complex and often ambivalent deployment of evolutionary psychology, focusing on "A Humble Remonstrance" (1884), "Pastoral" (1887), "The Manse" (1887), "Child's Play" (1878), "A Chapter on Dreams" (1888), and "Talk and Talkers" (1882). In these essays, Stevenson drew on evolutionist rhetoric, but he also destabilized many of its assumptions—assumptions about the nature and direction of the evolutionary process, and about the relations between "primitive" and "civilized" life.

The concept of evolution was central to Victorian science and was variously applied to the development of individuals, species, cultures, and societies. In the following century, evolutionism came to be exclusively associated with Charles Darwin, but Darwin's thesis was only one of many conflicting yet collectively influential theories of evolution (Bowler 1993). In the 1850s, '60s, and '70s, in what is now accepted as a development independent of Darwinism, sociocultural evolutionists including Herbert Spencer and E. B. Tylor presented secularizing accounts of humankind's mental and cultural evolution, exploring how language, religion, art, science, and morality had developed as part of a natural progression from savagery to civilization (Stocking 1987). The disciplines of evolutionary psychology and anthropology sprang essentially from this sociocultural evolutionism. Spencer was the founding father of the new psychology, and a subsequent generation of scientists, following his dictum that "Mind can be understood only by observing how Mind is evolved," interpreted psychology in terms not only of individual but of racial development (Spencer 1870–72, v. 1: 192; Rylance 2000: 203–50). Tylor's *Primitive Culture* (1871), meanwhile, established the fundamental assumption of anthropology, its belief in a unilinear scale of culture, where humans progressed from savagery, through barbarism, to civilization, and where modern "savages" represented a "survival" from the earliest condition of humankind. These evolutionist treatments of psychology and culture looked simultaneously backward and forward. Concerned with the legibility of the past in the present, they were nonetheless essentially progressive in their interpretation of evolution, celebrating what they viewed as the upward movement of the human mind (Spencer 1870–72, v. 1: 3; Tylor 1871, v. 2: 401–10).

Stevenson was preoccupied by the same questions that exercised his contemporaries within the field of evolutionary psychology: What was the rôle of culture (and specifically literature) in human mental and social development? How important was the influence of heredity? How far did the past live on, consciously or unconsciously, within the present? What were the relations of "savage" and "civilized" life? These questions, which are at the heart of much of Stevenson's writing, tapped into late-Victorian debate within the psychological discipline.

Not only did Stevenson share these intellectual preoccupations, he also moved in the same social circles as many prominent evolutionary scientists—most notably the folklorist Andrew Lang, the evolutionary psychologist James Sully, and the psychical researcher F. W. H. Myers—and he repeatedly discussed with them ideas about the unconscious basis of literature. Late-Victorian literary London, its clubs and periodicals, made these interdisciplinary associations possible. Sully wrote that "Although I was [Stevenson's] senior, the fact of our having joined the Savile [Club] at about the same time, and still more the synchronizing of our series of contributions to the Cornhill, made him seem in a curious way a brotherly companion." The nature of their intellectual engagement was suggested by Sully in his recollections of how he "wrote an article for an American review on the connection between imaginative writing and dreaming—a subject I was no doubt led to think about by a talk I had recently enjoyed with R. L. Stevenson at Skerryvore" (Sully 1918: 215, 194). Stevenson's work has been represented as unquestioningly "dramatizing" the scientific theories of evolutionists including Sully (Block 1982: 444). However, as Sully's remarks indicate, Stevenson's intellectual relationship with evolutionary scientists was clearly dynamic and reciprocal. It amounted to a creative dialogue, in which Stevenson was able to resist as well as affirm the tales told by evolutionary psychology.

Stevenson's engagement with evolutionist psychology emerges most clearly in the 1880s literary debate about "romance" and "realism." The clash between the supporters of "romance" and the defenders of "realism" was not a new contest of values, but it was one that took on renewed urgency in the context of arguments about the new "mass readership." Debate turned on questions about the advance of literature and the intellectual progress of contemporary readers. W. D. Howells defended Henry James's psychological realism as a more advanced, "new kind of fiction": "the stories were all told long ago," Howells wrote; readers now wanted analytic studies and should surrender the "childish . . . demand" for "finished" tales (Howells 1882, v. 1: 319, 323). Howells's progressivist emphasis chimed with the evolutionist narrative of psychological development. For while Spencer, Tylor, Sully, and others certainly recognized the primitive, sensual basis of literary pleasure, they did so within a framework that emphasized the passage toward a more civilized art. With increasingly peaceful social conditions, Spencer explained, art appealed to ever more refined and sympathetic feelings (Spencer 1870–72, v. 2: 648).

The champions of romance, however, saw psychological realism as a mark not of intellectual progress but of morbid overcivilization. Only adventure novels, Andrew Lang believed, could exert a truly popular appeal, attracting not just the highly cultured but, potentially, a mass readership. For Lang, the revival of "romance"—in novels by Stevenson, H. Rider Haggard, and others—appealed to savage "survivals" within human psychology. Declaring jubilantly that "Not for nothing did Nature leave us all savages under our white skins," he mocked the "Coming Man" as "bald, toothless, highly 'cultured,' and addicted to tales of introspective analysis" (Lang 1887: 689).

Stevenson similarly deployed evolutionist rhetoric to celebrate what he saw as the universal appeal of romance, suggesting that the pleasure derived from this form of narrative was rooted in humankind's primitive heritage. In "The Art of Fiction," Henry James mounted a subtle defense of realist novels that attempted to "reproduce" life (James 1884: 510). Stevenson responded with "A Humble Remonstrance," objecting to James's belief that "art . . . can successfully 'compete with life,'" and contending rather that the value of art lay in its *difference* from life. He overturned the hierarchy between serious novels that appealed to the intellect, and low-brow art that gratified the senses, suggesting that the romance was just as valuable as the Jamesian "novel of character." Stevenson's valorization of novels that appealed to the "sensual and quite illogical tendencies in man" challenged James's criticism of adventure novels and, specifically, of *Treasure Island* (Stevenson 1884: 281, 283, 286). James had suggested that a novel's success depended largely on whether it touched a reader's experience: "I have been a child," he wrote, "but I have never been on a quest for a buried Treasure" (James 1884: 518). Stevenson countered what he saw as James's narrow definition of experience, exclaiming that, in dreams at least, every child had hunted treasure, had "been a pirate, and a military commander, and a bandit of the mountains." *Treasure Island*, he claimed, stirred atavistic instincts: "The luxury, to most of us, is to lay by our judgment, to be submerged by the tale as by a billow" (Stevenson 1884: 287).

Stevenson, then, deployed evolutionist rhetoric to argue that "romance," being rooted in universal dreams and instinctual desires, had a deeper resonance and broader relevance than the "novel of character." Throughout the 1880s, Stevenson's essays returned, as if compulsively, to this central theme: the appeal of romance to the evolutionary unconscious. "Pastoral" (1887), which initially appears to be a gently evocative essay about childhood memories, unfolds as a call for a genuinely popular literary art, one that would embody a connection with humanity's primitive heritage. The essay affirms the importance of heredity in humans' ability to take pleasure in narrative, explaining that a "trade that touches nature, one . . . in which we have all had ancestors employed, so that on a hint of it ancestral memories revive, lends itself to literary use, vocal or written" (Stevenson 1887a: 102). This invocation of "ancestral memories" draws on the theory of "organic memory"—the idea, formulated by Spencer, Samuel Butler, and others, that individuals remembered their ancestors' experiences unconsciously, through the instincts (Spencer 1870–72, v. 1: 452; Otis 1994: 1–40). Stevenson's deployment of "organic memory" theory is inflected by a democratic rhetoric, an emphasis on the latent capacities of the common reader (thus the tale's fortune "lies not alone in the skill of him that writes, but as much, perhaps, in the inherited experience of him who reads"). Stevenson hails the romance as a truly popular form, judging that "novels begin to touch not the fine *dilettanti* but the gross mass of mankind, when they leave off to speak of parlours and shades of manner and still-born niceties of motive, and begin to deal with fighting, sailoring, adventure, death or child-birth; and thus ancient outdoor crafts and occupations, whether Mr. Hardy wields the shepherd's crook or Count Tolstoi swings the scythe, lift romance into a near neighbourhood with epic. These aged things have on them the dew of men's morning; they lie near, not so much to us, the semi-artificial flowerets, as to the trunk and aboriginal taproot of the race" (Stevenson 1887a: 102–3).

The sense of decadence conveyed by this metaphor of "semi-artificial flowerets" and vigorous "aboriginal taproot" suggests how Stevenson's deployment of "organic memory" theory undercut its conventionally progressivist assumptions. Theorists such as Spencer and Butler, despite their emphasis on the potency of the unconscious, retained a confident belief in the upward movement of the human mind (Spencer 1870–72, v. 1: 503; Otis 1994: 25, 40). By contrast, Stevenson detects, and celebrates, the primitive forces still potent within the most apparently refined and cultivated. With a mischievous glee, he describes his most admired literary critic, "a certain low-browed, hairy gentleman, at first a percher in the fork of trees, next (as they relate) a dweller in caves," and identifies him as, in Darwin's phrase, "Probably Arboreal."[1] In a deterministic move that scorns the pretensions of the "fine *dilettanti*," Stevenson reduces literary appreciation to ancestral influences. "Probably Arboreal" tops every family tree, and "in all our veins run some minims of his old, wild tree-top blood; our civilised nerves still tingle with his rude terrors and pleasures; and to that which would have moved our common ancestor, all must obediently thrill" (Stevenson 1887a: 103–4). These "rude terrors and pleasures," Stevenson suggests, can be rekindled by romance, and this resurgence of hereditary forces is viewed as a profoundly revitalizing experience.

"The Manse," published in the same year as "Pastoral" (1887), does not engage so directly with debates about romance. However, its concern with dormant primitive memory provides a comparable, if oblique, comment on what Stevenson saw as the function of romance—namely the arousal of primitive instincts. In this essay, Stevenson reflects on his ancestry, again using the trope of unconscious memory to link the individual present with a collective past. Recalling childhood visits to his grandfather's manse, he wonders what he has "inherited from this old minister." He invokes "our antenatal lives," explaining that "Our conscious years are but a moment in the history of the elements that build us" (Stevenson 1887b: 112, 116–17). This observation plays down the importance of conscious, rational elements in human life, strikingly echoing Samuel Butler's judgment, in *Life and Habit* (1878), that the "history of man prior to his birth is more important . . . than his surroundings after birth" (Butler 1878: 249). Stevenson's evocation of "antenatal lives" works to erode barriers between individuals, connecting them together in a collective psychological narrative that spans the generations. Thus he imagines joining in his grandfather's childhood games: "that, too, was a scene of my education. Some part of me played there in the eighteenth century." Indeed, he continues whimsically, "this *homunculus* or part-man of mine that walked about the eighteenth century with Dr. Balfour [his grandfather] in his youth, was in the way of meeting other *homunculos* [*sic*] or part-men, in the persons of my other ancestors. . . . as I went to college with Dr. Balfour, I may have seen the lamp and oil man taking down the shutters from his shop . . . and from the eyes of the lamp and oil man one-half of my unborn father, and one-quarter of myself, looked out upon us" (Stevenson 1887b: 114, 115–16).[2]

This sense that the line between individual and collective memory was blurred—and that the unconscious was not just personal but racial—was fundamental to nineteenth-century evolutionary psychology from Spencer onward (Small 2000: 67–68). But whereas Spencer and others usually saw the evolutionary past as prelude to an ever more civilized present, Stevenson viewed it as compensation for the present. It affords, in "The Manse," a heady sense of immortality, and translates personal identity from an impotent and effete present into a heroic past. Stevenson asks, "Are you a bank-clerk, and do you live at Peckham? It was not always so. And though to-day I am only a man of letters, . . . I was present when a skipper, plying from Dundee, smuggled Jacobites to France after the '15." Tracing his "antenatal" self further into the past, he lists all his vicarious experiences, declaring that "parts of me have seen life, and met adventures." The process moves from the individual, through the family, nation, human race, to the animal kingdom, culminating "in the still cloudier past." Returning to his favorite Darwinian phrase, Stevenson imagines that "the threads that make me up can be traced by fancy into the bosoms of thousands and millions of ascendants. . . . What sleeper in green tree-tops, what muncher of nuts, concludes my pedigree? Probably arboreal in his habits" (Stevenson 1887b: 117, 118).

The discovery of ancestral origins brings a thrilling sense of invigoration, although underneath this lies a potentially more unsettling perception of mysterious and uncontrollable hereditary forces. Stevenson's grandfather, a "grave, reverend" minister, is at the mercy of "an aboriginal frisking of blood that was not his; tree-top memories, like undeveloped negatives, lay dormant in his mind; tree-top instincts awoke and were trod down; and Probably Arboreal . . . gambolled and chattered in the brain of the old divine" (Stevenson 1887b: 119). It is a revealing passage, identifying the primitive forces still alive in the civilized figure of the "old divine," and threatening to collapse the forward-moving narrative of evolution. Outbreaks of unconscious memory figure as arbitrary primitive resurgences ("tree-top instincts awoke and were trod down"). The metaphor of "undeveloped negatives"—lying "dormant" but ready to be reawakened— also evokes the unpredictability of inherited instincts. This uncertainty brings Stevenson's vision closer to Darwin than to Spencer. In *The Variation of Animals and Plants Under Domestication* (1868), Darwin described the latent propensities harbored within organisms: written in "invisible characters," they are "ready to be evolved whenever the organization is disturbed by certain known or unknown conditions" (Darwin 1868, vol. 2: 36). Yet despite the uneasy frisson occasionally generated by the survival of a savage inheritance, Stevenson clearly celebrated the exhilaration which this afforded.

The appeal of the romance, he believed, lay in its capacity to trigger these bracing "tree-top memories," to develop the atavistic "negatives." Romance was not the only realm in which Stevenson believed primitive instinctual desires might be gratified; childhood make-believe, oral narratives, and dreams likewise embodied the primitive sources of the imagination. This interest in the origins of modern literature and culture was shared by many late-Victorians. For evolutionary psychologists, the childhood imagination, dream life, and oral tales were, like "savage" culture, representative of an earlier stage of evolutionary development (Lang 1889: xi; Sully 1893; Taylor and Shuttleworth 1998: 115). In his essays "Child's Play," "A Chapter on Dreams," and "Talk and Talkers," Stevenson scrutinized the evolution of imaginative processes in similar terms, but he also questioned the meliorist accent on gradual imaginative refinement, suggesting instead the vitality of primitive states of consciousness.

Stevenson's essay "Child's Play" (1878) is predicated on the evolutionist belief that children recapitulated the developmental stages passed through in the evolution of the race. Tylor wrote that "in our childhood we dwelt at the very gates of the realm of myth"; "Even in civilized countries," he continued, animism (the personification of inanimate objects, and for Tylor the mark of "primitive" psychology) "makes its appearance as the child's early theory of the outer world" (Tylor 1871, v. 1: 257–58). "Child's Play" mingles anecdotes about Stevenson's own childhood games with reflections on the imaginative processes at work in children's play. Echoing Tylor's vocabulary, Stevenson ruminates on children's "frame of mind," and finds himself quite disconcerted, exclaiming, "Surely they dwell in a mythological epoch, and are not the contemporaries of their parents." Like Tylor, Lang, and Sully, Stevenson describes how much of this primitive psychology is sloughed off on reaching adulthood; yet for him the imaginative impulse itself is not lost but merely redirected. The child's play, he declares, prefigures the adult's romance: "It is when we make castles in the air and personate the leading character in our own romances, that we return to the spirit of our first years" (Stevenson 1878: 357, 356).[3] This comparison draws on Spencer's belief in the similarity of the "play-impulse" and the "æsthetic sentiments." However, Spencer's narrative has a progressive impetus, figuring the "æsthetic sentiments" as a "higher" version of the "play-impulse" (Spencer 1870–72, v. 2: 627, 632). By contrast, Stevenson affirms the enduring vitality of the child's consciousness within civilized adults.

"A Chapter on Dreams" (1888) also dramatizes the persistence of pre-civilized states of consciousness. It furnishes a personal narrative in order to explore the affinities between dreams, myth-making, and the literary imagination, depicting the young Stevenson as composed of two distinct consciousnesses, a waking and a dreaming self. Evoking the involuntary nature of the unconscious, Stevenson describes his conscious self when asleep as the audience at a play, entertained by the "sleepless Brownies" who "manage man's internal theatre," and who provide inspiration for the tales that the waking Stevenson is able to write (Stevenson 1888: 194, 193).

These "Brownies" clearly personify Stevenson's creative unconscious. They are viewed through an evolutionary perspective as the myth-making savage that survives within a civilized human exterior: Stevenson laments, "I do most of the morality, worse luck! and my Brownies have not a rudiment of what we call a conscience." The belief that the human psyche harbored traces of many different developmental stages underlies his account of imaginative inspiration. Stevenson awkwardly distinguishes his Brownies from "myself—what I call I, my conscious ego, the denizen of the pineal gland unless he has changed his residence since Descartes." This hesitancy over "myself—what I call I" intimates that there is no such thing as a fully rational, conscious ego, and that Stevenson's Brownies may be in control more often than he imagines. He admits that "my Brownies . . . do one-half my work for me while I am fast asleep, and in all human likelihood, do the rest for me as well, when I am wide awake and fondly suppose I do it for myself" (Stevenson 1888: 198, 197).

While "A Chapter on Dreams" points to the survival of a vigorous primitive consciousness, elsewhere Stevenson suggested that this was in danger of being muffled by the civilized accretions of modern life. "Talk and Talkers" and "Talk and Talkers: A Sequel" (1882) contrast a spontaneous and original orality with modern print culture. Stevenson clearly shared the late-Victorian fascination with oral culture—a fascination that, Linda Dowling notes, drew on the new scientific belief that language was essentially constituted by sound, and that spoken dialects hence represented the most active, vital form of language (Dowling 1986: 61–65). Written literature, Stevenson argues in "Talk and Talkers," is the product of degeneration rather than progress, being "no other than the shadow of good talk" (Stevenson 1882b: 153). He depicts "good talk" as a rejuvenating struggle: "The aboriginal man within us, the cave-dweller, still lusty as when he fought tooth and nail for roots and berries, scents this kind of equal battle from afar; it is . . . a return to the sincerity of savage life from the comfortable fictions of the civilised" (Stevenson 1882c: 151). The opposition is between an authentic, primitive, and ferocious orality and a feeble and insincere modern literature (the "comfortable fictions of the civilised"). This perception of a degenerate modern literary scene clearly informed Stevenson's romance polemics. The revived romance form, for Stevenson, heralded at least a partial return to an unaffected oral culture: the "real art," he wrote in "A Humble Remonstrance," was that "of the first men who told their stories around the savage camp-fire" (Stevenson 1884: 284).[4]

Throughout the 1880s, then, Stevenson's romance polemics and other essays focused on the revitalizing potential of the imagination and its ability to reconnect modern individuals with the earliest stage of evolutionary development. This chapter has suggested that Stevenson and the evolutionary psychologists were engaged in a common endeavor to explore the hidden mysteries of the unconscious mind. It was an endeavor, however, marked by dissonance as well as consonance. While Stevenson's emphasis on the inherited and racial nature of imaginative processes chimed with evolutionist interpretations of human psychology, his depiction (and valorization) of primitive resurgences also undercut the narrative of smooth progress from "savagery" to "civilization."

This fundamental tension in Stevenson's deployment of evolutionary psychology is illuminated, finally, by the divergent evolutionist responses to "A Chapter on Dreams." F. W. H. Myers and James Sully both welcomed the essay as a recognition of the wide compass of the unconscious mind. Myers's reaction was one of wholehearted enthusiasm. In *Human Personality and Its Survival of Bodily Death* (1903), he hailed Stevenson's essay as a "description of the most successful dream-experiments thus far recorded." The essay seemed to confirm Myers's belief in the liberating value of states of altered consciousness. Stevenson's account of his independent dream life resonated with his own theory of a "subliminal Self" and endorsed his faith that creative inspiration represented a surge of unconscious energies, an "uprushing lava-stream from caves of hidden fire" (Myers 1903, v. 1: 14–15, 126, 90). However, Myers's unqualified appreciation of Stevenson's essay reflected his somewhat marginal position within British psychological thought. As a founding member of the Society for Psychical Research, he rejected the dominant evolutionist progressivism, emphasizing instead the importance and value of the unconscious mind.

James Sully's response was more equivocal. Sully, as he recalled in his 1918 autobiography, was intrigued by Stevenson's account of the unconscious nature of inspiration and began to investigate the nature of literary creativity. Having collected "personal testimonies" from many novelists, he concluded that "there are two pretty clearly marked types of novelist. Howell's [*sic*] attempt to make all fiction 'voluntary' activity . . . will not do in the face of Stevenson's account of how the little people, unknown to him, do all the weaving work." Sully also experimented with creative writing himself, and found it, as Stevenson described, a largely involuntary process. Yet here he reacted with less enthusiasm than Myers. His respect for the "creator of fiction," he noted, was diminished (though not his esteem for Stevenson's own literary work), and he decided that the "art of story-weaving," rather than being the sign of highly-evolved intelligence, was "a sort of trick" (Sully 1918: 194–95, 196–97). The intimation that literature might represent a primitive resurgence clearly disturbed Sully's confidence in a forward-moving evolutionary narrative.

Both Sully and Myers acknowledged a debt to Stevenson in their thinking about imagination. It is a debt that illustrates the complex interweaving of late-Victorian literary and scientific discourses, and suggests that Stevenson was able to engage critically and dynamically with evolutionist thought. Sully's rather wary, and more conventional, response to the essay's depiction of the revival of instinctual life indicates the ambivalence of Stevenson's evolutionism. While his essays drew on evolutionist belief in the primitive origins of literary pleasure and deployed a scientific vocabulary of "survivals" and "organic memory," they also undercut the progressive narrative of psychological development. Stevenson's essays—on romance, children's tales, dreams, and spoken narratives—celebrated the endurance of humankind's primitive heritage into the apparently refined present. In doing so, they unsettled the boundaries between "savagery" and "civilization," low and high culture, the senses and the intellect, and the unconscious and conscious mind.

NOTES

1. The phrase "Probably Arboreal" was a favorite of Stevenson's, and also occurs several times in "The Manse." It originated with Darwin, who observed, "We thus learn that man is descended from a hairy, tailed quadruped, probably arboreal in its habits" (Darwin 1871: 533).

2. Stevenson clearly echoes Laurence Sterne's *The Life and Opinions of Tristram Shandy, Gentleman.* Tristram Shandy describes himself as "The HOMUNCULUS," though Shandy employs the term in a more limited sense, as the minuscule human form believed to harbor in the spermatozoon (Sterne 1760: 6).

3. This description strikingly foreshadows Freud's portrayal, thirty years later, of the "growing child": "instead of playing, he now phantasies. He builds castles in the air and creates what are called day-dreams" (Freud 1908: 438).

4. For a discussion of the links between the late nineteenth-century romance revival and the cult of orality, see Fielding 1996: 132–51.

REFERENCES

Block, Ed. 1982. James Sully, Evolutionist Psychology, and Late-Victorian Gothic Fiction. *Victorian Studies* 25: 443–67.

Bowler, Peter J. 1993. *Biology and Social Thought.* Berkeley: Office for History of Science and Technology, University of California at Berkeley.

Butler, Samuel. 1878. *Life and Habit.* London: Trübner.

Darwin, Charles. 1868, 2nd ed. 1875. *The Variation of Animals and Plants Under Domestication.* 1998. Baltimore: Johns Hopkins University Press.

―――. 1871, 2nd ed. 1874. *The Descent of Man and Selection in Relation to Sex.* 1990. London: Folio Society.

Dowling, Linda. 1986. *Language and Decadence in the Victorian Fin de Siècle.* Princeton, NJ: Princeton University Press.

Fielding, Penny. 1996. *Writing and Orality: Nationality, Culture, and Nineteenth-Century Scottish Fiction.* Oxford: Clarendon Press.

Freud, Sigmund. 1908. Creative Writers and Day-dreaming (Der Dichter und das Phantasieren). In *The Freud Reader.* Ed. Peter Gay. 1995. London: Random House. 436–43.

Howells, W. D. 1882. Henry James, Jr. In James (ed. Halfmann & Lohmann) 1993, v. 1. 317–23.

James, Henry. 1884. The Art of Fiction. *Longman's Magazine* 4: 502–21.

James, Henry (ed. Ulrich Halfmann & Christoph K. Lohmann). 1993. *Selected Literary Criticism.* 3 vols. Bloomington: Indiana University Press.

Lang, Andrew. 1887. Realism and Romance. *Contemporary Review* 52: 683–93.

―――. 1889. *The Blue Fairy Book.* London: Longmans, Green & Co.

Myers, F. W. H. 1903. *Human Personality and Its Survival of Bodily Death.* 2 vols. London: Longmans and Green.

Norquay, Glenda. 1999. Introduction. In *R. L. Stevenson on Fiction: An Anthology of Literary and Critical Essays.* Edinburgh: Edinburgh University Press. 1–25.

Otis, Laura. 1994. *Organic Memory: History and the Body in the Late Nineteenth and Early Twentieth Centuries.* Lincoln: University of Nebraska Press.

Rylance, Rick. 2000. *Victorian Psychology and British Culture 1850–1880.* Oxford: Oxford University Press.

Sandison, Alan. 1996. *Robert Louis Stevenson and the Appearance of Modernism.* Basingstoke, UK: Macmillan.

Small, Helen. 2000. The Unquiet Limit: Old Age and Memory in Victorian Narrative. In *Memory and Memorials 1789–1914.* Ed. Matthew Campbell, Jacqueline M. Labbé, and Sally Shuttleworth. London: Routledge.

Spencer, Herbert. 1855, 2nd ed. 1870–72. *The Principles of Psychology.* 2 vols. London: Williams and Norgate.

Sterne, Laurence. 1760. *The Life and Opinions of Tristram Shandy, Gentleman.* Ed. Ian Campbell Ross. 1983. Oxford: Oxford University Press.

Stevenson, Robert Louis. 1878. "Child's Play." *Cornhill Magazine* 38: 352–59.

―――. 1882a. "A Gossip on Romance." In Stevenson 1904. 247–74.

―――. 1882b. "Talk and Talkers." In Stevenson (ed. Harman) 1992. 153–62.

―――. 1882c. "Talk and Talkers: A Sequel." *Cornhill Magazine* 46: 151–58.

―――. 1884. "A Humble Remonstrance." In Stevenson 1904. 275–99.

―――. 1887a. "Pastoral." In Stevenson 1904. 90–105.

―――. 1887b. "The Manse." In Stevenson 1904. 106–19.

―――. 1888. "A Chapter on Dreams." In Stevenson (ed. Harman) 1992. 189–99.

―――. 1904. *Memories and Portraits.* London: Chatto & Windus.

Stevenson, Robert Louis. 1992. *Essays and Poems.* Ed. Claire Harman. London: J. M. Dent.

Stocking, George W., Jr. 1987. *Victorian Anthropology*. New York: Free Press.

Sully, James. 1893. The Dream as a Revelation. *Fortnightly Review* n.s. 53: 354–69.

————. 1918. *My Life and Friends*. London: T. Fisher Unwin.

Taylor, Jenny Bourne and Sally Shuttleworth, eds. 1998. *Embodied Selves: An Anthology of Psychological Texts 1830–1890*. Oxford: Oxford University Press.

Tylor, E. B. 1871. *Primitive Culture: Researches into the Development of Mythology, Philosophy, Religion, Art, and Custom*. 2 vols. London: John Murray.

Robert Louis Stevenson and Nineteenth-Century Theories of Evolution

Crossing the Boundaries between Ideas and Art

Robert Louis Stevenson, a writer of wide and eclectic interests, has been seen as someone who made a serious effort "to account for the forces of science" (Paradis and Postlewait 1985: ix–x).[1] I contend that Stevenson attempted to do no such thing, and that this was especially true of his attitude toward Darwinism. Instead, he was concerned, through the medium of art, to defend the infinite scope and variety, autonomy and dignity of all life—and especially human life—in the face of what he saw as the new doctrine of evolution.[2]

Born into a family of distinguished engineers, the young Stevenson was originally destined to follow in his father's footsteps. By 1873, he had read a paper titled "On a New Form of Intermittent Light for Lighthouses" at a meeting of the Royal Society in Edinburgh that won him a silver medal, another paper "On the Thermal Influence of Forests" again at the Royal Society, and one on "Local Conditions Influencing Climate" at a meeting of the Scottish Meteorological Society. Stevenson was fairly well read in scientific subjects in general, and he was also familiar with theories concerning human evolution.[3] In his opinion, however, "Scientific men, who imagine that their science affords an answer to the problems of existence, are perhaps the most to be pitied of mankind" (Stevenson 1874–75: 249), and he believed that science carries the intellect "into zones of speculation, where there is no habitable city for the mind of man" (Stevenson 1892: 61).

There are a number of possible reasons for the decisiveness with which Stevenson expressed himself in this regard. First, he was aware of inconsistencies in scientific theories; second, he recognized that the realm of the subjective played as important a role in devising such theories as it did in any other branch of knowledge; and third, in an increasingly mechanized and industrial age, he was wary of "a vague notion that everything in the physical world goes deftly and perfectly, like the play of an ideal machine" (Stevenson 1874–75: 264). Finally, scientific ideas had to be expressed in language. Stevenson wrote that "Scientific language, like most other language, is extremely unsatisfactory" (248) and pronounced himself astonished at "how often there is no definite conception whatever, at the back of the most definite sounding words; and how often language is the cloak with which a man conceals, not his thought, but his want of thought" (251).

From the mid-nineteenth century, science, which supposedly deals with facts, may be said to have crossed a boundary from being specifically concerned with "the observation, identification, description, experimental investigation, and theoretical explanation of phenomena" (Pickett *et al* 2000: 1560) to participation in moral, ethical, philosophical, and even metaphysical debates. One of the scientific fields most involved in such debates was that of evolution. Ideas about evolution had existed in the works of poets and writers long before the age of Wallace and Darwin, and the publication of those ideas in the nineteenth century was met not so much with the shock of surprise as with that of recognition. Nevertheless, the ordered formulation of these ideas had confronted humanity with a "monstrous spectre" (Stevenson 1892: 62): a conception of man created not in the image of God but by Nature over the course of tens or perhaps hundreds of thousands of years.

Stevenson, however, seems to have believed that there was something more to man than the scientific perspective of his time allowed. In "Lay Morals," he contends that "Mankind, in the sense of the creeping mass that is born and eats, that generates and dies, is but the aggregate of the outer and lower sides of man" (Stevenson 1896: 557), and he describes man's inner essence as "This inner consciousness, this lantern alternately obscured and shining, to and by which the individual exists and must order his conduct [which] is something special to himself and not common to the race . . . I do not speak of it to hardened theorists: the living man knows keenly what I mean" (556–57). In this passage Stevenson might be describing conscience, rather than man's inner being or soul, but perhaps they were synonymous for him. Significantly, the passage is then followed by a quotation, not from the Bible but from the Roman Emperor and Stoic philosopher, Marcus Aurelius: "Perceive at last that thou hast in thee something better and more divine than the things which cause the various effects, and, as it were, pull thee by the strings" (557).

Often considered one of the least metaphysical of writers, Stevenson was actually as much interested in exploring "the problems of existence" as were other major writers, scientists, and philosophers of his day. Indeed, he states that, "You can keep no men long, nor Scotsmen at all, off moral, or theological discussion. These are to all the world what law is to lawyers; they are everybody's technicalities; the medium through which all consider life, and the dialect in which they express their judgments" (Stevenson 1882b: 89). Of life, Stevenson wrote that "where a life, low as it may be, has any upward tendency and does not progressively condescend with the baser parts of nature, if it be truly told, it may not only console but encourage others" (Stevenson 1880: 218). About death, too, he had something interesting to say, namely, "I do not admit immortality, but I cannot believe in death. . . . Cease to live I may; but not cease to be: it can only be a change of function" (Stevenson 1874–75: 254). Although he was highly critical of "the old [biblical] hypothesis about men" (264), he wrote to Adelaide Boodle on 17 January 1891: "I do believe with my heart and soul in a God, and a righteous God: what he wants of me, with what measure he will serve me, I know not, and I do not think it is my business to inquire, convinced it will be right" (*Ltrs* 7: 74). Stevenson's religious beliefs may well account for his "stout, though never narrow-minded" opposition to naturalist writers, for whom "The novelist becomes a natural scientist presenting human life as a purely objective phenomenon," and individual conscience is perceived to be "largely a pious delusion" (Good 1982: 50).

Stevenson's undoubted interest in evolutionary ideas are revealed in his works—indeed, Block goes so far as to claim that Stevenson's work, together with that of the evolutionary psychologist James Sully, "represents a significant sampling of the forms and perspectives upon which Victorian readers based their notions of evolution's usefulness as a scientific theory" (Block 1984: 465). Sully himself drew upon Stevenson's works, particularly *Strange Case of Dr. Jekyll and Mr. Hyde* (1886).

Stephen Arata (1996: 43) makes an important point when he states that Jekyll and Hyde is "an angry book" that "turns the discourses centering on degeneration, atavism, and criminality back on the professional classes that produced them." In Jekyll and Hyde, Stevenson's anger is directed at doctors and scientists in particular, and he subsequently goes out of his way in a succession of works to confront and examine the "monstrous spectre" of humanity raised by contemporary science.

In the poem, "A Portrait" (Stevenson 1887), in which he seems to go "the whole Orang" (as Himmelfarb so delightfully phrases it), we are confronted with the image of an orangutan who "Yet still, about the human pale, / [loves] to scamper, [loves] to race, / To swing by [its] irreverent tail / All over the most holy place" until "The unfailing sportsman" happens along to shoot it. The final memorable line: *"Thank God, and there's an end of that!"* humorously brings the poem to a close, happily and mirthfully debunks the notion of man's descent from the apes, and restores God and the status quo (in italics, no less). Like Benjamin Disraeli, Stevenson seems to have been "on the side of the angels." However, mention of the "unfailing sportsman" might well be intended to caution that nature in general, and brute nature in particular, had more to fear from the positively unsporting and predatory instincts of man himself who, oftentimes in the annals of history, has lived to kill rather than killed to live.

Stevenson writes to Georges Docquois, of "a small perfidy on the part of our scientists," since science has to "mind both its goat and its cabbages [i.e. have its cake and eat it too]. The goat is truth; the cabbages, vivisection. Thus we have an extraordinary sight . . . of a scientist who today tells us that animals don't suffer, and tomorrow bores us stiff with a vast tome on the temperatures/feeling of pain, as studied in animals" (*Ltrs* 7: 291). Clearly, in Stevenson's view, science frequently had to make unpleasant compromises, was often contradictory in its findings, and did not provide all—or even many—answers to the problems of existence.

The problem was the dogmatic absolutism of many scientists. For Stevenson, adversaries in conversational debate "must not be pontiffs holding doctrine, but huntsmen questing after elements of truth" (Stevenson 1882b: 90). Like many of his contemporaries, Stevenson did not so much object to scientific theories of evolution, and particularly Darwinian theories, as to the increasingly dogmatic way in which they were put forward as the new orthodoxy. While, in our own time, Wilson (1978: 201) has contended that "The core of scientific materialism is the evolutionary epic" (which, in his view, is "probably the best myth that we will ever have"), and that that epic "can be indefinitely strengthened up and down the line, but its most sweeping assertions cannot be proved with any finality," many scientists in the latter part of the nineteenth century were more rigid in their championship of the new doctrine of evolution. Darwinian ideas about evolution were completely compatible with Stevenson's views on life and death and religion (he deplored "prettified religion that would pretend the world is not a tragic battlefield"; *Ltrs* 7: 74), but he did take exception to a dogmatic stance on "natural selection," probably on the same grounds that he claimed to have no patience with "petty religion that takes the name and attributes of God for an election ticket" (*Ltrs* 7: 74).[4]

Stevenson reacts strongly against such ideas of racial, cultural, linguistic, and literary superiority and inferiority, and survival of the fittest, of the inexorable evolution of a single dominant form. His own work consists of a wonderful variety of written forms and linguistic modes: in "A Humble Remonstrance," he argues that "with each new subject the true artist will vary his method and change the point of attack" (Stevenson 1884: 86). That view may explain his frequent border crossings between genres and cross-fertilizations of art and ideas.

The variety of forms that Stevenson cultivates is clearly seen in *The Master of Ballantrae,* which is often considered the darkest of Stevenson's novels. His own last recorded comments of it were that it lacked "all pleasureableness" and was "imperfect in essence" (*Ltrs* 7: 384). Leslie Fiedler (1954: xix) finds this assessment of his novel "a strange judgment surely, for it is precisely a pleasureable story, a work of real wit: a tragedy seen through the eyes of a comic character." André Gide (1947: vol. 1:343) famously wrote that it is an "[o]dd book in which everything is excellent, but heterogeneous to such a degree that it seems the sample card of everything in which Stevenson excels." The oddness and heterogeneity of the text continue to pose problems for readers. Alexander B. Clunas has more recently commented that: "*Master* is a notably unstable text. It confounds generic unity, placing some of the definitive elements of Stevenson's earlier 'naïve' adventure stories within the main, by and large non-adventurous, narrative of Ephraim Mackellar. It requires readers to read across conventional boundaries between exotic romantic adventure and domestic drama, between desire and 'reality,' between *I* and *he*" (Clunas 1993: 55). Stevenson definitely requires his readers to read across conventional boundaries.

Stevenson intended *The Master of Ballantrae* to be "a story on a great canvas; it was to cover many years, so that [he] might draw [his] characters in the growth and the decay of life; and many lands, so that [he] might display them in changing and incongruous surroundings" (Letley 1983: x). Moreover, the tale repeatedly asks us to consider the evidence on both sides of a question, to decide who and what we believe. The randomness of the coin that sets the whole story in motion is the true symbol of James Durie's condition (Watson 1995: xi–xii). It is, in fact, the true symbol of the lives of all of the characters in Stevenson's novel. They are cast adrift in a nightmarish and indifferent universe, with "the lights all drifting, the compasses all awry, and nothing left to steer by except the stars" (Froude 1919, vol. 1:311). The world Stevenson depicts is cold, bleak, hostile, and godless. If its inhabitants survive, perhaps it is because their author permits them to retain a spark of that divinity of which Marcus Aurelius spoke.

For David Nash (2000: 44), "Religion was, in a very real sense, everywhere in Victorian England [by which one presumes that he actually means Victorian *Britain*], and it was confident enough to engage with society wholly on its own terms at least until the last years of the period." Nash further contends that, "Perhaps only in the area of popular culture was religion's role genuinely under threat, and it was this opening that secularists were to exploit." Himmelfarb (1996: 389), however, cites numerous examples of those whose religious beliefs were shaken, if not completely shattered, when they read Darwin's *Origin*, and she states that "the truly diabolical result of Darwinism [was] not the displacement of God entailed in the conventional loss of faith, but the substitution of Satan in the place of God, or even the Satanization of God himself. The perversion of faith rather than the loss of faith was the ultimate in heresy." In the light of Darwinian theory, mankind came to be perceived by many Victorians as having been demonized or utterly degraded.

In a letter to Sidney Colvin dated 20 November 1887, Stevenson describes his essay "Pulvis et Umbra" ("We are dust and shadows") as "a mere sermon" (*Ltrs* 6: 60). He also remarks that he might have called it "a Darwinian Sermon," given that it directly addresses Darwin's theory of evolution, which Stevenson portrays as "A new doctrine, received with screams a little while ago by canting moralists, and still not properly worked into the body of our thoughts" (Stevenson 1892: 65). He does not directly oppose the new doctrine, rather he contends that it "lights us a step further into the heart of [our] rough but noble universe" (65). He argues, in that gently ironic tone with which all readers of his essays and travel writings are familiar, that no matter in what stage of society or in what depth of ignorance, "human beings are condemned to some nobility" (Stevenson 1892: 65). Utilizing scientific and evolutionary metaphors, he relates of man that: "Of all earth's meteors, here at least is the most strange and consoling: that this ennobled lemur, this hair-crowned bubble of the dust, this inheritor of a few years and sorrows, should yet deny himself his rare delights, and add to his frequent pains, and live for an ideal, however misconceived"

(65). Having provided a various and extensive list of instances of human beings living for an ideal of goodness and perfectibility, and, having "ennobled" and restored some virtue and dignity to the aforementioned lemur, Stevenson turns his attention to the rest of creation to emphasize the interconnectedness of all life, before proceeding to state his own succinct credo. It runs as follows: "Let it be enough for faith, that the whole creation groans in mortal frailty, strives with unconquerable constancy: surely not all in vain" (66).[5] If, as Boethius claimed, philosophy has the power to console, then "Pulvis et Umbra" provided the consolation of Stevenson's spartan and unique wisdom, and many of his readers appear to have been comforted by it.

John William Cunliffe, critical though he was of Stevenson, noted that however deep or shallow we may find his philosophy, "What he had to say met with almost universal acceptance in his own generation, and he said it with a verbal felicity and an engaging personal touch which won him immediate popularity" (Cunliffe 1919: 87). If the purpose of art is to instruct and amuse, then Stevenson's art succeeds in doing both. As *writer*, rather than poet or novelist or essayist, he shows us that life and art (which is "a simplification of some side or point of life"; Stevenson 1884: 90) are unlimited, infinitely variable, and generally unpredictable, and that it is precisely in these characteristics that their charm and mystery lie. For Stevenson it is the astonishment in the face of such variety of life that remains of central importance: "Although the world and life have in a sense become commonplace to our experience, it is but in an external torpor; the true sentiment slumbers within us; and we have but to reflect on ourselves or our surroundings to rekindle our astonishment. No length of habit can blunt our first surprise" (Stevenson 1896: 552).

NOTES

1. This paper owes its genesis to discussions with friends and colleagues at a Nimrod Conference titled "The Shape of Discovery: Creative Writing and Science" at the University of Tulsa (October 2001), and a creative writing panel titled "From Prose to Poetry and Back Again" at the University of Wyoming's Conference on English (July 2001).

2. The Wallace-Darwin papers were read at the Linnean Society on 1 July 1858, and Darwin subsequently published *Origin of Species* (1859) and *The Descent of Man* (1871). Not only had Stevenson read Darwin, but he was also familiar with the ideas of Lyell, Galton, Haeckel, Hooker, Spencer, and Huxley, among others.

3. For example, he writes that he would willingly burn Haeckel's work and supply the matches himself (*Ltrs* 3: 209). As for Darwin, he claimed to have had no patience

with him for "making so much of Natural Selection" when on every page "he postulates 'spontaneous variations' or 'compensations of growth,' or 'correlated variations,' or something of the kind, as the material which his selection is to weigh in the balance and keep and cast away as useless; in other words, that all spontaneity, all inception, is independent of his own special doctrine" (Stevenson 1874–75: 260).

4. Adam Sedgwick, too, Darwin's teacher and friend, who held that creation was "a power I cannot imitate or comprehend; but in which I can believe, by a legitimate conclusion of sound reason drawn from the laws and harmonies of Nature," resented "the pretense that Darwin's theory was anything more than this" (Himmelfarb 1990: 352).

5. Elsewhere, Stevenson (1880: 218) wrote that "Even where there is no human dignity, there will be some human pathos; even when no great right has been done, and the being under review has merely struggled along the borderland of good and evil with conspicuous lapses, that struggle itself is something holy."

REFERENCES

Arata, Stephen. 1996. *Fictions of Loss in the Victorian Fin de Siècle.* Cambridge: Cambridge University Press.

Block Jr., Ed. 1984. Evolutionist Psychology and Aesthetics: *The Cornhill Magazine,* 1875–1880. *Journal of the History of Ideas* 45: 465–75.

Clunas, Alexander B. 1993. "A Double Word": Writing and Justice in *The Master of Ballantrae. Studies in Scottish Literature* 28: 55–74.

Cunliffe, John William. 1919. *English Literature During the Last Half Century.* 2nd ed. 1924. New York: Macmillan.

Fiedler, Leslie. 1954. Introd. to *The Master of Ballantrae,* by Robert Louis Stevenson. 1967. New York: Holt, Rinehart and Winston.

Froude, James Anthony. 1919. *Thomas Carlyle: A History of His Life in London, 1834–1881.* London: Longmans, Green & Co.

Gide, André. 1947–51. *The Journals of André Gide.* Trans. with an introduction and notes by Justin O' Brien. New York: Alfred Knopf.

Good, Graham. 1982. Rereading Robert Louis Stevenson. *The Dalhousie Review* 62 (1): 44–59.

Himmelfarb, Gertrude. 1959. *Darwin and the Darwinian Revolution.* 1996. Chicago: Ivan R. Dee.

Nash, David. 2000. Laughing at the Almighty: Freethinking, Lampoon, Satire, and Parody in Victorian England. In *The Victorian Comic Spirit: New Perspectives.* Ed. Jennifer A. Wagner-Lawlor. Aldershot: Ashgate.

Norquay, Glenda, ed. 1999. *R. L. Stevenson on Fiction: An Anthology of Literary and Critical Essays.* Edinburgh: Edinburgh University Press.

Paradis, James and Thomas Postlewait, eds. 1985. *Victorian Science and Victorian Values: Literary Perspectives.* New Brunswick, NJ: Rutgers University Press.

Pickett, Joseph P. et al. 2000. *The American Heritage Dictionary of The English Language.* 4th ed. Boston: Houghton Mifflin Company.

Stevenson, Robert Louis. [1874–75]. "Selections From His Notebook." Skerryvore Edition. Vol 25.

———. [1880]. "Memoirs of Himself." Skerryvore Edition. Vol. 25.

———. 1882a. "A Gossip on Romance." In Norquay 1999. 51–64.

———. 1882b. "Talk and Talkers: First Paper." Skerryvore Edition. Vol. 25.

———. 1884. "A Humble Remonstrance." In Norquay 1999. 80–91.

———. 1896. "Lay Morals." Thistle Edition, second issue. Vol. 22.

———. 1887. "A Portrait." In *Poems by Robert Louis Stevenson Including Underwoods, Ballads, Songs of Travel.* 1912. London: Chatto and Windus.

———. 1889. *The Master of Ballantrae.* In Stevenson 1995–96.

———. 1892. "Pulvis et Umbra." Tusitala Edition. Vol. 26.

———. 1995–96. *The Scottish Novels.* Edinburgh: Canongate Books.

Watson, Roderick. 1995–96. Introd. to *The Master of Ballantrae,* by Robert Louis Stevenson. In Stevenson 1995–96.

Wilson, Edward O. 1978. *On Human Nature.* Cambridge, MA: Harvard University Press.

Crossing the Bounds of Single Identity

Dr. Jekyll and Mr. Hyde and a Paper
in a French Scientific Journal

RICHARD DURY

Commenting on the origins of *Dr. Jekyll and Mr. Hyde,* Stevenson's wife suggested that the story evolved first of all from the writer's fascination with Deacon Brodie, combined with thoughts provoked by an article on psychology in a French periodical: "In the room in Edinburgh occupied by my husband as a child, was a bookcase and a chest of drawers made by the notorious Deacon Brodie—the respectable artisan by day, a burglar at night. . . . Years afterwards my husband was deeply impressed by a paper he read in a French scientific journal on sub-consciousness. This article, combined with his memories of Deacon Brodie, gave the germ of the idea that afterwards developed into the play, was used again in the story of Markheim, and finally in a hectic fever following a hemorrhage of the lungs, culminated in the dream of Jekyll and Hyde" (F. Stevenson 1905: xv, xvi).

The purpose of the present chapter is to shed some light on this unidentified "paper . . . on sub-consciousness" and the way it might be related to *Dr. Jekyll and Mr. Hyde.*

Judging by the evidence the most credible conclusion is that such an article simply does not exist: in April 1893, less than eight years after the writing and publication of *Jekyll and Hyde,* a New Zealand journalist asked Stevenson, "Had you heard of any actual case of double personality before you wrote your book?" and received the answer, "Never," followed by, "After the book was published I heard of the case of 'Louis V.,' the man in the hospital at Rochefort. Mr. Myers sent it to me" (Stevenson 1893).[1]

Stevenson's reply seems to allow no appeal: he had not been "deeply

FIGURE 3. Etching by Mirando Haz from *Dr. Jekyll Mr. Hyde and Company*, privately printed, 2002. Reproduced by kind permission of the artist.

impressed" by any such paper, had not even read such a paper, indeed he had *never* even *heard* of such a case.[2] It is a reply that is clearly in contrast with what Fanny Stevenson wrote in 1905, at a greater distance in time and as a witness rather than the person directly involved. If we add to these considerations the fact that elsewhere her testimony is not totally reliable (later in the preface, for example, she claims that the tale was written in three days and rewritten in another three, while Stevenson tells us that it was written over a space of about six weeks, *Ltrs* 5: 216), the rules of evidence should oblige us to take Stevenson's version as the most probable. Fanny could easily have confused an article read afterwards with an one read before, an article about a French psychological case with an article written in French. At this point, like the chapter on "Snakes in Iceland" ("There are no snakes in Iceland"), the present contribution could conclude, the shortest chapter in the book.

And yet, the French debate on consciousness and personality (carried on in monographs, lectures, general educated conversation, and papers in scientific journals) must still remain a significant part of the cultural context for the writing of *Strange Case of Dr. Jekyll and Mr. Hyde* and deserves further investigation.

As a student at Edinburgh University (1867–75), as a member of the Speculative Society (1869–73) and as a member of what we might call the "Fleeming Jenkin circle" (from 1871 to about 1878), Stevenson would have been exposed to contemporary ideas of nonunitary consciousness and personality. Indeed, his interest in psychological questions is clear: he was even secretary of the Psychological Society of Edinburgh for a short time in 1873 (*Ltrs* 1: 270n), a spiritualist society, it is true (despite its name), yet spiritualists were interested in the same phenomena of apparent changes in consciousness and personality in hypnotic and mediatic trances and in somnambulist states as were more scientific psychologists. In his first published book, *An Inland Voyage,* Stevenson makes a self-analysis of his feelings of alienation from his body as paddling his canoe becomes automatic, observing that "There was less *me* and more *not-me* than I was accustomed to expect" (Stevenson 1878a: 93). In "Crabbed Age and Youth" published in the same year he talks of how identity is never fixed: "we cannot even regard ourselves as a constant; in this flux of things, our identity itself seems in a perpetual variation; and not infrequently we find our own disguise the strangest in the masquerade" (Stevenson 1878b: 43–44); and later in "A Chapter on Dreams" (1888), he explores the unconscious creative processes involved in imaginative composition. His interest in psychological questions continues right through to the end of his life: in 1891 he asks to be sent William James's *Principles of Psychology* and Bourget's *Essai de psychologie contemporaine* (*Ltrs.* 7: 189, 198), and in 1893 we find him writing to F. W. H. Myers (founder of the Society for Psychical Research, of which Stevenson was a member) about "some experiences of mine . . . of a high psychological interest" (*Ltrs* 7: 331).

The most advanced studies of nonnormal and unconscious psychological states were being made by French doctors, and Stevenson could have learned more about this area of new ideas in the period 1873 to 1878 when he was in France for part of every year. It was indeed a moment of particular intellectual ferment: after the lifting of the 1874–76 clerically inspired ban on the teaching of psychiatry in Paris hospitals, the reestablished discipline developed year by year with new journals, monographs, institutions, and university chairs. In 1886 Frederick Myers says that multiplex personality has been studied "only of late years and mainly in France" (Myers 1886: 648).

The idea of a "consciousness" dates from Descartes, and "unconsciousness" was first discussed in detail by Leibniz (Ellenberger 1970: 28), and then explored in relation to dreams, sleep, hypnosis, and various drugged (and later in hysteric) states. It was recognized that the unconscious life of dreams involved a state without conscious volition in which new thoughts may be evolved, as represented in Diderot's *Le rêve de d'Alembert* (written 1769) and attested in Coleridge's preface to "Kubla Khan" (1816); in 1798 P.-J.-G. Cabanis claimed that even without dreams "the mind never sleeps" (Richardson 2001: 40). In the sleeping and dreaming state the influence of the body and particularly sexuality was often dominant, as indicated by sexual dreams, nocturnal emissions (alluded to in Diderot's dialogue), or waking to find "[la bête] éveillée et très éveillée" [the beast awake, very awake indeed] (as de Maistre puts it, in typically Shandean fashion; 1795, ch. 39).

The concept of the unconscious, explored by Romantic poets and further elaborated by the German philosophers von Schubert in *Die Symbolik des Traumes* (1814), Carus in *Psyche* (1846) and Hartmann in *Philosophie des Unbewußten* (1869), undermined any sense of a simple and single identity ruled by will and reason, an idea as disconcerting to contemporary received ideas as any of the theories of Darwin.[3] These early nineteenth-century models have little of the Freudian conflictual unconscious about them and are concerned with the primacy of will over reason, automatic responses, unremembered states, somatic consciousness, and the creative unconscious (cf. Richardson 2001: 57–65), the latter brilliantly elaborated on by Stevenson himself in "A Chapter on Dreams." Many of the published French psychological case studies illustrated aspects of the unconscious: F. W. H. Myers says in 1885 that "the hypothesis of an unconscious self . . . has been independently urged by several German writers of high repute, and has received illustration and corroboration from a great number of French experiments" (Myers 1885b: 123).

An important area of study after 1840 was that of multiple and double consciousness (or personality), and around 1880 it had become one of the questions most debated by psychiatrists and philosophers (Ellenberger 1970: 156).

A second consciousness could be simply the body, opposed to the spirit or soul or mind (in a tradition going back at least to St. Paul), with a will of its own, so already with an element of a separate personality. Xavier de Maistre in *Voyage autour de ma chambre* (1794) proposes an opposition, instead, of spirit and animal: "Je me suis aperçu, par diverses observations, que l'homme est composé d'une âme et d'une bête. Ces deux êtres sont absolument distincts" [I have noticed, in various observations, that man is composed of a soul and a beast. These two beings are completely distinct] (ch. 6). "On s'aperçoit bien en gros que l'homme est double" [It is clear that man, generally speaking, is double] and that the animal part has its own wishes and individuality. These two "créatures hétérogènes" coexist in unresolved opposition: the soul can impose its will on the animal, but then "par un fâcheux retour, celle-ci oblige très souvent l'âme d'agir contre son gré" [by a troubling return, the latter often obliges the soul to act against its wishes] (ch. 6). In chapter 39, de Maistre even gives a dialogue of mutual accusations between the spirit and the beast, the latter clearly identified with sexuality since it has become dominant during sleep: "C'était le matin à l'aube du jour . . . et déjà *elle* [la bête] était éveillée" [It was dawn and it (the beast) was already awake] under the effect of exciting nocturnal visions. "Enfin, *elle* était éveillée et très éveillée, lorsque mon âme se débarrassa elle-même des liens du sommeil" [In short, it was awake, very awake indeed, as my soul loosened itself from the constraints of sleep]. Here we have several affinities with Jekyll's "Full Statement": the simple summarizing formulation of "l'homme est double" [man is double] reminds one of "man is not truly one, but truly two" (Stevenson 1886: 35); the temporarily dominated animal that then imposes itself "by a troublesome return" has similarities in Jekyll's vain attempt "to be done with" Hyde; and the drowsy waking state when the beast is quite definitely awake has a parallel in Jekyll's waking to a gradual languid awareness of the hand of Hyde.

The "second self" could also be the unconscious. F. W. H. Myers argues that automatic writing is not due to extrahuman agencies but to a "second center of mentality" (1885b: 122) and he postulates "*a secondary self*—if I may coin the phrase—. . . a latent capacity . . . of developing or manifesting a second focus of cerebral energy which . . . may possess, for a time at least, a kind of continuous individuality, a purposeful activity of its own" (1885a: 27); this is (and Myers again uses italics) "a *secondary or inner self,* which is . . . thus far . . . independent that it can acquire knowledge which the primary self has no means of reaching . . . a secondary self possessing our brains, as it were, in a kind of sleeping co-partnership, and utilizing our members when it pleases him, for his private ends" (28). Here, the "secondary self" referred to in the third person, who uses our limbs "when it pleases him" sounds very much like Jekyll talking of Hyde as a separate being.

The idea of alternating personality had existed since the time of the mesmerists, who observed that the hypnotized personality was often more lively than the normal one and who saw that memory could be carried over from one mesmeric séance to another ("periodic amnesia," Ellenberger 1970: 177). The same idea is behind the idea of an independent personality or consciousness under the influence of drugs: an autonomous life under the influence of opium plays a central part in *The Moonstone* by Wilkie Collins, in which he refers to a "case" in Elliotson's *Human Physiology;* Dickens in *Edwin Drood* (1870) presents a drug-addict with two lives and two memories; and Stevenson in "A Chapter on Dreams" talks self-analytically of a sequence of dreams with the memory of one dream carried over to the next, so that he began "to lead a double life—one of the day, one of the night" (Stevenson 1888: 43).

French philosophers also pursued the idea of multiple consciousness, an idea that apparently appealed to Stevenson more than mere doubleness.[4] In 1868, J.-P. Durand coined the term "polypsychisme" in *Polyzoïsme ou pluralité animale chez l'homme* in which he claimed that the human organism was made up of anatomical segments each with an individual "I," with consciousness and memory, all under a "chief-I." Two years later, Hypolite Taine, in *De l'intelligence,* talks of "a basic plurality of the *me*" and compares the mind to a theater where different plays are being performed at the same time but only one is illuminated (Carroy 1993: xii)—a comparison that reminds us of Stevenson's repeated references to the "theatre of the brain" in "A Chapter on Dreams." And in 1885 Ribot (*Maladies de la personnalité* 1885: 170–72) says that the *me* is only a temporary coordination of elements.

The series of French studies on double personalities begins in May 1876 with the famous case of Félida in "Amnésie périodique, ou doublement de la vie" [Periodic amnesia, or doubled life] by Etienne Eugène Azam.[5] After publication in a Bordeaux medical journal it was republished in the Paris *Revue scientifique,* a twenty-four-page weekly publication that republished articles and reports from other journals, covering all areas of science, the kind of publication that might have been read by any educated reader. (We have now begun to look through some scientific journals of the period in search of a likely candidate for the famous "paper," without any strong commitment to its existence.) The article was given prominence—it is the first article on the front page—and sparked off a series of contributions of similar cases, objections and replies in this and other journals. The case aroused such interest in experimental psychology that Paul Janet claimed that Félida was the real founder of the professorial chair in the subject at the Collège de France (1888) (cf. Carroy 1993: x, xi). Myers refers in 1886 to "Dr. Azam's often quoted patient, Felida X.," and assumes that the case is widely known in Britain: "Felida's name . . . is probably familiar to most of my readers" (1886: 654, 648).

The case involved a young woman who, in early observations in 1858, has a first state in which she is morose and talks little; she then suffers a transitional phase for a few minutes in which she feels sharp pain at the temples and collapses into a sleeplike state, after which she enters a second state (with no trace of hallucination or delirium)[6] in which she is light-hearted and sociable (she becomes "gaie et sa vivacité touche à la turbulence, son imagination est plus exaltée" [lively, and her vivacity is almost excessive, her imagination is raised to a higher level]; Azam 1876: 482). Sometimes Félida goes to sleep in her "normal state" but wakes in her second state (485). The second state is also associated with a less repressed sexuality: while still engaged to her future husband, she became pregnant in her second state, she refuses to understand the reason for her subsequent illness while in her first state, but acknowledges it in her second state (482). The second state lasts an hour or two, and then another crisis phase brings her back to the first state again.

Azam says that his title offers two alternative explanations ("periodic amnesia" or "doubled life"), between which he leaves to the reader to choose, but the editor of the review had already made up his mind, since he puts "Un Cas de dédoublement de la vie" [A Case of Doubled Life] as the running title on both verso and recto pages, and indeed the same is true of Azam since he presents the case as "l'histoire d'une jeune femme . . . tourmentée par une altération de la mémoire . . . telle qu'il est permis de se demander se cette jeune femme n'a pas deux vies" [the story of a young woman . . . tormented by such an alteration of memory . . . that one may ask oneself if this young woman does not perhaps live two lives] (481), and he refers to "cette sorte de seconde vie" [this sort of second life].

As Azam observed Félida over the years, the second state "has extended itself at the expense of the other" (488): the second state has become almost totally dominant, and he wonders if (what he calls) the "normal state" will disappear in a few years time, and Félida would become "une autre personne" [another person].

The Félida case has some affinities with Stevenson's story: the alternating personalities, the repressed personality contrasting with the more lively and less sexually repressed one, the painful passage from one to the other, the occasional spontaneous change during sleep to the second personality, and the growing and possibly complete dominance of the second personality-state.

Dr. Azam himself also has some affinities with Dr. Jekyll, as he practices hypnotism as a therapy, in a period when it was outlawed from serious medicine,[7] and expresses impatience with established medical science: for the majority of his colleagues who believed that Félida was playacting "la science était faite, et tout ce que en est dehors du cadre connu ne pouvait être que tromperie" [science had reached a final state, and everything outside its known boundaries could only be a fraud] (483). This reminds us of Jekyll's condemnation (while still in the person of Hyde) of Lanyon: "you who have so long been bound to the most narrow and material views, you who have denied the virtue of transcendental medicine" (Stevenson 1886: 46).

Nevertheless, the case has important differences from the Jekyll and Hyde case: the change is involuntary (where Jekyll's transformation is originally voluntary), in one state Félida does not remember the other state (where Jekyll and Hyde share memory), and of course the second state does not involve criminal or sadistic acts like those of Hyde. Another important difference is that (in Stevenson's last chapter) the doctor is not only the narrator, but also the subject of the case, doubly doubled.

Part of the ensuing debate about Félida took place in *La revue scientifique* itself: in the 10 June issue (574–75) Paul Janet writes of "La notion de la personnalité" in the light of the Félida case and mentions other striking cases of "la double personnalité." On 15 July 1876 (69–71) Dr. Dufay cites a similar case: Mlle. R. L. enters a trance state when she refers (in the third person) to her waking self as stupid ("quand moi est bête" [when me is stupid], 69). In this state she talks freely of certain things but asks the doctor not to tell this "à l'autre" [the other one] because "moi sait qu'elle ne veut pas confier cela à vous" [me knows she doesn't want to tell you that].

In the 16 September issue, Azam (again given the front page and the first article) answered criticisms and summarized the case. This is now presented in the title as "Le dédoublement de la personnalité. Suite de l'histoire de Félida X***" (Doubling of the personality. Continuation of the story of Félida X***).

The following year, Azam has a third front-page article in *La revue scientifique,* again with the running title "Le dédoublement de la personnalité," in which he summarizes the case again, adds a few more details, and comments on the amount of discussion it has caused.

By 1878, Azam leaves behind the idea of amnesia and titles his article in *La revue scientifique* simply "La double conscience" [Double consciousness]. In this more theoretical contribution, he claims that the Félida case "présente, à son plus haute degré, le phénomène de la double conscience, de la double personnalité" [displays the phenomenon of double consciousness, of the double personality, in its clearest form] (194). The case now calls into question the very notion of a single personality and identity: "Ainsi se trouve posé le problème redoutable de l'unité de moi et peut-être ébranlée la croyance à la personnalité, à l'individualité" [In this way the huge and difficult question is raised of the unity of the me, shaking perhaps belief in the personality, in individuality] (194).

Another journal that might have caught the eye of any educated reader is the *Revue philosophique de la France et de l'étranger,* founded and edited by the French pioneer psychologist Ribot. This, like the *Revue scientifique,* included original articles as well as reports and summaries of other periodicals and covered a wide area of interest. The second issue (July–Dec. 1876) reports on Azam's first article and on Dufay's contribution. The third issue, for the first half of 1877, reports on an article by W. G. Davies in *Mind,* January 1877, in which he is said to claim that "la double conscience (considérée comme une affirmation primitive) révèle directement et clairement l'existence d'un non-moi à titre de fait immédiatement vérifié" [double consciousness (taken as an assumption) directly and clearly reveals the existence of a non-*moi* as an immediately verified fact] (547). Issue no. 4 contains a report on an article by M. Laveran on a sea captain "tourmenté par une illusion singulière: il croit qu'il est *dédoublé* en deux personnes. Il voit sans cesse à côté de lui un autre lui-même" [tormented by a singular illusion: he believes he is *doubled* in two persons. At his side he constantly sees another self]. The same number has an article by Th. Galicier, another case history of a patient who saw himself doubled, saying "ce n'est pas moi qui suis ici" [it's not me who's here] and "je suis un autre" [I am someone else] (75). Galicier sees "cet autre moi" [this other me] as the body, the "moi périphérique" [the peripheric me], and supplies an anecdote of a personal experience of feeling doubled: called from his sleep to go to a patient, he is walking painfully and wearily and finds himself saying "tais-toi, mon pauvre corps, tais-toi" [there-there, poor body, be quiet]. He then recalls his exploration of the situation: "Quelque chose d'insolite me frappant dans cette circonstance, l'idée me vint d'analyser ce qui se passait en moi tout en cherchant à ne pas dissiper le reste de sommeil qui m'influençait encore" [Something unusual struck me in this situation, and it occurred to me that I should analyze what was happening in me while at the same time trying not to lose the remains of the sleep that still held me in its influence] (75). This seems close to Jekyll's self-analytical search for a psychological explanation of another phenomenon of waking, the feeling of being in another house: "I smiled to myself, and, in my psychological way, began lazily to inquire into the elements of this illusion, occasionally, even as I did so, dropping back into a comfortable morning doze" (Stevenson 1886: 54). It is clear that Stevenson is influenced by the typical presentation of this type of self-analysis in psychological literature (and that we will find again in Freud), even if there is no basis for saying that he read this particular article.[8]

Returning now to Fanny Stevenson's reference to "a paper he read in a French scientific journal on sub-consciousness," we can see that (forgetting the 1893 interview for a moment) we will never be able to identify the article in question: there were too many French scientific journals with too many articles touching on the unconscious in the most likely period (1876–78),[9] and even the two scientific reviews with nonspecialist appeal carried several articles on the subject in this period. Nevertheless, the most likely candidate is one of the articles on Félida, because the case was so widely discussed in this period (cf. Naugrette 1995–96: 152; Naugrette 2000: 283).[10]

We return empty-handed from our search for the famous article, but (like Naugrette 1995–96, on a similar quest but with a different itinerary) we have made an interesting journey. It is clear from what we have seen and from Stevenson's writings that he was acutely interested in contemporary ideas on nonunitary consciousness and personality, including theories of multiple and double consciousness and personality. It is indeed likely—despite the interview—that he had also read about actual cases illustrating these ideas.

What now becomes interesting is to account for Stevenson's rather brusque "Never" in 1893, and for this we need to look at the whole of the text. Here we find that in the first three-quarters of the interview he is cooperative and gives long answers about the best authors to read for someone aspiring to a literary career (Hammerton 1910: 182–84). In notable contrast are his answers to the three questions at the end of the interview:

> In conclusion, the interviewer asked Mr. Stevenson if he had noticed the loss of memory case in Melbourne, and, if so, whether he did not find it interesting as an illustration in real life of the existence of the double personality dealt with in *The Strange Case of Dr. Jekyll and Mr. Hyde?*
>
> "Yes," said Mr. Stevenson, "it is certainly a very extraordinary affair."
>
> "Had you heard of any actual case of double personality before you wrote your book?"
>
> "Never," replied the author. "After the book was published I heard of the case of "Louis V.," the man in the hospital at Rochefort. Mr. Myers sent it to me."
>
> "Was it not an extraordinary coincidence that you should have anticipated in a work of fiction, at least so far as your own knowledge was concerned, the discoveries of science in regard to the existence of double personality?"
>
> "I don't know that it is altogether established yet by scientific men. They are only on the threshold of the subject. My profound conviction is that there are many consciousnesses in a man. I have no doubt about it—I can feel them working in many directions." (Stevenson 1893)[11]

Not only are the replies here notably shorter than the previous ones, they are also notably evasive: (i) the reporter wants to know if Stevenson thinks the Melbourne case is an interesting illustration of the double personality in *Jekyll and Hyde,* and Stevenson says only that the case is an interesting one; (ii) the reporter returns to the question of links between double personality cases and Jekyll, and Stevenson flatly denies that he had heard of any such case before writing the text, adding additional information (as a kind of compensation) about the case read afterwards (but avoiding any mention of connection with the text); (iii) a third attempt is made to get Stevenson to admit to a link between, if not case-histories, at least scientific theories of double personalities and Jekyll, which Stevenson parries by questioning the truth-value of the reporter's implied statement about "the discoveries of science," attenuating the effect of this move by volunteering (as before) additional information about multiple consciousness (while still avoiding the suggestion of any link with Jekyll). In these noncollaborative replies one thing is clear: Stevenson simply does not want to discuss connections between double-personality cases and Jekyll and Hyde.[12]

Stevenson undoubtedly had read or heard of double-personality cases, and those we have looked at show some interesting affinities with *Dr. Jekyll and Mr. Hyde* in narrative elements, phraseology, and in the style of psychological self-analysis. However, this psychological theme is only one of several in a text that deliberately invites interpretation yet systematically impedes it. Stevenson's "Never" has to be interpreted in context—it tells us less about his interests in psychology than about his views of *Dr. Jekyll and Mr. Hyde:* he refuses to collaborate with the reporter because he does not wish to provide a single key to a story that is intended to remain enigmatic, like human existence, like human consciousness itself.

NOTES

1. Probably Myers 1886 (which interestingly shows the influence of *Dr. Jekyll and Mr. Hyde* in some of its lexical choices, cf. Mighall 2002: 175), in which he discusses the "Louis V[ivet]" case in detail. The case had been described by Ribot in *Maladies de la mémoire* (1881) and by Camuset in *Annales médico-psychologiques* (1882).

2. We leave aside the possibility that Stevenson did read an article on "subconsciousness" (Fanny's term) but not one on "double personality" (the term used by the journalist), since any study of subconsciousness relevant to *Dr. Jekyll and Mr. Hyde* must have involved the idea of a double (or multiple) consciousness (and "consciousness" and "personality" can be seen as referring to subjective and objective views of closely related phenomena).

3. F. Bonatelli in an article in an Italian periodical in 1875, reported in the *Revue philosophique* I (Jan.–June 1876), 318, as "Etude sur la philosophie de l'inconscient," actually refuses to discuss Hartmann's idea of multiple consciousness because it is too materialist to deserve refutation and is deeply repugnant to the "intime persuasion que nous avons de notre indivisible unité" [deep conviction that we have of our indivisible unity].

4. See Stevenson (1886: 48) ("I hazard the guess that man will be ultimately known for a mere polity of multifarious, incongruous and independent denizens") and also the end of the 1893 New Zealand interview at the end of the present chapter ("My profound conviction is that there are many consciousnesses in a man"). Stevenson's formulation in *Jekyll and Hyde* may have influenced Wilde in *Dorian Gray,* when he rejects the ego as something simple and sees man as "a complex multiform creature" (Wilde 1891b: 175).

5. For accounts of Azam's publications on Félida, see Carroy 1991a: 103–9, 1992a passim, 1992b: 126–27. Here, as elsewhere, any translations are by the author of the present chapter. There were several early "double consciousness" cases published in British and American journals, starting with Mitchell's 1816 study of Mary Reynolds, "A Double Consciousness, or a Duality of Person in the Same Individual." The index catalogue of the Library of the Surgeon-General's Office of the U.S. Army (Washington: Government Printing Office), 1st series, lists six "double consciousness" case-studies in British and American journals in the 1840s.

6. In the version published in book form, at this point Azam inserts the simple summarizing formulation, "Félida est autre, voilà tout" [Félida is other, that's all] (1887: 68).

7. On three occasions between 1837 and 1880 the French Académie des Sciences condemned research into "animal magnetism" as nonscientific (cf. Ellenberger 1970: 119, 763).

8. Stevenson was also familiar with other types of medical texts (in English, not only French, scientific journals), as can be seen from Lanyon's description of the transformation from Hyde to Jekyll, which according to Wilde "reads dangerously like an experiment out of the *Lancet*" (Wilde 1891a: 15). Fanny Stevenson subscribed to the *Lancet* in 1884 (and for an uncertain period after that) and read it eagerly (Osbourne 1924: 49–50).

9. The periodicals catalogue of the Bibliothèque Charcot at the Hôpital de la Salpêtrière in Paris lists eighteen French medical periodicals in print in the 1870s, excluding marginal publications (journals of mesmerism, etc.).

10. The fact that the most famous case and many other cases of double personality were female, and that hysteria was long associated with women can only add to the female associations of Jekyll and Hyde: (i) Hyde is "closer than a wife" to Jekyll, walks "with a certain swing" and weeps "like a woman" (Stevenson 1886: 61, 38, 38); (ii) Jekyll's hand is "white and comely," he is viewed at a window by two male flâneurs, claims that Hyde views him as a "cavern" of refuge, talks of "the agonized womb of consciousness," describes the pains of the first transformation in a way that recalls childbirth, and in the end constantly feels Hyde "struggle to be born" (54, 31, 55, 49, 50, 61). The psychoanalytic aspects of this situation ("le moi matriciel") are examined by Naugrette (1987: 63–66).

11. My thanks to Katherine Linehan of Oberlin College for kindly supplying me with a copy of this interview.

12. Of relevance here may be what Eugene Limedorfer (with information from Stevenson's stepdaughter) says: "In his later years Stevenson did not like to refer at all to Jekyll and Hyde. He always said that the writing of the story was such a strain on him he could never forget it" (Limedorfer 1900: 58).

REFERENCES

Azam, Etienne Eugène. 1876a. Amnésie périodique, ou doublement de la vie. *Revue scientifique*, 2 série, 5 année, No. 47 (20 May 1876): 481–89. Originally published as Névrose extraordinaire, doublement de la vie in *Mémoires et Bulletins de la Société de médecine et de chirurgie de Bordeaux*, 1876, 1er et 2ème fasc.; also published in abridged form in *Annales médico-psychologiques* [Paris], 5 sér., 16: 5–35; republished in Azam 1887.

———. 1876b. Le dédoublement de la personnalité. Suite de l'histoire de Félida X***. *Revue scientifique*, 2 sér., 6 année, No. 12 (September 16): 265–69.

———. 1877. Le dédoublement de la personnalité et l'amnésie périodique. *Revue scientifique*, 2 sér., 7 année, No. 25.

———. 1878. La double conscience. *Revue scientifique*, 2 sér., 8 année, no. 9 (August 31, 1878): 194–96.

———. 1887. *Hypnotisme, double conscience et altération de la personnalité*. Préface par J.-M. Charcot. Paris: Baillière.

Carroy, Jacqueline. 1991a. *Hypnose, suggestion et psychologie: l'invention de sujets*. Paris: Presses Universitaires de France.

———. 1991b. Dédoublements. l'énigmatique récit d'un docteur inconnu. *Nouvelle revue de psychanalyse* 41: 151–71.

———. 1992a. Entre mémoire et oubli: les deux vies de Félida. *Revue internationale de psychopathologie* 5: 73–80.

———. 1992b. Le savant et ses doubles. Docteurs Jekyll et Misters Hyde du siècle dernier. *Frénesie* 10: 125–42.

———. 1993. *Les personnalités doubles et multiples. Entre science et fiction*. Paris: Presses Universitaires de France.

Ellenberger, Henri F. 1970. *The Discovery of the Unconscious*. New York: Basic Books. French translation: *Histoire de la découverte de l'inconscient*. Paris: Fayard. 1994.

Hammerton, J. A. 1910. *Stevensoniana: An anecdotal life and appreciation of Robert Louis Stevenson*. Edinburgh: John Grant.

Limedorfer, Eugene. 1900. The Manuscript of Dr. Jekyll and Mr. Hyde. *The Bookman* 12: 52–58.

Maistre, Xavier de. 1794. *Voyage autour de ma chambre*. 2000. Paris: Editions Mille et une Nuits/Fayard.

Mighall, Robert. 2002. Diagnosing Jekyll: The Scientific Context to Dr. Jekyll's Experiment and Mr. Hyde's Embodiment. In R. L. Stevenson, *The Strange Case of Dr. Jekyll and Mr. Hyde and Other Tales of Terror*. Ed. Robert Mighall. Harmondsworth: Penguin. 145–61, 175–78.

Myers, F. W. H. 1885a. Automatic Writing. *Proceedings of the Society for Psychical Research* 3 (January 30, 1885): 1–63.

———. 1885b. Further Notes on the Unconscious Self. *Journal of the Society for Psychical Research* 2 (22) (December 1885): 122–31.

———. 1886. Multiplex Personality. *Nineteenth Century* 20 (November 1886): 648–56. Also in *Proceedings of the Society for Psychical Research* 4 (1886–87): 496–97, 499–500, 503–4.

Naugrette, Jean-Pierre. 1987. *Robert Louis Stevenson: l'aventure et son double*. Paris: Presses de l'Ecole Normale Supérieur.

————. 1995–96. Le texte et son double: le cas de M. P. et du Dr. Forsyth. *Otrante* 8: 149–59.

————. 2000. l'Étrange cas du doutor Pereira et du docteur Cardoso: Essai sur la fonction cognitive et politique d'un mythe littéraire. *La Licorne* [Université de Poitiers] 55: 277–92.

Richardson, Alan. 2001. *British Romanticism and the Sciences of Mind.* Cambridge: Cambridge University Press.

Stevenson, Fanny van der Grift. 1905. Strange Case of Dr. Jekyll and Mr. Hyde. In *Registration Prefaces to Robert Louis Stevenson's Works.* New York: Charles Scribner's Sons. Also as Prefatory Note in Tusitala Edition. Vol. 5. xv–xviii.

Stevenson, Robert Louis. 1878a. *An Inland Voyage.* Tusitala Edition. Vol. 17.

————. 1878b. "Crabbed Age and Youth." Tusitala Edition. Vol. 25. 39–50.

————. 1886. *Strange Case of Dr. Jekyll and Mr. Hyde.* In *Strange Case of Dr. Jekyll and Mr. Hyde: An Authoritative Text, Backgrounds and Context, Performance Adaptations, Criticism.* Ed. Katherine Linehan. 2003. New York: W. W. Norton & Company.

————. 1893. Mr. R. L. Stevenson on Reading and Literature: An Interview. *Argus* ("Wellington, April 11"). Clipping in Stevenson's mother's scrapbooks, vol. 5, 163–64. Monterey Stevenson House. Partly reprinted in Hammerton 1910. 182–84.

Wilde, Oscar. 1891a. The Decay of Lying. In *Intentions.* 1945. London: The Unicorn Press.

————. 1891b. *The Picture of Dorian Gray.* Ed. Peter Ackroyd. 1985. Harmondsworth: Penguin.

Note: At the proofs stage of the present volume I learned of a forthcoming study of relevance to this essay, surveying the reporting of the Félida and other French "double personality" cases in the *Cornhill Magazine* and *Mind* in the second half of the 1870s: Stiles, Anne. Forthcoming. Robert Louis Stevenson's "Jekyll and Hyde" and the Double Brain. *Studies in English Literature* 46 (4) (autumn 2006).—R. D.

FIGURE 4. Etching by Mirando Haz from *Dr. Jekyll Mr. Hyde and Company*, privately printed, 2002. Reproduced by kind permission of the artist.

"City of Dreadful Night"

Stevenson's Gothic London

LINDA DRYDEN

In his study of crowds, published in translation in Britain in 1896, Gustave Le Bon warned of the atavistic nature of crowd behavior, declaring that "an individual in a crowd resembles primitive beings" (Le Bon 1895: 3). In 1886 *Jekyll and Hyde* had concentrated on individual duality, separating the moral from the immoral in an exploration of the human psyche; some years later, Le Bon attributed the bestial behavior exhibited by Hyde to entire groups of people. Stevenson had exploited the popular notion of "the beast within" to create a horrifying vision of one divided soul; by the 1890s the fear of this inner beast had become a hysteria, not just about the degenerative capabilities of the individual but of the whole race. Le Bon's fear that "all our ancient beliefs are tottering and disappearing, while the old pillars of society are giving way one by one" (1895: xiv–xv) is prefigured in the downfall of that professional "pillar of society," Jekyll. In showing Jekyll increasingly under the control of Hyde, Stevenson gave fictional form to an emerging anxiety of the late nineteenth century: the perception that the race itself was succumbing to degenerative tendencies that threatened the very fabric of society. Using gothic narrative motifs, Stevenson touched a nerve in the middle-class sensibility, and as William Greenslade (1994: 84) says, "Jekyll and Hyde provided a timely myth."

Metropolitan and Imperial Anxiety

In 1885 W. T. Stead's "The Maiden Tribute of Modern Babylon" sensitized British public consciousness to vice in lower and upper classes, and Hyde can be seen as symbolizing the metropolitan anxiety about moral dissipation in the heart of the city. Furthermore, it was Stead who first suggested a Jekyll and Hyde parallel in the Ripper murders, which prompted a rash of similar allusions to Stevenson's novel (Walkowitz 1992: 206). The *East London Advertiser* invokes Hyde in its predications of more atrocities to come: "On 8 September the Advertiser again warned that 'the murderous lunatic, who issues forth at night like another Hyde to prey upon the defenceless unfortunate class' would attack again, and that 'three successful murders will have the effect of whetting his appetite further'" (Fishman 2001: 210). In the wake of Annie Chapman's murder at the hands of the Ripper, the *Globe*, on 8 September 1888, also invoked Stevenson's story; now "Life—or rather death—was imitating art, because the 'obscene Hyde' took no more 'intense delight in murder for murder's sake' than did the Whitechapel assassin" (Curtis 2001: 127). The connection, whipped up by the press, between the Ripper Murders and Jekyll and Hyde curtailed Richard Mansfield's famous staging of the story, "because Hyde's behavior came too close for comfort to the Ripper's reign of terror": "Audiences emerging from the theater in September occasionally heard newsboys in the Strand crying 'Another 'Orrible Murder,'" and rumours soon connected Mansfield to the crime" (Curtis 2001: 78).

By the 1880s the London population of 4.5 million was mushrooming, and its vastness inspired panic. After the first Ripper murder the *Advertiser* gave voice to public fears: "The circumstances of this awful tragedy are not only surrounded with the deepest mystery, but there is also a feeling of insecurity to think that in a great city like London, the streets of which are continually patrolled by police, a woman can be foully and horribly killed almost next to the citizens peacefully sleeping in their beds, without a trace or clue being left of the villain who did the deed" (Fishman 2001: 210). Hyde's nocturnal criminality echoes public insecurity engendered by the expanding city even before the awful events in Whitechapel in the summer and autumn of 1888. The anxiety also had a class-dimension: the Bryant and May matchgirls strike of the same year pressed home the point that the proletariat was a constant presence on the city's streets.

The reader infers that it is highly likely that Jekyll/Hyde's activities included sexual exploits. The contemporary reader would have thought of sadistic relationships with child prostitutes as among the possible vices that Jekyll/Hyde indulged in during his nightly forays into the nether world of London: "The Maiden Tribute," a sensational press exposé of the child prostitution trade in London, appeared in the summer of 1885, and Henley had forwarded the installments to Stevenson. The coincidences are too compelling to ignore. Hyde's trampling of the child in the dead of night has suggestive undertones of the abuse of children perpetrated by the "gentlemen" of the city, exposed by Stead. Witnessing this savagery, Enfield is coming back "from some place at the end of the world" (Stevenson 1886: 7), suggesting the East End, and a possible affinity with Hyde in vice. Judith Walkowitz (1992: 122) believes that Stead's example caused some writers to locate "sexual danger in the dark corners and subterranean spaces of the London Labyrinth." In this sense degeneracy and what was perceived as moral insanity were linked, especially in their sexual aspects, to the East End's teeming population.

Mass population was seen to entail mass moral and spiritual corruption. In some quarters this led to a desire for selective breeding and even extermination to preserve the physical and spiritual "health" of the nation. The East End became "Africanized" in the popular imagination, and the Ripper reportage helped to concretize that sense of the "otherness" of the poorer parts of East London, an image which the East End press tried to play down (Curtis 2001: 35, 120). When Enfield speaks of having come from "some place at the end of the world" (Stevenson 1886: 7), allusions to the far-flung corners of the Empire are discernable. It is not unreasonable to conjecture that this allusion is to a place characterized by an "otherness" borne of the largely non-British community of the East End. Hyde would therefore come to represent more than the metropolitan criminal mentality, and sexual predator; his deformed physical presence, could be seen as standing for the imagined threats to European civilization. And since Hyde is part of Jekyll, then Victorian fears of racial degeneration become even more real, because Hyde reveals the potential atavistic nature present in each of us. A Victorian belief in the essential "soundness" of the British race becomes, as result, seriously undermined by the possibility of a suppressed Mr. Hyde skulking in each individual.

Hyde-ing in the City

Raymond Williams argues that the city is an unknowable space, as opposed to the knowable rural community (Williams 1973: 165). The divide between town and country is not simply a matter of geography: it depends on individual experience, and, more crucially, on a sense of community. Jekyll and Hyde dwells upon the geography of the late-Victorian city in ways that highlight a duality in the city itself. By the 1880s London had become, for many writers, a place of fear and darkness, a labyrinthine hell, as vividly figured in James Thomson's "City of Dreadful Night" (1874), where "The street-lamps burn amidst the baleful glooms / Amidst the soundless solitudes immense / Of rangèd mansions dark and still as tombs." Thomson imagines how the masses of the city wander or sit "foredone and desolately ponder / Through sleepless hours with heavy drooping head" (Thomson 1874: 738). Zero, the eponymous dynamiter of *The Dynamiter* (Stevenson 1885b: 203), seeks to destroy the metropolis for political ends. "Here . . . you behold this field of city, rich, crowded, laughing with the spoil of continents; but soon, how soon, to be laid low!" It will be a day of retribution for the greed of Empire: "'Blaze!' he cried, 'blaze, derided city! Fall, flatulent monarchy, fall like Dagon!'" (Stevenson 1885b: 203). Zero is quite mad, but his hatred of the metropolis reflects contemporary perceptions of the European city, and London in particular, as a modern day Babylon; and, as Kelly Hurley (1996: 165) says, "That these dyna-miters are essentially comic bumblers should not obviate the fact that the threat of urban terrorism was perceived a very real one at the *fin de siècle*."

Fiction and reality merged when Stead invoked *Jekyll and Hyde* as a model for the "Ripper Murders." The vastness and anonymity of the city helped to mask the Ripper's identity, a cover that Jekyll also exploits with relish: "I was the first that could thus plod in the public eye with a load of genial respectability, and in a moment, like a schoolboy, strip off these lendings and spring headlong into the sea of liberty. But for me, in my impenetrable mantle, the safety was complete. Think of it—I did not even exist!" (Stevenson 1886: 60). To the fellow-members of the middle-class community, any transgressive acts of Jekyll are "hidden," officially nonex-istent; and yet "The Maiden Tribute" had effectively proven that men lead-ing double lives were, in reality, prowling the city streets. Stead exposed a metropolitan reality, and Hyde becomes a product of both metropolitan imagination and the metropolitan experience. The division of self in *Jekyll and Hyde* is linked to the fragmented social and physical aspects of the city. Hyde is a *flâneur* who becomes a sinister and threatening city phe-nomenon. The city breeds its own deviant types, like Hyde. In Utterson's imagination, therefore Hyde embodies the nocturnal threat of Victorian London; it is little wonder that he became so closely linked in the public imagination with that other nocturnal criminal, Jack the Ripper. Stead's "Maiden Tribute" is also called to mind: Utterson's nightmare involves the abuse of a child at every street corner. When Jekyll decides to lay aside his alchemy, and with it Hyde, it seems as if his dreadful alter ego has disappeared, like the Ripper, into thin air: "From the time he had left the house in Soho on the morning of the murder, he was simply blotted out" (31). The sprawling metropolis, which breeds criminals, also has the capacity to conceal them from view, as if providing sanctuary to the criminals it creates.

Duality, Light and the City

The physical city has a multiple personality: its daytime and nighttime faces strongly reinforce the sense of duality in *Jekyll and Hyde*. By day the street behind Jekyll's house bustles with commerce and traffic, a knowable community in Williams's sense. An atmosphere of gaiety and invitation pervades the by-street where the shop fronts stood "like rows of smiling saleswomen." Even on Sundays, with the shops closed, the thoroughfare "with its freshly-painted shutters, well-polished brasses, and general cleanliness and gaiety of note, instantly caught and pleased the eye of the passenger" (6). Human presence in the city can be reassuring, as well as threatening: a friendly face is the counterpoint to Le Bon's murderous crowds; Utterson considers it of therapeutic value: "I feel as if the presence of a friend might do him good" (35). When Utterson and Enfield see Jekyll's "expression of such abject terror and despair as froze the blood," they cannot speak until "they had come into a neighbouring thoroughfare, where even upon a Sunday there were still some stirrings of life" (36).

At night the city can assume an even more gothic atmosphere. The strange and the supernatural, and often the criminal, occur under cover of night. When Utterson first confronts Hyde it is ten o'clock in the evening, all the shops are closed, and the bystreet that houses Jekyll's old dissecting-room is "very solitary, and in spite of the low growl of London from all around, very silent" (4). "Domestic sounds" emanate from the surrounding houses, but the atmosphere on the street is one of quiet emptiness. The heightened sensibility of gothic narratives is invoked by the echoing of Hyde's footsteps as he arrives on the scene. Hyde's demeanor compounds the gothicism: his appearance "went somehow strongly against the watcher's inclination" (4). He shrinks back, hisses, and snarls "with a savage laugh," like a cornered animal, dangerous and unpredictable, with something of the uncanny that links him to the villain of gothic literature (14).

Nocturnal prowlers like Hyde are commonly the stuff of gothic fiction: Frankenstein's monster spurns daylight; Dracula is, physically, a creature of the night who can not risk exposure on the thronged sunlit streets.

Night is the domain of the "other," camouflaging identity and criminal activity. At night the gothic monster penetrates "safe" domestic environments. The monster kills Elizabeth in Frankenstein's own bedchamber; Dracula vampirizes women in their bedrooms; Utterson imagines the urban monster Hyde as summoning Jekyll from his own bed. Hyde precipitates Lanyon's death in his own parlor and murders Carew in the street outside a gentleman's house. At the very center of his home, Jekyll awaits death at the hands of Hyde. Metropolitan anxiety about criminal activity goes to the heart of the domestic sphere in the modern gothic novel, where the urban monster leaves the streets of low-life London to attack citizens in or near their own homes.

As Fishman (2001: 194) observes, the nocturnal East London streets were notorious for violence: "Nocturnal predators were on the prowl, ready to pounce on some naïve victim who ventured out alone. A German innocent, John Kolisky, was strolling along the Commercial Road at 4.30 a.m., the morning of 12 February [1888]. He was followed silently by a William Ryan, who suddenly seized him by the throat, struck him a violent blow in the eye, and with the aid of an accomplice, cut his pockets and extracted all his money (£4 14s)." Such robberies led to public calls for a rapid installation of street lighting in the East End to deter criminal activity—appeals that were only increased in the wake of the Ripper Murders.[1] The *Star*, on 1 October 1888, even invoked the threat to the British Empire: "Above all, let us impress the moral of this awful business on the consciences and the fears of the West End. The cry of the East End is for light—the electric light to flash into the dark corners of its streets and alleys, the magic light of sympathy and hope to flash into the dark corners of wrecked and marred lives. Unless these and other things come, Whitechapel will smash the Empire, and the best thing that can happen to us is for some purified Republic of the West to step in and look after these fragments" (Curtis 2001: 263).

Light, daylight, moonlight, or artificial light, is the enemy of the evildoer; yet lamplight illuminates Hyde's trampling of the child, moonlight his murder of Carew. Visiting Lanyon to collect the powders, Hyde fears discovery when a policeman approaches with his bull's-eye lantern open. Hyde shuns the day, and Jekyll recognizes danger by daylight: when he awakens as Hyde, it is in the yellow light of a mid-morning London. His most terrifying moment comes when, sitting on a bench in Regent's Park in full daylight, he realizes he has transformed into Hyde: "A moment before I had been safe of all men's respect, wealthy, beloved—the cloth laying for me in the dining-room at home; and now I was the common quarry of mankind, hunted, houseless, a known murderer, thrall to the gallows" (Stevenson 1886: 6). For Hyde the streets that were the location of his nocturnal wanderings are now fraught with terror.

Street lighting began to be introduced in London from the 1680s. Before that, as Stevenson, himself noted in "A Plea for Gas Lamps," nighttime pedestrians carried their own form of lighting: "But sun, moon, and stars abstracted or concealed, the night-faring inhabitant had to fall back— we speak on the authority of old prints—upon stable lanthorns two storeys in height. Many holes, drilled in the conical turret-roof of this vagabond Pharos, let up spouts of dazzlement into the bearer's eyes; and as he paced forth in the ghostly darkness, carrying his own sun by a ring about his finger, day and night swung to and fro and up and down about his footsteps. Blackness haunted his path; he was beleaguered by goblins as he went; and curfew being struck, he found no light but that he travelled in throughout the township" (Stevenson 1878: 189).

By the early nineteenth century, gas lighting abounded: "The spread of gas lighting made the streets safer by night. Pall Mall had been illuminated as early as 1807; by 1841, it was claimed, 'the metropolis now burns gas in every square, street, alley, lane, passage, and court,' and thereby 'half the work of the prevention of crime was accomplished'" (Porter 1998: 300). But this illumination did not extend into the East End, even in the last quarter of the nineteenth century. Amid the general disapproval of Police Commissioner Warren's handling of the Ripper murders, there were numerous calls for increased lighting in the dark courts and alleyways of Whitechapel. After the first two murders, the editorial writer for the *Daily Telegraph* on 1 September 1888 even "urged the police to install 'the latest scientific appliances'—namely side-street telephone boxes like those used by the New York City police to improve communications'" (Curtis 2001: 119).

The city lamps engendered that sense of security that Stevenson recorded in his own poem "The Lamplighter": "But I, when I am stronger and can choose what I'm to do, / O Leerie, I'll go round at night and light the lamps with you! / For we are very lucky, with a lamp before the door, / And Leerie stops to light it as he lights so many more" (Stevenson 1885a: 40). The cheerful lilt of the verse echoes the leavening effect of lamplight for the young poet.[2] These were gas lamps, not the sickly sodium lights of the sprawling suburbs that Betjeman was later to deplore. "A Plea for Gas Lamps" was an invective against the installation of electric lighting in the cities. Paris was lit by " new sort of urban star" that "now shines out nightly, horrible, unearthly, obnoxious to the human eye; a lamp for a nightmare!" (Stevenson 1878: 192).

In the London of Jekyll and Hyde, Stevenson uses street lighting for a variety of effects. In the "dismal quarter of Soho" where Hyde lives, the atmosphere is so gloomy that the lamps seem never to have been extinguished, suggesting the older gas lighting. The overall effect is of "a district of some city in a nightmare" (Stevenson 1886: 23), recalling Thomson's "City of Dreadful Night." Lamplight here compounds the nightmarish quality and danger of the place. When Enfield encounters Hyde, it is in the uncomfortably empty lamp-lit spaces of London at dead of night, and, unexpectedly, the lamps serve to heighten the sense of isolation and fear: "I was coming home from some place at the end of the world, about three o'clock of a black winter morning, and my way lay through a part of town where there was literally nothing to be seen but lamps. Street after street, and all the folks asleep—street after street, all lighted up as if for a procession, and all as empty as a church—till at last I got into that state of mind when a man listens and begins to long for the sight of a policeman" (7). This type of illumination seems precisely that to which Stevenson objects. In "A Plea for Gas Lamps" he deplores the imminent installation of electric lighting in London: "A sedate electrician somewhere in a back office touches a spring—and behold! From one end to another of the city, from east to west, from the Alexandra to the Crystal Palace, there is light!" The "monstrous city," as he calls London, "flashes into vision." Prefiguring Hyde's crimes, Stevenson claims that such a "light as this should shine only on murders and public crime, or along the corridors of lunatic asylums, a horror to heighten horror" (Stevenson 1878: 192).

Soho remains in a perpetual state of murky twilight, its inhabitants more like specters than solid forms; Hyde's crimes in the more open spaces of the city are viewed as under a spot light, where law-abiding citizens look on, appalled at such brutality in their neighborhood. The point is that in Soho, criminal activity is tolerated and flourishes; it is in the nature of place, as reflected in the swirling mists that obscure and envelop vice and crime. Hyde belongs here, among the degenerate population who will ask no questions, or turn a blind eye to his activities. On entering the "upper" world of the well-to-do, the mists roll away, city spaces are floodlit, and the light shines on his violence, "a horror to heighten horror." His crimes, the trampling of the child and the murder of Carew, occur under the lamplight designed to reduce crime or enable its detection. The fact that such illumination does not deter Hyde's brutality is even more sinister:

like Le Bon's crowd, Hyde acts on instinct when he tramples or murders, and his consciousness of personal danger only kicks in after the deed.

The London Labyrinth

The London of Jekyll and Hyde, even during the day, is a Janus-faced metropolis. In contrast to the more salubrious district of Jekyll's home, Hyde haunts the dark spaces of the city and the nightmarish space of Soho where prostitution and vaguely criminal activities are suggested. At nine in the morning it wears the aspect of dusk:

> It was by this time about nine o'clock in the morning, and the first fog of the season. A great chocolate-coloured pall lowered over heaven, but the wind was continually charging and routing these embattled vapours; so that as the cab crawled from street to street, Mr Utterson beheld a marvellous number of degrees and hues of twilight; for here it would be dark like the back-end of evening; and there would be a glow of a rich, lurid brown, like the light of some strange conflagration; and here, for a moment, the fog would be quite broken up, and a haggard shaft of daylight would glance in between the swirling wreathes. The dismal quarter of Soho seen under these changing glimpses, with its muddy ways, and slatternly passengers, and its lamps, which had never been extinguished or had been rekindled afresh to combat this mournful reinvasion of darkness, seemed, in the lawyer's eyes, like a district of some city in a nightmare. (Stevenson 1886: 23)

The location of Hyde's abode is seemingly a living hell surrounded by "a low French eating-house," ragged children, and "many women of many different nationalities passing out, key in hand, to have a morning glass" (23).

Peter Ackroyd (2000: 435) describes *Jekyll and Hyde* as the greatest novel of London fog in which "the fable of changing identities and secret lives takes place within the medium of the city's shifting insubstantial mists." The isolation that the fog engenders is for Ackroyd "the condition of living in London—to be 'cut off,' isolated, a single mote in the swirl of fog and smoke. To be alone among the confusion is perhaps the single most piercing emotion of any stranger in the city." Ackroyd mentions how Elizabeth Barrett Browning spoke of the fog blurring the cityscape, "as if a sponge had wiped out London." Fear of invisibility prompted radical techniques to counteract the effect of the fog: "That is precisely why architects decided to clothe buildings in bright red brick and shining terracotta so that they would remain visible; the features of nineteenth-century building, which may seem vulgar or gaudy, were attempts to stabilise the identity and legibility of the city" (Ackroyd 2000: 435). The physical city then, according to Ackroyd, has an identity crisis of its own. *Jekyll and Hyde* dramatizes the very essence of late-nineteenth-century city life: its duality is figured in the discrete personalities of Jekyll/Hyde; its shifting and merging identities figured in Jekyll's increasing inability to stabilize his own identity.

This is not a perception of London that is confined to Stevenson's imagination: it is a persistent portrayal of the city that emerges in numerous fictional representations, and particularly in the modern gothic novel. Prendick in Wells's *The Island of Doctor Moreau*, sees London inhabitants who eerily recall Moreau's Beast People: "I would go out into the streets to fight with my delusion, and prowling women would mew after me, furtive craving men glance jealously at me, weary pale workers go coughing by me, with tired eyes and eager paces like wounded deer dripping blood, old people, bent and dull, pass murmuring to themselves, and all unheeding a ragged tail of gibing children" (Wells 1896: 186–87). Here the metropolis is metaphorically a jungle, populated by predatory beings, like Le Bon's crowds, that act not on reason but on instinct. When Hyde blindly tramples the child or gleefully thrashes Carew to death he behaves in a manner more animal than human; his rapacity is that of a metropolitan beast.

A complex image of the city thus begins to emerge. For Cedric Watts, it is the "striking contrasts" that London can accommodate within a few square miles that makes it so "enabling" for writers: "Soho and Buckingham Palace; sordid squalor and majestic opulence; working-class tenements and the Houses of Parliament; downtrodden masses and the centre of imperial power" (Moore 1992: 27). These are the contrasts contained within the metropolis that Stevenson exploits in his gothic tale of duality: Jekyll's respectable home and Lanyon's comfortable fireside oppose Hyde's Soho residence. Hyde does not belong in Jekyll's district; hence his surreptitious entry to the house by the back door. The novel never mentions Jekyll having been in Soho. The servants admitting visitors to the two homes further strengthen this dichotomy: Hyde's obsequious landlady with her "evil face, smoothed by hypocrisy" fits her seedy surroundings and has none of the discretion of Jekyll's or Lanyon's butlers. Introduced to Inspector Newcomen of Scotland Yard, a "flash of odious joy appeared on the woman's face": "'Ah!' said she, 'he is in trouble! What has he done?'" (Stevenson 1886: 4). Poole's priorities are to protect his master; this woman actively seeks Hyde's apprehension. Loyalty, human compassion, decency: symptoms of civilized human existence are absent in the underworld of Soho.

Its London setting and social concerns identify *Jekyll and Hyde* as a novel about the late-nineteenth-century metropolis. London was, and remains, representative of the metropolitan experience. A city as vast as this lends itself to the suggestiveness and impressionism in the artistic sense that Stevenson implies in "A Humble Remonstrance," allowing the artist to "shut his eyes against the dazzle and confusion of reality" and to "regard instead a certain figmentary abstraction" (Stevenson 1884: 159). In Stevenson's modern gothic tale, in the heart of Britain, the center of the Empire, lurk the dangerous impulses, destabilizing influences, and social fissures that are implied in Jekyll's metamorphosis into Hyde. The duality of the city and its dwellings, the imprint of personality left on inanimate objects and personal spaces become a cipher in which we read the complexity of the human personality. It can be a space of light and gaiety, but in *Jekyll and Hyde*, Stevenson's metropolis is a "City of Dreadful Night."

NOTES

1. Fishman records that the "Whitechapel Board of Works were debating the extension of gas lamps into the dimly-lit alleys and culs-de-sac of Spitalfields on the eve of the Ripper's first attack!" (2001: 209).

2. The situation of the family house at 17 Heriot Row could have inspired Stevenson in his description of the murder of Carew. The upper floors of the house look down onto the street lit by the lamp outside.

REFERENCES

Ackroyd, Peter. 2000. *London: The Biography*. London: Chatto & Windus.

Booth William. 1890. *In Darkest England and the Way Out*. London: International Headquarters of the Salvation Army.

Curtis, L. Perry. 2001. *Jack the Ripper and the London Press*. New Haven, CT: Yale University Press.

Fishman, William. 2001. *East End 1888*. London: Hanbury.

Greenslade, William. 1994. *Degeneration, Culture and the Novel 1880–1940*. Cambridge: Cambridge University Press.

Hurley, Kelly. 1996. *The Gothic Body: Sexuality, Materialism, and Degeneration at the Fin de Siècle*. Cambridge: Cambridge University Press.

Le Bon, Gustave. 1895. *Psychologie des foules*. 1982. *The Crowd: A Study of the Popular Mind*. Atlanta, GA: Cherokee Publishing Company.

Moore, Gene. ed. 1992. *Conrad's Cities: Essays for Hans van Marle*. Amsterdam: Rodopi.

Porter, Roy. 1998. *London: A Social History.* Cambridge, MA: Harvard University Press.

Stevenson, Robert Louis. 1878. A Plea for Gas Lamps. In *Virginibus Puerisque and Other Papers.* 1924. London: Chatto & Windus. 189–193.

———. 1884. A Humble Remonstrance. In *Memories and Portraits, Other Essays and Reminiscences.* 1925. London: Heinemann. 155–168.

——— 1885a. *A Child's Garden of Verses.* 1984. London: Treasure Press.

——— (with Fanny Van de Grift Stevenson). 1885b. *More New Arabian Nights: The Dynamiter.* London: Longmans, Green & Co.

———. 1886. *Strange Case of Dr. Jekyll and Mr. Hyde.* In *The Strange Case of Dr. Jekyll and Mr. Hyde and Other Tales of Terror.* Ed. Robert Mighall. 2002. Harmondsworth: Penguin.

Thomson, James. 1874. The City of Dreadful Night. In *The New Oxford Book of English Verse.* 1972. London: Oxford University Press.

Walkowitz, Judith. 1992. *City of Dreadful Delight: Narratives of Sexual Danger in Late-Victorian London.* Chicago: University of Chicago Press.

Wells, H. G. 1896. *The Island of Dr Moreau.* n.d. London: Daily Express Fiction Library.

Williams, Raymond. 1973. *The Country and the City.* London: Chatto & Windus.

Pious Works

Aesthetics, Ethics, and the Modern Individual
in Robert Louis Stevenson's
Strange Case of Dr. Jekyll and Mr. Hyde

RICHARD J. WALKER

On 13 May 1871, Jean-Nicolas-Arthur Rimbaud—Charleville malcontent, budding anarchist, future Communard, poet of precocious talent, and not yet seventeen—corresponded with his old schoolmaster Georges Izambard. In what has become known as the "seer" letter, Rimbaud set out his manifesto for modern poetry claiming "Je est un autre" ["I is another," "I is somebody else"]. Graham Robb, in his authoritative study of Rimbaud, observes that the statement that "has often been treated as a poetic E = mc²" (Robb 2000: 81). Rimbaud's equation is clearly provocative, and as a result has been read in many different ways, "from the banal to the fantastic" as Robb goes on to point out. It certainly attempts to challenge the assumption of a coherent and autonomous individual identity in Western thought, one that can be traced back to Descartes' "Cogito ergo sum" from that seminal document for modernity *Discourse on Method* (1637), an equation that continues to provoke debate among philosophers and critical theorists in the twenty-first century. For the purposes of the present essay, Rimbaud's statement is important for the way it disturbs the prevailing concept of the sincerity of the lyric in nineteenth-century British poetry. As a result it also problematizes meditations on the seemingly insoluble connection between art and ethics that critical writing of the century strives to sustain. Significantly enough, Rimbaud's equation also evokes the theme of doubleness that haunts cultural representation in nineteenth century Britain, one that is evoked in dynamic if problematic ways in *fin*

FIGURE 5. Etching by Mirando Haz from *Dr. Jekyll Mr. Hyde and Company*, privately printed, 2002. Reproduced by kind permission of the artist.

de siècle writing, and in particular Robert Louis Stevenson's classic tale of "I" being "somebody else," *Strange Case of Dr. Jekyll and Mr. Hyde* (1886).

Arguably, it is the Romantic poet William Wordsworth, in his preface to the second edition of *Lyrical Ballads* (1800), who first attempts to establish and consolidate a connection between ethics and aesthetics for nineteenth-century culture in Britain. His vision of a coherent and morally instructive culture is one that—whether we agree with it or not—still remains resonant today, regardless of developments in critical theory in the academy from the mid-twentieth century onward. Wordsworth claims that "the human mind is capable of being excited without the application of gross and violent stimulants, and he must have a very faint perception of its beauty and dignity who does not know this" (Wordsworth 1800: 243).

For Wordsworth, culture needs to have an ethical dimension; but he sees the modern reader's mind reduced to a "savage torpor" because "the increasing accumulation of men in cities, where the uniformity of their occupations produces a craving for extraordinary incident, which the rapid communication of intelligence hourly gratifies. To this tendency of life and manners the literature and theatrical exhibitions of the country have conformed themselves. The invaluable works of our elder writers (I had almost said the works of Shakespeare and Milton) are driven into neglect by frantic novels, sickly and stupid German tragedies, and deluges of idle and extravagant stories in verse" (243).

This statement can come across as the grumblings of a conservative, provincial, little-Englander: it seems to be nostalgic for a "Golden Age" of English Literature (offering the talismans of Shakespeare and Milton), it laments urbanization over "natural" life and bewails the influence of technology on the modern world. In effect, for culture to have both an aesthetic and ethical value it should be "natural," incorporating "the spontaneous overflow of powerful emotions" as Wordsworth famously put it (242). In effect it is possible to argue, as Neil Sammells does, that the equation "nature plus culture equals an ethical life" turns the interaction between all three into "a kind of moral gymnasium" (Sammells 1997: 313). However, it is often easy to overlook how important Wordsworth's words are in establishing a correspondence between aesthetics and ethics; and it is in the correlation between the two that his vision becomes interesting with regard to this debate. What Wordsworth suggests is that modern culture is affected by a malaise, and one that is not only "sickly," if not "stupid," but intrinsically "evil" (Wordsworth 1800: 243). In effect he posits a series of boundaries, based upon doubling, that haunt cultural criticism and theory in the nineteenth century, through the twentieth. and no doubt on into the twenty-first: "High" *contra* "Low," "Good" *contra* "Bad," "moral" versus "immoral," "healthy" versus "sickly." What is particularly significant is that what Wordsworth identifies as the source of "evil," as the cultural malaise, is "frantic novels, sickly and stupid German tragedies"; in short it is not just popular culture that is to blame, but the gothic novel in particular. It is, of course, the gothic novel that, apart from giving birth to a variety of popular literary subgenres from science fiction to the detective novel, emerges as the "penny dreadful" in Victorian culture and leads Stevenson to allude to his gothic text, *Jekyll and Hyde*, in a self-deprecating way as his own "shilling shocker" (Masson 1922: 213). Stevenson's description of the novel, as flippant as it may be, is a significant one; it allows the text to enter the literary marketplace, therefore removing it from the world of creative integrity privileged by Wordsworth, and one where bourgeois self-interest is the only law. Indeed, as Inspector Newcomen puts it in the hunt for the murderous Hyde, "money's life to the man," (Stevenson 1886: 50) and Hyde's trampling of a little girl, which opens the strange case, evokes Marshall Berman's "modern men and women" who "may well stop at nothing": "free from fear and trembling, they are free to trample down everyone in their way if self-interest drives them to it" (Berman 1983: 115).

In this light, Hyde can be read as "boorish" (Miller 1985: 211); his crimes are petty, malicious, and self-indulgent. Indeed, it is possible to read Hyde not only as the industrial bourgeois of Marx and Engels' *Communist Manifesto*—who experiences "uninterrupted disturbance" and "everlasting uncertainty" (Marx and Engels 1848: 83), manifest in the fluidity of identity between Jekyll and Hyde and in the strange, shifting nature of Hyde's appearance itself—but also as the "philistine" of Matthew Arnold's *Culture and Anarchy*, the uncultured and bourgeois product of utilitarian thought. It is Arnold whose work most clearly sustains the correlation between aesthetics and ethics in nineteenth-century debates on culture. Picking up on Wordsworth's ideas in the preface to *Lyrical Ballads*, Arnold argues for a conception of culture that is moral, cathartic, instructive, and beautiful; in effect culture should be "the endeavor to know the best and to make this knowledge prevail for the good of all mankind" (Storey 2001: 18). In effect culture should consist of "Sweetness and Light" rather than sourness and dark, and, as he puts it the preface to *Poems* (1853), modern culture should evade the "doubts" and "discouragement" and return to the "disinterested objectivity" of classical verse (Arnold 1853: 115). Such a program would seem certain to exclude the gothic "shilling shocker." The

Wordsworthian and Arnoldian critical position therefore propagates a theory that advocates coherence and an ethical dimension to culture through establishing a binary opposition between good and bad, high and low, pious and impious, inside and outside with, of course, an emphasis on privileging the center ("High" culture) over the margins (popular culture).

Ironically, neither Wordsworth nor Arnold, the high priests of ethical aesthetics, are averse to their own, maybe unwitting, forays into the territory of the uncertain and disruptive divided self that haunts nineteenth-century literature. This is the area of Rimbaud's declaration "Je est un autre," a statement that deconstructs both Cartesian self-affirmation and the sincerity and authenticity of Wordsworthian lyricism. The same can be said of Stevenson's *Strange Case*, where Jekyll's inability to speak the self ("He, I say—I cannot say, I"; Stevenson 1886: 94) uncannily echoes the Rimbaldian equation of otherness. Wordsworth experiences similar self-division in book two of *The Prelude* of 1805 where, recollecting his childhood experiences, he finds that:

> so wide appears
> The vacancy between me and those days
> Which yet have such self-presence in my mind
> That sometimes, when I think of them I seem
> Two consciousnesses—conscious of myself
> And of some other being. (2: 28–33)

Arnold's experience of doubling is perhaps more problematic than the gulf between mature and infant self evoked by Wordsworth. In the aforementioned preface to *Poems* of 1853, Arnold discusses his disillusionment with modern culture, and finds that "the dialogue of the mind with itself has commenced; modern problems have presented themselves" (Arnold 1853: 115). More significantly, in the lyric "The Buried Life," the poetic voice knows that

> the mass of men conceal'd
> Their thoughts, for fear that if revealed
> They would by other men be met
> With blank indifference, or with blame reproved;
> I knew they lived and moved
> Trick'd in disguises, alien to the rest
> Of men, and alien to themselves. (Arnold 1852: 84)

This sense of insincerity, of the modern individual existing "Trick'd in disguises," results in the speaker expressing the desire to unearth the authentic self. The expression of this desire is significant:

> But often, in the world's most crowded streets,
> But often, in the din of strife,
> There rises an unspeakable desire
> After the knowledge of our buried life. (85)

The experience takes place in the "crowded streets" of the modern metropolis, not the bucolic environment typical to the Wordsworthian lyric, and the quest for this alternative "authentic" self has a distinctly gothic flavor, involving as it does an "unspeakable desire"—reminding us once again of the double-haunted Jekyll's inability to speak the self. Taking into consideration the fact that Wordsworth and Arnold, determined custodians of high-minded and serious culture, both acknowledge the presence of another, divided and possibly secretive self, perhaps we are a bit too condemnatory of the monstrous, atavistic, deviant, anarchic, criminal, insane, and boorish Hyde.

The cultural boundaries established by Wordsworth and sustained by Arnold are troubled by the French poet and critic Charles Baudelaire, one of the few writers that Arthur Rimbaud confessed to admire. It is Baudelaire who "cancels the distinction between High Art and other cultural forms: the imagery of advertising is as powerful and worthy of note as the 'masterpieces' in the salons" (Sammells 1997: 310). It is also Baudelaire who, albeit filtered through Walter Benjamin's essays on the French poet and nineteenth-century France, starts to theorize the *flâneur*, the strolling idler, the "hero" of modern life, the modern individual. It is clearly possible to read the *flâneur* as bourgeois dandy—Benjamin describes him as "unwilling to forego the life of a gentleman of leisure" (Benjamin 1983: 54)—and can therefore be equated with Richard Dellamora's description of the dandy as philistine parasite: "Dandyism was associated with middle-class uppityism . . . the Dandy is too relaxed, too visible, consumes to excess while producing little or nothing" (Dellamora 1990: 198–99).

If the dandy/*flâneur* does consume "to excess . . . producing little or nothing" we are back to the reading of Hyde as "boorish" bourgeois self-interest incarnate. However, Baudelaire's evocation of the fluidity of aesthetics, ethics, and individualism is much more complex than Dellamora's reading of the dandy suggests; indeed it is Baudelaire's stress, in his own art and criticism, on "fluidity . . . gaseousness . . . and vaporousness" that troubles the certainties of nineteenth-century cultural debate discussed so far and, as Marshall Berman puts it, paves the way for "the primary qualities in the self-consciously modernist painting, architecture and design, music and literature, that will emerge at the end of the nineteenth century" (Berman 1983: 144). It is Baudelaire who, in Madan Sarup's opinion, is the "writer associated with the heroic transfiguration of the ephemeral and fleeting moment" (Sarup 1996: 89), and who inspires Michel Foucault to contradict the ethics of self found in Arnold's "The Buried Life": "Modern man, for Baudelaire, is not the man who goes off to discover himself, his secrets and his hidden truth; he is the man who tries to invent himself. This modernity does not "liberate man in his own being"; it compels him to face the task of producing himself" (Foucault 1984: 41).

It is, perhaps, unfair to compare Baudelaire, sower of *Les Fleurs du mal,* a collection of poesy that suggests that art can be sickly or evil and which collapses the high vs. low debate that still troubles the academy, with Stevenson, author of *A Child's Garden of Verses.* That said, it is clear that Stevenson's *Strange Case of Dr. Jekyll and Mr. Hyde* evokes the fluid and vaporous aesthetic of modernity and individualism found in Baudelaire. After all, the Stevenson of *Jekyll and Hyde* is—ironically, considering his emphasis on romance as a creative medium—like Baudelaire, Rimbaud, and later, Oscar Wilde, anti-romantic in that he sets his novella in a macabre and phantasmagoric city. Utterson finds himself, like Baudelaire, in "a district of some city in a nightmare," and "As the cab drew up before the address indicated, the fog lifted a little and showed him a dingy street, a gin palace, a low French eating-house, a shop for the retail of penny numbers and two-penny salads, many ragged children huddled in the doorways, and many women of many different nationalities passing out, key in hand, to have a morning glass; and the next moment the fog settled down again upon that part, as brown as umber, and cut him off from his blackguardly surroundings" (Stevenson 1886: 48).

More significantly, the "boorish" Hyde has an antiestablishment bent and an adaptable fluidity that challenges the prevailing and monolithic construction of culture in the nineteenth century, one that can be traced in the lineage that emerges with Wordsworth and Arnold and is maintained in the twentieth century with F. R. Leavis. In short Hyde, like the sinister Baudelaire, can be read as avant-garde artist/critic; after all he has "a kind of black, sneering coolness . . . like Satan," and has "Satan's signature upon [his] face" (32). He is also clearly a gentleman ("no gentleman but wishes to avoid a scene" he states with provocative coolness when faced with blackmail after trampling the little girl at the start of the novel), and with an apartment "furnished with luxury and good taste" with "carpets of many plies and agreeable in colour" is very much the dandy (32, 49).

That said, perhaps most significantly: of the three crimes of Hyde alluded to specifically by Stevenson, one is an act of literary criticism: "There were several books on a shelf . . . and Utterson was amazed to find . . . a copy of a pious work for which Jekyll had several times expressed a great esteem, annotated, in his own hand, with startling blasphemies" (71).

This act of blasphemous, irreverent, and unethical marginalia contradicts the earnest eulogies of culture and criticism by Wordsworth and Arnold. In addition, it establishes Stevenson's Hyde as operating on the boundaries of cultural criticism and good taste; indeed, it is possible that his "boorish" philistinism is seen as such from the perspective of a priggish, hypocritical, and similarly philistine Jekyll.

The cultural milieu of the late nineteenth century in Britain, more familiarly referred to as the fin de siècle, is characterized by an influx of French influences, associated in particular with the symbolist poetry of Baudelaire and Rimbaud. The heady amorality of their poesy allows the *décadent* Oscar Wilde to announce, from the margins of his own sickly "shilling shocker" *The Picture of Dorian Gray*, that "pious works" have no aesthetic value at all: "There is no such thing as a moral or an immoral book. Books are well written or badly written. That is all" (Wilde 1891: 21).

In such a context, Hyde, like the amoral and aloof satanist of Baudelaire's *Les Fleurs du mal*, is other, challenging the received wisdom of hegemonic cultural criticism from and in the margins; indeed, symbolically killing God by defacing Jekyll's "pious work." Also, like the self-consciously displaced Rimbaud (who incidentally also found himself holed up in London) he is a "perfect little monster" (Robb 2000: 26): Rimbaud the Communard advocated burning down the Louvre, for him a symbol of French bourgeois cultural complacency, Hyde defaces Jekyll's talismanic "pious work" with blasphemous scribblings. In effect, Hyde's marginalia anticipate Wilde's work on art and criticism in "The Decay of Lying" (1891), an essay (if it can be called that) clearly indebted to Baudelaire, which "champions an art which is unnatural, unhealthy and untruthful: in effect, an art which is subversive of all political, cultural and social institutions and discourses which solidify or ossify into the 'natural' state of affairs" (Sammells 1997: 309).

This "art" is clearly the opposite of the Wordsworthian and Arnoldian equation between aesthetics and ethics discussed earlier. Stevenson's Hyde therefore, through his gloss on Jekyll's pious work and the very fluidity of his otherness, like Baudelaire, Rimbaud, and Wilde, contributes to the questioning of cultural hegemony in the late nineteenth century. Stevenson's *Strange Case* (and its monster), whether Stevenson intended it or not, is placed on the boundaries of nineteenth-century British culture and, with its emphasis on insincerity, duplicity, and uncertainty, paves the way, as Marshall Berman puts it, for the "numerous fragmentary ways" of twentieth-century modernism. It is, after all, to Baudelaire's *Les Fleurs du mal*, with its opening address to the author's double, that Eliot goes for his unreal city in "The Waste Land," a poem in which he also alludes to Stevenson's "Requiem" and perhaps also (in the line "Nor under seals broken by the lean solicitor") to Stevenson's lean solicitor Utterson (Satpathy 1999), often sealing and unsealing in his vain attempt to control texts and meaning.

REFERENCES

Arnold, Matthew. 1852. The Buried Life. *Empedocles on Etna, and Other Poems.* In *Selected Poems and Prose.* Ed. Miriam Allott. 1978. London: Dent.
————. 1853. Preface. In *Selected Poems and Prose.* Ed. Miriam Allott. 1978. London: Dent.
Benjamin, Walter. 1955. *Charles Baudelaire. Ein Lyriker im Zeitalter des Hochkapitalismus.* 1983. *Charles Baudelaire: A Lyric Poet in the Era of High Capitalism.* London: Verso.
Berman, Marshall. 1983. *All That Is Solid Melts into Air: The Experience of Modernity.* London: Verso.
Dellamora, Richard. 1990. *Masculine Desire: The Sexual Politics of Victorian Aestheticism.* Chapel Hill: University of North Carolina Press.
Foucault, Michel. 1978.Was ist Aufklärung? Ed. Paul Rabinow. 1984. What Is Enlightenment? In *The Foucault Reader.* Harmondsworth: Penguin.
Marx, Karl, and Friedrich Engels. 1848. *Manifest der Kommunistischen Partei.* Ed. A. J. P. Taylor. 1985. *The Communist Manifesto.* Harmondsworth: Penguin.
Masson, Rosaline, ed. 1922. *I Can Remember Robert Louis Stevenson.* Edinburgh: Chambers.
Miller, Karl. 1985. *Doubles: Studies in Literary History.* Oxford: Oxford University Press.
Robb, Graham. 2000. *Rimbaud.* London: Picador.
Sammells, Neil. 1997. Oscar Wilde at Centuries' End. In *Writing and Victorianism.* Ed. J. B. Bullen. London: Longman. 306–27.
Sarup, Madan. 1996. *Identity, Culture and the Postmodern World.* Edinburgh: Edinburgh University Press.
Satpathy, S. 1995. An Allusion to Stevenson in The Waste Land. *Papers on Language and History* 31 (3): 286–90.

Stevenson, Robert Louis. 1886. *Strange Case of Dr. Jekyll and Mr. Hyde.* 1979. In *Dr Jekyll and Mr Hyde and Other Stories.* Ed. Jenni Calder. Harmondsworth: Penguin.

Storey, John. 2001. *Cultural Theory and Popular Culture: An Introduction.* Essex, NJ: Prentice Hall.

Wilde, Oscar. 1891. *The Picture of Dorian Gray.* Ed. Peter Ackroyd. 1985. Harmondsworth: Penguin.

Wordsworth, William. 1800. Preface. *Lyrical Ballads.* 2nd ed. In *The Norton Anthology of English Literature.* vol. 2, 7th ed. Ed. M. H. Abrams et al. New York: W. W. Norton, 2000.

Dr. Jekyll and Mr. Hyde

A "Men's Narrative" of Hysteria and Containment

JANE V. RAGO

In Western cultural imagination, Stevenson's *Strange Case of Dr. Jekyll and Mr. Hyde* has become a metaphor, almost the very name for the duplicitous self. The categorical tradition of the good/bad, normal/deviant construction of the subject is revealed in the numerous attempts to fix Hyde's identity. Critics have read Hyde as a figure of perverse violence and male sexuality, as the illicit pleasures of homoeroticism, as a frightful blurring of gender roles linked to the New Woman, as the degenerate, as an Irish Frankenstein's monster, as an embodiment of the horror of addiction, and as the atavistic criminal who "passes" as a gentleman.[1] All of these readings of Hyde construct him, on some level, as something other than Jekyll, or, more specifically, as something other than the gentlemanly medico-juridico-scientific world that comprises the text. This gentlemanly caste is depicted through the respected and professional men in the text: Utterson, the "protagonist" of the text, is a lawyer, Enfield, the "well known man about town" (Stevenson 1886: 8), "the great Dr. Lanyon of Cavendish Square, that citadel of medicine" (15), and Henry Jekyll, "M.D, D.C.L, LL.D, F.R.S" (14).

Even if Hyde is constructed as the necessarily dark side of the bourgeois professional man, as the other side of the same coin, there remains a tendency to posit Hyde as fundamentally different, out of control, the anarchist of the city streets of London.

As the work of these critics suggest, the focus of Stevenson's novella resides in the professional world's attempts to represent and fix Hyde's identity

FIGURE 6. Etching by Mirando Haz from *Dr. Jekyll Mr. Hyde and Company*, privately printed, 2002. Reproduced by kind permission of the artist.

into a known subject. This attempt to fix Hyde's identity comprises the action of the text: Utterson, a representative of the social world that seemingly excludes Hyde, skulks about the shadows and fog of nighttime London, in accord with his private watchword—"If he be Mr. Hyde, I shall be Mr. Seek" (17), so that Hyde does not create a public scene, understood as a scandal, for Dr. Jekyll. In this chapter, I shall argue that the transgression of Hyde lies not in his otherness but rather in his sameness. The professional medico-juridico-scientific world of the text is enmeshed in the gentlemanly rituals of authoritative discourse. It is precisely this discursive regime that Hyde threatens, and this results in a panic of representation and self-implication that surrounds the professional world. The problem of Hyde originates for us not in the space of London, nor in the "Story of the Door," but in the sealed and enclosed will of Jekyll that so bothers Utterson. It is through Hyde's very condition of possibility, or his relation to writing, that he threatens to disrupt and denaturalize the tenuous practice of the professional world that maintains an authoritative and unseen gaze, through which they can author-ize deviance and normativity. What makes Hyde so threatening within this schema is that he is not an atavistic other but rather he is a gentleman, a part of this very same masculine order of the text. The threat of self-implication that Hyde poses is the crux of the narrative structure of the text. There exists, on the part of the professional order (personified by Utterson), at once a paranoid and a cynical response to Hyde: a deliberate misrecognition of Hyde in the various attempts to interpellate him as "other" that (it is cynically recognized) necessarily must fail (cf. Žižek 1989). This dialectical reaction is apparent in the frantic attempts to "other" Hyde that fail because they are, on one level, fully intended to fail, in order to justify ongoing efforts to construct a normative identity.

In late-Victorian London (as elsewhere), this medico-juridico-scientific world relied upon its own perceived authority to control representations of identity through the dialectically related acts of looking and constructing a discourse of visual description. The authoritative gaze of this professional world is premised on the authority to write—and the assumption that the writing subject remains outside the field of vision—relying on its own invisibility as the default setting of normativity. Hyde defies visual description in the narrative and disrupts the authoritative gaze, so he remains deliberately unspoken; yet there is a discursive explosion that frantically and obsessively tries to fix Hyde's identity as deviant. This textual hysteria revolves around the threat of interpellation turned back in on itself and culminates in a crisis of representation through a misrecognition of Hyde and the dislocation of deviance from his body onto the text. In other words, what is hysterical and deviant about *Dr. Jekyll and Mr. Hyde* is not the pathology of Hyde, but the normative ideological practices of invisibility and silence that enshroud the text.

Stephen D. Arata links this need to identify Victorian bodies with the discourse of degeneration that was prevalent toward the end of the nineteenth century. He writes, "because degenerative illness presented itself to the interested observer as a series of marks and symptoms to be interpreted, certain aggressive forms of reading were required to make sense of the evidence. The text to be read took many shapes—bodies, cells, cultures, nations, races, historical periods, as well as works of literature" (Arata 1996: 19). What this discourse of degeneration provided was an aggressive practice that could mark various bodies as deviant. Yet degenerative illness did not present itself to the interested observer as "marks and symptoms to be interpreted"—rather these marks and symptoms were constructed by the very act of aggressive reading. The medico-juridico-scientific networks' expansion of the discourse of degeneration from aggressively reading bodies to include "works of literature" now allowed for the marks of deviance to be evinced in language itself.[2] The fantasy is that "if imaginative writing was often figured as a product of disease, that disease was made visible through the hermeneutic expertise of the professional, whose own writing was untainted by . . . various pathologies" (Arata 1996: 20).[3] The perception of the untainted nature of the professional serves two functions: on one hand, it maintains a naturalizing authority to construct marks of deviance, and by doing so remaining unrepresented, the invisibility of the "normal," and on the other hand it blurs bodies into text and text into bodies via rendering language at once the site of disease and the means to contain that very same disease. In Stevenson's novella, the professional world struggles to maintain its authority through its own controlling invisibility (attempting to see Hyde) and silence (attempting to write Hyde)—negotiating Hyde illustrates this crisis in representation, or how to know Hyde-as-one-of-us.

The Scene

According to Kellen Williams (1996: 417), "Utterson's quest is remarkably akin to late nineteenth-century medical and scientific attempts to give the deviant body and its untoward pleasures what Foucault has described as 'analytical, visible, and permanent reality.'" In other words, Hyde must be made visible to Utterson so that the latter may remain invisible to society at large. The very act of seeking to find a deviant body reinforces the myth of the unrepresentability of the normal in the authoritative gaze. Within the narrative, Hyde does invite being seen. Although he creeps about at night and can literally disappear (when he becomes Jekyll), he is perpetually observed and curiosity is piqued to know who this monstrous gentleman is. Starkly illustrating the power of the ideological gaze of the normative professional, Utterson has a "curiosity to behold the features of the real Mr. Hyde. If he could but once set eyes on him, he thought the mystery would lighten and perhaps roll altogether away, as was the habit of mysterious things when well examined" (Stevenson 1886: 17). In desiring to set eyes on Hyde, Utterson is relying upon the authority of the normative gaze, deliberately positing him as "mysterious" and reinforcing the ideological fantasy of an authoritative, objective reading of the body. To see Hyde is to position him as other merely by observing, categorizing, and interpellating him into an objective, scientific regime of knowledge.

In this manner Utterson can then fantasize about controlling how to represent Hyde to the world—the ultimate act of containment.

If Hyde's vague nighttime atrocities (whether murder, trampling little girls, or unspecified acts of sexual excess/perversity) became publicly linked to Jekyll, then Utterson would quite literally be placed under scrutiny. All of the "gentlemen" in the text have a vague and unspecified past that threatens scandal. Indeed, shortly after encountering (seeing) Hyde, Utterson's thoughts turn away from Hyde's activities-as-other and toward himself "scared by the thought, [Utterson] brooded awhile on his own past . . . he was humbled to dust by the many ill things he had done" (20–21). Immediately, Utterson squirms under this self-implication, the awareness that Hyde's actions reflect his own—Hyde-as-same. Our first encounter with Hyde already positions him not as other but as same—he is a gentleman, albeit a depraved one, but of the bourgeois male social order nonetheless. Arata makes a similar claim: "Edward Hyde may not be an image of the *upright* bourgeois male, but he is decidedly an image of the bourgeois male" (1995: 238). Arata goes on to say, however, that Hyde is really an atavistic other who "passes" as a gentleman (1995: 240). Although, in a sense, all identities and nominations, such as "gentleman" and "other" are acts of passing and performativity, I am suggesting that Hyde does not pass as a gentleman, he *is* a gentleman, and this is precisely where the anxiety of the text is located—in trying to contain this paradox of Hyde-as-same.

Enfield describes how Hyde "trampled calmly over" (Stevenson 1886: 9) a girl in the middle of the night (note that Enfield is prowling the night streets as well), "But there was one curious circumstance. I had taken a loathing to *my gentleman* at first sight" (9, italics mine). The language used is of a communal and social identity, "my gentleman," thus implying that Enfield recognizes Hyde as one of his own. The scene continues with Enfield and the doctor (called in to treat the trampled girl) threatening to "make such a scandal out of this as should make his name stink from one end of London to the other"; however, "all the time . . . we were keeping the women off him as best we could, for they were as wild as harpies" (10). Already Enfield assumes Hyde speaks his own "language" by threatening a scandal—only a gentleman, one of Enfield's own social standing, would regard a scandal (literally being talked about, placed under scrutiny) as a serious threat. Furthermore, although they detest Hyde, the men close about him to protect him from the wild and harpylike women. This is one of only three scenes that involve women; as the wild and beastlike "harpies" they represent the "other" that becomes the means to reintegrate Hyde, as gentleman, into a professional world of gentlemanly power and values. Hyde responds to the men's threat of scandal with "No gentleman but wishes to avoid a scene" (10). With that, the three men retire to a private room to await dawn in private, away from the public's scrutiny, draw up bank statements in order to pay off the girl's family, and thus buy silence.

Prisonhouse of Language

Stephen Heath situates *Jekyll and Hyde* solely in the realm of a masculine discourse: "Now at the end of the century Stevenson provides a text—perhaps *the* text—for the representation of men and sexuality, excluding women and so the sexual and so the hysteria and then finding the only language it can for what is, therefore, the emergence of the hidden male: the animal, the criminal, *perversion*. Perversion is men's narrative and their story" (Heath 1986: 104). Without question, *Jekyll and Hyde* is a "men's narrative," but there is no "emergence of the hidden male." In fact the entire text is an attempt to render the "normal" male invisible and silent so that he may retain the authority of defining what is deviant and other. Since the normal reinforces the very myth of the other against which it must define itself, the text's overt attempts to preserve the medico-juridico-scientific codes of invisibility and silence have to fail—thus erupting in the sexual and the hysterical.

Nineteenth-century hysteria was a discursive function within medical texts that was intimately bound up with the naturalization of the power of the medical gaze. The medical gaze, as one of the many "surface networks of power" (cf. Foucault 1975), primarily located hysteria within the female body. As much as hysteria was eventually acknowledged as affecting both men and women, gender asymmetry at the site of representation functioned to map hysteria onto and in the woman's body. For example, medical professionals, students, and curious observers went to the famous Tuesday lectures at the Salpetrière hospital when Charcot presented and commented on the condition of hysterical patients. Interestingly, although Charcot recognized and treated the male hysteric, he never actually used the male hysteric for his staged performances of hysteria during his thirty-year tenure as a neurologist in Paris. These induced performances, therefore, constructed the female body as that which is always a spectacle, a window to a tortured soul. It is significant, in this regard, that Max Nordau, in *Degeneration*, posits that most hysterics were actually men. He argues that hysteria is the first step toward degeneration and that the hysteric man shows an "utter inability to resist suggestion, especially when it comes to him via the strong rhetorical patterns of language" (Nordau 1892: 29). What is important here is that Nordau is linking masculine hysteria to language, as opposed to the body, as seems to be the case in feminine hysteria. Implicit, then, in Nordau's description is the sense that through a discursive regime male hysterics could still be reasoned with. When it came to the degenerate criminal, however, the subject was most often described as atavistic, which implied something other than human. Hyde, as gentleman, undermines the putative distinctions between the deviant as object of the scientific gaze and the gentleman-deviant as a member of the community that marshals the discourse of objective reason with the aim of defending its prerogatives. To recognize deviance in Hyde as a gentleman requires knowledge that one should pretend not to have, yet to ignore it is to risk accepting the degenerate into one's own society. Recognition here is trapped, as in the recognition of the homosexual, ensnared by "the ultimate phrase of knowingness, 'It takes one to know one.' Interpretive access to the code that renders homosexuality legible may thus carry with it the stigma of too intimate a relation to the code and machinery of its production. . . . Though it can become, therefore, as dangerous to read as to fail to read homosexuality, homosexuality retains in either case its determining relationship to textuality and the legibility of signs" (Edelman 1994: 13). *Jekyll and Hyde* frantically attempts to read Hyde as other in an act of containment that necessarily produces an overdetermined discourse that seeks—and fails—to interpellate, or visibly mark, Hyde: it is precisely because he won't be spoken that he must be written. The narrative is an imperfect act of containment: the text seeks to build a "prisonhouse of language"[4] around Hyde and provides him the means to escape.

Scattered throughout the narrative is a Hyde who, while visibly described in detail, still defies description: "Mr Hyde was pale and dwarfish, he gave an impression of deformity without any nameable malformation, he had a displeasing smile, he had borne himself to the lawyer with a sort of murderous mixture of timidity and boldness, and he spoke with a husky, whispering and somewhat broken voice, but not all of these together could explain the hitherto unknown disgust, loathing and fear with which Mr Utterson regarded him" (Stevenson 1886: 19). This passage echoes almost all of the encounters we have with Hyde in that these descriptions are actually a de-articulation of Hyde. Although his physique is described, there is still some unexplained and unstated vagueness—Hyde's signification fails to signify who he is: Utterson fails to utter Hyde. The act of reading Hyde's body is dislocated from the physical into the discursive, into a textual hysteria that seeks to contain what it ironically creates. Williams posits that "the systematic linking of the aberrant to the ineffable, the pathological to the unspoken, suggests that what makes Hyde's 'unexpressed deformity' so scandalous is, precisely, that it remains 'unexpressed' . . . and will remain a liability only so long as it eludes the proper name" (Williams 1996: 421). However, the narrative of the text is driven by an imposed silence and the willed de-articulation of Hyde. To give Hyde his "proper name" (gentleman, self, part of professional world) would be the ultimate scandal, and this is precisely what the text seeks to contain. It is not that Hyde *cannot* be spoken, but that they *won't* speak him—they (above all Utterson) deliberately misrecognize him, because to name him would be to re-present themselves as part of this schema of invisibility and silence.

At the end of the first chapter, Utterson and Enfield literally make a pact of silence regarding anything to do with Hyde: "Mr Utterson sighed deeply, but never said a word . . . 'Here is another lesson to say nothing,' said he [Enfield]. 'I am ashamed of my long tongue. Let us make a bargain never to refer to this again.' 'With all my heart,' said the lawyer. 'I shake hands on that, Richard'" (Stevenson 1886: 13). This passage sets up the entire text's attempt at silence. Paradoxically, the novel is, of course, about Hyde. In an attempt to negotiate this pact of silence with the anxious need to identify Hyde, the spoken becomes displaced into the written forms that comprise the narrative. The text contains references to and extracts from many authoritative documents: a bank check, letters, a depositional report by a doctor, a self-observation case-study, a fragment of a newspaper account, and entries from a book of experiments. These are all official documents that seek to contain and identify Hyde and therefore silence "the arbitrary and tenuous nature of the relationship between any signified and signifier" (Edelman 1994: 8) without having to speak Hyde. To do so would be too close to making Hyde visible, and his legibility would serve to interpellate/implicate Utterson. So in attempting to write Hyde in the "official" discourse of the homosocial world (akin to the official criminal confessions of Havelock Ellis, the official sexual confessions of the medical profession, the official bankruptcy notices of the economic world, and so on) Hyde-as-other "is made to bear the stigma of writing or textuality as his identity . . . by a masculinist culture eager to preserve the authority of its own self-identity through the institution of homographesis" (Edelman 1994: 16).

This moment of de-articulated anxiety is specifically located in the move from what is (not) said to what is written—Hyde, in not being spoken, is transferred into the act of writing, the act of representation through writing. After witnessing the metamorphosis of Hyde into Jekyll, Lanyon becomes ill. When pressed about the incident, Lanyon insists upon not speaking: "'I wish to see or hear no more of Dr Jekyll . . . Some day, Utterson, *after I am dead*, you may perhaps come to learn the right and wrong of this. *I cannot tell you*'" (Stevenson 1886: 36, italics mine). Again, there is not an inability to speak Hyde, there is a self-imposed silence to de-articulate him. Lanyon knows the story but will not speak it. A week later, Lanyon dies from the shock of finding himself obliged to identify Hyde-as-Jekyll (the ultimate self-implication), and Utterson receives an envelope "addressed by the hand and sealed with the seal of his dead friend. 'PRIVATE: for the hands of J. G. Utterson ALONE and in the case of his predecease *to be destroyed unread*'" (37). Inside is a written confession, and a duplicate copy of Jekyll's will, to be opened only on the condition of Jekyll's disappearance. The professional world will not identify (speak) Hyde, and so they attempt to transcribe him into a graphic representation that they alone write and they alone read in order to contain his threat of rupture. This cordons Hyde inside a legitimate written form; the will and the confession are sealed around the subject of Hyde.

The embedded silence and invisibility of the text maintain such an ideological hold that these documents are lethal—they can only be read after the author has died or disappeared; in other words, after the author is out of reach of Hyde's contagion. The hysterical attempts to perform and maintain normative identities occlude a reading that posits Hyde strictly as other. Lanyon's illness verges on the hysteria that is constantly below the surface and yet must be seen as a crisis of representation that must be disarticulated from the body and onto the text. What is hysterical is this wild compulsion performed by the male professional to see and be unseen, to be silent and yet to write profusely, to create a paradox that then must be contained in an effort to name the other that renders the self invisible and therefore natural, normal, and unrepresentable. Ironically, in constructing Hyde, the medico-juridico-scientific world of Utterson threatens to be deconstructed and therefore denaturalized as normative by exposing the perverse relationship patriarchy has with identity—controlling textual representations of sexuality while remaining invisible itself, as ultimately un-represented.

NOTES

1. Veeder 1988, Williams 1996, Doane and Hodges 1998, Davidson 1995, Hirsch 1988, Wright 1994, and Arata 1995, respectively.

2. Perhaps the most striking and famous example of this would be Max Nordau's seemingly all-inclusive work, *Entartung* of 1892 (*Degeneration*, 1895), wherein entire literary movements are indicative of degeneration and deviance through their linguistic structure alone.

3. What is relevant here is that Arata's remarks liken the literary critic, as a professional, to the doctor, the lawyer, etc. through a sense of the "professional"—the homosocial order of the time that was imbued with authority.

4. To borrow the title of one of Fredric Jameson's early works, *The Prisonhouse of Language* (1972).

REFERENCES

Arata, Stephen D. 1995. The Sedulous Ape: Atavism, Professionalism, and Stevenson's Jekyll and Hyde. *Criticism* 37 (2): 233–59. Reprinted in Arata 1996, 33–53.
———. 1996. *Fictions of Loss in the Victorian Fin de Siècle*. Cambridge: Cambridge University Press.
Davidson, Guy. 1995. Sexuality and the Degenerate Body in Robert Louis Stevenson's *The Strange Case of Dr Jekyll and Mr Hyde*. *Australasian Victorian Studies Journal* 1: 31–40.
Doane, Janice, and Devon Hodges. 1989. Demonic Disturbances of Sexual Identity: The Strange Case of Dr. Jekyll And Mr/s. Hyde. *Novel: A Forum in Fiction*. 23 (1): 63–74.
Edelman, Lee. 1994. *Homographesis: Essays in Gay Literary and Cultural Theory*. New York: Routledge.

Foucault, Michel. 1975. *Surveiller et punir. Naissance de la prison.* English translation: *Discipline and Punish: The Birth of the Prison.* Trans. Alan Sheridan. 1977. New York: Vintage Books.

Gilmour, Robin. 1981. *The Idea of the Gentleman in the Victorian Novel.* London: George Allen & Unwin.

Heath, Stephen. 1986. Psychopathia Sexualis: Stevenson's Strange Case. *Critical Quarterly* 28 (1–2): 93–108.

Hirsch, Gordon. 1988. Frankenstein, Detective Fiction, and Jekyll and Hyde. In Veeder and Hirsch 1988, 223–46.

Nordau, Max. 1892. *Entartung.* English translation: *Degeneration.* 1895. Repr., Lincoln: University of Nebraska Press, 1968.

Stevenson, Robert Louis. 1886. *Strange Case of Dr. Jekyll and Mr. Hyde.* In R. L. Stevenson. *The Strange Case of Dr. Jekyll and Mr. Hyde and Weir of Hermiston.* Ed. Emma Letley. 1987. Oxford: Oxford University Press.

Veeder, William. 1988. Children of the Night: Stevenson and Patriarchy. In Veeder and Hirsch 1988, 107–60.

Veeder, William, and Gordon Hirsch, eds. 1988. *Dr. Jekyll and Mr. Hyde after One Hundred Years.* Chicago: University of Chicago Press.

Williams, M. Kellen. 1996. "Down with the Door, Poole": Designating Deviance in Stevenson's *Strange Case of Dr Jekyll and Mr Hyde. English Literature in Transition* 39 (4): 412–29.

Wright, Daniel. 1994. "The Prisonhouse of my Disposition": A Study of the Psychology of Addiction in Dr. Jekyll and Mr. Hyde. *Studies in the Novel* 26 (3): 254–67.

Žižek, Slavoj. 1989. *The Sublime Object of Ideology.* New York: Verso.

Consumerism and Stevenson's Misfit Masculinities

DENNIS DENISOFF

At the end of the nineteenth century, a matrix of mutually reinforcing cultural values privileged a masculinity characterized by responsibility, industry, and new money. And yet, as Martin Green notes in *Dreams of Adventure, Deeds of Empire*, despite the glorification of a mature, productive masculinity, it was "a striking feature of late Victorian culture that its emotional focus was on boys" (Green 1980: 389). Adventure literature such as Stevenson's often offered men a temporary escape into the world of their childhood, thereby giving them a safe site of release that would make sure the hegemony was maintained in the world of day-to-day business. Not surprisingly, when Stevenson began imagining the exciting exploits that would make up *Treasure Island*, his father was as eager as his twelve-year-old stepson to give input (Dillard 1998: ix).

Stevenson's support for boyish virility over bourgeois adult masculinity is even apparent in works that cannot be easily characterized as youth-oriented, such as the 1882 story collection *New Arabian Nights*. Not only do these stories have none of the exotic adventure of the dangerous and uncivilized that can be found in *Treasure Island* (1883) and *Kidnapped* (1886), but they also lack the novels' central symbolic protagonists—fledgling boys like Jim Hawkins and David Balfour. As I hope to demonstrate, however, the absence of the adolescent rascals accentuates the actual presence of their youthful qualities and values in adult culture. The pervasive "shrug-of-the-shoulders fatalism" among the urban males in Stevenson's work (Saposnik 1974: 21) suggests a deeper cultural grumbling at the constrictions

286

of the economic model of the masculine ideal, one that was not to be allayed by an evening of cerebral swashbuckling. In *New Arabian Nights*, the disgruntled young professionals that populate the stories challenge the naturalized conflation of commercialism with masculine virtue, a merger that Stevenson saw fostering the derogation of not only certain types of literature as juvenile but also certain types of men.[1]

Middle-Class Masculinities

Generally speaking, as individuals move toward adulthood, their social and economic responsibilities increase, and so too do the constrictions on their gender identities. In *Female Masculinity*, Judith Halberstam discusses the concept of tomboyism and the understandable desire in young females "for the great freedoms and mobilities enjoyed by boys" (Halberstam 1998: 6). The phenomenon is socially sanctioned when read as a reflection of a girl's "independence and self-motivation" but becomes punishable when it appears to be "the sign of extreme male identification," a concern that is drastically heightened when a tomboy reaches puberty. In "Virginibus Puerisque" Stevenson locates the same regulatory system in his era and critiques its confinement of girls within the "glass house" of a false doctrine defined by women's intrinsic innocence and purity.[2] In the essay, Stevenson implies that, while girls are being prepared for an adult life of subordination and accommodation, the energy and spirit of boys is harnessed to support the traditional family model and the economic system that it serves. But, as Stevenson asks, "our boyhood ceased—well, when? not, I think, at twenty; nor, perhaps, altogether at twenty-five; nor yet at thirty; and possibly, to be quite frank, we are still in the thick of that arcadian period" (Stevenson 1881: 15). "How are you," Stevenson asks of the bachelor, "the apostle of laxity, to turn suddenly about into the rabbi of precision; and after these years of ragged practice, pose for a hero . . .?" (21). While a girl loses rights to freedom and daring, a boy is forcefully encouraged to channel his liberties into the economic system such that he ultimately contributes not only to his own prosperity but also to that of the capitalist hegemony. It is young men, therefore, who most obviously suffer from the conflict between these age-associated masculinities.

James Eli Adams (1995) has demonstrated the growth during the Victorian era of a masculine ideal that supported bourgeois values by combining the gentlemanly restraint generally associated with the upper class with a business-minded mental rigor located, it was suggested, among white-collar workers. Many people who remembered with nostalgia a child-hood of boyish adventure, however, would have found the persona of the gentlemanly professional too constrictive. This led the image of the boy to personify, as Martha Vicinus puts it, "a fleeting moment of liberty and of dangerously attractive innocence, making possible fantasies of total contingency and total annihilation. For men, the boy suggested freedom without committing them to action" (Vicinus 1999: 83). Not surprisingly, at the same time that the image of the reserved white-collar male became more common, so too did boys' adventure literature, as compensation or even counteraction. But, as Vicinus's wording implies, the literature was more a form of escapism than a source of identification.

The main masculine persona available to the late-Victorian bourgeois male remained that of the controlled, productive capitalist. But when, during the latter half of the century, the ethos of the economy shifted its focus from production to consumption and the seemingly passive role of the consumer, this source of gender identification found itself with new difficulties. Max Nordau was stating a familiar view when he argued that the notion of productivity for the good of society is the essential, biolog-ical stimulus within all healthy organisms. For him, the rise of commod-ity culture was "a stigma of degeneration," an illness, a "buying craze," and he goes on to chastise all those people who participate in "the present rage for collecting, the piling up, in dwellings, of aimless bric-à-brac" (Nordau 1892: 27). Individuals who focus on consumption, he concludes, are too interested in themselves, and this narcissism operates at the expense of the health, prosperity, and (re)production of society in general.

Nordau's main target in his critique of consumerism and deviant pas-sivity is male artists like Oscar Wilde and Charles Baudelaire. Regenia Gag-nier has, conversely, put a rebellious spin on the self-interest and public display of such men, arguing that they used their dandiacal performances to react against "a bourgeois ethos of productivity and domestic reproduc-tion, rejecting masculine virility itself" (Gagnier 1999: 129).[3] The dandy image discussed by Nordau and Gagnier is indeed heavily entwined with that of the aesthetes of the Aesthetic Movement, but (as Nordau feared) it also attracted other members of the middle class who did not subscribe wholeheartedly to the masculine image of the restrained gentlemanly professional. It is this more general persona that takes central stage in Steven-son's stories. While the author's work does reflect values that were popu-larized through the Aesthetic Movement, his characters do not follow the likes of Wilde in boldly challenging "masculine virility." They may act unconventionally, but their primary reason is never simply to "épater les bourgeois." They never discuss issues of aesthetics and for the most part avoid epigrammatic wit and discussions of style and décor. The men-about-town in *New Arabian Nights* are less invested in aesthetics or sexual politics, and more interested in locating some fresh source of excitement in a society bent on eliminating the possibilities of unforeseen stimuli. Stevenson is not portraying a specific persona such as the dandy-aesthete but, more broadly, youthful adventurousness chafing within the ill-fitting garb of the gentlemanly professional.

Masculine Misfits and Cheap Tarts

In Stevenson's adventure novels, the conflict of masculinities within adults is often delineated through an age-based contrast. The narratives of *Kidnapped* and *Treasure Island*, for example, each depict a boy attaining an education in manly qualities from a person who is himself cast away from the dominant system. While the boys come across as rather stalwart and responsible, the cultural castaways are mature in years but youthful in spirit. This discordant pederastic model where a youth learns from an elder who is not conventionally virtuous and wise can be read as a threat to the dominant reproductive ideology. However, from a perspective more in line with Stevenson's oeuvre, the homosocial culture and devotions offer a sympathetic portrayal of males in search of others who refuse to sacrifice their masculinity to the traditional family narrative and the capitalist economic model that it helps sustain.[4]

Katherine Linehan has noted that Stevenson's "attraction to carefree male fellowship contends through his adult life against a principled concern to promote male maturity of vision about the social and psychological realities of relations between the sexes" (Linehan 1997: 35). Focusing on the author's representations of heteronormative institutions, Linehan locates a conflict in Stevenson's work between, on one hand, premarital communities that reinforce "youthful extremes of egoism" and "male temptations . . . towards self-centered immaturity" and, on the other, conventional cross-sexual relations leading to the institution of marriage, which embody a more mature attitude toward social responsibility and gender equality (35–36). Peter Stearns offers some historical grounding within which we can situate Linehan's image of heterosexual love. He notes that, in the nineteenth century, "economics declined as a criterion for male selection, to be sure, and men and women both had greater freedom of choice. But that they married for love is uncertain. Sexual attraction, yes; desire for a companion-partner, without question. But love as basis or result of marriage was probably as accidental as it had been in preindustrial society" (Stearns 1990: 92). In accord with Stearns's insights, Stevenson does not claim that the realization of heterosexual monogamy is the singular ideal toward which all individuals should aspire. Instead, in "Virginibus Puerisque," it is idealization itself that he questions, pointing out the inevitable conflicts of any relationship due to the flaws of all individuals: "Faith is built upon a knowledge of our life, of the tyranny of circumstance and the frailty of human resolution. . . . you yourself are compacted of infirmities, perfect, you might say, in imperfection" (Stevenson 1881: 24–25).

The concept of individuality is also central to Stevenson's notion of love. When he declares that "love is so startlingly real," he does so while associating it with a "consciousness of *personal* existence" (1878: 96; emphasis added). He goes on to note that "Whitman's ideal man must not only be strong, free, and self-reliant in himself, but his freedom must be bounded and his strength perfected by the most intimate, eager, and long-suffering love for others" (96). The language obviously echoes Whitman's notion of fraternity, but it also brings to mind the centrality of empathy to the model of aestheticism that Walter Pater had advocated in *The Renaissance* (1872), which was published only a few years prior to Stevenson's essay. As in Pater's aesthetics, Stevenson's description of love makes sure that individuality remains a key element of mutual admiration and affection. Stevenson does not propose that cross-sexual monogamy is superior to or more mature than other forms of love: this can be seen not only by the context of Whitman but also by the reference to the "love of others" rather than one other, and by his articulation of a high regard for freedom and self-reliance. Of equal importance, Stevenson questions the notion that, with age, one experiences superior models of devotion or respect. Damage is not caused by the pleasures of youth and independence, he implies, but results from the constriction and denial of feelings through the stifling veneration of such images as the gentlemanly businessman.

In various works, Stevenson derogates the capitalist tinge that had permeated the image of the gentleman. Most obviously, the pirates of *Treasure Island* repeatedly refer to themselves euphemistically as "gentlemen of fortune" (1883: 62). The appropriately named Long John *Silver* himself distinguishes between being a gentleman of fortune and retiring as a "gentleman in earnest" (62), suggesting the sham quality Stevenson recognized in the money-based model. The weakness in such constructions of gentlemanliness is apparent in Silver's tendency to use the term to fit his situation. Trying to "make terms" with Captain Smollett after leading a mutiny against him, Silver claims to discern that the captain is a gentleman and thus true to his word (112). Elsewhere, however, he threatens to *force* young Jim Hawkins to become a gentleman (assumedly "of fortune") (162). Later, needing Jim's cooperation, he tells the boy that, since the pirate's previous threat, the boy has somehow managed to become a young gentleman on his own (177). Meanwhile Benjamin Gunn, having turned more savage and more noble during his three years marooned on the island, prides himself on being able to differentiate a gentleman of fortune from a "gen'leman born" (90). The discourse of the pirates of *Treasure Island* embodies the duplicity accommodated by the modern persona of the middle-class gentleman. Here and elsewhere in his works, Stevenson exposes the performance of restraint, altruism, and perseverance as often a charade that obscures insincerity and greed. At the same time, we are encouraged to admire, at least to some degree, characters such as Alan Breck in *Kidnapped* precisely for their boyish daring and idealism.

By combining images of excess with contemporary, urban characters, *New Arabian Nights* offers unique insights into Stevenson's attitude toward his society's culture of masculinity. The collection consists of three connected stories collectively titled "The Suicide Club" and three more titled "The Rajah's Diamond." In many of the pieces, the author depicts young, pleasant men who find themselves overwhelmed by the weight of an adventurous challenge to their identities. In the "Story of the Physician and the Saratoga Trunk," for example, the wealthy but conservative man-about-town Silas Q. Scuddamore is described as suffering from curiosity. Stevenson first presents Silas's curiosity as an absurd "foible" (1882: 45) and then seems to accept the daring with which the character himself endows it. The hero's decision to attend a dance is described with the following hyperbole: "Curiosity and timidity fought a long battle in his heart; sometimes he was all virtue, sometimes all fire and daring; and the result of it was that, long before ten, Mr. Silas Q. Scuddamore presented himself in unimpeachable attire at the door of the Bullier Ball Rooms, and paid his entry money with a sense of reckless deviltry that was not without its charm" (47). "The lights and the crowd at first rather abashed our young adventurer," we are told, "and then, mounting to his brain with a sort of intoxication, put him in possession of more than his own share of manhood. He felt ready to face the devil, and strutted in the ballroom with the swagger of a cavalier" (47–48).[5] Although the adventure is far from daring,

Silas's swollen manhood draws him to overconfidence and miscalculations that ultimately lead to him finding his bed occupied by the corpse of a handsome young duelist. Earlier in the narrative, Silas had taken the advice of one of the murderer's accomplices and lied to the hotel porter, saying that just such a man would be arriving to his room to collect a debt; thus the wealthy youth has framed himself as a financially pressured murderer. The remainder of the story involves his fumbling efforts to unburden himself of the duelist's body and its romantic symbolism of daring and adventure.

In "Story of the Bandbox," the incompetent "gentleman" Harry Hartley is similarly described as "unfitted alike by nature and training" and "not the man to lead armaments of war, or direct the councils of a State" (109). The incompetent fellow is soon fooled into delivering a box of stolen jewelry. After a series of comic mishaps down suburban alleys, whatever jewels Harry has kept from spilling along the way are stolen from him. The story ends with the original owner of the goods hauling our hero to the police station. Notably, the jewels belong to a Major-General and the most precious stone—the Rajah's Diamond—had been given to him as a gift for some secret service fulfilled. The central gem is thus rooted in mysterious glories of imperialist exploits. Like Silas's misadventures with the dead duelist, Harry's incompetence in managing the bandbox of jewels symbolizes the inability of the modern youth to take on such adventures. Having been raised without the skills or strengths required to deal with the unexpected, these urban young men are easy dupes to the unethical, and they fumble the goods as soon as events move away from the conventional narrative of middle-class life. In both stories, Stevenson ends with a tongue-in-cheek comment to the reader, whom he seems to see as an armchair adventurer—a conservative who may have some yearning for the unknown and unexpected—but who ultimately chooses the familiar. Silas, we are assured in the final paragraph, eventually met with a comfortable career in which he mounts "the ladder of political fame," having already attained the position of "Sheriff of his native town" in New England (78). Meanwhile, the police ultimately compliment Harry on "the probity and simplicity of his behaviour" and let him go. His misfortune leads a maiden aunt to leave him enough money in her will to marry and move away "exceedingly content, and with the best of prospects" (141). Having proven themselves lacking in the qualities that would allow them to function outside conventional bourgeois culture, both men are rewarded for resigning themselves to comfortable, unexciting lives as cogs in the economic machinery.

It is in "The Adventure of the Hansom Cab," the second story in the "Suicide Club" trilogy, that such comic characterization takes on its most despondent air. In this piece, a mysterious man has hired cab drivers to pick up any well-dressed single men they can find and deliver them to a party. Preference is given to those with a military air. The drivers come upon dozens of these past heroes wandering the streets of the London night in search of "the shadow of an adventure" in "this . . . the great battlefield of mankind" (80), as one such man describes it. Dismissing the guests whom he feels display insufficient gentlemanliness or bravery, the host asks the final four "to render me a dangerous and delicate service; dangerous because you may run the hazard of your lives" (90). Two of the men are too scared, but the remaining pair goes through with the adventure and succeed without injury. The text for its part, however, inflicts a critical wound on Victorian society in general through its depiction of all these gentlemen whose past careers involved bravery and risk but who now find themselves wandering the lonely streets of London, unfulfilled by lives of redundant conformity and yet frightened to return to the sphere of uncertainty by which they had defined their masculinity.

Educated and adequately moneyed, the innumerable men that frequent the gaming parties and other urbane bachelor gatherings in the stories of *New Arabian Nights* seem to lack the final impetus for realizing their desire for adventure. Even the young men who do search for daring stimuli by joining suicide clubs or engaging in trysts with mysterious women act half-heartedly. The fatalism underlying these comic works is most fully realized in "The Story of the Young Man with the Cream Tarts." The piece is riddled with young men who are part of the urban middle-to-upper classes on whom capitalism relied. The bachelors often have enough money to support themselves comfortably, but their wealth is not growing. Indeed, while all the members of the Suicide Club appear secure as far as money goes, not only the most popular but also the most readily accepted excuse for joining is perceived financial difficulty. Ironically, one must pay forty pounds to become a member. "Accursed life," declares one character, "where a man cannot even die without money!" (11). The extreme of such despair is especially notable because virtually all of the members of the club are quite young. As the narrator comments, most are "in the prime of youth. . . . Few were much above thirty, and not a few were still in their teens" (23). "Poetical boys" (36), the president of the club calls these men who now suffer a crisis of masculinity after having been squeezed into an off-the-rack bourgeois identity.

The Suicide Club was founded precisely to offer an alternative to young urban males who could not bare a life of bourgeois conformity. "A large number of our fellow-men," explains the man with the cream tarts, "have grown heartily sick of the performance in which they are expected to join daily and all their lives long" (14). The very industriousness of the era exacerbates the men's own sense of passivity and worthlessness. As the eponymous character explains, railroads eliminated the challenges of travel by giving individuals access to distant locations. To accommodate the resultant separation between friends, the telegraph was invented. Even vertical travel has been gutted of exertion, thanks to the invention of the elevator. "There was one more convenience lacking to modern comfort," opines the speaker, "the back stairs to liberty; . . . Death's private door" (14). The economic demand for responsible masculinity fosters an industrial streamlining of lives that devalues creative energy and individuality. Innovation, these stories propose, results in a cultural cohesion that gradually eliminates the need for innovation and, with it, the masculine qualities that the hegemony initially encouraged.

Prince Florizel of Bohemia, the main upper-class male of "The Story of the Young Man with the Cream Tarts," offers an especially astute demonstration of the mismanaged authority of a dominant form of masculinity. The prince finds it easy to perform a range of identities, adapting "not only his face and bearing, but his voice and almost his thoughts, to those of any rank, character, or nation" (4). Stevenson emphasizes the dangerous ambiguity of the character's identity by making him literally a citizen of Bohemia, bringing to mind the bohemianism that many Victorians found unsettling. Fulfilling the roles of both a bohemian and a gentleman, the prince's adeptness at self-fashioning undermines efforts to essentialize the middle-class masculine identity as the primary model from which other forms of manliness are subordinate deviations. In one scene, upon learning the danger of being a member of the Suicide Club—that is, accepting the risk of becoming a murderer or a murder victim—the prince's level-headed sidekick whispers "One bold stroke . . . and we may still escape" (31). But this, the only hint of adventurous daring in the entire story, is immediately curtailed by the prince's declaration that they must remain gentlemen and follow through on their gamble. Prince Florizel thus sees no problem in using the code of gentlemanliness to justify his sacrifice of ethical values and a respect for life. "Alas!" he cries, "to be bound by an oath in such a matter! to allow this wholesale trade in murder to be continued with profit and impunity!" (33). The prince's crisis of conscience

has here taken on a distinctly capitalist air, with the conflict being between, on one hand, ideals of humanity and, on the other, a commercial
system of trade and profit to which the prince had given his pledge before
being fully informed of the repercussions. However, when he himself draws
the card marking him as the next victim, he conveniently uses the rhetoric of gentlemanliness to circumvent his murder. He concludes that the
president of the club has forfeited the contract by organizing a business
that profits from the deaths of males pining for adventure. Under threat
of being murdered, the prince now allows an ethical conclusion to override the authority of the industry in death to which the prince had pledged
himself. The rhetorical shift allows him to retain his status as gentleman
even though he breaks his pledge.

For bourgeois youths such as the man with the cream tarts, who do not
have the same class- and wealth-based privileges, such masculine drag is
an unaffordable pleasure. Indeed, at the beginning of the story, we find the
man with the cream tarts struggling to maintain even one image of himself. He is described as laughing "louder than was natural in a person of
polite breeding." "His hands trembled violently," we are told, "and his
voice took sudden surprising inflections, which seemed to be independent
of his will" (8). The anxieties signified by these awkward gestures arise from
the man's sense of his identity as lacking in substance. He may describe
himself as "a person full of manly accomplishments," but when the only
example he offers is "a duel about nothing" (9), the claim rings hollow.
The combat may suggest bravery, but there is nothing for the man to
defend and, because his accomplishments are in fact empty gestures, the
character continues to hunger for greater proofs of his virility.

Stevenson's resolution to the story is pessimistic and carries the same
tinge of sarcasm found in the "Story of the Physician and the Saratoga
Trunk" and the "Story of the Bandbox." The wealthy prince alleviates
the despondency of all the other members of the Suicide Club simply by
offering them employment and remuneration. We are also lead to assume
that they are all suddenly satisfied by this financial liquidity, having no
aspiration for productivity. In the closing paragraph, the narrator informs
us that the young man with the cream tarts takes the opportunity to
become "a comfortable householder in Wigmore Street, Cavendish Square"
(43). So consumer culture has overridden productive energy as the driving force behind not only mass-market capitalism but also the characters' lives. We are left with the eponymous hero stupidly gorging himself
on pastry in a sickening effort to demarcate some sense of individuality.

He is nothing less than Stevenson's symbolic derogation of the ideal consumer, a man spending his time filling himself with cream tarts while remaining unfulfilled. In a sense, the character and the other middle-class males of his society are themselves cream tarts, a tray of identical, unsatisfying men who take the space of individuals but contribute nothing of originality to their society. They have become fodder for consumer culture itself, subordinated to the commodities they consume. Or to paraphrase Walter Benjamin (1936), they are the embodiment of the individual in the age of mechanical reproduction. In the twentieth century, Benjamin would welcome the democratization of aesthetics that technological reproduction allowed. In *New Arabian Nights*, Stevenson argues against the rise of commodity culture as much as he critiques the productivist ethos that it replaced. Bourgeois capitalism, Stevenson proposes, does not only homogenize taste but individuals as well.

NOTES

1. For discussions of Victorian attacks on adventure literature as dangerous to society and the economic order, see Dunae 1979 and Haining 1975. Contemporary critiques can be found in Greenwood 1869 and Oliphant 1858.

2. In light of Stevenson's essay, R. H. W. Dillard's speculation that females were as attracted by *Treasure Island* as boys is appropriate. "Girl readers, most likely, have all along been as pleased by the absence of stereotypically weak and timid females as boys," writes Dillard, "Girls' active imaginations find Jim Hawkins a much more congenial companion and role model than the kinds of girls who too often appeared in both boys' and girls' books of the late nineteenth century" (Dillard 1998: ix).

3. For further discussion of the rise of consumerism in relation to British literature and art, see Dowling 1995, Freedman 1990, and Gagnier 2000.

4. I use the term "pederastic" in its classical sense as referring to the pedagogical relationship between an older and younger man, where the former attains inspiration from the health, vitality, and beauty of the latter while offering him instruction and elucidation. The appropriateness of the model is reinforced by the corollary to the pederastic ideal in popular models of friendship for Victorian boys. Vicinus (1999) notes that boys' literature and culture harmonized with this model by including "narratives of physical hardship, spiritualized love, and idealistic self-sacrifice" among men. Male-male idolization and devotion found reinforcement from various sources, including the rhetoric of imperialism, apprenticeship models for artistic and craft-based careers, and classical literature. A summary of such influences can be found in Richards 1987. Important readings of Stevenson's writings—especially *Treasure Island*, *Kidnapped*, and *Strange Case of Dr. Jekyll and Mr. Hyde*—in relation to homosexuality and homosociality can be found in Fiedler 1960, Koestenbaum 1991, Sedgwick 1990, and Williams 1996.

5. The elegant expression combined with winking complicity with the reader here is an example of the decidedly camp nature of the whole text (see Dury 2003).

REFERENCES

Adams, James Eli. 1995. *Dandies and Desert Saints: Styles of Victorian Masculinity.* Ithaca, NY: Cornell University Press.

Benjamin, Walter. 1936. Das Kunstwerk im Zeitalter seiner technischen Reproduzierbarkeit. 1968. The Work of Art in the Age of Mechanical Reproduction. In Walter Benjamin (ed. Hannah Arendt). *Illuminations.* New York: Shocken.

Dellamora, Richard, ed. 1999. *Victorian Sexual Dissidence.* Chicago: University of Chicago Press.

Dillard, R. H. W. 1998. Introduction. In Stevenson 1883: vii–xv.

Dowling, Linda. 1995. *The Vulgarization of Art: The Victorians and Aesthetic Democracy.* Charlottesville: University of Virginia Press.

Dunae, Patrick. 1979. Penny Dreadfuls: Late Nineteenth-Century Boys' Literature and Crime. *Victorian Studies* 22: 133–50.

Dury, Richard. 2003. Le caractère camp des Nouvelles Mille et Une Nuits. In *R. L. Stevenson & A. Conan Doyle. Aventures de la Fiction.* Ed. Gilles Menegaldo and Jean-Pierre Naugrette. Rennes: Terre de Brume. 119–40.

Fiedler, Leslie. 1960. Introduction. *No! In Thunder.* 1972. New York: Stein and Day.

Freedman, Jonathan. 1990. *Professions of Taste: Henry James, British Aestheticism, and Commodity Culture.* Stanford, CA: Stanford University Press.

Gagnier, Regenia. 1999. Production, Reproduction, and Pleasure in Victorian Aesthetics and Economics. In Dellamora 1999. 127–45.

———. 2000. *The Insatiability of Human Wants: Economics and Aesthetics in Market Society.* Chicago: University of Chicago Press.

Green, Martin. 1980. *Dreams of Adventure, Deeds of Empire.* London: Martin Secker.

Greenwood, James. 1869. *Seven Curses of London.* Boston: Fields, Osgood.

Haining, Peter. 1975. Introduction. *The Penny Dreadful.* London: Victor Gollancz.

Halberstam, Judith. 1998. *Female Masculinity.* Durham, NC: Duke University Press.

Koestenbaum, Wayne. 1991. *Double Talk: The Erotics of Male Literary Collaboration.* New York: Routledge.

Linehan, Katherine. 1997. Revaluing Women and Marriage in Robert Louis Stevenson's Short Fiction. *English Literature in Transition* 40 (7): 34–59.

Nordau, Max. 1892. *Entartung.* English Translation 1895. *Degeneration.* Repr., Lincoln: University of Nebraska Press, 1993.

Oliphant, Margaret. 1858. The Byways of Literature: Reading for the Million. *Blackwood's Edinburgh Magazine* 84 (Aug. 1858): 200–16.

Richards, Jeffrey. 1987. "Passing the Love of Women": Manly Love and Victorian Society. In *Manliness and Morality: Middle-class Masculinity in Britain and America, 1800–1940.* Ed. J. A. Mangan and James Walvin. New York: St. Martin's Press. 102–5.

Saposnik, Irving S. 1974. *Robert Louis Stevenson.* New York: Twayne.

Sedgwick, Eve. 1990. *The Epistemology of the Closet.* Berkeley: University of California Press.

Stearns, Peter N. 1990. *Be a Man! Males in Modern Society.* New York: Holmes and Meier.

Stevenson, Robert Louis. 1878. "The Gospel According to Walt Whitman." In *Familiar Studies of Men and Books.* 1912. New York: Charles Scribner's Sons. 81–110.

———. 1881. "Virginibus Puerisque." In *Virginibus Puerisque and Other Papers*. 1925. London: Macmillan. 1–47.

———. 1882. *New Arabian Nights*. 1913. New York: Current Literature.

———. 1883. *Treasure Island*. Ed. R. H. W. Dillard. 1998. New York: Penguin.

———. 1886. *Kidnapped*. 1994. London: Penguin.

Sussman, Herbert. 1995. *Victorian Masculinities: Manhood and Masculine Poetics in Early Victorian Literature and Art*. Cambridge: Cambridge University Press.

Vicinus, Martha. 1999. The Adolescent Boy: Fin-de-Siècle Femme Fatale? In Dellamora 1999. 83–106.

Williams, M. Kellen. 1996. "Down With the Door, Poole": Designating Deviance in Stevenson's *Strange Case of Dr. Jekyll and Mr. Hyde*. *English Literature in Transition*. 39 (4): 412–29.

"Markheim" and the Shadow of the Other

MICHELA VANON ALLIATA

At the core of "Markheim" (1885), a short, but highly concentrated story, is a ruthless and apparently gratuitous crime and its aftermath leading to the murderer's final confession. Through a web of intertextual references ranging from Dostoevsky, Shakespeare, and Poe, Stevenson explores both the psychology of crime and the ethics of guilt. Skillfully constructed and related with extraordinary dramatic power, this tale that investigates the idea that human freedom is exhibited in an extreme act, a murder, also articulates typical late-Victorian anxieties concerning degeneration, criminality, and post-Darwinian fascination with regression.

The almost satanic quality permeating "Markheim"—when Stevenson finished it, he said that "to be clear of 'Markheim' is like a ton's weight off my neck" (*Ltrs* 5: 44)—testifies to Stevenson's unceasing concern with moral ambiguity and with the strands of violence and irrationality in the human psyche.

In its suspense and swiftness of development, "Markheim" resembles the genre of the modern thriller. However, its emphasis on the conflicts in the human will, on the dialectics of pride, and on the problem of evil makes the tale closer to a moral fable. Frightening forces are internalized and thus become part of the inscrutable workings of the human mind. Confronted with the dark forces of his nature, the title character of the story meets a tragic destiny he is powerless to evade.

The form adopted seems close to that of Poe's "The Black Cat," "The Tell-Tale Heart," and "The Imp of the Perverse": that hybrid of essay and tale, which foregrounds the "innate and primitive principle of human action" (Poe 1984: 827). In Poe's stories one also finds the crime without a clear motive, the *act gratuit*. The calm murder and the compulsive confession in "The Imp of the Perverse" is seen by Stevenson, in a perceptive essay, as "an important contribution to morbid psychology" (Stevenson 1875: 112). (Poe's dark protagonist is also found in Dostoevsky's *Crime and Punishment*, Gide's *Les caves du vatican*, and Camus's *L'étranger*.) In "Markheim" the impulse to kill is a supreme act of hubris and is followed, as in "The Tell-Tale Heart," by the need for release, by an equally irresistible impulse to confess.[1]

In Stevenson, however, the emphasis lies more in the dynamics of self-incrimination and on the protagonist's tortured consciousness than on the motive of perversity. His Presbyterian heritage with its idea of predestination and sense of sharply overdefined opposition between good and evil led him to graft the analysis of the psychology of the killer onto one of his most abiding preoccupations, that of duality. Herdman suggests (1990: 16) that although the ultimate reasons for the "heightened Scottish awareness of duality" of both Hogg and Stevenson "may lie deep in the national psyche and history, a proximate causation in the schematic polarities of Calvinist theology can scarcely be put in doubt." A further and crucial question arising from his Calvinist background is the possibility of repentance, an idea central to the Christian conception of the working redemption.

This exploration of divided consciousness is further developed in *Dr. Jekyll and Mr. Hyde*. In this later work the personified conscience of "Markheim" becomes an independent character, whose uncontrollable violence and apelike fury correspond to Lombroso's characterization of the typical criminal personality (Mighall 1999: 148).

Like *Dr. Jekyll and Mr. Hyde*, "Markheim" testifies to Stevenson's abiding responsiveness to the language of dreams, long before Freud's epoch-making theory of dreams and the unconscious, that place where the desires that can't be fulfilled are repressed. Fanny reported that her husband was "deeply impressed by a paper he read in a French scientific journal on sub-consciousness."[2] This article, "combined with the memories of Deacon Brodie" who was publicly a respectable person but privately a thief and rakehell, "gave the germ of the idea that afterwards developed into the play, was used again in the story of "Markheim," and finally, in a hectic fever following a hemorrhage of the lungs, culminated in the dream of Jekyll and Hyde" (F. Stevenson 1905: 338).

The tale begins *in medias res*, close to the climax of the action. The reader hears a conversation, one that began before his arrival on the scene, between Markheim and his interlocutor.

> "Yes," said the dealer, "our windfalls are of various kinds. Some customers are ignorant, and then I touch a dividend on my superior knowledge. Some are dishonest," and here he held up the candle, so that the light fell strongly on his visitor, "and in that case," he continued, "I profit by my virtue."
>
> Markheim had but just entered from the daylight streets, and his eyes had not yet grown familiar with the mingled shine and darkness in the shop. At these pointed words . . . he blinked painfully and looked aside.
>
> The dealer chuckled. "You come to me on Christmas Day," he resumed, "when you know that I am alone in my house, put up my shutters, and make a point of refusing business. Well, you will have to pay for that; you will have to pay for my loss of time, when I should be balancing my books. (Stevenson 1885: 129)

It is Christmas Eve and Markheim, "the nephew and sole heir of a remark-able collector" has entered an antique dealer's shop. Although he is not very young, he embodies numerous psychological traits associated with youth such as impulsiveness, courage, eagerness to live, and a certain melancholic rudeness. While the action itself remains comparatively simple, centered on the two characters and revolving around a limited series of events, the dramatic appeal of the story derives from a sophisticated viewpoint. "Mark-heim" is a symbolic narrative where the action is seen through the eyes of a reflector figure. The point of view is of crucial importance to the total effect. Stevenson aimed at capturing the consciousness of his internal focalizer, a killer. What indeed makes the tale compelling is precisely the fact that the reader sees the victim through the killer's eyes and is made, in a way, an accomplice in his crime. The reader, like the protagonist, is engaged in an act of interpretation that involves the evaluation of his motives. He is being prepared to consider him, if not a "Justified Sinner," at least an "unwilling sinner" (148), an allusion to St. Paul (Romans 7:19).

The opening paragraph plunges the reader into the mind of a man about to commit murder, into the dynamics that propel him to crime. Indeed, the whole structure of the tale is based on the consciousness of its protagonist. Through the brief opening dialogue, the reader is given an accurate portrayal of the dealer and is immediately introduced to the des-olation of a life marked by the sole logic of profit and money. Meanness appears as his most prominent trait. The "little pale, round-shouldered" dealer engrossed in "balancing [his] books" even on Christmas Eve, is an avaricious misanthrope impervious to any sentimental promptings. Consistently, his language is pragmatic and businesslike. Words such as "profit," "dividend," "pay," and "business" recur insistently in this dialogue to emphasize his calculating aridity, driving the reader into the awareness of the fact that "the little man" is primarily an embittered and selfish man.

The effect of the initial passage centered on the unnamed dealer—and how significant it is that one never knows him by his name, only by his occupation—powerfully, though obliquely, highlights something shady about Markheim too. The pawnbroker's question—"You can give, as usual, a clear account of how you came into the possession of the object?" (130)—reveals that the two men know each other well and that they are used to doing business together. But it is the sentence "when a customer cannot look me in the eye, he has to pay for it" (130) that alerts the reader that this time Markheim has not come on business, but with an evil intent.

In "the mingled shine and darkness" of the shop, Markheim's attitude toward the rapacious and colorless man, oscillates between feelings of "infinite pity" and "horror" (130). The utilitarian, unimaginative dealer drives him almost insane. As in Poe's "The Cask of Amontillado," the fated victim appears to his killer as both a tempter and a torturer. Hounded by the dealer and pressed by time, a powerful structural element of the story, he makes clear that this time he has not come to sell but to buy a present for his lady. Before reaching the climax of the tale, it is worth considering this passage that adds relevant information on Markheim. His statement that his uncle's cabinet is "bare to the wainscot" may suggest that he is a thief and that, not unlike the dealer, he is avaricious himself if he thinks that "a rich marriage is not a thing to be neglected" (130). What precipitates the action and Markheim's murderous rage in a crescendo of tension, highlighted by the dealer's "dry and biting voice" and by "the ticking of many clocks" obsessively marking the passing of time, is a mirror, "the fifteenth-century hand-glass" he is offered: "'A glass? For Christmas? Surely not?' 'And why not?' cried the dealer . . . Markheim was looking upon him with an indefinable expression. 'You ask me why not?' he said. 'Why, look here—look in it—look at yourself! Do you like to see it? No! nor I—nor any man'" (132).

The dealer's harshness and lack of understanding of Markheim's rejection of the glass—he attributes it to mere vanity ("Your future lady, sir, must be pretty hard favored")—further exasperates Markheim. The anxiety and horror conveyed by the mirror as a merciless and implacable reminder of "years, and sins and follies—this hand-conscience!" (132), derives from the fact that it is the symbol *par excellence* of the double—an instrument for self-revelation, as it is in Shakespeare, a device of deceit but also a tool for truth.[3] Here it becomes an extension of Markheim's haunted soul, making him painfully aware of his past, his mistakes, and finally of his mortality. The following comment by Markheim identifies the dealer as a selfish, unloving man, someone who, like Dickens's Scrooge, the archetypal miser, has never lived, has never loved, but has devoted all his life to the pursuit of money: "Not charitable? . . . not pious; unloving, unbeloved; a hand to get money, a safe to keep it. Is that all? Dear God, is that all?" (132).

"A Christmas Carol" is an important intertext for "Markheim," which is a Christmas story too, in that it was written for the Christmas anthology *The Broken Shaft* with a shipboard frame situation that is a variant of the Victorian tradition of people gathering around the fire on Christmas Eve to tell and listen to ghost and mystery stories (Waters 1997: 72–73). Stevenson even seems to be parodying Dickens when Markeim, playing for time and half-genuinely but half-tauntingly trying to be friendly with the dealer, says "Let us be confidential. Who knows, we might become friends?" This seems quite close to the genuine appeal to Scrooge by his nephew at the beginning of "A Christmas Carol": "I want nothing from you; I ask nothing of you; why cannot we be friends?" (Dickens 1843: 56). In Stevenson's more pessimistic vision, however, there is no redemption. The dealer, to Markheim's despair, repeatedly shows his disdain for sentiments, like Scrooge, by labeling them "nonsense": "'Ah, have you been in love? Tell me about that.' 'I,!' cried the dealer. 'I in love! I never had the time, nor have I the time to-day for all this nonsense. Will you take the glass?'" (Stevenson 1885: 132–33).

The dealer's unmarried status is also important, as it was for Scrooge, for it further establishes the notion that he is a hard-hearted man who has excluded from his life any sentimental values: they would inhibit his main purpose, which is to make and keep money.[4] The pawnbroker represents an attitude to life that was anathema to Stevenson: the shunning of all opportunities for adventure and romance in favor of dull security and stability. Markheim's anguished plea of *carpe diem* falls on deaf ears: "life is so short and insecure that I would not hurry away from any pleasure—no, not even from so mild a one as this. We should rather cling, cling to what little we can get, like a man at a cliff's edge" (133). When the dealer at these words invites him either to make his purchase, or walk out of his shop,

Markheim pretends to agree but soon after he savagely plunges a dagger into his back. In its economy, swiftness, and unity of tone, the narrative moves to its well-managed climax revealing Stevenson a master of the compact short story.

> The dealer stooped once more . . . his thin blond hair falling over his eyes as he did so. [He] drew himself up and filled his lungs . . . many different emotions were depicted together on his face—terror, horror, and resolve, fascination, and a physical repulsion; and through a haggard lift of his upper lip, his teeth looked out.
>
> Markheim bounded from behind upon his victim. The long, skewer-like dagger flashed and fell. The dealer struggled like a hen, striking his temple on the shelf, and then tumbled on the floor in a heap" (133–34).

From this moment on, the register of the tale changes radically. From the initial realistic, everyday-like atmosphere, the movement of the narrative, becomes fantastic. Action is internalized, while the elements of realism are reduced to a functional minimum so as to highlight its symbolic tone. Structurally the short story appears divided into two parts. The first, which appears a study in terror after the manner of Poe, revolves around the preannounced murder, and a steady accumulation of detail increases the suspense to a notable intensity. The second, instead, rich in psychological undertones, is pervaded by an hallucinatory quality. It has been argued that this structural division mirrors Markheim's ambivalence in that he sums up the characteristics of both the man of action and of the man of thought (De Propris 1992: 11). With the internalization of the setting in Markheim's own mind, the tale becomes an investigation of psychological duality. After the murder, instead of hurrying to rob the dealer of his money and run away, Markheim seems to have lost any stimulus to act. His infirmity of purpose is similar to Macbeth's after his murder of Duncan.

What the reader sees are the terrors of the haunted murderer who awaits his own doom in a state of pulsating suspense and for whom the surroundings are transformed into an objectification of his own guilt-ridden conscience. Alone in the shop "full of shadows" and mirrors in which he sees "his face repeated and repeated, as if it were an army of spies" (Stevenson 1885: 135), he begins to realize what he has done. His eyes, like a camera, rest on "the pool of blood" where the victim's body lies "humped and sprawling, incredibly small and strangely meaner than in life" (134). This sight startles him into an awareness of "the thousand faults of his design."

Again, as in *Macbeth*, the tale is a statement of evil and a portrayal of a battle fought entirely in the soul of its protagonist: "Ay, dead or not, this was still the enemy. 'Time was that when the brains were out,' he thought; . . . Time, now that the deed was accomplished—time, which had closed for the victim, had become instant and momentous for the slayer" (135).

Stevenson's quotation of Macbeth's words after he has seen the ghost of Banquo (*Macbeth* 3.4.77–78), signals that Markheim, like Macbeth, is obsessed by the incessant flow of time. The ticking of the clocks are ominous to him since what has been done cannot be revoked. Stevenson's perception of the killer's fear is relentless. In its sympathetic viewpoint, the narrative tone has the power of entering into the obscurities and vertiginous horrors of the murderer's psyche. Through the use of metaphors that testify to Stevenson's abiding predilection for the sea—"the room was filled with noiseless bustle and kept heaving like a sea" (Stevenson 1885: 134)—he follows Markheim's inexorable descent into a world inhabited by guilt: "brute terrors, like the scurrying of rats in a deserted attic, filled the more remote chambers of his brain with riot" (136).[5]

Though guilty, Markheim is certain that God understands and forgives him. "His act," he admits, "was doubtless exceptional, but so were his excuses, which God knew; it was there, and not among men, that he felt sure of justice" (143). As with Hogg's "Justified Sinner" and Dostoevsky's Raskolnikov, the resentful student who kills a greedy old pawnbroker for money, Markheim's hubris and impulse to gratify his drives make him attempt to justify his murder. Thus he says: "I was born and I have lived in a land of giants; giants have dragged me by the wrists since I was born out of my mother—the giants of circumstance" (147).

This belief that evil actions do not necessarily stain the character of the good man echoes an idea that runs through *Crime and Punishment*. Stevenson read the novel and enjoyed it so much that he called it "the greatest book I ever read easily in ten years . . . Many find it dull. Henry James could not finish it: all I can say, it nearly finished me. It was like having an illness" (*Ltrs* 5: 220–21). In his enthusiastic admiration, he wrote that Dostoevsky was "simply immense: it is not reading a book, it is having a brain fever, to read it" (*Ltrs* 5: 151). Raskolnikov, whose "uncircumscribed, protoplasmic humanity" filled him with "wonder" (*Ltrs* 5: 221), is a man of immense pride who, although he has only contempt for society, for the "herd," wants to acquire power over it for its own good. This leads to his plan of murder for money and to Dostoevsky's exploration of the Napoleonic theme, the theory that there are a few extraordinary men who stand

above the law—an idea that appears demeaned by the victim's own meanness as well as by the unheroic quality of the murderer's undertaking (Prina
1994: ix).

Dostoevsky's novel is a powerful influence behind" Markheim" for other
reasons as well. In both works the protagonist murders an old pawnbroker and believes he is justified and thus suffers no moral harm. Money is
also a central issue to both stories.

Tension reaches a climatic frenzy. Markheim's nerves "jerk[ed] like a
hooked fish" while his mind "trembled on the brink of lunacy" (Stevenson
1885: 136, 137). Stricken with fear, "he beheld, in galloping defile, the dock,
the prison, the gallows, and the black coffin" (136). As Stevenson wrote,
"the note of the picture" is "the deadly fear, strained hearkening and startling looking around of the murderer" (*Ltrs* 5: 36). Wandering through the
premises in search of the dealer's hidden wealth, Markheim, no longer
master of himself, fears for his own sanity. His feeling that he is not alone,
that he is being watched by unseen eyes, is communicated through a series
of powerful images: "One hallucination in particular took a strong hold
on his credulity. . . . But here, within the house, was he alone? He knew
he was; he had watched the servant set forth sweethearting, in her poor
best. . . . Yes, he was alone, of course; and yet, in the bulk of the empty
house about him, he could surely hear a stir of delicate footing—he was
surely conscious, inexplicably conscious of some presence . . . and now it
was a faceless thing, and yet had eyes to see with; and again it was a shadow
of himself" (Stevenson 1885: 137–38).

While the shadow is "still lingering and shivering," Markheim draws
near the body of his victim. The sight of his face "shockingly smeared with
blood about one temple" (139) fills him with nausea, carrying him back in
time to a day in his childhood when, "divided between interest and fear,"
he beheld in a fair booth reproductions of notorious murder scenes. This
analepsis, while producing an effect of dramatic intensification, contains
an oxymoron emblematic of Stevenson psychological insight: "The thing
was as clear as an illusion" (140).

Markheim's process of redemption is not achieved yet. At best he felt "a
gleam of pity for one who had been endowed in vain with all those faculties that can make the world a garden of enchantment. . . . But of peni-
tence, no, not a tremor" (141).

Time increasingly becomes an interior and psychological dimension in
a paranoid orchestration highlighted by the loud beating of the rain.
Behind this tale there is also the ethical insight of Hawthorne's major tales

and his guilt-ridden characters. Markheim reaches the upper drawing room of the house where the money might be hidden. In another reminder of Macbeth who has violated the natural order, Markheim fears "the laws of nature" (143). The confused state of the drawing room, full of "pier-glasses, in which he beheld himself at various angles, like an actor on a stage" (144)—seems a projection of his disordered soul.

He is still searching when a visitor enters the room. He appears while Markheim is thinking of "children afield, bathers by the brookside, ramblers on the brambly common, kite-flyers in the windy and cloud-navigated sky" (145), an image of open-air cheerfulness that contrasts with the claustrophobic atmosphere pervading the murder scene. He wonders if it is "the dead man walking," or "the official ministers of human justice" ready "to consign him to the gallows" (145). But the visitor looks and smiles at him "as if in friendly recognition" (146). The description of the mysterious shadow, a thing that bears a likeness to himself ("at times he thought he knew him"), and yet seems a supernatural presence ("this thing was not of the earth and not of God"; 146), reveals that he is a double of Markheim. The mysterious visitant who materializes in the story as a sort of *deus ex machina* is a doppelganger, Markheim's second self. The human shadow and reflection have always been seen as "extensions of the personality and have carried a numinous charge" (Herdman 1990: 2).

The dialogue between the two, structured as a moral argument, suggests that Markheim's double is his worse self that magnifies his propensity to evil, but at the same time, being a projection of his conscience, calls forth his better side, becoming the agent of his own redemption. Claiming to know his innermost thoughts, the visitor talks with Markheim reviewing his past life and the motives for his actions. The voice of his conscience has now become a mirror in which he is made to see his own soul. He appears as a demon tormentor, a persecutory self, a "devil" (146) that has come to usurp his functions, forcing him to face the truth: "My life is but a travesty and slander on myself. I have lived to belie my nature" (147). By stressing the unfixedness of human nature, Stevenson undermines Markheim's appeal to natural tendencies as a reason for disposing entirely with moral categories and denying moral responsibility.

At first Markheim continues his rationalizing, but the self-deceptive excuses he advances in his defense ("I was a bondslave to poverty, driven and scourged"; 151) fall in their turn before the pressing arguments of the alter ego who taunts him with the idea that he "will never change," forcing him "to behold [himself] for what [he] is" (154). When the bell rings announcing the return of the maid, the shadow urges Markheim to kill her, ransack the house, and make good his escape. But Markheim, dismissing the stranger, "confronted the maid upon the threshold with something like a smile. 'You had better go for the police,' said he: 'I have killed your master'" (155).

Thus Markheim surrenders himself to the authorities. Stevenson seems to have taken from Dostoevsky the idea of the confession. But although there are close thematic analogies, it would be unfair to claim that Stevenson's story is simply a retelling of Dostoevsky: The final lines stress notes of despair and damnation; the punishment for murderers was more severe in England than in Russia: Raskolnikov, as a consequence of his crime, goes to Siberia for seven years of penal servitude, while Markheim will be hanged. "He is not choosing between suicide and surrender as Raskolnikov is, because for Markheim, surrender can only mean a kind of suicide" (Eigner 1965: 130–31). Like so many of Stevenson's life deserters, he embraces his death courageously and with quiet desperation: "His past went soberly before him; he beheld it as it was, ugly and strenuous like a dream, random as chance-medley—a scene of defeat. Life, as he thus reviewed it, tempted him no longer" (Stevenson 1885: 155).

For Dostoevsky, Christianity was one of the forces preventing self-destruction. His central obsession was God, whom his characters seek through pain, evil, and humiliation. In Stevenson's Calvinistic view, instead, there is no salvation since human nature is inescapably evil, and thus any attempt to act according to virtue is doomed to failure. The double was central to his apprehension of reality, for his mind was cast in the mold of a morally conceived dualism. Protestant theology provides the dominant discourse of the tale, contributing to its almost Manichean division between the powers of good and evil. As in *Dr. Jekyll and Mr. Hyde*, the world of "Markheim" is one of sharply etched moral oppositions. Its most pervasive imagery is that of light and shadow. The conclusion of the tale, while suggesting an antinomian perspective, shows that it was precisely the moral dimension that he most unequivocally aimed at.

Yet, the subtlety of penetration with which Stevenson explores Markheim's rebellious mind, Promethean audacity, mocking contempt, frailty, and despair allowed him to overcome the constraints of a strict moral Manicheism. Duality was for Stevenson a precision tool of psychological penetration that allowed him to explore the ambiguities of human behavior and the coexistence in one person of conflicting motives.

Markheim, who is thirty-six years old, as Stevenson was at the time he wrote the story, is a sort of double of the author himself who grew up in the Calvinistic confines of nineteenth-century bourgeois Edinburgh. Markheim's "thirst of pleasure" (151), and disposition to be guided by chance, his readiness to place himself in a position of challenging fate (he regularly speculates on the stock exchange) and thus attain to an absolute freedom from the laws of nature that are binding on ordinary men, express Stevenson's fascination with transgression, regression and reversion—with the idea that division of the self results from the repressive forms of Victorian morality.

Stevenson anticipated Freud's most important theory on the workings of the mind torn between what in *Civilization and Its Discontents* he called the "pleasure principle" and the "reality principle," an idea that was taken up in *Dr. Jekyll and Mr. Hyde*, his uncanny and arresting story of crimes and guilty secrets involving a respectable member of Victorian society. Through the potion he has himself compounded in order to release his evil side, Dr. Jekyll undergoes a radical transformation that allows him to forget the restrictions of social codes and indulge in forbidden pleasures. Thus he is turned into a primitive, unrepressed, and much more happy being—the sadistic Mr. Hyde who follows at will the pleasure principle and its commands to do whatever feels good, rather than subordinate pleasure to what needs to be done.

However, Stevenson's tale is revolutionary not only in this idea of the split personality but in the underlying implication that good and evil cannot be kept separate and are indeed indissolubly part of man's nature. Markheim's proclivity toward fatalism, and his disposition to be guided by chance, become a metaphor for Stevenson's sense of a frightening ambiguity inherent in human behavior, rendering impossible any reliance on reassuring Christian values.

The striking modernity and freshness of approach pervading "Markheim" and its surprising ending, allowed Stevenson to transform an allegorical tale into a subtle investigation of man's inscrutable drive to self-annihilation. Allied to Stevenson's love of romance and adventure, there was firmly embedded in his nature a brooding sense of evil fostered by his background and the acknowledgment of the thin line separating rational from irrational conduct.

Thus Stevenson, in a tale full of strong emotional resonances, enabled himself and his readers to experience the uncanny experience of the irrational, the widening gap between good intentions and self-annihilating drives. A proto-existentialist code of courage and fatalism in the face of nothingness, an unsettling notion that, while positing the existence of a blind, meaningless, and incoherent universe, seems ultimately to anticipate the poetics and ethics of the absurd espoused by Camus and Kafka, for whom desire for comprehension ends in denial and frustration and for whom man is a stranger to himself.[6]

NOTES

1. In this tale, as well as in "The Black Cat," Poe is "less interested in the *commission* of crimes than in the *confession* to them. These are not so much stories of crime and detection as of crime and confession" (Benfey 1993: 36).

2. For more on the "French scientific journal," see Dury in this volume.

3. "Early man viewed the mirror with awe. A pool of water or a piece of polished metal had the power to show him a duplicate of himself that he identified as his spiritual double, or soul. It revealed to him the phantom form of his being that lived on after he died, preserving his ego and giving him a confronting sense of immortality. At the same time it made him uneasily aware of his eventual bodily death when his soul decided to leave his body" (Goldberg 1985: 3). See also Eco 1985.

4. In this connection, "Markheim" bears an affinity with "Will o' the Mill," a short story rich in allegorical overtones in which Stevenson explored the dichotomy between "the desire for security and order and the quest for emotional fulfilment" (Hammond 1984: 79).

5. For the significance of marine metaphors for Stevenson, see Villa "Quarreling with the Father" in this volume.

6. Although the notion of judgment and retribution are foreign to the protagonist of Camus's *L'étranger*, the second part of the novel, just like "Markheim," is completely taken up with Meursault's state of mind while waiting for execution, arraignment, trial, and punishment.

REFERENCES

Benfey, Christopher. 1993. Poe and the Unreadable: "The Black Cat" and "The Tell-Tale Heart." In *New Essays on Poe's Major Tales*. Ed. Kenneth Silverman. Cambridge: Cambridge University Press. 27–44.

De Propris, Fabio. 1992. Introd. to R. L. Stevenson, *Markheim*. Ed. Fabio De Propris. Rome: Salerno Editrice.

Dickens, Charles. 1843. *A Christmas Carol*. Ed. Marisa Sestito. 2001. In *Un canto di Natale. Con testo a fronte*. Venezia: Marsilio.

Eco, Umberto. 1985. Sugli specchi. In *Sugli specchi e altri saggi*. Milan: Bompiani.

Eigner, Edwin M. 1965. *Robert Louis Stevenson and Romantic Tradition*. Princeton, NJ: Princeton University Press.

Goldberg, Benjamin. 1985. *The Mirror and Man*. Charlottesville: University Press of Virginia.

Hammond, J. R. 1984. *A Robert Louis Stevenson Companion*. Basingstoke, UK: Macmillan.

Herdman, John. 1990. *The Double in Nineteenth-Century Fiction.* London: Macmillan.

Mighall, Robert. 1999. *A Geography of Victorian Fiction. Mapping History's Nightmares.* Oxford: Oxford University Press.

Poe, Edgar Allan. 1984. *Poetry and Tales.* Ed. Patrick F. Quinn. New York: The Library of America. 826–32.

Prina, Serena. 1994. Introduzione. In *Feodor Dostoevskij: Delitto e castigo.* Milan: Mondadori.

Stevenson, Fanny van der Grift. 1905. Prefatory Note [to *Strange Case of Dr. Jekyll and Mr. Hyde*]. Vailima Edition (1922–23). Vol 7. 337–42

Stevenson, Robert Louis. 1875. "The Works of Edgar Allan Poe." Vailima Edition (1922–23). Vol. 24. 107–17.

———. 1885. "Markheim." Vailima Edition (1922–23). Vol. 11. 129–55.

Waters, Catherine. 1997. *Dickens and the Politics of the Family.* Cambridge: Cambridge University Press.

PART IV

Textual and Cultural Crossings

Masters of the Hovering Life

Robert Musil and R. L. Stevenson

ALAN SANDISON

To justify mentioning in the same breath Robert Musil—the Robert Musil of *The Man Without Qualities*, that is—and Robert Louis Stevenson might seem, on the face of it, to require some ingenious argument. On reflection, though, we may be just a little too ready to apologize for juxtaposing Stevenson with a writer of such high cultural seriousness as Musil. Might it not, perhaps, signal a failure in comprehension on our part?

Superficially, there would appear to be some mildly interesting, if rather adventitious, affinities between the two. Both were the sons of engineers, both gave themselves—for varying periods but with almost equal distaste—to the study of engineering, both proved themselves inventive: Stevenson with his paper "On a New Form of Intermittent Light in Lighthouses" for which he got a medal; Musil with his invention (and patenting) of a chromatometer, which was still in use in the 1930s. Both were determined to be writers.

Less superficially, there is a certain amount of internal evidence to suggest that Musil, too, had played the sedulous ape—with Stevenson as his mentor. (Compare, for example, the description of the state of Kakania in part 1, chapter 8, with the description of the state of Grünewald in the first three pages of *Prince Otto*.) What really draws them together, however, is the importance they both attach to the essay and the practice of essay writing.

One of the obstacles that has, for most of the twentieth century, impeded the proper evaluation of Stevenson's work, is that his essays have tended to be both separated from, and overshadowed by, his fiction. I say "tended" advisedly for there have been a number of critics—particularly reviewers—who *did* recognize their importance to his oeuvre; and these were particularly conspicuous in the early days of his fame. In an unsigned review in *The Scottish Leader* in 1892 of *Across the Plains*, a volume of twelve essays, the author asks if it is in the essay that Stevenson's true strength and vocation will be found. He goes on: "Is it among the romancers, with Scott and Dumas, that Mr Stevenson will stand, or among the essayists, the pleasant prattlers and gossips of literature, with Montaigne, and Addison and Lamb?" (Maixner 1981: 380). To number Stevenson among "prattlers" like these puts the reviewer's condescension in perspective; nonetheless, his conclusion is clear: "While his fiction is sound and brilliant beyond all question, the best part of his work . . . has been done in the region of desultory imaginative prose." Stevenson is "a delightful egotist—as entertaining in his way as Montaigne himself" (how casually he asperses the great progenitor of the modern essay!). "What justifies it all is, of course, that about the effect there is nothing vulgar: an air of delicate mockery saves everything, and we close the book, knowing that Mr Stevenson, to give us a charming essay, has been exploiting and exaggerating himself, and laughing at himself, too, and at us all the time" (381).

Richard Le Gallienne takes a far more serious and considered view of the essay and announces firmly at the beginning of his 1892 review in *The Academy* that "Mr Stevenson's final fame will be that of an essayist, nearest and dearest fame of the prose-writer." He makes a particularly perceptive point both about the nature of the essay and the nature of Stevenson's essay writing: "In the essay, no octave-spanning architecture has to be considered, with a half heart which would fain be at the floriation of niche and capital." While such architecture, he acknowledges, is no doubt the prerogative of the magnum opus, the essayist "cannot but feel the essential . . . limitation of the greatest monuments of art, monuments which attain their air of majestic completion, simply by shutting out the moon and the stars." As he continues, expanding his metaphor, he helps to define Stevenson the essayist: "The essayist is essentially a son of Shem, and his method is the wayward travel of a gypsy. He builds not, but he pitches his tent, lights his fire of sticks, and invites you to smoke a pipe with him over their crackling. While he dreamily chats, now here now there, of his discursive way of life; the sun has gone down, and you begin to feel the sweet influences of the Pleiades" (Maixner 1981: 387).

Le Gallienne's point about the "unroofed" or incomplete nature of the essay, expanded to catch up notions of fragmentariness and wayward traveling, lies at the core of the essay form and is crucial to an understanding of its appeal to Stevenson—the writer whose romances (we scarcely need reminding) are themselves characterized by inconclusiveness and wayward traveling.

The essay may be necessarily a fragment, but that very fact demands that its author must concern himself closely with the integrity of its structure. This was a challenge that Stevenson recognized and enjoyed meeting. As he himself said of the essay (or the "short study"): "Short studies are, or should be, things woven like a carpet, from which it is impossible to detach a strand." Even what is wrong "has its place there forever, as a part of that technical means by which what is right has been presented" (Stevenson 1882: xiv). Open-roofed the form may be, but it must conform strictly to its own logic, in which its structure will be defined. ("Let no one confine his attention to the matter," his acknowledged master, Montaigne, advises readers of his essay "Of Books," "but to the shape I give to it. Let them see, in my borrowings, whether I have been able to choose the means of improving the idea" (Montaigne 1580: 342).

Thus is the essay's necessary subjectivism made subordinate to certain laws, but in a way that allows the personal voice free play. And this personal voice is an essential quality: "What [the writer of short studies] can't vivify," Stevenson declares roundly, "should be left out" (Stevenson 1882: xiv), and the vivifying comes in his case through the constant deployment of the personal voice in digression, anecdote, and aphorism. These were devices he could well have learned from Montaigne, as others have done since. Susan Sontag, in her fine essay, "Writing Itself: On Roland Barthes", describes Barthes as being "irrepressibly aphoristic." It is a phrase one might well apply to Stevenson, and the comparison becomes more attractive when Sontag goes on: "Barthes' strengths as an aphorist suggest a sensibility gifted, before any intervention of theory, for the perception of structure. A method of condensed assertion by means of symmetrically counterposed terms, the aphorism displays the symmetries and complementarities of situations or ideas—their design, their shape. Like a markedly greater feeling for drawings than for paintings, a talent for aphorism is one of the signs of what could be called the formalist temperament" (Sontag 1982: 65).

That "formalist temperament" was amply recognized by many of the reviewers of Stevenson's essays—sometimes as a matter for praise, sometimes for blame. What several of them also criticized was something that came with the territory—Stevenson's subjectivity. Yet, as Sontag says of the formalist temperament, "What characterizes such a sensibility . . . is

its reliance on the criterion of taste, and its proud refusal to propose anything that does not bear the stamp of subjectivity. Confidently assertive,
it nevertheless insists that its assertions are no more than provisional. . . .
Indeed adepts of this sensibility usually make a point of claiming and
reclaiming amateur status" (65). Again Sontag could well have instanced
Montaigne, the common ancestor of both Barthes and Stevenson: "I make
no doubt that I often speak of things which are better treated by the masters of the craft, and with more truth. What I write here is purely an essay
of my natural faculties. . . . Let him who is in search of knowledge fish for
it where it lurks; there is nothing I so little profess. These are fancies of my
own, by which I endeavor to make known, not things, but myself" (Montaigne 1580: 342).

Stevenson employs the same tactic, frequently apologizing for his naiv-
eté (as he does in his extremely interesting preface to *Familiar Studies of
Men and Books*). Dogmatic? Perish the thought! He is merely chatting,
isn't an expert on anything, and is really only there to amuse you in an idle
hour. As Sontag says of Barthes, "this is seduction as play, never violation";
and she adds: "All of Barthes' work is an exploration of the histrionic or
ludic; in many ingenious modes, a plea for savor, for a festive (rather than
dogmatic or credulous) relation to ideas. For Barthes, as for Nietzsche, the
point is not to teach us something in particular. The point is to make us
bold, agile, subtle, intelligent, detached. And to give pleasure" (Sontag 1982:
72). Just like Stevenson, we might say.

In the essays, the Stevensonian "self" repeatedly appears as one of the
dramatis personae, a harlequin figure, teasing and subversive. So its utterances come tinged with the same iridescent suggestion of incalculable
possibilities, and a readiness to back away from an apparently dogmatic
assertion with the apology "well, after all I'm only a fiction." As Glenda
Norquay writes in her introduction to her anthology of Stevenson's essays:
"The essays create little fictions within themselves, playing with the narrative 'I': in several instances, Stevenson begins talking about a third-
person character until finally 'admitting' that this person he knows so
well is of course himself" (Norquay 1999: 2). In fact, reading Stevenson's
essays helps to justify Barthes' celebrated appeal: "let the essay avow itself
almost a novel: a novel without proper names" (Barthes 1975: 120). It also
helps us to identify this self and its protean capacities as the locus of all
possibilities—nothing closed off, nothing ever finally concluded, no roof
overhead to block out the stars. All illustrative, I would argue, of a master
hoverer.

I have, in the approved tradition of the essay, followed a slight detour on my way to *The Man Without Qualities* to take in Roland Barthes because Barthes is by far the most committed exponent and the most searching anatomist of the essay form in our time. In his inaugural address to the Collège de France as the first holder of the Chair of Literary Semiology, Barthes claimed that he had "produced only essays, an ambiguous genre in which analysis vies with writing" (Barthes 1978: 457). The self-deprecation smacks very slightly of an attitude he condemns in his own essay "Blind and Dumb Criticism"; despite that "only" we can be in no doubt of the importance he attaches to the genre, or of his own brilliant practice in it. The odd thing is that, so far as I can discover, he makes no reference to the only other contemporary writer who took the essay form equally seriously: Robert Musil.

In his brilliant magnum opus, *The Man Without Qualities*, Musil interpolates lengthy essays on all sort of things within the realm of ethics and aesthetics. Perhaps "integrates" would be better than "interpolates" for these essays cannot be extracted from the text like nuggets; they are not there to add editorial variety but to intensify the book's meaning while defining the author's literary theory and his chosen novelistic practice. His argument is about open-endedness, and the essay, in its moral and aesthetic universe, enshrines the continuously exploratory. He is as hostile as Barthes or Stevenson to the closing of the roof (whether by dogma or scientific fact) that shuts out the vista of infinite possibilities. Ulrich in *The Man Without Qualities* tells us that he coins the word *Essayismus*, "essayism," precisely to cover "the sense of possibility, the imaginative in contrast with pedantic precision" (Musil 1930–43: 646). The fluidity and mobility that are hallmarks of his moral and intellectual world find their ideal form in the essay. It is the form best suited to accommodating the human mind "which secretly detests everything with pretensions to permanence, all the great ideas and laws and their little fossilized imprint, the well-adjusted character. It regards nothing as fixed, no personality, no order of things . . . everything has the value it has only until the next act of creation" (163). There is an echo here of Stevenson ("God, if there be any God, speaks daily in a new language by the tongues of men; the thoughts and habits of each fresh generation and each new-coined spirit throw another light upon the universe and contain another commentary on the printed Bibles," Stevenson 1896: 32); and it recurs again in one of his neatly summarizing aphorisms when he insists that "faith must never be more than an hour old" (Musil 1930–43: 829).

Trying to describe the young man "hesitantly ventur[ing] into life" Ulrich reflects: "The drive of his own nature to keep developing prevents him from believing that anything is final and complete":

> He suspects that the given order of things is not as solid as it pretends to be, no thing, no self, no form, no principle, is safe, everything is undergoing an invisible but ceaseless transformation, the unsettled holds more of the future than the settled, and the present is nothing but a hypothesis that has not yet been surmounted. . . . Hence he hesitates in trying to make something of himself; a character, a profession, a fixed mode of being, are for him concepts that already shadow forth the outlines of the skeleton, which is all that will be left of him in the end. He seeks to understand himself differently, as someone inclined and open to everything that may enrich him inwardly, even if it should be morally or intellectually taboo. (269–70)

Ulrich has dubbed this attitude to life "living hypothetically," but he now connects it with a concept he admits is "oddly named": it is the concept of the essay. He goes on:

> It is more or less in the way an essay, in the sequence of its paragraphs, explores a thing from many sides without wholly encompassing it . . . that he believed he could most rightly survey and handle the world and his own life. The value of an action or a quality, and indeed its meaning and nature, seemed to him to depend on its surrounding circumstances, on the aims it served. . . . In this way an open-ended system of relationships arises . . . [and all that is] seemingly solid in this system becomes a porous pretext for many possible meanings; . . . and man as the quintessence of his possibilities, potential man, the unwritten poem of his existence, confronts man as recorded fact, as reality, as character. (270)

Incompleteness, potentiality, and mobility are depictions of his moral vision as they were for Stevenson who railed against the realists' "insane pursuit of completion" (Stevenson 1883: 74). They are a defining characteristic of the essay too: as Réda Bensmaïa writes in his introduction to *The Barthes Effect,* "it is not at all fortuitous or accidental that the notions of incompleteness and inexhaustibility have been associated with Montaigne's essays and through them with the Essay as a specific genre" (Bensmaïa 1986: xxx). This is precisely what recommended the essay to Musil, convinced as he was that the moral norm is no longer to be seen "as a set of rigid commandments but rather as a mobile equilibrium that at every moment requires continual efforts at renewal" (Musil 1930–43: 272). All systematizing thought is repudiated in Ulrich's position—indeed, it is anathema to him, hence his distaste for philosophers. ("Philosophers are despots who have no armies to command, so they subject the world to their tyranny by locking it up in a system of thought," 272). His commitment to "essayism" is entirely of a piece with this:

> The accepted translation of "essay" as "attempt" contains only vaguely the essential allusion to the literary model, for an essay is not a provisional or incidental expression of a conviction capable of being elevated to a truth under more favorable circumstances or of being exposed as an error . . . ; an essay is rather the unique and unalterable form assumed by a man's inner life in a decisive thought. . . . Terms like true and false, wise and unwise, are . . . inapplicable, and yet the essay is subject to laws that are no less strict for appearing to be delicate and ineffable. There have been more than a few such essayists, masters of the inner hovering life, but there would be no point in naming them. Their domain lies between religion and knowledge, between example and doctrine, between *amor intellectualis* and poetry; they are saints with and without religion, and sometimes they are simply men on an adventure who have gone astray. (273)

Ulrich repeatedly postulates—frequently in the intercalated essays—both mobility and equilibrium, searching for a harmonious point of balance between certain contrarieties to which, as in the example just quoted, he gives many different names. It is a state, perhaps a space, an unassertive, undogmatic, and imaginative space neither true nor false, neither rational nor irrational. He is particularly hostile to attempts to turn the "living wisdom" of the essayists

> into knowledge to live by and thus extract some "content" from the notion of those who were moved: but about as much remains of this as of the delicately opalescent body of a jellyfish when one lifts it out of the water and lays it on the sand. The rationality of the uninspired will make the teachings of the inspired crumble into dust, contradiction, and nonsense, and yet one has no right to call them frail and unviable unless one would also call an elephant too frail to survive in an airless environment unsuitable to its needs . . . [T]he underlying problem presented itself to Ulrich not at all intuitively but quite soberly, in the following form: A man who wants the

truth becomes a scholar; a man who wants to give free play to his subjectivity may become a writer; but what should a man do who wants something in between? (274)

In his search for the balanced life, Ulrich is trying to discover a synthesis which will result in what he termed "das rechte Leben," by which, it
has been speculated, he meant not just the morally right but also the creative life excluding neither the scientific attitude nor that rooted in areas
of human experience lying outside the boundaries of strict empirical enquiry (Peters 1978: 11). Characteristically, though, his conviction that in
the space that allowed some sort of creative reciprocity of thinking and
feeling, he would realize a domain of "total insight" into the moral life,
remains somewhat tentative. And interestingly he links this state of being
to the essay: "as little as one can make a truth out of the genuine elements
of an essay can one gain conviction from such a condition" (Musil 1930–
43: 275). The link with the essay has been made both explicitly and implicitly throughout what is itself an interpolated essay. Given his definition of
the essayist as a master of the hovering inner life, we have the outline of
an answer to his question "What should a man do who wants something
in between?" Write essays, would seem to be the solution!

Where is Stevenson in all this? The short answer is: everywhere. The
terms in which Musil modulates and advances the definition of the essay
form well beyond that supplied by their common ancestor, Montaigne,
explain much of Stevenson's own attraction to it and no small measure of
his moral and aesthetic vision. What Musil identifies in it as being of prime
relevance to the moral, intellectual, and creative life of his times, describes
precisely the appeal of that same form to Stevenson's protomodernist sensibility. (For more on the latter, see Sandison 1996.) Stevenson, too, is one
of the masters of the hovering life.

When the young firebrand Hans Sepp assails Ulrich, exasperated at
never being able to pin him down, he shouts: "Can you tell me one single, solid, ultimate value from which you, for instance, take your bearings
in life?" Ulrich only answers him with another question: "Is it really utterly
impossible for you to live without some ultimate value?" (527). Stevenson
is equally elusive on the same issue (for which he was repeatedly criticized
by some of the best reviewers), but when he depicts someone who has no
doubt about the ultimate value he embraces—like Attwater in *The Ebb-
Tide* or Justice Weir in *Weir of Hermiston*—that someone is a person to
fear, just as some in *The Man Without Qualities* show signs of fearing Hans

Sepp or what he, in the 1930s, might come to stand for. Absolutes that anchor people in the sea-bed of their prejudices are as suspect for Stevenson as they are for Musil. He would have agreed with Ulrich (and, indeed, says something very like it himself) when the latter reflects on the failure of everyone to get to the bottom of Moosbrugger's problems: "The truth is not a crystal that can be slipped into one's pocket, but an endless current into which one falls headlong" (582). Heretically, Stevenson had proposed in "Crabbed Age and Youth," that youth's capacity for error is a healthy sign, for it teaches us that all error and not just verbal error is simply "a strong way of stating that the current truth is incomplete" (Stevenson 1878: 48), which is not really far from Musil's argument that "the immoral achieves its divine right by being a drastic critique of the moral! It shows us that life has other possibilities" (Musil 1930–43: 1040).

The differences between Musil's generation and Stevenson's (Musil was born in 1880) were, of course, considerable, as was the cultural context. However, the determination to be fair to intellectual enquiry and analysis as well as to feeling was certainly common to both. As Musil himself defined it, his challenging, hypothesizing, undogmatic essayism was directed at "a *possible* person" and "a *possible* world": an "essayistic way of thinking which tended to fall between the subjectivity of the self and the impersonality of objective truth" (Pike and Luft 1990: xxii). Fluidity, provisionality, and a constant emphasis on the need for renewal characterize his outlook: "each new experience escapes the formula of previous experiences, and is at the same time formed in their image. What we call our spiritual and intellectual being finds itself continually in this process of expansion and contraction. In it art has the task of ceaselessly reforming and renewing the image of the world and of our behaviour in it, in that through art's unique experiences, it breaks out of the rigid formulas of ordinary experience" (Musil 1925: 206). Stevenson's denunciation of the stultifying effects of "rank conformity" are recalled when Musil rounds upon the formulaic tendency as "the enemy of the saint as well as the artist, of the scholar as well as the legislator" (206).

For Musil, the essay provided an ideal bridge: "For me," he writes in "On the Essay," "ethics and aesthetics are associated with the word essay." It is "the strictest form available in an area were one *cannot* work precisely" (Musil 1914: 48). Like Stevenson, he is attracted to ideas and thinking but only as these are embedded in a process of lived experience. In fact, Stevenson's concept and practice of the essay conforms in large measure to Musil's view of it as "an intermediate and mediating form of discourse

between morality and life and between science and art" (Luft 1990: 48).
The last two terms have both to be interpreted and understood broadly
and in the light of Musil's own description: "[The Essay] takes its form
and method from science, its matter from art." He explains why he believes it preferable to say "from art" and not "from life," then goes on:
"The essay seeks to establish an order. It presents not character but a connection of thoughts, that is, a logical connection, and it proceeds from
facts, like the natural sciences, to which the essay imparts an order. Except
that these facts are not generally observable, and also their connections are
in many cases only a singularity. There is no total solution, but only a
series of particular ones. But the essay does present evidence, and investigates" (Musil 1914: 49).

Thought for Musil, however, is never an exclusively rational process:
"There are trains of thought that really only work through the mode of
feelings. For a person who has no ear for them they are completely confusing and incomprehensible. But here it is nevertheless visibly a matter of
an entirely legitimate means of understanding, even if it is not of binding
general validity" (Musil 1914: 50). He talks of a sudden "lightninglike re-
forging of a great complex of feeling . . . by means of the idea, so that one
suddenly understands the world and oneself differently" and adds "[o]n a
smaller scale [this] is the constant movement of essayistic thought." Within
the circle of the essay, he concludes in a sentence that might well have
come from Stevenson, "lies the human branch of religion" (51).

For Stevenson, from a very different background, there is never any
prospect that the idea will dominate; to him, hovering comes more easily,
one might say. Yet, the poles of their discourse are surely very similar
though the accentuation may be different. For Stevenson, the essay is a
means of his giving expression to a carefully-deployed subjectivism of
which Musil would not have disapproved since it is reined in by an equally
careful cultivation of the idea—even, it could be said, by a healthy degree
of subservience to its necessary logic. It is this consideration that makes
one want to argue with passion that Stevenson the essayist is wholly inseparable from Stevenson the novelist if we would appreciate his real significance. He did not intercalate his essays with the novel, as Musil did, but
the two different sides of his head, as Kipling put it, are represented in the
essay and the novel. In the latter he readily obeys different rules, which are
those Ulrich reflects upon in *The Man Without Qualities*: "it struck him
that when one is overburdened and dreams of simplifying one's life, the
basic law of this life, the law one longs for, is nothing other than that of

narrative order, the simple order that allows one to say: 'First this happened and that happened.' It is the simple sequence of events in which the overwhelmingly manifold nature of things is represented, in a unidimensional order . . . which calms us; that celebrated 'thread of the story' which is, it seems, the thread of life itself" (Musil 1930–43: 708–9).

It was a law Stevenson was intensely conscious of, and it structures all of his major tales of adventure. But the essays are *not* directed at simplifying one's life—that is the difference: they allow their author to expand and to express a more diverse mental and moral universe (which some of his fictional works like the *Arabian Nights* volumes or *The Ebb-Tide* also do). In them he can probe the vagaries of human behavior, philosophize, challenge orthodoxies and traditional practices, conduct experiments, redefine his own moral system, even extract moral and literary value from the exercise of a wit that may, at first glance, seem like mere caprice. But all of the "truths" he explores and investigates there have this in common with Musil: they are fluid, infused with skepticism, demand continual revision ("every scruple, every true dissent, every glimpse of something new, is a letter of God's alphabet," Stevenson 1896: 32), and contemn the formulaic—*and* they are rooted in human experience. Just one extract will have to serve to encapsulate the most important elements in *his* essayism (and conveniently demonstrate his affinity with Musil's thinking). It is to be found in his essay "Books Which Have Influenced Me" at the point where he is talking about the gift of reading and its essential concomitant—that "free grace"

by which a man rises to understand that he is not punctually right, nor those from whom he differs absolutely wrong. He may hold dogmas; he may hold them passionately; and he may know that others hold them but coldly, or hold them differently, or hold them not at all. Well, if he has the gift of reading, these others will be full of meat for him. They will see the other side of propositions and the other side of virtues. He need not change his dogma for that, but he may change his reading of that dogma, and he must supplement and correct his deductions from it. A human truth, which is always very much a lie, hides as much of life as it displays. It is men who hold another truth, or, as it seems to us, perhaps, a dangerous lie, who can extend our restricted field of knowledge, and rouse our drowsy consciences. (Stevenson 1887: 67–68)

Musil and Stevenson together make hovering respectable.

REFERENCES

Barthes, Roland. 1975. *Roland Barthes par Roland Barthes.* English translation: *Roland Barthes by Roland Barthes.* Trans. Richard Howard. 1977. New York: Hill and Wang.

———. Leçon inaugurale au Collège de France. 1978. English translation: Inaugural Lecture, Collège de France. In *A Roland Barthes Reader.* Ed. Susan Sontag. 1982. London: Vintage.

Bensmaïa, Réda. 1986. *Barthes à l'essai: Introduction au texte réfléchissant.* English translation: *The Barthes Effect: The Essay as Reflective Text.* Trans. Pat Fedkiew. 1987. Minneapolis: University of Minnesota Press.

Luft, David S. 1990. Headnote to "On the Essay." In Musil 1990.

Maixner, Paul, ed. 1981. *Robert Louis Stevenson: The Critical Heritage.* London: Routledge & Kegan Paul.

Montaigne, Michel de. 1580. Des Livres. English translation: Of Books. In *The Essays of Montaigne.* Trans. E. J. Trechmann. 1946. New York: Modern Library.

Musil, Robert. 1930–43. *Der Mann ohne Eigenschaften.* English translation: *The Man Without Qualities.* Trans. Sophie Wilkins and Burton Pike. 1995. London: Picador.

———. 1914. Über den Essay. English translation: On the Essay. Trans. Burton Pike and David S. Luft. 1990. In Musil 1990.

———. 1925. Ansätze zu neuer Ästhetik. English translation: Toward a New Aesthetic. Trans. Burton Pike and David S. Luft. 1990. In Musil 1990.

Musil, Robert. 1990. *Precision and Soul: Essays and Addresses.* Ed. Burton Pike and David S. Luft. Chicago: University of Chicago Press.

Norquay, Glenda, ed. 1999. *R. L. Stevenson on Fiction. An Anthology of Literary and Critical Essays.* Edinburgh: Edinburgh University Press.

Peters, Frederick G. 1978. *Robert Musil: Master of the Hovering Life.* New York: Columbia University Press.

Pike, Burton, and David S. Luft. 1990. Introduction. In Musil 1990.

Sandison, Alan. 1996. *Robert Louis Stevenson and the Appearance of Modernism.* London: Macmillan.

Sontag, Susan. 1982. Writing Itself: On Roland Barthes. In *Where the Stress Falls: Essays.* London: Jonathan Cape, 2002.

Stevenson, Robert Louis. 1878. "Crabbed Age and Youth." Tusitala Edition. Vol. 25. 39–50.

———. 1882. "Preface, By Way of Criticism." In *Familiar Studies of Men and Books.* Tusitala Edition. Vol. 27. xi–xxiv.

———. 1883. "A Note on Realism." Tusitala Edition. Vol. 28. 69–75.

———. 1887. "Books Which Have Influenced Me." Tusitala Edition. Vol. 28. 62–68.

———. 1896. "Lay Morals." Tusitala Edition. Vol. 26. 1–49.

Whitman and Thoreau as Literary Stowaways in Stevenson's American Writings

WENDY R. KATZ

Stevenson's *The Amateur Emigrant* and *The Silverado Squatters*, the works based on his 1879–80 journey to America, are, for several critics, the products of a travel experience that altered not only the man but also his writing.[1] J. C. Furnas says that the American travel writings "have a new energy and pith," and he suggests that Stevenson "might never have come so far had he lacked the physical and emotional shock treatment that America afforded him" (Furnas 1980: 101, 104). According to James D. Hart, who restored previously omitted material in his edition of the American works, *From Scotland to Silverado*, the trip follows a trajectory "from youth to maturity." Stevenson's famously uncomfortable journey, ill health, and new marriage, with its consequent burden of writing to support a family, developed a "mood of maturity, and a sense of substance" in his works (Hart 1966: xxxvi, xxxvii).[2] Andrew Noble, in his edition of the American texts, *From the Clyde to California, Robert Louis Stevenson's Emigrant Journey*, also uses the word "maturity" to characterize the American works, introducing the figure of the "boundary" to describe the national, class, and personal frontiers traversed during the year in America. Of *The Amateur Emigrant*, he maintains: "This is a book concerned with crossing multiple, inter-connected boundaries: from Scotland to America; from being an upper-middle-class, slightly spoiled writer to mixing with a far lower social stratum; from being single to becoming married" (Noble 1985: 6). The experience, so the argument runs, formed a new and better writer.

The creative gains that result from coming through painful realities are substantial. Stevenson (*Ltrs* 3: 75) himself was convinced of the quality of *The Amateur Emigrant*, writing from California a letter to Colvin in mid-April 1880 that "I shall always think of it as my best work" (*Ltrs* 3: 75).[3] Noble agrees that *The Amateur Emigrant* is Stevenson's preeminent work: "The journey West had hurt Stevenson into great prose; into the creation of a book which, arguably, he was not to equal" (Noble 1985: 13). The trip to America, undertaken to reunite with Fanny in California, was an immersion course in the privation and misery of emigrant steam and rail travel. As almost everyone who has written about it concedes, the reality was a chastening corrective to Stevenson's romantic view of the New World. "For many years," Stevenson explains in *The Amateur Emigrant*, "America was to me a sort of promised land." It had, moreover, the added appeal of release from constraint and convention: "the war of life was still conducted in the open and on free barbaric terms" (Stevenson 1895: 105).[4] The emigrants he observed, however, were hardly brave seekers of the golden land of democracy and equality; they were largely life's failures. "The more I saw of my fellow-passengers," writes Stevenson, the subdued enthusiast, "the less I was tempted to the lyric note" (43).

It seems reasonable to approach the American travel writings, as others have done, by examining the details of Stevenson's life as they emerge from letters or other accounts of this period. I would like, however, to explore the texts from the perspective of literary influence. It is not my intention to minimize the importance of Stevenson's actual experience, the near-steerage accommodations on ship, and the cramped, airless, and miserable circumstances of his emigrant train.[5] Nonetheless, I wish to argue that Stevenson relied on more than his personal experience of the journey for his texts, and that for much of what appears in them he drew on his reading of American literature, and two works in particular. First, there is Walt Whitman's *Leaves of Grass* (1855), which holds a central place in Stevenson's essay "Books Which Have Influenced Me" as having "tumbled the world upside down" (Stevenson 1887a: 82). Equally important as an influence on the American writings is Henry David Thoreau's *Walden* (1854).

To some extent emigrant and nonemigrant travelers alike project an imaginative idea of the places to which they travel. For those with a literary bent, the mental images of places and people derive from books. In Stevenson's case, *Leaves of Grass* and *Walden*, I would suggest, helped to shape the imagination that created the American travel books. The evidence for my case comes not only from the traces of these works in the travel books but also from Stevenson's essays on Whitman and Thoreau.

Stevenson's "The Gospel According to Walt Whitman," written before the American trip, was published in *New Quarterly Magazine* in October 1878, although an earlier version existed as far back as 1873. "Henry David Thoreau: His Character and Opinions," written in San Francisco during December/January 1879–80, approximately when Stevenson was finishing the first part of *The Amateur Emigrant*, was published in *Cornhill Magazine* in June 1880.[6] Both essays were later included in *Familiar Studies of Men and Books* (1882), supplemented by a preface in which Stevenson offers what he perceives are more balanced and positive views and declares, regarding Thoreau, that "I have scarce written ten sentences since I was introduced to him, but his influence might be somewhere detected by a close observer" (Stevenson 1880: 28). Whitman and Thoreau, I propose, are Stevenson's literary stowaways, literary travelers lodged by memory and admiration and released to help articulate his experience of a nation and its people. As Stevenson observes in a discussion of stowaways on board the *Devonia*, "When the stowaway appears on deck he has but one thing to pray for: that he be set to work" (Stevenson 1895: 81). Both Whitman and Thoreau, once perceived, can be seen hard at work, shaping Stevenson's texts, informing their tone, and focusing points of discussion.

The intertextual byroads that run through this discussion of imagining America and American influence reach across the border of Anglo-American literary relations, a useful context in which to begin treatment of the way that Whitman and Thoreau help shape Stevenson's American texts. Specifically, recurrent and related images of sunrise and dawn, carried over from Whitman and Thoreau to Stevenson, counter the more dispiriting realities of the actual experiences related and provide a literary shorthand for American optimism. Robert Weisbuch (1986: 109), in his study of Anglo-American relations, *Atlantic Double-Cross*, develops a compelling argument in this regard involving a binary of cultural time, or what he calls "British lateness and American earliness." British "lateness" manifests itself in a sense of loss, the mythology of the Fall, and images of darkness and night, whereas American "earliness" appears in a sense of hope, a transcendent time, and images of dawn, sunrise and morning.[7] Weisbuch's discussion provides a framework for the interconnecting images of sunrise in Stevenson, Thoreau, and Whitman.

Walden, for example, begins with Thoreau's epigraph that he does "not propose to write an ode to dejection [as does Coleridge], but to brag as lustily as chanticleer in the morning, standing on his roost, if only to wake my neighbors up" (Thoreau 1854: 84). His morning world is a call to consciousness, and he concludes *Walden* with another image of sunrise, and another call to consciousness: "Only that day dawns to which we are awake" (333). Between these bracketing images, he remarks that he is "a worshipper of Aurora," getting up early to bathe in the pond as "a religious exercise." Morning is "the most memorable season of the day," he writes, and again, "We must learn to reawaken and keep ourselves awake, not by mechanical aids, but by an infinite expectation of the dawn"(88, 89, 90).

Leaves of Grass is just as insistent on morning and sunrise. Like Thoreau, Whitman singles out daybreak, when "Seas of bright juice suffuse heaven" (Whitman 1891–92: 54, l. 556) as that season of the day that is most important. "To behold the day-break" (54, l. 550) is also to observe a matching interior awakening: "Dazzling and tremendous how quick the sun-rise would kill me, / If I could not now and always send sun-rise out of me. / We also ascend dazzling and tremendous as the sun" (54, ll. 560–62). The sun is the sign of promise, a guarantee of the future. For Stevenson, too, the sunrise becomes an image to invoke an American voice and spirit in the midst of the emigrant reality. Thoreau and Whitman furnish him with a literary strategy to lighten and lift the spirit of his work.

The Amateur Emigrant makes good use of the sunrise convention. Like Thoreau, Stevenson uses it to end his text. The misery of sick passengers, airless spaces, poor diet, and the flat, endless space of the plains, all those "maturing" experiences that sharpened Stevenson's prose style, give way to a more optimistic aesthetic reality: sunrise. The decidedly grim penultimate chapter of *The Amateur Emigrant*, "Despised Races," examines the racial hatred toward both the Native American, "over whose own hereditary continent we had been steaming all these days" (Stevenson 1895: 149–50), and the Chinese, confined to their own rail car on the train and, like the Native Americans, frequently maligned by fellow passengers. But this dismal tone ultimately yields to something more upbeat. As his train moves into California, Stevenson (157) insists on the prospect of the dawn to strike his final note:

> I am usually very calm over the displays of nature; but you will scarce believe how my heart leaped at this [the dawn]. It was like meeting one's wife. I had come home again. . . . all the passengers on board, threw off their sense of dirt and weariness . . . , and thronged with shining eyes upon the platform, and became new creatures within and without. The sun no longer oppressed us with heat,—it only shone laughingly along the mountain-side. . . . At every town the cocks were tossing their clear notes into the golden air, and

crowing for the new day and the new country. . . . The next day before the dawn we were lying to upon the Oakland side of San Francisco Bay. The day was breaking . . . everything was waiting, breathless, for the sun. . . . and suddenly . . . the city of San Francisco, and the bay of gold and corn, were lit from end to end with summer daylight.

Stevenson doesn't need the sunrise to end *The Silverado Squatters*, an inherently sunnier book, yet readers sense the difference made by his concluding with a transformed image of "American earliness," a picture of evening and nightfall that he describes as "the dawning of the stars" (Stevenson 1884: 275).[8] In the outdoor world, Stevenson maintains, "though the coming of the day is still the most inspiriting, yet day's departure, also, and the return of night, refresh, renew, and quiet us" (275).[9]

More obvious tributes to Whitman and Thoreau come in the democratic voice that sets the tone of Stevenson's American works. It is Whitman's gift, Stevenson had already noted in his essay on the American poet, to be able to give significance to "ordinary and even commonplace lives" (Stevenson 1878: 82). Stevenson cannot manage the staggering catalogue of Americans that Whitman offers in *Leaves of Grass*, but the various characters he describes offer a pictorial survey of the American common people that is marked by a Whitmanesque sense of acceptance, tolerance and, very often, affection. Notable figures are his shipboard acquaintance Jones, the sick man, the fiddler, and the stowaways, along with his California friends, the Kelmars and the Hansons. In his preface to *Leaves of Grass*, Whitman contends that the "genius of the United States is . . . in the common people." Everything about them, their "manners speech dress friendships" and their "delight in music," is "unrhymed poetry" (Whitman 1891–92: 712). Stevenson, seemingly following Whitman's lead, devotes a chapter of *The Amateur Emigrant* to steerage types and another to steerage scenes, describing in full the "manners speech dress friendships" of the passengers on the *Devonia* along with their "delight in music" as shown in their regular evening concerts.

Not surprisingly, Stevenson finds that he is won over by the common people, this especially on the shipboard leg of his journey. The physical unpleasantness aside, the "steerage conquered me; I conformed more and more to the type of the place not only in manner but at heart" (Stevenson 1895: 92). The manners of the steerage passengers are "as gentle and becoming as those of any other class that I have had an opportunity of studying." He moves among his fellow passengers "in a relation of equality"(94).

The emigrant train experience is a different story, but he draws on Whitman here as well, allowing for a Whitmanesque tolerance of its shortcomings. Stevenson records in his essay that Whitman portrays his neighbors with a realistic hand, "accepting without shame the inconsistencies and brutalities that go to make up man, and yet treating the whole in a high, magnanimous spirit" (Stevenson 1878: 80). Whitman himself explains his attitude in *Leaves of Grass*: "Through me many long dumb voices, / Voices of the interminable generations of prisoners and slaves, / Voices of the diseas'd and despairing" (Whitman 1891–92: 53, ll. 508–10).[10] In the rail section of his journey, where crowds, incivility, and disorder prevail, Stevenson finds himself accepting the "misery and danger" as he does the shared soap, washing tin, and towel (Stevenson 1895: 113, 130). Similarly, he tries to treat his fellow passengers with the generous spirit he observes in Whitman, looking "for the human rather than the bestial in this Yahoo-like business of the Emigrant train" (142).

Although Thoreau presents his celebrated picture of the common person in the "Canadian wood-chopper," a portrait Stevenson admires (Stevenson 1880: 111), the democratic tone that Thoreau sets and Stevenson recreates emphasizes not the collective mass but the free individual, the "different drummer" (Thoreau 1854: 326). Happiness itself is democratized, gloriously open to anyone, without reference to class or material possessions; it comes from within: "Every man is the lord of a realm beside which the earthly empire of the Czar is but a petty state" (321). This Thoreauvian individuality resonates in particular in *Silverado Squatters*, where Stevenson's playful remark that he is the "lord" of Silverado is strongly suggestive of *Walden*, as is his narrative account of arranging for food, shelter, and fuel. Presiding both as "squatters" (Thoreau 1854: 54; Stevenson 1884: *passim*), Thoreau and Stevenson enjoy the spiritual freedom of their modest estates. Thoreau's quotation of William Cowper's lines from "Verses Supposed to be Written by Alexander Selkirk," "I am monarch of all I survey, / My right there is none to dispute" (Thoreau 1854: 82), are also alluded to by Stevenson,[11] and its sentiment is echoed by a very similar Latin epigraph to *The Silverado Squatters*,[12] in which text we also find repeated references to Stevenson's family as "lords of Silverado." There seems to be a clear affinity between Walden and Stevenson's presentation of the miners' camp, especially in the similar spirit of independence from the rest of the world and in the emphasis on simple physical activities, Thoreau's famous work with his ax finding an echo in Stevenson's work with pick and shovel.

Yet a third area of influence is apparent in the social commentary that

Stevenson offers in such passages as his discussion of "despised races" mentioned above. Thoreau and Whitman are also social critics. They see a nation in process and, in a spirit of constructive criticism, identify unreservedly the contradictions of a society that promises much but still runs on getting and spending. Stevenson writes of Whitman as "a theoriser about society before he was a poet" (Stevenson 1878: 77), and claims that in Thoreau's "criticism of life as it goes on in our societies . . . he best displays the freshness and surprising trenchancy of his intellect" (Stevenson 1880: 105). Stevenson, too, finds opportunities to assume the mantle of social commentator, most compellingly on the subjects of race and class. He writes of the patronizing saloon passengers who examine Stevenson and his steerage acquaintances as if they were less than human: "We had been made to feel ourselves a sort of comical lower animal" (Stevenson 1895: 56). He has little confidence in the commercial integrity of those who manage the transport of the laboring British populace across America: "The whole business [of the train] was a nightmare while it lasted, and is still a nightmare to remember. If the railway company cared—but then it does not" (115).[13] Thoreau and Whitman, for whom nature rather than money makes the more eloquent appeal, establish a mode of social discourse that Stevenson admires and employs.

Finally, there are discernible echoes in Stevenson's texts that resonate with Thoreau and Whitman. In *The Amateur Emigrant*, Stevenson's emphasis on "nature" and "simple pleasures" as watchwords seems to come directly from *Walden*. "Nature is a good guide through life, and the love of simple pleasures next, if not superior, to virtue" (66). For Thoreau, of course, nature and the simple life are the keys to spiritual well-being. Also reminiscent of *Walden* and Thoreau's description of his house, the digging of his cellar, its dimensions, costs, and the like are the passages describing the labor that goes into setting up and provisioning the Silverado camp. Likewise, the re-creation of visitors, animals, insects, sounds, silence, odors, the close observation of the natural landscape, and the recounting of daily household tasks and activities—"how the days passed and what pleasure we took in them"(Stevenson 1884: 268)—seem to come straight out of *Walden*, from Thoreau's chapters on "Visitors" and "Brute Neighbors." In *The Amateur Emigrant*, Stevenson's chapter on "Personal Experience and Review" resembles Thoreau's "Where I Lived, and What I Lived For" in *Walden*. One particular passage, in which Stevenson (1895: 99) discusses "the human side of economics," seems to have its roots in "Economy," the first chapter of *Walden*. Stevenson considers the worker, whose "thoughts, hopes and fears . . . lie nearer to necessity and nature [than those of a wealthy merchant]. They are more immediate to human life" (99). Thoreau's concerns with necessity in "Economy" are more fully developed, but the similarities of the two writers remain insistent.

In the same way, Stevenson seems to find sources in Whitman for specific passages that he develops. For example, Stevenson devotes an entire chapter in *The Amateur Emigrant* to his encounter, as he walks with friends Jones and O'Reilly, with a sick man on deck, and to the efforts made to seek medical help and offer comfort. In *Leaves of Grass*, Whitman refers to "a sick man . . . borne to the hospital" (Whitman 1891–92: 36, l. 158) and reports of "bringing help for the sick" (74, l. 1021), illustrations of a compassion that perhaps commends itself as material on which to build. Stevenson, the traveler, who claims to have been "not only travelling out of my country in latitude and longitude, but out of myself" (Stevenson 1895: 90), sounds much like Whitman, who insists on being a life-traveler tramping his "perpetual journey"(Whitman 1891–92: 83, l. 1202) pointing to roads of self-discovery. Stevenson's emphasis on the national diversity of the emigrants he sees may also have its source in Whitman's relentless variety of people in *Leaves of Grass*. The emigrant concerts, Stevenson writes, "cheered our way into exile with . . . the songs of all nations" (Stevenson 1895: 46), a multinational chorus consistent with Whitman's remark that he is "One of the Nation of many nations" (Whitman 1891–92: 44, l. 334). Stevenson's comment on the rich nomenclature of place in America is similarly reminiscent of Whitman: "The names of the States and Territories themselves form a chorus of sweet and most romantic vocables: Delaware, Ohio, Indiana . . . there are few poems with a nobler music" (Stevenson 1895: 117). Here, Whitman's intoning of American place names, of Tennessee, Arkansas, Vermont, Maine, Texas, and California, for example, appears to furnish fuel for Stevenson's remarks. Stevenson's inclusion, in *The Amateur Emigrant*, of a letter from the son of his San Francisco landlady, a young boy who reports his own harrowing experiences traveling across to California, reminds readers of Stevenson's account of Whitman's letter to the mother of a Civil War soldier whom Whitman had tended just before the young man died (Stevenson 1878: 89–90). Whitman's letter sheds light on the poet's humanity; the young boy's letter that Stevenson quotes has the effect of sounding a similar note of loving-kindness, a virtue that accrues value in Stevenson's travels. Finally, in a segment on change in the new land, Stevenson seems even to adopt a Whitmanesque cadence: "This stir of change and these perpetual echoes of the moving footfall haunt the land. Men move eternally, still chasing Fortune; and, Fortune found, still wander" (Stevenson 1884: 219). With its alliteration, repetition, and incantatory phrasing, this has clear affinities with the Whitmanesque line.

Stevenson did not need to go to American literature or America to discover nature writing, the common person, or social criticism. These were available in and integral to Wordsworthian romanticism, and Wordsworth is duly acknowledged in "Books Which Have Influenced Me" (Stevenson 1887a: 87). Even so, the American writers, who carried on their own dialogue with English romanticism, seem to have the best claim for strongest influence on his American travel books. Stevenson's attraction to Whitman and Thoreau is understandable: all three were unconventional, somewhat eccentric men, impatient with what Thoreau calls "the ruts of tradition and conformity" (1854: 323). No less reasonable, it seems to me, is the presence of Whitman and Thoreau as Stevenson attempts to assimilate the experience of his various border crossings. If the actual experience refined and developed the writer, it seems apparent from the evidence above that its imaginative reconstruction was shaped by the transmission, absorption, and recombination of literary experience. From Whitman and Thoreau, Stevenson learned much about how to "write" American. From them he encountered a forward-looking optimism, an appreciative regard for the variegated spirit of democracy, and the responsibility to speak critically of the developing society; in short, a nation and its ideology. Stevenson's American writings are not simply personal narratives; they are texts mediated by other texts, eyes opened to America by admired Americans.

NOTES

1. *The Amateur Emigrant* is comprised of two parts: "From the Clyde to Sandy Hook" covers the ocean journey to New York, and "Across the Plains" covers the train trip to California.

2. Unfortunately, Hart observes (1966: xxxvii), this maturity and substance remained hidden from readers. The first part of *The Amateur Emigrant* was withheld from publication until after Stevenson's death, and the second part was published with deletions, first in *Longman's Magazine* (July and August 1883) and then in book form as part of *Across the Plains With Other Memories and Essays* (1892).

3. Other letters, admittedly, indicate less enthusiasm for the work, but the mid-April 1880 letter is emphatically clear on this point.

4. References to *The Amateur Emigrant* are from Noble's edition of 1985. Noble's text does not indicate passages deleted in 1894 that he restores from the manuscript. These are clearly indicated as inserts in James D. Hart's 1966 edition, which is otherwise

based on the 1894 Edinburgh Edition and follows Stevenson's last changes. Roger Swearingen transcribes Stevenson's original manuscript in his 1976 two-volume limited edition of the book.

5. Likewise, I want to resist bending the available material to suit my argument, as is the case, it seems to me, in Peter Conrad's *Imagining America*. In his disappointing analysis of the American texts, he describes Stevenson's journey as "gratuitously idealistic. . . . Stevenson's title admits the element of chivalric imposture: as an emigrant he is an amateur, and at Silverado he fatuously squats in a landscape of desolation which is not the picturesque ruin he expected" (Conrad 1980: 108). Conrad writes of the way that several writers "imagine" America, yet these reconstructed mentalities, as in this case, are not always convincingly based on textual evidence.

6. For further clarification of publication history, see separate entries for the Whitman and Thoreau essays, *The Amateur Emigrant* and *The Silverado Squatters* in Swearingen 1980: 12–13, 33, 72; 47–48; 42–46, 81; 75–76.

7. Weisbuch's analysis also applies to Stevenson's verse lines from the "New York" chapter of *The Amateur Emigrant* subsequently included in *Underwoods* with the title "In the States": "You speak another tongue from mine, / Though both were English born. / I towards the night of time decline: / You mount into the morn. // Youth shall grow great and strong and free / But age must still decay: / To-morrow for the States— for me, / England and yesterday!" (1887b: 62, ll. 5–12).

8. All subsequent references to *The Silverado Squatters* are to Andrew Noble's 1985 edition. *The Silverado Squatters* appeared originally in *Century Magazine* in November and December 1883. Some passages from the magazine publication (and included in Stevenson [ed. Noble] 1985) were not included in the 1884 first edition or in the Edinburgh Edition.

9. In the same passage that ends *The Silverado Squatters*, the cabin, lit from within, "seemed literally bursting with light" (Stevenson 1884: 275).

10. The 1855 edition has the line "Voices of prostitutes and of deformed persons" after "slaves" and before "Voices of the diseas'd" (Whitman 1855: 48, l. 511).

11. Describing Rufe Hanson's desire to "jump the claim" on the mine, Stevenson ironically quotes "His right there was none to dispute" (Stevenson 1884: 263).

12. The epigraph comes from Cicero's *De Officiis* and is translated by the Loeb Classical Library as follows: "Some of them, too, lived in the country and found their pleasure in the management of their private estates. Such men have had the same aims as kings—to suffer no want, to be subject to no authority, to enjoy their liberty, that is, in its essence, to live just as they please."

13. In his essay "San Francisco," Stevenson refers to the Stock Exchange, as "the heart of San Francisco: a great pump we might call it, continually pumping up the savings of the lower quarters into the pockets of the millionaires upon the hill [i.e. Nob Hill]" (Stevenson 1883b: 201).

REFERENCES

Conrad, Peter. 1980. *Imagining America*. New York: Oxford University Press.
Furnas, J. C. 1980. Stevenson and America. In *Robert Louis Stevenson, A Critical Celebration*. Ed. Jenni Calder. Totowa, NJ: Barnes and Noble.

Hart, James D. 1966. Introduction. In Stevenson 1966.

Noble, Andrew. 1985. Introduction. In Stevenson 1985.

Stevenson, Robert Louis. 1878. "The Gospel According to Walt Whitman." In Stevenson 1956.

———. 1880. "Henry David Thoreau: His Character and Opinions." In Stevenson 1956.

———. 1883a. Across the Plains: Leaves from the Notebook of an Emigrant between New York and San Francisco. *Longman's Magazine* 2 (July–Aug 1883).

———. 1883b. "San Francisco." In Stevenson 1985.

———. 1884. *The Silverado Squatters.*

———. 1887a. "Books Which Have Influenced Me." In Stevenson 1910.

———. 1887b. *Underwoods.* New York: Charles Scribner's Sons.

———. 1892. *Across the Plains With Other Memories and Essays.* London: Chatto & Windus; New York: Scribner's.

———. 1895. *The Amateur Emigrant.* Edinburgh Edition. Vol. 3. In Stevenson 1985.

———. 1910. *Essays in the Art of Writing.* London: Chatto & Windus.

———. 1956. *Familiar Studies of Men and Books, Virginibus Puerisque, Selected Poems.* London: Collins.

———. 1966. *From Scotland to Silverado, Comprising The Amateur Emigrant, The Silverado Squatters and Four Essays on California.* Ed. James D. Hart. Cambridge, MA: Harvard University Press.

———. 1976. *Amateur Emigrant, With Some First Impressions of America.* 2 vols. Ed. Roger Swearingen. Ashland: Lewis Osborne.

———. 1985. *From the Clyde to California, Robert Louis Stevenson's Emigrant Journey.* Ed. Andrew Noble. Aberdeen: Aberdeen University Press.

Swearingen, Roger G. 1980. *The Prose Writings of Robert Louis Stevenson, A Guide.* Hamden, CT: Archon Books; London: Macmillan.

Thoreau, Henry David. 1854. *Walden.* Ed. J. Lyndon Shanley. 1971. Princeton, NJ: Princeton University Press.

Weisbuch, Robert. 1986. *Atlantic Double-Cross, American Literature and British Influence in the Age of Emerson.* Chicago: Chicago University Press.

Whitman, Walt. 1855. *Leaves of Grass.* Ed. Malcolm Cowley. 1959. *Leaves of Grass: The First (1855) Edition.* New York: Viking Penguin.

———. 1891–92. *Leaves of Grass.* Ed. Sculley Bradley and Harold W. Blodgett. 1973. New York: Norton.

The Pirate Chief
in Salgari, Stevenson,
and Calvino

ANN LAWSON LUCAS

Piracy entered modern Western prose narrative in the seventeenth century with the autobiographer Alexander Exquemelin, and in the eighteenth century with the novelist and biographer Daniel Defoe.[1] But arguably the two most influential creators of fictional pirates worked at the end of the nineteenth century, presenting their singular inventions to the public almost simultaneously between 1881 and 1884: they were Robert Louis Stevenson in Britain and Emilio Salgari in Italy; the first book edition of *Treasure Island* in 1883 coincided with the beginning of Salgari's newspaper serial, *La Tigre della Malesia* (*The Tiger of Malaysia*), which in volume form would be rechristened *Le Tigri di Mompracem* (*The Tigers of Mompracem*).[2] Both novels unleashed a long history of imitation, parody, and intertextuality, and—in Salgari's case—a lifelong series of sequels; each presented the figure of an extraordinary leader of pirates, destined to become part of his nation's cultural mythology. Salgari, the Italian past master of adventure, would later, in 1898, create a second piratical superhero in *Il Corsaro Nero* (*The Black Corsair*), with similarly seminal results. While the Black Corsair is a familiar type (indeed he is the epitome of the aristocratic European pirate), Salgari's first pirate prince (created when the author was only twenty-one) is a markedly original creation, a character even more unexpected than Long John Silver, and one who appears to have nothing in common with him except—in the broadest terms—piracy. On the other hand, Salgari's later pirate, the funereal and noble freebooter, and RLS's silver-tongued ruffian do have one thing, or perhaps two, in common. They both conduct their depredations in the general region of the Caribbean (or Spanish Main), the "Corsaro Nero" at the end of the seventeenth century and Silver in the eighteenth; originating in the lands of their first readers, both these Europeans voyage across the globe and are of no fixed abode, yet each has a special connection with a particular islet.[3]

By contrast, Salgari's first pirate, Sandokan, was a Borneo sultan's son dispossessed by British colonial activity, who, with his followers, has taken to the life of the exiled offshore sea-marauder, seeking vengeance and the restitution of his throne and territory. Though piracy was historically endemic there, indeed more so than in the West Indies since it was an indigenous way of life, in terms of the Western cultural mythology of pirates, Sandokan's archipelago, the East Indies, was and still is the stranger and more exotic location. Set in the era of the White Rajahs of Sarawak, this was recent, almost topical, piracy: the action of the first novel opens with the date 1849.[4] Like Silver and the later Black Corsair, Sandokan, too, has a focal islet, Mompracem, off the northwestern coast of Borneo, like Stevenson's an invented island in a region where many abound. However, the island was not a historical necessity for Sandokan's way of life any more than it was for Silver's trade, because the Dayak pirates of Borneo were more often than not river pirates, living in jungle villages inland: the pirate island in both cases is a cultural construct that links the pirate tradition back to Defoe's other Great Idea, the castaway (consciously evoked by Stevenson in the figure of Ben Gunn, and by Salgari in a nonpiratical, later novel of the East Indies, *I Robinson italiani*, The Italian Crusoes).[5] In each case, the writer makes the concept of the island integral to the character and role of the pirate chief: their mastery of their island's advantages and dangers is ultimately compromised, even negated, by near-failure; throughout, the threat to this mastery comes not only from other humans but from the natural world, represented in the microcosm of the islands and their surrounding seas. The indissoluble link between pirate chief and island, and the ultimately superior power of the island, are implied by the changes of title adopted by both authors: the preliminary title identifying the central character ("The Sea Cook," "The Tiger of Malaysia") gives way to the definitive title emphasizing the totemic place (*Treasure Island, The Tigers of Mompracem*).[6]

Treasure Island and Mompracem, then, rather than representing historical pseudoreality, are symbolic spatial expressions of isolation, unreliable refuge, confinement, embattlement, danger, and fear without end because the means of escape from adversity may easily be lost. The narrative difference between the two pirate islands is that Stevenson's is temporarily populated by the two enemy groups who play cat-and-mouse with each other amid its natural camouflage, unable entirely to overcome or to escape each other, whereas Sandokan's enemies, the English colonists, are symmetrically confined in their own small—and real—island of Labuan, so that repeated voyages are an essential part of the conflict. Both narratives are dependent on the idea of the sea voyage, but these journeys have a different shape and meaning in the two novels. Here symmetry plays its part in *Treasure Island*, with starting and finishing voyages to and from the island, and a climactic semicircular voyage—a partial circumnavigation of the island—at its heart. These events also follow the pattern of the traditional folk- or fairy tale: the hero leaves home, successfully faces a series of perils, then returns home reestablished either socially or psychologically or both.[7] The voyages of Sandokan's flotilla and of the British navy, by contrast, are to and fro (between the two alien islands), not once but several times, shifting not only the scene but the balance of power alternately from one group to the other. Unlike Squire Trelawney or even the desperado Silver, Sandokan is not optimistic—he knows his deeds are desperate—but he is nevertheless unrealistic in defying his powerful enemy and fate (Salgari 1900: 6–7, 266–73). The repeated journeys express symbolic and psychological states: the voyage out, or sortie, advancing toward and into the enemy island, brings success; but the return, or retreat, to the supposed refuge of Mompracem brings disaster. This narrative is asymmetrical: it ends with a further flight by sea, this time away from the failed refuge, away from failure, into an unknown future (Salgari 1900: 273).

If Mompracem and Treasure Island are inventions, on the contrary, Salgari had strict recourse to history in his presentation of the Black Corsair's more substantial island of Tortuga, the headquarters of buccaneer activity as described by Exquemelin (1969: 67–69, 89 ff). But, in the two fictions the island has a different function. The Black Corsair is most frequently at sea aboard his galleon, his floating palace, which is his focal but mobile location; mainland Venezuela provides the target for his aggression and the island of Tortuga is—as in history—a kind of pirates' naval base and, *in extremis*, safe-haven to which, in need, the Corsair can repair. On the other hand, Sandokan's *praho* is not his home, and the island of Mompracem is both improvised home and fortress: the fabled "Tiger" has made this his lair, where he plans his exploits, where he keeps his flotilla of *prahos* and has settled his village of pirates, and from which he radiates outward on expeditions; however, his existence there is temporary and intended as a stage towards a return to his real home. Treasure Island is for the time being the goal, the desired destination, the solution to life's problems or mysteries, while Salgari's pirate islands are not a goal or a solution but a temporary expedient. The most important voyages narrated go toward and around one (Treasure Island), away from another (Mompracem), and leave the third (Tortuga) to one side. The concept of home is an important element in the stories of both Sandokan and Silver: Sandokan wants to return to his original home, while Silver wants to move on and establish a new one. To the "Corsaro Nero" the concept is irrelevant: he is destined forever to be "away" and in motion, buffeted hither and thither by the waves. This is why the stability (albeit transgressive) of Tortuga is marginal to his existence, as an exile from all society.

The pirates associated with the archetypal islands can be distinguished from one another in a great variety of ways: social status, personality, the nature of their piracy, and the roles they play in the narrative, among others. While there is a broad and approximate foundation in history lying behind the invention of both Salgari's Sandokan and Stevenson's Silver, each of these great pirate figures is intimately related to cultural history, in particular the literary history of piracy writing and to the two opposed branches of this tradition. Whereas Long John Silver's forbears engaged in the lowlife, picaresque adventures of the likes of Defoe's Captain Singleton, Sandokan is descended from tragic, orientalist, aristocratic models, in the Byronic manner.[8]

Clearly in terms of both social status and motivation in piracy, Silver and Sandokan could hardly be more different, one the potentate and the other a plebeian, one a rich exile, surrounded by and scorning treasure, who pursues a reckless political quest, and the other a venal, scheming, ruthless predator whose single aim is self-enrichment and self-preservation. Yet both have identities other than that of pirate; both have left behind another activity that likewise expressed leadership, the capacity to command, but also (and conversely) a more humane, more responsible persona, Sandokan as heir to a throne, Silver as a pub landlord. Silver is a more complex character than Sandokan, and his maritime role is made all the more unpredictable by his trade and rank as ship's cook: it is by force of character and intelligence that this menial asserts himself as a leader of men; he is a natural leader, while Sandokan had been born and trained to lead. Silver has a long history as a pirate, and there are many references back to past experiences; Sandokan's piratical experience seems at first to have been short (and the bitterness of the disinherited is still acute), and yet the dates, given in narrative asides, show his exile to have lasted a decade already. The recollected past is his earlier, privileged life, but though supposedly fighting to regain it, in reality his days of Borneo piracy are nearly at an end, not through heroic success against the enemy, but through heroic defeat. Both narratives, then, possess a substantial "antefatto" or story-before-the-story, and both pirate chiefs aim to win their freedom from piracy and withdraw from it into peaceful comfort.

As befits the distinction between humble buccaneer and freedom-fighting prince, Silver and Sandokan are physical opposites, one maimed and plain-faced, the other impressively handsome. Both characters established archetypal visual images, but these sometimes betray the original and, moreover, it is often in the forgotten descriptive grace-notes that the genius of these two pirate chiefs' creation lies. The first description of Sandokan (in the revised and definitive version for young readers of 1900) presents him as tall and elegant, powerfully built, with a proud, energetic, masculine face of strange beauty. He has long hair, a black beard, lightly bronzed skin, a high forehead, fine eyebrows, and very black eyes that attract attention, dazzle, and cause the onlooker to lower his gaze; his mouth is small, his teeth shine like pearls, and . . . these teeth are filed into sharp points, so resembling the teeth of a wild beast (Salgari 1900: 6). Even the resplendent and refined Sandokan, then, is not *whole*, any more than Silver is, and possesses a physical characteristic that shocks and is redolent of the abnormal, the barbaric, the transgressive. In general, an essential element in the physical representation of Silver and Sandokan is that these figures confound expectations: the sea-cook turns physical disadvantage into strategic weapon;[9] the beauty of the oriental prince is contaminated by voluntary disfigurement, his civilized persona by the call of the wild. He is known, of course, in the manner of the Tamil Tigers, as the "Tiger of Malaysia," and the metaphorical association runs as a refrain through the text.

Not only physically but morally these two pirate chiefs surprise and unnerve the reader. Silver's moral ambiguity is fully recognized, the late-romantic hero Sandokan's less so, still less the moral culpability of the decadentist superman, the Black Corsair. Long John's criminal personality is counterbalanced by his apparently genuine, fatherly kindness to the young boy in the enemy camp. Sandokan's plans are all but wrecked by his love-at-first-sight for a young English girl, the niece of his sworn enemy. Similarly the "Corsaro Nero" falls for the daughter of his mortal foe, though without knowing who she is. These relationships are all versions of the age-old literary nexus of conflict between the affections and duty; each situation is resolved in a different way: for Silver, focused on gold, the natural order and enmity are restored; Sandokan, defeated in his primary purpose of anticolonial war, instead wins his love; the Black Corsair gains nothing, clinging to military honor, and rejecting and punishing his innocent ladylove. In no case does "winner take all," although Silver comes closest to this: Jim is but a passing sympathy, perhaps motivated somewhat by Silver's self-interest and the potential for advantage.

Sandokan and Silver, then, seem to be poles apart: derived from aesthetically, ideologically, and sociologically opposite genres of narrative literature, the social status and physical appearance of these two pirate chiefs are widely divergent, as are their practical and moral objectives. In moral terms, Silver is driven by self-serving venality, Sandokan by principle; Silver is the aggressor, Sandokan the victim. Yet it is in the context of morality that there is the greatest rapprochement between them, of crucial importance in terms of literary efficacy: in short, both characters are deeply morally ambivalent, and it is this that especially endears them to the reader. Silver is ostensibly the villain (though a deal more attractive than the respectable adults and, moreover, successful in his enterprise), while Sandokan is supposedly the hero (though vanquished in the final catastrophic battle and put to flight). Silver's deep-dyed and murderous criminality is clear, and yet his kindness to Jim, his skill in moderating the excesses of his companions and directing their behavior, his intelligent and characterful conversation, all this attracts the interest, sympathy and approbation of the reader. Sandokan's moral persona is also complex: although he is the endangered hero, whose success and safety the reader desires, this nobleman of exceptional powers is capable of self-pitying despair, of the profligate wasting of his comrades' lives, and—worse—of behaving dishonorably. The Englishman who has saved Sandokan's life, and offered him unstinting hospitality and friendship, is rewarded by the Tiger's treachery and warfare in pursuit of his love affair and his destiny.[10] If Sandokan is not a wholly admirable paragon of rectitude, the Black Corsair's acts have no moral justification at all, at any rate by modern standards. Like Sandokan, he has been wronged, but whereas Sandokan can legitimately hope to regain his stolen patrimony, the "Corsaro Nero" cannot restore his executed brother; the whole purpose of his piracy is not financial or personal gain, but revenge, and this indomitable and cultivated hero is even willing to kill the woman he loves in pursuit of his vendetta.[11] Ambivalence and transgressiveness are therefore essential features of all these characters and, in their presentation, the concepts of both hero and villain take on new and more equivocal attributes.

Half a century after these qualified heroics, and in the shadow of a world war rather than the dazzle of the age of empire, the novice novelist Italo Calvino affectionately and repeatedly paid tribute to his literary hero, Robert Louis Stevenson. Intertextuality was to become one of his literary hallmarks and his second novel would be a light-fantastic play upon the Jekyll and Hyde theme.[12] But, already in his first novel of 1947, *Il sentiero dei nidi di ragno* (*The Path to the Spiders' Nests*), a nonrealist fiction of the Italian Resistance movement, he incorporated allusions to Kipling, Hemingway, Collodi's *Pinocchio*, and above all to *Treasure Island*.[13] This too is an adventure story with a boy at its center, in which the fighting men are flawed, bizarre, sometimes murderous, often morally contradictory.

For Calvino, the political affiliations and moral distinctions of World War II were as arbitrary and ambiguous as those of any adventure story. Unlike much of the contemporaneous, neorealist war writing, Calvino's novel deliberately sets out to demystify and deconsecrate—to honor the heroism of the partisans, but not through conventional heroics. His partisans are misfits, outcasts from the main organization, but they, like pirates, are tough, undisciplined fighting men without uniforms, who sing traditional songs to keep their spirits up. Though in the mountains, they too have a sea-cook, Mancino, who dotes on a pet bird, a hawk instead of a parrot. Like Long John's parrot "Captain Flint," the hawk is named after a human hero of its owner, in this case the French Revolutionary, Babeuf. The cook's own code-name implies left-handedness, but his main disability is intellectual and psychological: a devout Trotskyite among moderate Communists, he is the true parrot of this tale, repeating over and over and unquestioningly the slogans he has learned, foisting them upon his comrades whether they listen or not. There is no island here but, in the isolation of the partisan encampment hidden in the hills, Mancino is doubly isolated as a noncombatant extremist and, unlike Silver, he is utterly impotent, utterly peripheral, a gnomelike figure without support for his cause. There is, however, treasure—not gold, but a gun—a treasure buried in the earth by one character and dug up treacherously by another whose lust for weapons obliterates other loyalties. Like Stevenson's buried treasure, it is the pistol that sets the narrative's chain of events in motion, that causes the landlocked voyage of discovery, of danger and defeat to take place; when, on the return journey the treasured pistol is safely recovered, home is in sight, but "home" in this instance is the promise of peace, democracy, and normality.

I am not sure whether my brief remarks on the pirate inventions of Salgari and Stevenson amount to a study of mere coincidence, or of the 1880s' *zeitgeist*, or of the potential for identifying common sources. Certainly *Le Tigri di Mompracem* is in no way derived from *Treasure Island* and, even though *Il Corsaro Nero* belongs to the same literary geography, its literary sociology and mood are far distant from those of Stevenson's novel. On the other hand, the direct descent of Calvino's *Il sentiero dei nidi di ragno* from *Treasure Island* is not in doubt, as indicated by Calvino himself in his later preface; it is unlikely, however, that Calvino bore Salgari's piratical writings in mind, even though they were read by generations of Italian adolescents. Nevertheless, the two Italian writers share a viewpoint not to be found on Spy-glass Hill: they both clearly enunciate political opinions. While *Treasure Island* may indeed incorporate a study in personal power (wily and determined, Long John Silver overcomes the detriments of his social and physical state), it does not offer any commentary on the creation of Empire and imperial power, upon which the story is ultimately dependent. Even if largely ignored until recently, what remains perhaps the most astonishing of Salgari's characteristics—in novels written between 1880 and 1911, when Italy itself was engaging in its first colonialist adventures—is the fact that all his narratives with colonial settings, including *Le Tigri di Mompracem*, espouse the cause of the indigenous freedom-fighters or favor other losing parties in the colonialist strife and, moreover, cast the representatives of imperial power, of whatever nationality, as the villains, the enemy.[14] For Salgari, it is not so much Sandokan's activity as pirate chief that makes him a hero as his status as a defiant victim of imperialism.

NOTES

1. Alexander O. Exquemelin (or Esquemeling, or Oexmelin), ca. 1645–1707, was possibly French, from Harfleur, and in later life settled in Holland. He served with the French West India Company in Tortuga from 1666 for three years, then enlisting with the buccaneers apparently as a barber-surgeon, returning to Europe in 1674. His account of the life and exploits of the buccaneers, including Morgan and L'Olonnais, was first published in Dutch as *De Americaensche Zee-Roovers* in 1678, then in German (1679), Spanish (1681), English (1684), and French (1686); it was to become a major source-book for fictions of piracy. Some indications of Salgari's debts to Exquemelin are given in Ann Lawson Lucas, *La ricerca dell'ignoto. I romanzi d'avventura di Emilio Salgari* (Firenze: Olschki, 2000), 88–91. Daniel Defoe's *The King of Pyrates*, on the life of the real Captain Avery, was published in 1719, the same year as *The Life and Strange Surprising Adventures of Robinson Crusoe, of York, Mariner*; it was followed in 1720 by his novel, *The Life, Adventures and Piracies of the Famous Captain Singleton*. Defoe may also be the true author of *A General History of the Robberies and Murders of the most notorious Pyrates* by 'Captain Charles Johnson' (1724).

2. Emilio Salgari (Verona 1862–Turin 1911), published his earliest adventure novels as serials for adult readers in daily newspapers (1883–94). After publication in a children's newspaper in 1891, he became the leading adventure writer for the young in Italy, remaining popular and culturally influential to this day, although serious critical appraisal began to assert itself only in the 1980s. Before *La Tigre della Malesia* (1883–84), Salgari had published only a short novel, *Tay-See*, set in French Indochina, and serialized in the same Veronese daily *La Nuova Arena* (1883), and a long short story, "I selvaggi della Papuasia," published in a Milanese travel journal, *La Valigia* (1883). *Le Tigri di Mompracem*, the revised version of *La Tigre della Malesia*, was not published as a book for the young until 1900 (Genova: Donath), although a sequel presenting the same pirate hero had preceded it.

3. The "Corsaro Nero" is, unusually in Salgari's repertoire of eighty-one novels, an Italian, the Cavaliere Emilio di Roccanera, lord of Ventimiglia.

4. This was the period when Labuan, a small island off the northwestern coast of Borneo was officially ceded to the British Crown as the first true colony of Britain in the region (the Dutch held Southern Borneo); however, the first "White Rajah," James Brooke, who had arrived in Borneo in 1839, was already well established, from 1841, as a regional administrator for the Malay sultanate of Brunei. Though he does not appear in person in *Le Tigri di Mompracem*, he is an *éminence grise* several times mentioned.

5. *I Robinson italiani* (Salgari 1896) is a hybrid between the original *Robinson Crusoe* and *The Swiss Family Robinson* (J. D. Wyss, *Der schweizerische Robinson*, Zurich, 1812–13), since it has a group of three male castaways (a knowledgeable passenger, a sailor, and a cabin boy) marooned on an island in the Sulu Sea.

6. *Treasure Island* was first published as a serial in *Young Folks* starting in October 1881.

7. The classic analysis establishing this outline and, within it, thirty-one universal functions of the folktale, is to be found in Vladimir Propp, *Morphology of the Folktale*, trans. L. Scott (Austin: University of Texas Press, 1968), 19–24, and the thirty-one functions are quoted in *The Classic Fairy Tales*, ed. Maria Tatar (New York and London: W. W. Norton, 1999), 382–87.

8. It is the Byronic tradition, the late romantic, or even decadentist vision that links Salgari's two heroic pirates, in other respects very different from each other. For further discussion of the "Corsaro Nero" as aristocratic, decadentist superman, see Ann Lawson Lucas, "Decadentism for Kids: Salgari's Corsaro Nero in context" in *Children's Literature and the Fin de Siècle*, ed. Roderick McGillis (Westport, CT: Praeger, 2003).

9. As when, observed by Jim Hawkins in the woods of the island, the previously amiable and avuncular Silver viciously murders the seaman, Tom, using his crutch as projectile (Stevenson 1883: 89).

10. Lord Guillonk is the uncle of the English girl loved by Sandokan, but when he is told that the stranger is the notorious "Tiger" his friendship and protection are withdrawn (Salgari 1900: 66–68).

11. When the Black Corsair discovers the parentage of his sweetheart, he recognizes that he is trapped between his passionate love and his sworn commitment to avenge his brother's death; the latter takes precedence, and he therefore abandons the noble young lady on the high seas aboard an open boat (Salgari 1898: 254–58).

12. Italo Calvino, *Il visconte dimezzato* (1952); the cloven viscount, split in two by a cannon ball, wreaks havoc on his community through his evil half and a different kind of havoc through the good half.

13. Calvino's 1964 preface records some of his deliberated references especially to English-language literature (Calvino 1947: 7–30).

14. This is so much the case that Salgari's opinion of a nation may be reversed by the political circumstances described: in *Le stragi delle Filippine* (Genova: Donath, 1897), the Spanish colonialists in the Philippines are the enemy, whereas in *La capitana del Yucatan* (Genova: Donath, 1899) a heroic Spanish lady runs guns to defend Cuba from the imperialism of the United States in the Spanish-American war.

REFERENCES

Calvino, Italo. 1947. *Il sentiero dei nidi di ragno.* Torino: Einaudi. English translation: *The Path to the Spiders' Nests.* Trans. A. Colquhoun, revised by M. McLaughlin. 1998. London: Jonathan Cape.

———. 1952. *Il visconte dimezzato.* Torino: Einaudi. English translation: *The Cloven Viscount.* Trans. A. Colquhoun. 1992. In *Our Ancestors.* London: Minerva.

Exquemelin, Alexander O. 1969. *The Buccaneers of America.* Harmondsworth: Penguin.

Lawson Lucas, Ann. 2000. *La ricerca dell'ignoto. I romanzi d'avventura di Emilio Salgari.* Firenze: Leo S. Olschki.

Salgari, Emilio. 1883–84. La Tigre della Malesia. *La Nuova Arena* [Verona]. Preface by Roberto Fioraso. 1991. *La Tigre della Malesia.* Torino: Viglongo.

———. 1896. *I Robinson italiani.* Genoa: Donath.

———. 1898. *Il Corsaro Nero.* Genoa: Donath.

———. 1900. *Le Tigri di Mompracem.* Genoa: Donath.

Stevenson, Robert Louis. 1883. *Treasure Island.* Ed. Wendy Katz. 1998. Edinburgh: Edinburgh University Press.

Murder by Suggestion

El sueño de los héroes *and* The Master of Ballantrae

DANIEL BALDERSTON

It was a slightly odd experience for me to be at the Stevenson Conference in Gargnano. I finished a dissertation on Borges and Stevenson in 1981 and published it in Spanish in Argentina in 1985, and apart from an occasional reference to Stevenson's work (and its importance to Borges) I haven't really worked on the Scottish writer since. I was quite surprised to learn that some kind people—some of whom are here—had consulted the microfilm version of my dissertation, just as I was surprised to find my interviews with Borges and Bioy Casares (from 1978) in French translation[1] in the volume of L'Herne that Michel Le Bris devoted to Stevenson in 1995 and to find a somewhat misleading reference to my "thèse, hélas inédite" [alas unpublished thesis] in Le Bris's *Pour saluer Stevenson* (2000)—my book had, as I've mentioned, been published by a major Argentine publisher in 1985, but obviously its Spanish language version didn't find its way to many Stevenson scholars. Today I'm going to talk not about Borges but about his friend and close collaborator Adolfo Bioy Casares (1914–1999), whose work in the crucial period of their collaborations (roughly 1940 to 1955) provides important evidence of Borges's ideas about narrative theory and favorite reading. Bioy has long been known to have been enthusiastic about Stevenson—he mentions him in several essays and interviews—but his own fiction has not been examined much for evidence of the relation. So here goes.

In 1943, Borges and Bioy Casares included an excerpt from Stevenson's *The Master of Ballantrae* in their first anthology of crime fiction (*Los mejores cuentos policiales*). They titled it "La puerta y el pino" ("The Door and the Pine Tree"), a title they invented themselves, because in the original the tale comes in the middle of a chapter titled "Mr Mackellar's Journey with the Master" (the eighth chapter in some editions, the ninth in others). In their headnote they call Stevenson "el preclaro escritor escocés" [the eminent Scottish writer], and comment: "Escribía con felicidad, pensaba con precisión e imaginaba con lucidez" [He wrote joyfully, thought precisely, and imagined lucidly].[2] The list of Stevenson's fiction in the headnote consists of the stories of the *New Arabian Nights* and *Island Nights' Entertainments*, as well as *Dr. Jekyll and Mr. Hyde* and only four of the novels: *Treasure Island*, the unfinished *Weir of Hermiston*, and two of the books written in collaboration with Lloyd Osbourne, *The Wrecker* and *The Ebb-Tide*. Two secondary works are listed: Chesterton's book *Robert Louis Stevenson*, and Sir Walter Raleigh's *R. L. Stevenson*, one of the first works of criticism to appear after Stevenson's death.

The excerpt from *The Master of Ballantrae* is clearly a detective story, though a highly unusual one, especially when it is considered in relation to the detective story of the time, dominated by the figures of Auguste Dupin and Sherlock Holmes: that is, by the figure of the detective, an individual marked by his mannerisms and opinions, whose way of conducting an inquiry into a case takes precedence over the original crime of violence. Borges, in an article on the detective fiction of Chesterton, says that one of the rules of detective fiction is "primacía del cómo sobre el quién" [predominance of the how over the who] (Borges 1935: 93), but the Holmes stories tend to stress the *who* and *how* of the detective more than the identity of the criminal and the mechanics of the crime. The Stevenson story, by way of contrast, dispenses with the detective altogether, and even with any discussion of the prehistory (or motivation) of the crime or of its later consequences: that is, with the investigation that normally takes precedence in the classic detective story. The story plunges us directly into the working out of a crime, a murder that is a pure act of imagination or, as De Quincey says, "one of the fine arts."

In the Stevenson novel, the narrator (an unimaginative old servant, Mackellar) is forced to cross the Atlantic in company of the Master of Ballantrae, the evil older brother of his master, Henry Durie, whom he insists on seeing as purely good in contrast to the monstrosity of the brother. In the middle of a storm, the Master "must tell me a tale, and show me at the same time how clever he was and how wicked. . . . [T]his tale, told in a high key in the midst of so great a tumult, and by a narrator who was one moment looking down at me from the skies and the next peering up from under the soles of my feet—this particular tale, I say, took hold upon me in a degree quite singular" (Stevenson 1889: 209). Borges and Bioy (who we must assume are the translators for lack of evidence to the contrary) provide a fairly faithful translation of the tale, omitting only occasional references to Mackellar and the Master, and sharpening the effect of the tale as a whole by isolating it from its context.

The Master's story consists of four distinct moments or scenes and includes only two characters: a count (a friend of the Master) and a German baron, whom the count hates for some undisclosed reason. The first scene shows the count riding outside of Rome one day and discovering an ancient tomb by a pine tree. He enters a door in the tomb, takes the right fork of a passage, and barely escapes falling down a deep well. Reflecting on the event, he asks himself: "a strong impulse brought me to this place: what for? what have I gained? why should I be sent to gaze into this well?" (210). In the second scene he makes up a dream about himself and the baron, in order to tempt the baron to enter the tomb; besides describing the place, he says that when the baron entered the door and turned to the right, "there was made to you a communication, I do not think I even gathered what it was, but the fear of it plucked me clean out of my slumber, and I awoke shaking and sobbing" (212). The third scene shows them riding together, passing the tomb, and the count feigning an attack of fright—which he will not explain, but which is sufficient motive for the baron to look around and recognize the place from the description of it in the supposed dream. On their return to Rome, the count "took to his bed and gave out he had a touch of country fever" (213). The fourth scene is the briefest of all: "The next day the baron's horse was found tied to the pine, but himself was never heard of from that hour." And the Master, "breaking sharply off," adds: "And now, was that a murder?" (213).

The tale, brief and understated as it is, is structurally quite complex. The first and last episodes involve only one of the two characters, first with the near death of the count, and later with the death of the baron. In each case the approach to the well provokes a question and a story: the count's questions about why he has been brought there (which he answers by making up a plot, and by slightly changing his experiences in making of them a "dream," which satisfies his own and the baron's wishful thinking in different ways), and the Master's question whether the death of the baron was a murder (which provokes Mackellar to try to kill the Master by pushing him overboard, but which even in the fragment published in

Borges and Bioy's anthology demands an answer from the reader, a sequel, or supplement). The second and third episodes mirror each other in a similar fashion. Both consist of excursions on horseback by the two characters together, first in a fiction (the count's "dream"), and later in fact. In both the count pretends (the dream, the attack), and the pretense allegedly portends ill for him (he wakes in a fright from his "dream," he takes to bed after the excursion). And in both episodes something mysterious is communicated without being stated: in the "dream," according to the count, "there was made to you a communication," but he doesn't know what it was; during the excursion, the count refuses to say what has upset him, and his silence serves to "make a communication."

The story's success depends on its being told in an understated way, that is to say, on the narrator's keeping silent about a number of essential issues (the motive for the tale, the communication from the well, the exact manner of the baron's death, the question of whether or not this was a murder). Thus, the reader has to fill in the gaps, to supplement what is given by work of the imagination, to answer the questions posed by the text. The reader is made to perform the same mental operations that the count performed when he concocted the plan; the tale is a question directed at the reader, and challenging his or her morality by stating baldly: if murder can be accomplished by the mere power of suggestion, then what is the reading of imaginative literature but the enactment in the mind of every kind of crime? And the question is a telling one within the frame tale of *The Master of Ballantrae*: the narrator, staid old Mackellar, after listening to the Master's tale, answers it in his own way by trying to shove him overboard. Such, indeed, is the power of suggestion.

The tale functions within the whole of *The Master of Ballantrae* as an only too literal *mise-en-abyme:* a story within a story that, by mirroring the whole of which it is a part, but only in essence, in outline, serves to reveal the shape of the whole more clearly.[3] The hatred that the Master feels for his brother Harry, and which is repaid in kind, is as unmotivated as the count's hatred for the baron and as lethal. In the tale the Master dramatizes the immense power of suggestion (which allows him, in the novel as a whole, to control his brother so completely that the latter ends an abject parody of himself), as well as the moral ambiguity of that suggestion. He forces Mackellar to confront the question, at the very moment when the narrative is passing from home and Scotland to the American wilderness, of who is responsible when violence is done—the author or the actors. Even after the excursion into the wilderness that has left both brothers

dead, Mackellar is left with the question of who is to blame for the tragedy, if blame is to be assigned; and by abnegating his role when he presents
a simplified view of the story to the reader, in which the Master is villain
and Henry is martyr, he passes the question along to us.

Speaking of the famous "problem of the closed room" in the history
of crime fiction, Borges says: "En alguna página de algunos de sus catorce
volúmenes piensa De Quincey que haber descubierto un problema no
es menos admirable (y es más fecundo) que haber descubierto una solu-
ción" [In some page of one of his fourteen volumes De Quincey affirms
that to have discovered a problem is no less admirable (and is more fruit-
ful) than to have discovered a solution] (Borges 1938: 24). He credits Poe
(in "The Murders in the Rue Morgue") with having discovered the problem of the closed room; I don't know whether to credit Stevenson with
the *discovery* of the problem of murder-by-suggestion in the tale we have
been discussing, but can affirm with confidence that it was a problem that
was fruitfully and passionately explored in the crime fiction of Borges
and Bioy Casares (and in that of their joint creation Honorio Bustos
Domecq). To cite a few examples: Borges's "La muerte y la brújula" (1943)
explores the manipulation and eventual murder of the detective by the
criminal, who bases his plot initially on some chance events (just as the
count begins with his chance experience of discovering the tomb), which
he later elaborates into a complicated system;[4] Bustos Domecq's "Las pre-
visiones de Sangiácomo" (1942)[5] tells of the enormously intricate plot by
which a father forces his supposed son (who is actually the product of an
adulterous relation on the part of his wife) to commit suicide;[6] Borges's
"Abenjacán el Bojarí, muerto en su laberinto" (1951) recounts the trap set
by Zaid, servant of Abenjacán, for his master, using the telling symbols of
the labyrinth and the spider web. However, the closest parallel to "La puerta
y el pino" is Bioy Casares's novel *El sueño de los héroes* (1954), the whole
of which can be viewed as an attempt to answer the questions posed by
Stevenson's brief text, or to pose those questions in a different, more insistent, way.

El sueño de los héroes is the story of a young Argentine man, Emilio Gauna,
who becomes obsessed with a mysterious event in his past, until the obsession leads to his death. Shortly before carnival in 1927, Gauna wins a lot
of money at the races, which he decides to spend in a three-day drinking
spree with a number of friends, led by an older father figure, Sebastián
Valerga, who is at once sinister and brave. Toward the end of the three days,
Gauna's hold on the situation becomes increasingly loose, and when he is

found in the Bosque de Palermo, he has vague, contradictory memories of what has happened to him, including one very intense memory of something that did not happen—a fight at knife-point between him and Valerga. Three years pass, during which Gauna gets married and draws away from the group and from Valerga; then, during carnival in 1930, Gauna again wins a sum of money and decides to try to repeat the earlier experiences, hoping to penetrate the mystery of the third day of the 1927 carnival. Valerga and his friends play along with his obsession, and on the third day of the 1930 carnival, after an approximate repetition of the earlier spree, Gauna faces Valerga in the Palermo woods, each with knife in hand, and is killed by him. The narrator explains that the first time Gauna was protected by the intercession of a sorcerer, Taboada, whose daughter will become Gauna's wife; the second time Taboada is dead, and the events take the course they were fated to take the first time when Taboada interrupted them.

The parallels with the Stevenson story are numerous and striking. Bioy also uses the motif of the asymmetrical repetition of a series of events, which the first time almost leads to death (that of the count, and that of Gauna), and which the second time does lead to death (of the baron, of Gauna). The driving force of the middle portion of the novel, as of the tale, is the principal character's fascination or obsession with his near death, which leads to investigations and plans that include other people. In both fictions one person controls another by the power of suggestion, leading him to his death in a very subtle way, so that it appears that it is always the latter who is seeking his own death. Control is exerted over the victim by the suggestion that something was communicated to him, or was about to be communicated, at the moment of the near death: I have already cited the count's remark, and although Valerga doesn't say anything so explicit, his conduct leaves Gauna "muy resuelto a ver lo que había entrevisto esa noche, a recuperar lo que había perdido" [very decided to see what he had glimpsed that night, to recover what he had lost] (41). And in both stories, this hidden communication spurs the victim on, working on his curiosity (that is to say, on an incomplete faculty of the imagination, since it cannot recapture the whole communication except by leading to the death of the "curioso impertinente"), until the moment of his death, on the outskirts of a great city.[7]

Furthermore, in both the motif of the dream is of utmost importance. The count invents a dream to tantalize the baron, by giving him a vicarious sense of *déjà vu* when they "chance" to pass the tomb in the course of their excursion. Gauna, toward the end of the second carnival, dreams "the dream of the heroes" that gives the book its title: in his dream the heroes play a card game to decide who will have the right to walk down a red carpet and take his place on a throne as the greatest of the heroes (212). At the end of the book, Gauna recalls the red carpet and understands that it is spread for him (239): as a brave man, but also as a dead one, since the red is that of his own blood. Both dreams serve to inspire the victims to hurry on to their encounter with death, which will reveal the significance of the dreams and of the heroes (though it must be added that we are privy not at all to the baron's point of view at the decisive moment, so we cannot say with confidence whether he meets death with Gauna's resolution and conviction of his own courage—and one suspects that he has no time to reflect on these questions before sliding into the slimy hole).

Furthermore, *El sueño de los héroes* makes an enigmatic question of the death of the hero, much as the Master's tale ends with the question: "And now, was that a murder?" Is the death of Gauna the death of a hero or that of a suicide? Or is it murder? Bioy and his narrator leave these questions open at the end. In his review of the book, Borges touches on the enigmatic nature of the ending:

> Al final se revela que este mentor es un hombre siniestro; la revelación nos choca y hasta nos duele, porque nos hemos identificado con Gauna, pero confirma las fugaces sospechas que inquietaron nuestra lectura. Gauna y Valerga se traban en un duelo a cuchillo y el maestro mata al discípulo. Ocurre entonces la segunda revelación, harto más asombrosa que la primera; descubrimos que Valerga es abominable, pero que también es valiente. El efecto alcanzado es abrumador. Bioy, instintivamente, ha salvado el mito. ¿Qué pasaría si en la última página del Quijote, don Quijote muriera bajo el acero de un verdadero paladín, en el mágico reino de Bretaña o en las remotas playas de Ariosto? (Borges 1955: 89)

> [At the end it is revealed that this mentor is a sinister man; the revelation shocks and even pains us, because we have identified with Gauna, but it confirms the passing suspicions that disturbed our reading. Gauna and Valerga have a knife fight and the master kills the disciple. Then the second revelation occurs, which is much more surprising than the first one: we discover that Valerga is odious but is also brave. The effect that is achieved is striking. Bioy, instinctively, has saved the myth. What would happen if on

the last page of Don Quixote the hero were to die beneath the sword of a true paladin in the magic kingdom of Briton or on the remote beaches of Ariosto?]

The reference to Don Quixote and heroic legend is far from casual. Gauna, like Don Quixote, has sought the death of a hero, and through his obsession has been granted some measure of fulfillment. But Bioy is kinder to his hero than is Cervantes:[8] he doesn't demand that his hero wake up and die sane according to the norms of the everyday world, granting him instead access to the heroic world of myth.

If we consider the Master's little tale as part (a *mise-en-abyme*) of the whole of *The Master of Ballantrae*, we notice some further parallels with *El sueño de los héroes*. Both novels are concerned with a relation between two people marked by animosity and attraction: the antagonists need each other to be themselves, to fulfill their destinies. This rivalry leads first to the near murder of one by the other (Henry's duel with the Master, whom he leaves for dead, and Valerga and Gauna's shadowy duel in the first carnival, which allegedly only happens in Gauna's imagination), and then to death (of both brothers in the Stevenson novel, of Gauna in *El sueño*). The stronger of the two rivals—and the older in both cases—is evil ("siniestro," as Borges says in his review), and yet strangely brave and attractive, a heroic figure after all. And the victim in both cases is the focus of the narrators' sympathy, yet that sympathy is highly ambivalent—Mackellar insists on taking Henry's part throughout, but portrays his weaknesses only too clearly, while the enigmatic narrator of *El sueño de los héroes* seems to take Gauna's part and yet makes fun of him throughout the novel (as do Gauna's "friends" in the group).

An important difference between *El sueño de los héroes* and both the Stevenson pieces we have been considering—the whole of *The Master of Ballantrae*, and the interpolated story of the count and the baron—is that Valerga's evil influence on Gauna is offset in Bioy's novel by the protection afforded him by the sorcerer Taboada, while both the baron and Henry are helpless before their adversaries, although Henry has the benefit of Mackellar's common sense and good advice. The existence of Taboada as well as Valerga—a good as well as a bad influence—gives Gauna freedom to resist the call of death, a freedom not granted the baron or Henry Durie. His destiny is equivocal (more so, perhaps, than he is ready to admit), as the sorcerer points out to him: "En ese viaje no todo es bueno ni todo es malo. Por usted y por los demás, no vuelva a emprenderlo. Es una hermosa memoria y la memoria es la vida. No la destruya" [On that journey not everything is good and not everything is evil. For your own sake and that of others don't try to take it. It is a beautiful memory and memory is life. Don't destroy it] (47–48). So when he chooses to repeat the earlier adventure, it is a choice, an act of will on his part, a decision to obliterate a memory *qua* memory by realizing or enacting it.

The juxtaposition of "La puerta y el pino" and *El sueño de los héroes* is useful because it helps us interpret a number of factors that would otherwise be difficult to discuss. In the Stevenson tale we are given a skeletal form of the intricate plot of the Bioy novel: a chance event that almost leads to death, the elaboration of that event by means of imagination and memory, and a repetition of it leading to death. By contrasting the dynamics at work in the earlier tale, which is acted out by only two characters, with that of the group of characters in *El sueño*, we can see more clearly the specific kinds of complexity introduced by the figures of Taboada, Clara, and Larsen, and the ambivalent nature of Gauna. More importantly, the intertext of "La puerta y el pino" serves to explain the presence of elements of the detective story in *El sueño de los héroes*, as well as the deviations from the norms of the genre: Gauna's investigations lead to his own death (as in "La muerte y la brújula"); the initial act of violence turns out to be a mere rehearsal of the final one; and the process of revelation or explanation that usually pertains to the detective is—with the death of Gauna—fulfilled by the narrator instead, though the latter's explanations may not be completely convincing.

Moreover, the noting of the similarities between Bioy's novel and "La puerta y el pino" points up the need to study Bioy's (as well as Borges's) interest in Stevenson, an interest that should not surprise us, in view of the close association of Borges and Bioy and of Borges's fondness for Stevenson's fiction, but which has not been explored up to now.[9] It also serves to explain the inclusion of the Stevenson story in an anthology with the provocative title *Los mejores cuentos policiales*, since Stevenson's treatment here of some elements of the detective story—stressing the plotting or imagination of a crime more than the investigation of it,[10] omitting the superfluous character of the detective, and achieving a high degree of ambiguity—anticipates the experiments with the genre some half-century after Stevenson's death in Samoa by the Argentine writers Borges, Bioy Casares, Bianco, and H. Bustos Domecq.

NOTES

1. The interviews were also published in the original English in Balderston 1999.

2. This glowing comment is very different in tone from the other headnotes in the volume, which tend to be mere lists of biographical and bibliographical data.

3. The classic example of this device, discussed in Borges 1949, is the play within the play in *Hamlet.*

4. The story further resembles "La puerta y el pino" in its open ending: Lönnrot's posing of a geometrical problem at the end invites the reader to go on with the story in much the same way as the Master's posing of the final question.

5. This story, co-authored by Borges and Bioy under the pseudonym of Honorio Bustos Domecq, appeared in *Seis problemas para don Isidro Parodi* (1942), and is included in Borges et al. 1979.

6. "Sangiácomo" is similar to "La puerta y el pino" (unlike the other stories mentioned here) in that no murder is committed directly: the baron's death, like Sangiácomo's, could be interpreted as suicide.

7. The Italian name of the park where Gauna meets his death, Palermo, perhaps is meant to recall the Italy of Stevenson's story, though of course it is also a real park in Buenos Aires, and the neighborhood is central to Borges's early poetry.

8. Cf. the comments in Borges 1956 on Cervantes's final cruelty to his hero, a note that is almost contemporary to his review of Bioy's novel.

9. The only critic I know of who touches on Stevenson's anticipations of some of Bioy's fiction is Julio Matas (1978: 123).

10. Cf. Borges's review of Bianco's *Las ratas:* "su tema es la prehistoria de un crimen, las delicadas circunstancias graduales que paran en la muerte de un hombre" (Borges 1944: 76). Dorothy L. Sayers included the same extract, titled "Was It Murder?" in *Tales of Detection: A New Anthology* (1936), which Borges reviewed in *El Hogar* (19 Feb. 1937).

REFERENCES

Balderston, Daniel. 1985. *El precursor velado: R. L. Stevenson en la obra de Borges.* Buenos Aires: Editorial Sudamericana.

———. 1999. Interviews with Borges: Buenos Aires, August–September 1978. *Variaciones Borges* 8: 187–215.

Bioy Casares, Adolfo. 1954. *El sueño de los heroes.* 1969. Buenos Aires: Emecé.

Borges, Jorge Luis. 1935 Los laberintos policiales y Chesterton. *Sur* 10: 92–94. In del Carril et al. 1999: 126–29.

———. 1938. [Column.] *El Hogar* (March 4, 1938): 24.

———. 1944. [Review of José Bianco's *Las ratas.*] *Sur* 111. In del Carril et al. 1999: 271–74.

———. 1949. Magias parciales del Quijote. *La Nación* (November 6, 1949): 1. In *Otrás inquisiciones.* 1952. Buenos Aires: Sur. 55–58.

———. 1955. [Review of Adolfo Bioy Casares's *El sueño de los heroes.*] *Sur* 235. In del Carril et al. 1999: 284–86.

————. 1956. Análisis del último capítulo del "Quijote," *Revista de la Universidad de Buenos Aires* 1: 28–36.

————. 1974. *Obras completas.* Buenos Aires: Emecé.

————, et al. 1979. *Obras completas en colaboración.* Buenos Aires: Emecé.

————, and Adolfo Bioy Casares, eds. 1943. *Los mejores cuentos policiales.* Buenos Aires: Emecé.

del Carril, Sara Luisa, and Mercedes Rubio de Socchi, eds. 1999. *Borges en Sur 1931–1980.* Buenos Aires: Emecé.

Le Bris, Michel. 2000. *Pour saluer Stevenson.* Paris: Flammarion.

————, ed. 1995. *Robert Louis Stevenson.* Paris: l'Herne (Les Cahiers de l'Herne, 66).

Matas, Julio. 1978. Bioy Casares o la aventura de narrar. *Nueva Revista de Filología Hispánica* 27:112–23.

Sayers, Dorothy, ed. 1936. *Tales of Detection: A New Anthology.* London: Dent.

Stevenson, Robert Louis. 1889. *The Master of Ballantrae.* Thistle Edition, second issue. Vol. 9.

CONTRIBUTORS

Robert Louis Abrahamson, collegiate professor of English with the University of Maryland University College's European Division, has lived under the shadow of RLS all his life. His doctorate was on Scottish literature, and more recently he has focused his teaching on various literary forms of myth. He is presently working on a stage production of Stevenson's Fables.

Richard Ambrosini, professor of English literature, Università di Roma Tre, has worked in the past on Joseph Conrad, writing two books (*Conrad's Fiction as Critical Discourse*, 1991; *Introduzione a Conrad*, 1991), and translating into Italian *An Outcast of the Islands* (1994) and *The Secret Agent* (1996). After translating *Treasure Island* (1996), he wrote a monograph on Stevenson (*R. L. Stevenson: la poetica del romanzo*, 2001). His other area of interest is English poetry (*Il piacere della poesia inglese*, 2000).

Stephen Arata is associate professor of English at the University of Virginia and the author of *Fictions of Loss in the Victorian Fin de Siècle* (1996). His recent publications include Broadview Literary Texts editions of William Morris's *News from Nowhere* and George Gissing's *New Grub Street*.

Daniel Balderston is professor of Spanish and Portuguese at the University of Iowa. He is the author of five books on Borges and has edited several books on sexuality studies. His most recent books are *Voice Overs:*

Translation and Latin American Literature (co-edited with Marcy Schwartz, 2002), *El deseo, enorme cicatriz luminosa: ensayos sobre homosexualidades latinoamericanas* (2004), *Encyclopedia of Latin American and Caribbean Literature* (co-edited with Mike Gonzalez, 2004) and *Sexualidades en disputa* (co-authored with Jose Quiroga, 2005).

Oliver S. Buckton is associate professor of English at Florida Atlantic University, Boca Raton. His recent publications include an article on Stevenson in *Nineteenth Century Literature,* and *Secret Selves: Confession and Same-Sex Desire in Victorian Autobiography* (1998). He is currently working on a book-length project on Stevenson's travel writing, focusing on the relation between fiction and nonfiction in Stevenson's South Seas literature.

Jenni Calder, formerly of the National Museums of Scotland, has written widely on Robert Louis Stevenson, including *RLS: A Life Study* (1980) and many essays, introductions, and the like. She has published on Scottish, English, and American literary and historical subjects. Her book *Beyond Scotland—Canada* (2003) will be followed by *Beyond Scotland—the USA* (2005). Also recent is *Not Nebuchadnezzar: In Search of Identities* (2005).

Ann C. Colley is professor of English at Buffalo State College. Her most recent book is *Robert Louis Stevenson and the Colonial Imagination* (2004). Others include *Nostalgia and Recollection in Victorian Culture* (1998), *Edward Lear and the Critics* (1993), *The Search for Synthesis in Literature and Art* (1990), and *Tennyson and Madness* (1983). Professor Colley has published essays in various journals including *Victorian Literature and Culture, Victorian Poetry, Word & Image,* the *Journal of Pre-Raphaelite Studies,* and the *Kenyon Review.*

Dennis Denisoff is Research Chair in Victorian Literature and Culture at Ryerson University, Toronto. He is the author of *Aestheticism and Sexual Parody: 1840–1940* (2001) and *Sexual Visuality from Literature to Film, 1850 to 1950* (2004). He has edited *The Broadview Anthology of Victorian Short Stories* (2004) and co-edited the essay collection *Perennial Decay: On the Aesthetics and Politics of Decadence* (1999). His second novel, *The Winter Gardeners,* was published in 2003.

Stephen Donovan is a postdoctoral researcher at Blekinge Institute of Technology, Karlskrona, Sweden. His research interests include literary modernism, media history, and late-Victorian colonialism. His *Joseph Conrad and Popular Culture* will be published in September 2005.

Linda Dryden is reader in literature and culture at Napier University, Edinburgh. She has published numerous articles on Joseph Conrad as well as papers on popular culture. Her monograph *Joseph Conrad and the Imperial Romance* appeared in 2000, followed by *The Modern Gothic* and *Literary Doubles: Stevenson, Wilde and Wells* in September 2003. Dr Dryden is currently co-editor of a volume dedicated to the serialization of Conrad's fiction, and is co-editor with Rory Watson of the *Journal of Stevenson Studies*.

Richard Dury is associate professor of English language at Bergamo University in Italy; apart from publications on English language history he has published various articles on Stevenson as well as *The Annotated Dr. Jekyll and Mr. Hyde* (1993, 2005) and a critical edition of *Dr. Jekyll and Mr. Hyde* for Edinburgh University Press (2004). He is editor of the Robert Louis Stevenson web site (www.unibg.it/rls).

Gordon Hirsch is professor and associate chair of the English Department at the University of Minnesota. He has published essays on the travel literature of Robert Louis Stevenson and is co-editor of *Dr. Jekyll and Mr. Hyde After One Hundred Years* (1988). He has also published essays on other nineteenth-century authors, including Austen, Carlyle, Carroll, Dickens, Eliot, J. S. Mill, Mary Shelley, and Tennyson.

Liz Farr, a senior lecturer in English at the University of Plymouth, has just completed a thesis, "Robert Louis Stevenson's Essays: Aesthetics, Masculinity and the Literary Marketplace," at Birkbeck College, University of London. Her essay on Stevenson's essays of travel and youth has been published in a special edition of *Nineteenth-Century Prose* (Fall 2002), devoted to the nineteenth-century picturesque.

Robbie B. H. Goh is an associate professor and chair of the Department of English Language and Literature at the National University of Singapore. He teaches and writes on nineteenth-century literature, critical theory, popular culture, and Asian studies. Recent works include *Theorizing the Southeast Asian City as Text* (co-edited, 2003), *Sparks of Grace: The Story of Methodism in Asia* (2003), and *Singapore Space and the Dialogics of Culture* (2005).

Nathalie Jaëck is a lecturer at Bordeaux University, France, specializing in late-nineteenth-entury fiction. After a PhD on Arthur Conan Doyle and the Sherlock Holmes stories, she has published numerous papers on Doyle, Stevenson, Dickens, and Conrad.

Wendy R. Katz is professor of English literature at Saint Mary's University, in Halifax, Nova Scotia, Canada. She is the author of *Rider Haggard and the Fiction of Empire* (1987), and *The Emblems of Margaret Gatty, A Study of Allegory in Nineteenth-Century Children's Literature* (1993). She is the co-editor of *Introduction to Literature: British, American and Canadian* (2004, 5th edition), and the editor of the EUP critical edition of Stevenson's *Treasure Island*. She is currently working on a project on Stevenson and America.

Ann Lawson Lucas was senior lecturer in Italian at the University of Hull and, recently, visiting research fellow at the Institute for Advanced Studies in the Humanities, University of Edinburgh. Her main research field is nineteenth-century children's literature in Italy. Recent publications include a monograph on Salgari and an edition of three of his novels. She is now preparing a monograph on the fortunes of Salgari, including the repercussions of political patronage under Fascism.

Caroline McCracken-Flesher, professor of English literature at the University of Wyoming, publishes widely on Scottish literature and culture, and on the film/literature connection. Publications include *Possible Scotlands: Walter Scott and the Story of Tomorrow* (2005) and an edited volume, *Culture, Nation and the New Scottish Parliament* (forthcoming).

Manfred Malzahn has worked in seven countries in Europe, Africa and Asia, and is currently professor of English literature at United Arab Emirates University. He has published widely, but by no means exclusively, on Scottish literature; his other publications range from contemporary African writing to twentieth-century German history.

Jean-Pierre Naugrette is professor of English literature at the University of Paris III-Sorbonne Nouvelle. He has published *Robert Louis Stevenson: l'aventure et son double* (1987), along with numerous articles and essays on Stevenson, the fiction of adventure, and the Victorian detective story from Collins to Doyle. He has recently co-edited the proceedings of the Cerisy International Conference on R. L. Stevenson and A. Conan Doyle (2003) and has published two novels.

Glenda Norquay is professor of Scottish literary studies at Liverpool John Moores University. She has edited *R. L. Stevenson on Fiction* (1999) and has published widely on Scottish fiction, national identities, and women's suffrage fiction. She is currently working on a study of Stevenson's reading practices.

Ralph Parfect wrote his doctoral thesis on violence in the works of Robert Louis Stevenson. He has lectured at King's College London on Victorian and twentieth-century literature, and is currently working on a study of violence in a range of late Victorian writers.

Jane V. Rago is a doctoral candidate at West Virginia University. Her dissertation on the relations between scientific discourses and feminism in late nineteenth-century England, focusing on the work of Robert Louis Stevenson, New Women Fiction, and leftist political narratives.

Julia Reid is lecturer in British social and cultural history at the University of Liverpool. Her research interests are in Victorian science and culture, and recent publications include articles on Stevenson and evolutionary science. She is currently preparing for publication a book titled *Robert Louis Stevenson, Science, and the Fin de Siècle*.

Alan Sandison is emeritus professor of the Department of English and Communication Studies at the University of New England, Armidale, Australia. He has published widely on late-nineteenth- and early-twentieth-century writers. His works include *The Wheel of Empire* (1967), *The Last Man in Europe: An Essay on George Orwell* (1973), *Robert Louis Stevenson and the Appearance of Modernism* (1996) and (with Robert Dingley), *Histories of the Future Studies in Fact, Fantasy and Science Fiction* (2001).

Ilaria B. Sborgi has a PhD in English and American literature from the University of Florence, Italy. She wrote her dissertation on Robert Louis Stevenson and his writings on the South Seas and has published essays on this topic, on detective fiction, feminist history, and the English writer Dorothy Nevile Lees.

Olena M.Turnbull teaches English at Kirkcaldy High School, Scotland. She has published work on Scott, Henry James, and Robert Louis Stevenson. She is currently working on a book based on her doctoral thesis on Henry James's criticism of British and American women writers (University of Tulsa, 2002).

Michela Vanon Alliata is associate professor of English literature at the University of Venice. She has published works on James, Hawthorne, Melville, Brockden Brown, Stevenson, Atwood, and Trevor. She is author of *Il giardino delle delizie. L'immaginario visivo di Henry James* (1997) and editor of *Desiderio e trasgressione nella letteratura fantastica* (2002), to which she contributed an essay on Stevenson's "The Bottle Imp." She is currently working on a book on supernatural and gothic fiction.

Luisa Villa is professor of English literature at the University of Genova, Italy. She has published widely on Victorian and early modernist literature. Her publications include books on Henry James (*Esperienza e memoria*, 1989), George Eliot (*Riscrivendo il conflitto*, 1994) and resentment in late Victorian fiction (*Figure del risentimento*, 1997). Together with Marco Pustianaz she recently co-edited *Maschilità decadenti* (2004) and is currently working on the representation of colonial warfare.

Richard J. Walker is senior lecturer in English literature at the University of Central Lancashire. He has published works on Australian popular culture, the gothic, is co-editor of *Inhuman Reflections: Thinking the Limits of the Human* (2000) and author of *Labyrinths of Deceit: Culture, Modernity and Identity in the Nineteenth Century* (2005). He is currently working on a study of aesthetics, ethics, and the avant-garde in nineteenth-century English and French poetry.

Mirando Haz [Amedeo Pieragostini] has produced several series of etching inspired by writers (including Dickens and James), and his works are among the collections of leading museums (such as the Calcografia in Rome and the Bibliotèque Nationale et Cabinet des Estampes in Paris). The complete catalogue of *Mirando Haz: l'opera incisa* was published in Milan in 1999 by Nuages, with an introduction by Carlo Bertelli. Quotations for his engravings have been published annually in the Prendi international catalogue from 1974 on, and he has an entry in the *Dictionnaire Bénézit de peintures, graveurs etc.* The images reproduced in this volume were first exhibited at the RLS 2002 conference at Gargnano.

INDEX OF
STEVENSON'S WORKS

GENERAL INDEX

Sun (New York), 200, 210
Survivor, 92
Sutherland, John, 68
Swearingen, Roger G., 58, 336
Sweet, Matthew, 70
Swinnerton, Frank, xvi
Symonds, John Addington, 13, 161

Tacitus, 14
Taine, Hypolite, *De l'intelligence*, 242
Taylor, Lady Theodosia, 20
Tembinok, 205–8
Tennyson, Lord Alfred, 14; *Maud*, 14
Thackeray, William Makepeace, *The Newcomes*, 19–20
Theroux, Paul, 162
Theweleit, Klaus, 112, 119
Thomson, James, "City of Dreadful Night," 256, 260
Thoreau, Henry David, xxvi, 14, 328–36; *Walden*, 328–30, 332–33
Thurn, E. F., 188
Times Literary Supplement, The, xv
Times, The, 34
Tit-Bits, 73
Tolstoy, Leo, 219
Tonti, Lorenzo, 84, 91
Tontine: What It Is; How It Works, 87
Trebilcock, Clive, 85
Treble, James H., 85
Tribune (New York), 87
Turner, Rev. George, 188
Twain, Mark (Samuel Langhorne Clemens), 13, 14, 161–63; *The Adventures of Huckleberry Finn*, 13, 161–62
Tylor, Edward Burnett, 23, 33, 216–17, 222; *Primitive Culture*, 155, 216, 222

Valigia, La, 346
Veeder, William, 111, 117, 119, 284
Vicinus, Martha, 288, 296
Villa, Luisa, 109
Villon, François, 14, 44, 174, 178
Virgil, 14

Walford, Cornelius, 85

Walkowitz, Judith, 73, 254
Wallace, Alfred Russell, 229
Wallace, Christopher, *The Resurrection Club*, 134
Warner, Alan, *Morvern Callar*, 134; *These Demented Lands*, 134
Warner, Marina, 155
Warren, Sir Charles, 259
Waters, Catherine, 303
Watson, Roderick, 232
Watts, Cedric, 262
Watts, Isaac, 14
Weber, Carl Maria von, *Der Freischütz*, 193
Weisbuch, Robert, 329, 336
Wells, Herbert George, 139, 262; *The Island of Doctor Moreau*, 262
Whitman, Walt, xxvi–xxvii, 14, 328–36; *Leaves of Grass*, 328, 331–32, 334
Wilde, Oscar, 34, 43, 46, 72, 163, 165, 249, 271–73, 288; "The Decay of Living," 272; *The Picture of Dorian Gray*, 46, 163, 249, 272
Williams, Kellen, 278, 282, 284, 296
Williams, Raymond, 255, 257
Wilson, Edward O., 231
Wollstonecraft, Mary, 107
Wood, Naomi, J., 170–71
Woolf, Leonard, xiv–xv
Woolf, Virginia, xv
Wordsworth, William, 14, 267–72, 335; "Preface" to *Lyrical Ballads*, 267–68; *The Prelude* (1805), 269
Wright, Daniel, 284
Wright, Thomas, "On a Possible Popular Culture," 71
Wyss, Johann David, *The Swiss Family Robinson*, 346

Yeats, William Butler, 179
Young Folks, 60–62, 346
Young Ladies' Journal, 31

Zelizer, Vivian A., 84, 87
Žižek, Slavoj, 277
Zola, Émile, 48, 50, 53, 57; "Les romanciers naturalistes," 48; *Vérité*, 57